Criminal Courts in Theory, Research, and Practice

A READER

First Edition

MARC GERTZ

Florida State University

CHRISTI METCALFE

University of South Carolina

Bassim Hamadeh, CEO and Publisher

Jennifer McCarthy, Acquisitions Editor

Gem Rabanera, Project Editor

Miguel Macias, Senior Graphic Designer

Alexa Lucido, Licensing Associate

Christian Berk, Interior Designer

Natalie Piccotti, Senior Marketing Manager

Kassie Graves, Director of Acquisitions and Sales

Jamie Giganti, Senior Managing Editor

ISBN: 978-1-5165-0401-5 (pbk) / 978-1-5165-0402-2 (br)

Criminal Courts in Theory, Research, and Practice

A READER

Contents

SECTION 3. COURTROOM WORKGROUPS

SECTION 4. EARLY PHASES OF CASE PROCESSING

SECTION 7. THE IMPACT OF APPELLATE COURTS

Introduction

Purpose of the Book

In many circumstances, criminal courts do not operate in legally expected ways. The overwhelming majority of cases are not resolved by jury trials, but rather by pleas of guilty. Prosecutors and defense attorneys actually cooperate more than they serve as adversaries. Similarly situated offenders do not always get the same sentences. Sometimes, legally irrelevant factors of a case, such as race and sex, influence defendants' sentences. Appellate judges often produce decisions in line with law-making majorities, even though they are protectors of minority rights. Public opinion has an impact on the court system despite its supposed independent and apolitical nature.

It is our belief that it is difficult to teach many of these legal paradoxes within the trial and appellate courts without students understanding that criminal courts are social systems subject to demands and pressures that alter their expected behavior. Therefore, in this book, we set out to focus on three specific aspects of courts. One, criminal courts are subject to organizational pressures to process cases efficiently. These pressures can alter the legally prescribed roles of judges, prosecutors, and defense attorneys. Two, criminal courts are composed and ran by people who are subjective and often have their own ideological viewpoints that can sway decision-making. Despite how hard the actors within the court system try to remain objective, they can never escape unconscious biases and leanings that can lead to disparate case outcomes. Three, the system is continuously pressured by those outside of it. For the court, this involves a consideration of the demands placed on them by defendants, victims, the police, legislatures, and the community. Balancing these demands will inevitably influence their decisions.

This book is designed to be a primary text or a supplemental reader for an undergraduate course in criminal courts or a supplemental text for a graduate course. As a primary text for undergraduates, the book provides a structural foundation for the study of key areas pertaining to the criminal court system, and supplemental readings or books can be assigned as warranted in more specialized or specific topic areas. The book can also be used as a supplementary text to a more traditional criminal courts textbook in an undergraduate class or as a basis for introducing some of the key pieces in the courts literature for a graduate class. We have brought together various readings, including many foundational theoretical pieces, as well as empirical research and Supreme Court cases that we believe are demonstrative of the three areas of focus mentioned above and further elucidate specific themes highlighted in each of the book's sections.

Organization of the Book

The book is divided into seven sections. Section 1 focuses on legal ideologies that form the basis of the court system. Specifically, the section details the difference between a realist versus traditionalist approach to the law and how the both are manifested within criminal courts. Emphasis is also placed on realist and traditionalist mechanisms within case processing, tying these ideologies to the crime control and due process models of criminal justice.

Sections 2 through 5 discuss criminal trial courts. Section 2 provides an organizational basis for explaining plea bargaining. Focus is placed on the organizational goals within the court that contribute to the predominant use of pleas, as well as the resulting cooperative nature among judges, prosecutors, and defense attorneys in pursuit of these goals. The influence of outsiders is also emphasized with attention paid to how outside forces can disrupt case processing norms. Section 3 highlights the importance of courtroom workgroups, including workgroup dynamics that can influence case outcomes. These dynamics include incentives of individual actors, familiarity among the members within workgroups, and influence of prosecutors. The debate regarding representation by public versus private defense attorneys is also discussed.

Section 4 addresses the earlier phases of case processing, including the decision to prosecute, detention, and plea bargaining. Factors influencing the decision to prosecute are reviewed, as well the debate surrounding detention and the pros and cons of the plea bargaining process. Section 5 focuses on sentencing, beginning with a discussion of varying sentencing ideologies and reasons for punishment. The section then reviews several theoretical viewpoints that can explain why organizational and extralegal factors influence sentencing even after accounting for legal factors.

Finally, Sections 6 and 7 concentrate on appellate courts. Section 6 calls attention to the powers and limits of appellate decision-making and the various forces that influence these decisions, particularly in the context of the explained powers and limits. Section 7 addresses the impact of appellate court decisions and the situations in which the appellate courts can have a greater influence in the community.

"Stat Help!" Feature

Some of the readings include regression tables reporting empirical findings (i.e., logistic regression, ordinal logistic regression, Tobit regression, and ordinary least squares (OLS) regression). We think it is important to acquaint students with the empirical literature in the field, especially policy-relevant studies, and recognize that familiarity with academic writing can be a valuable asset. We acknowledge, though, that some students reading this book do not necessarily have the skill set (at least not yet) to interpret the regression tables. In response to this concern, we have included a "Stat Help!" feature to the book with editorial commentary to assist students in a basic interpretation of the tables. The commentary suggests where students should focus their attention in the tables and offers examples to help with interpretation.

CRIMINAL COURT IDEOLOGIES

Introduction

In his book, *The Nature of the Judicial Process,* Justice Benjamin Cardoza said that "we may try to see things as objectively as we please. Nonetheless, we can never see them with any eyes except our own." This statement exemplifies the notion of legal realists who stress the subjectivity inherent in the interpretation and application of the law, even among judges who we often view as independent from politics. Legal realism presented a contrast to legal traditionalism, a view that largely assumes judges can be completely objective and free from their own subjective biases. Much of our understanding of criminal courts from a sociological perspective, including many of the theories that attempt to explain decision-making at various phases of case processing, focuses on the inherent realism within the criminal court system. Therefore, in studying criminal courts, it is essential to begin with these legal traditions.

Legal Traditionalism vs. Legal Realism

In a traditionalist perspective, law can be seen as the foundation of decision-making within the criminal court system, such that all decisions can be made on the basis of the law alone. It is this perspective that provides the groundwork for the Socratic Method in law schools, where law is best understood by studying existing cases.

Judges are expected to make decisions on a particular issue after thoroughly reviewing precedent, or prior cases relevant to the issue at hand. In this search, judges are assumed to remain completely objective, almost to the point of being mechanic and robot-like. If this is in fact the case in the criminal court system, similarly situated offenders should always get similar sentences. Also, any errors that occur within the lower courts will of course be reviewed and corrected in the upper appellate courts, so as to ensure that every criminal defendant receives a just and fair process.

While judges do rely on precedent to inform their decision-making, in "Courts on Trial," Jerome Frank acknowledges that there are different ways to interpret case law, and these interpretations can often be based on subjective factors, including judges' social, economic, and political backgrounds. As he states, "judges are human and share the virtues and weaknesses of mortals." Therefore, the search for precedent to inform decision-making may be jaded by personal biases, both conscious and unconscious, such that judges often make a decision and then find the precedent supportive of that decision. In this context, similarly situated offenders would not get similar sentences, especially since different judges may emphasize different legal rules. So, as Frank states, "if we look for a constant in all mature human societies, we will discover at least this one: the constancy of the inconstancy in judicial fact-finding."

From a realist perspective, judges can often be susceptible to political and social changes, including changes in public opinion. This is best exemplified by the decisions of the segregation cases, included in the readings "Dred Scott v. Sandford," "Plessy v. Ferguson," and "Brown v. Board of Education." In isolation, these cases can be seen as a reflection of precedent and existing law, which is traditionalist in nature. However, the progression of these cases is difficult to explain without a reliance on legal realism. The transition from case to case demonstrates the change in society and culture, such that the Supreme Court becomes a reflection of the changing norms. A more recent example can be seen with the right to marriage among same-sex couples. The decision in *Obergefell v. Hodges* can partly be attributed to prior precedent but largely reflects a change in public opinion and attitudes regarding marriage to which the majority of the justices sympathized. Accepting this reality requires a recognition that judges are humans, and as such, can never act to the equivalent of robots. Grounded in the propositions of legal realists, criminal courts will always, to varying degrees, be a reflection of local community values, attitudes, and norms.

Focusing on Trial Courts

An important recognition by realists, and less emphasized by traditionalists, is the fact that the trial courts, or the courts of original jurisdiction, are just as important, or even more relevant, than the appellate courts. The truth is that most cases do not make it on appeal, unlike the segregation cases, and are, therefore, not reviewed and corrected in the appellate courts, as traditionalists espouse. Frank refers to this unrealistic take on the court system as the "upper court myth." Trial court judges will view many more cases, most of which will never come before another judge. About 95% of cases get plea bargained in the criminal court system, and when they plea, defendants give up (in virtually all circumstances) their right to appeal. Therefore, we know that at least 95% of cases that come to the trial courts will not make it on appeal.

In this context, we should not only focus on the leanings and influences of judges, but also the biases of the other court actors, including prosecutors and defense attorneys. These actors are of particular importance in the early phases of case processing, including dismissals, detentions, and pleas, as will be discussed further in Section 4. In "Two Models of the Criminal Process," Herbert Packer identifies competing ideologies by which criminal justice actors, including judges, prosecutors, and defense attorneys, operate. These actors may place more emphasis on due process, or the fair and reasonable treatment by the state or federal government in matters of life, liberty, or property. Alternatively, more focus may be placed on crime control, including the apprehension of criminals and the repression of criminal conduct.

The processing of criminal cases in any given court can be seen on a continuum between due process and crime control, often possessing elements of both. Case processing will vary depending on the ideology of focus—with due process lending to a system focused on trials and crime control to a system focused on pleas of guilt. The former is tied more to the ideals of legal traditionalism, while the latter is more realistic in nature. Given that so many cases are resolved through a plea, it could be argued that the actors lean more towards a system that is crime-control oriented, often relying on informal methods of fact-finding and "assembly line" justice. However, there still remains a certain level of formality to the system that is based in the ideals of respecting justice, due process, and fairness, often creating "obstacles" in efficient case processing.

The Jury System

Because of their beliefs in how courts operate, legal realists would be wary of some of the accepted procedures in the criminal courts. For example, Jerome Frank was not confident in the jury system. According to the Sixth Amendment, "the accused shall enjoy the right to a speedy and public trial, by an impartial jury of the State and district wherein the crime shall have been committed." Traditionalists would stand by the importance of a jury, especially as part of the right to due process. The jury is supposed to represent people more similar to the defendant and not necessarily tied to the criminal justice system. The actors, to a certain extent, are influenced by their involvement in the system, so including people from outside the court community attempts to remedy this scenario.

If the concern among realists, though, is that decisions are often made based on subjective leanings, a jury adds even more subjectivity to the process. Each member of the jury brings his or her own biases, making it even more unlikely that similar offenders will get similar sentences. Members of the jury also lack the legal knowledge necessary to fully understand most cases. Even further, it is often unlikely that a jury is completely representative, and therefore, may be biased against particular defendants. If the defendant is black, for instance, and the jury is 90 percent white, it is questionable whether this distribution represents an "impartial jury" of the defendant's peers.

Some of these concerns may be eased if the jury system operated differently. The issue of impartiality and lack of knowledge regarding the law could be remedied with a specialized jury or trainings for jury service in schools. Further restrictions could also be added to the voir dire process to ensure that the jury represents a cross-section of the community and is truly a representation of the defendant's peers. The Supreme Court has already taken initiative in this area over the years in an attempt to prevent discrimination in the selection of jurors that can affect the fairness of the process (e.g., *Batson v. Kentucky; Powers v. Ohio; Georgia v. McCollum; Edmonson v. Leesville Concrete Company, Inc;, J.E.B. v. Alabama ex rel T.B.*). There is even the possibility of abandoning jury trials altogether, except maybe in serious cases. With so few cases going to trial, it can be argued that we have largely moved away from a jury system. In the end, juries may only create more uncertainties for the court actors and defendants. In this context, the value added by a jury to the criminal process becomes questionable.

Selection from Courts on Trial

Are Judges Human?

Jerome Frank

That judges are human and share the virtues and weaknesses of mortals generally—that fact you may think so obvious as scarcely to deserve discussion. Why then do I discuss it? Because, among American lawyers, until fairly recently, that fact was largely tabu. To mention it, except in an aside and as a joke, even in gatherings of lawyers, was considered bad taste, to say the least. That tabu dominated most legal education during the 19th century and the early part of the 20th. Above all, it controlled what lawyers said to non-lawyers in publications and in public addresses. The Bar spoke to the laity as if the human characteristics of judges had little or no practical consequences. And when, not very long ago, some few of us ventured to violate that tabu, a considerable part of the legal profession called us subversive, enemies of good government, disturbers of "law and order."

No doubt, some of the lawyers who today support that tabu do so because, somehow, either they believe, more or less, that judges are super-human or that the human-ness of judges has virtually no effect on how courts decide cases. Such self-deceivers are not hypocrites but unquestionably sincere men. They come within my category of the second class of wizards. The same cannot be said, however, of some of those lawyers who deplore the public revelation that judges are not demi-gods or, at any rate, do not serve as almost flawless conduits of the divine. The deplorers, fully cognizant of the realities of court-house government, want to conceal them from the public. Their attitude is basically anti-democratic.

That sort of attitude received its best articulation in Plato's Republic. Plato, a totalitarian, who detested democracy, depicted the best state as a dictatorship by a handful of intellectuals. His guardians—or, more accurately, "guards"—were to be absolute rulers. They must, said Plato, have the privilege of employing "useful lies," "opportune falsehoods," for "the public good." Wrote Plato: "I mean ... that our rulers will find a considerable dose of falsehood and deceit necessary for the good of their subjects." Paul Shorey defines such a Platonic "opportune falsehood" as "an ingenious device employed by a superior intelligence to circumvent necessity or to play providence to the vulgar." In Plato's ideal state, the few on top were to handle the multitude as if they were children, children to be duped—or rather, doped—with "magnificent lies."

That, I say, is the spirit of some of those who, themselves aware of the truth, wish to hide from the American public the human qualities of our court-house government. In one way or another, they seek to disseminate and perpetuate what they regard as an "opportune falsehood." Thanks to Hitler, we have come to recognize the utilization of such "ingenious devices" as the essence of fascism. If we cherish democracy, we must not tolerate that sort of deception of the public "for its own good." We must eliminate the myth or legend that judges arc more—or less—than human.

Vigorous attacks on the myth about the non-human-ness of judges came in this country in the early twentieth century from some of the lawyers and legal thinkers who were interested primarily in the legal rules applied by the upper courts in important constitutional and labor cases. These thinkers demonstrated that the legal rules applicable to such cases were by no means as fixed and certain as they would be if the legend of the superhuman origin of decisions were true, that the formulation or interpretation of rules often varied with the particular judges who sat in particular cases. These students of the judicial process said that no judge was a mere judicial slot-machine, that the idea of a "mechanical jurisprudence" was an absurdity. Writers such as Pound, Frankfurter and Powell substituted so-called "sociological jurisprudence." They noted, for instance, that John Marshall's interpretation of the Constitution differed from Taney's, or Waite's from Field's; and that, on careful examination, the differences between judges often showed up as not merely differences in pure reasoning.

The key to the differences, most of these writers maintained, was to be found in the differing social, economic, and political backgrounds of the several judges. For the legal rules express social policies, and (said the "sociological" legal school) a judge's conception of such policies responds more or less to his social, economic and political outlook, which usually derives from his education, his social affiliations, his social environment.

The sociological school had its predecessors in the "historical school" of legal thinkers which had absurdly emphasized the Time Spirit,[1] and also in the Marxists and others who exploited the economic interpretation of the judiciary, with its deterministic explanations of all court decisions as inevitable derivatives of the class-biases of members of the bench.[2] Less radical, but no less vehement forerunners were such critics of high-court decisions as Teddy Roosevelt: T.R., having appointed men to the Supreme Court, knew from first-hand knowledge that judges were not fungible, like grains of sand or particles of wheat, that the pronounced economic and political views of the man within the judge sometimes influence the judge's decisions.

But the sociological jurisprudes, although they gave weight to the economic factors, were not economic determinists. They made a nicer, less crude, analysis than their predecessors of influences affecting judges. Among the influences they recognized were the judges' professional legal education and experience, and the power of judicial tradition. They observed that many a judge, as he develops, changes (or learns to keep in check) his personal social philosophy, often because of the judicial conventions, sometimes because he is persuaded by his fellow judges, sometimes because of the pressure of events. Far more keenly than their forerunners, the sociological jurisprudes perceived that they were talking about psychology, the psychology of judges.

Thus, in 1931, Professor (now Mr. Justice) Frankfurter, writing of the Supreme Court, explicitly mentioned the "psychological factor" and said that the judges' "unconscious" plays "an enormous role in the exercise of the judicial process, particularly where it closely touches contemporary economic and social problems." A brilliant younger member of this school, Felix Cohen, in 1935[3] asserted that, although

---

1   For criticism of this notion of the Time Spirit, see Frank, *Fate and Freedom* (1945) Reading 7; Frank, "A Sketch of An Influence," in the volume, *Interpretations of Modern Legal Philosophies* (1947) 189, 218–22.

2   See Reading XXV.

3   F. S. Cohen, 'Transcendental Nonsense and the Functional Approach," 35 *Col. L. Rev.* (1935) 809. Felix Cohen is one of our foremost "rule skeptics." His lack of "factskepdeism" appears, for instance, in his failure to mention jury cases.

"there is a large element of uncertainty in actual law," yet "actual experience" reveals "a significant body of predictable uniformity in the behavior of courts," that "reasonably certain predictions" of decisions are possible. He said that such prediction "is not a question of pure logic but of human psychology, economics and politics," and that "the motivating forces which mold legal decisions" can be found in "the political, economic and professional background and activities of our various judges."

But note the rather severely limited scope of the psychological explorations of this school: (1) To the exclusion of virtually all else, they dwell on the rule-element in decisions or on the social policies behind the rules. (2) They therefore center their interest on decisions of upper courts. (3) They restrict the relevant judicial motivations almost entirely to those caused by the social, economic, political and professional influences affecting upper-court judges.

Frankfurter, for example, said that the "psychological factor is, of course, of infinitely greater significance where a court possesses the powers of our Supreme Court." Cohen, looking for "predictable uniformity in the behavior of courts," underscores the "social forces"[4] behind decisions, and discounts the effect of the "individual personality" of the judge; he dismisses attempted studies of individual judges' quirks, because (Cohen says) such studies had not produced any "significant results." I could quote similar views expressed by Pound, Powell, and other adherents of this school. Some of them have dwelt on the alleged uniformitarian effects of the similar education and professional experiences of the several judges.

The reader probably suspects what I regard as the flaws in this approach. Those who adopt it seek— and find—uniformities in the legal rules or in the social policies back of those rules. They ignore, however, that vast majority of decisions of cases in which social, economic, political and professional considerations are entirely, or almost entirely, absent, and where the rules are clear, the facts alone being in dispute. These thinkers, since their interest is in upper courts (where the facts are "given" by the trial courts), fail to take into account the numerous psychological factors in the non-rule element of the decisional process—that is, in trial-court fact-finding.[5] When they reject, as not "significant," any studies of the individual personalities of judges (especially of trial judges) which do not fall into the category of social-economic-political-professional influences, they do so, one suspects, because, most "significantly," the existence of those undiscoverable personal quirks knocks galley west the hope of discovering that "predictable uniformity in the behavior of courts" without which there can be no "reasonably certain predictions" of decisions of most law-suits not yet commenced.[6]

The sociological school has made important contributions, has illuminated the methods of upper courts, and has valuably suggested improvements in those methods. But it has been too frock-coated, too preoccupied with "judicial statesmanship" in the so-called "higher" courts. The consequence of its aloofness from the trial courts has not been fortunate. For the chief impediments to adequate court-house government, to decent administration of justice, would remain even if there should disappear all the difficulties encountered in constitutional cases, in the interpretation of statutes, and in the contriving and revision of judge-made rules. "Sociological jurisprudence" has long been the fashion in the law schools, with the more sophisticated lawyers, and among writers of books on history, economics and political science. This fashion has led to a general disregard by educated non-lawyers of the impact of the idiosyncratic personalities of trial judges on the overwhelming majority of cases they decide, when they sit without juries, cases affecting the lives of citizens, cases which turn on questions of fact such as these: How fast was Smith driving? Did Robinson and Sullivan make an agreement for the purchase and sale of 1,000

---

4   For criticism of the glib determinism which the words "social forces" often imply, see Frank, *Fate and Freedom* (1945) Reading 1.

5   Yet, like most "rule-skeptics," they disclose, here and there, some marginal disquietude about the "personal element" in such fact-finding.

6   Patterson, referring to the notion that a "judge's digestion" may affect his decision, says: "Since judges suffering from indigestion do not have any uniform predilections, as far as I know, this theory never got very far." Patterson, *Introduction to Jurisprudence* (2d ed. 1946) 222–23. Earlier, Patterson seems to have considered a judge's "peculiar drives and preferences" important; see "Logic in the Law," *90 un. of Pa. L. Rev.* (1942) at 893–894.

tins of salmon? Was old lady Tompkins in her right mind when she deeded her house to Will Playboy? Into the answers to such questions the differing personalities of trial judges enter with a vengeance and in ways about which sociological jurisprudence has been all but silent.

It is not difficult to expose the weakness of the "sociological approach": Assume that two trial judges have precisely the same social, economic and political background, that therefore (ex hypothesi) they have precisely the same social outlook, and that, accordingly, having the same attitude towards social policies, they would arrive at the same notion of the legal rule applicable to a given set of facts. It does not at all follow that, if they both heard the same witnesses, they would reach the same decision. Why? Because it is very, very far from certain that the two judges would believe and disbelieve the same witnesses, and consequently, that they would "find" the "facts" identically.

You see what I'm driving at: The influences operating on a particular trial judge, when he is listening to, and observing, witnesses, cannot be neatly caged within the categories of his fairly obvious social, economic and political views. Even the older psychology would suggest that these pigeon-holes are insufficient. See, for instance, Spencer's *Study of Sociology* in which he considers at length the obstacles to dispassionate judgment; he includes impatience, irrational irritation in the presence of unpleasant truths which are disappointing cherished hopes, hates, antipathies, awe of power, loyalty to the group. Francis Bacon included in his "Idols" those of the "Den," that is, errors due to causes peculiar to a specific individual. The "new psychology," Freudian or otherwise, properly emphasizes these peculiarly individual factors.[7] These uniquely, highly individual, operative influences are far more subtle, far more difficult to get at. Many of them, without possible doubt, are unknown to anyone except the judge. Indeed, often the judge himself is unaware of them.

When it comes to "finding" the "facts" in law-suits where the oral testimony is in conflict, these obscure idiosyncracies in the trial judge are bafflingly at work. The judge's sympathies and antipathies are likely to be active with respect to the witnesses. His own past may have created plus or minus reactions to women, or blonde women, or men with beards, or Southerners, or Italians, or Englishmen, or plumbers, or ministers, or college-graduates or Democrats. A certain facial twitch or cough or gesture may start up memories, painful or pleasant. Those memories of the trial judge, while he is listening to a witness with such a facial twitch or cough or gesture, may affect the judge's initial hearing, or subsequent recollection, of what the witness said, or the weight or credibility which the judge will attach to the witness' testimony.

Ranyard West, a practicing psychiatrist and also a close student of matters legal, makes some comments pertinent here. He writes of the "formation of prejudice from fantasy, a process deeply hidden from all but the most penetrating introspection. ... " The "mental processes involved" have two stages: In early life, each person has fantasies "compounded out of (a) genuine observations made by him as a young child, (b) perversions of truth introduced by misapprehended observations, and (c) pure inventions of the mind, imposed by the early emotional life of the child upon the real or semi-real figures around him" which "arouse his primitive and incoherent passions." In the adult period, "the unconscious mind" achieves an "identification ... between personalities of ... adult experiences and these ... fantasy figures of infancy." The "realities of infancy ... bias the tastes and judgments" of the adult, providing the "unconscious prejudices" of adult life. "We meet the persons, situations, and causes, X, Y, Z of our adult life; and to our conscious appraisement of them is contributed a factor from our unconscious memories, which judges them as if they were the A B C of some forgotten, far-off experiences of childhood." Many of us therefore often "do not see things and people as they are." In "the very act of labeling an experience we must needs go on and identify it with some fantasy or other, and docket it accordingly." Once "unfavorable unconscious

---

7   I am here lifting a passage from my book, *Law and the Modern Mind* (1930) 338–339 There I also said (p. 106): "In the first place, all other biases express themselves in connection with, and as modified by, these idiosyncratic biases. A man's political or economic prejudices are frequently cut across by his affection for or animosity to same particular individual or group, due to some unique experience he has had; or a racial antagonism which he entertains may be deflected in a particular case by a desire to be admired by someone who is devoid of such antagonism."

identification occurs, we falsify ... our judgments ..." of others. It is, says West, by no means easy for a man to "realize and feel the scope of his own prejudicial judgments," to "appreciate fully the measure of ... prejudice" in his own life.

Now the trial judge is a man, with a susceptibility to such unconscious prejudiced "identifications" originating in his infant experiences. Sitting at a trial, long before he has come to the point where he must decide what is right or wrong, just or unjust, with reference to the facts of the case as a whole, he has been engaged in making numerous judgments or inferences, as the testimony dribbles in. His impressions, colored by his unconscious biases with respect to the witnesses, as to what they said, and with what truthfulness and accuracy they said it, will determine what he believes to be the "facts of the case." His innumerable hidden traits and predispositions often get in their work in shaping his decision in the very process by which he becomes convinced what those facts are. The judge's belief about the facts results from the impact of numerous stimuli—including the words, gestures, postures and grimaces of the witnesses—on his distinctive "personality"; that personality, in turn, is a product of numerous factors, including his parents, his schooling, his teachers and companions, the persons he has met, the woman he married (or did not marry), his children, the books and articles he has read.

[...]

In sum, we may (for the sake of argument) assume judicial uniformity in judicial use of all the legal rules. But when it comes to the fact-component of decisions, uniformity may easily be absent in lawsuits in which the orally testifying witnesses disagree. If so, then—what? Then, in any one of the vast majority of juryless cases of that kind, the decision will depend on the peculiar personality of the particular trial judge who happens to be sitting.[8] "Art," said Zola, "is nature through the medium of a temperament." One may say the same of that segment of nature constituting the facts of a lawsuit.[9]

It is sometimes suggested that the hidden biases of divers judges will correct each other and largely cancel out. So said Cardozo.[10] That is partly true of judges sitting together in deciding a case. But that suggestion cannot be true of many trial judges sitting in separate courtrooms and separately making findings of fact in separate law-suits.

Studies of the restricted sort of background factors which interest the "sociological" school give some help, within limits, in prophesying how upper-court judges will decide some types of cases.[11] But they will give slight help in fore-knowing what trial judges will do in "contested" cases.[12] Even where the oral testimony is not conflicting, predictions of trial judges' decisions are not always easy, since such judges are not robots. Practicing lawyers, therefore, attempt to learn the idiosyncrasies of particular trial judges: Judge Brown is known as a former railroad lawyer, who, fearful of showing favoritism, leans over backwards and is likely to be unduly hostile to railroads. Judge Green, who for years had served in the office of the city's Corporation Counsel, is partial to municipalities. Judge Blue is markedly puritanical. Armed with such

---

8   Fromm, *Man For Himself* (1947) makes an important distinction between "temperament" and "character." But I have ignored that distinction in this book because it is not germane to my discussion.

9   One should add that, in a law-suit, the facts are seen through many temperaments, i.e., those of the witnesses and the trial judge; in a jury trial, one must add the jurors' temperaments.

10   "The eccentricities of judges balance one another." Cardozo, *The Nature of the Judicial Process* (1921) 112.

11   For a pioneering study of that type, see Haines, "General Observations on the Effect of Personal, Political and Economic Influences in The Decision of Cases," 17 *Ill. L. Rev.* (1923) 98. See also the several detailed biographies of Justices of the United States Supreme Court. Compare Frank, Book Review, 54 *Harv. L. Rev.* (1941) 905–06.

12   For an attempted study in that field, see Schroeder, "The Psychologic Study of Judicial Opinions," 6 *Calif. L. Rev.* 89. Schroeder was overly optimistic; he asserted that every opinion of a judge "amounts to a confession." For criticism of his article, see Frank, *Law and The Modern Mind* (1930) 113–14.

Even the most detailed studies of individual trial judges will be of little aid in prophesying how they will react to particular witnesses; consequently they will be of little value in predicting how those judges will find the facts on which they base their decisions. See the discussion, infra, of Lasswell and McDougal, Reading XIV.

information, lawyers try to have (or avoid having) some cases tried before certain judges. Knowledge of that character might be called "rules for decision" by Judge Brown, Green, Blue, Yellow, Purple, etc. It is perhaps conceivable that such data can be skillfully organized in great detail. But even such data will seldom, if ever, be enough when the oral testimony is in conflict.

[...]

Selection from Courts on Trial

The Upper-Court Myth

Jerome Frank

In legal mythology, one of the most popular and most harmful myth is the upper-court myth, the myth that upper courts are the heart of court-house government. This myth induces the false belief that it is of no importance whether or not trial judges are well-trained for their job, fair-minded, conscientious in listening to testimony, and honest. In considerable part, this belief arises from the fallacious notion that the legal rules, supervised by the upper courts, control decisions. But the false belief about the unimportance of the trial judge's activities is also encouraged by another tenet of the upper-court myth, i.e., that the upper courts on appeals can and will safeguard litigants against the trial judge's mistakes concerning the facts.[1] I think that by now the reader knows how delusional that notion is, knows that, when the oral testimony is in conflict as to a pivotal issue of fact, and when some of that testimony supports the trial court's (express or implied) finding on that issue, then the upper court ordinarily has to accept that finding. Usually it can refuse to do so only if it appears in the written or printed record of the trial that the finding was the product of the trial judge's incompetence, unfairness or dishonesty. Such matters, however, show up in such a record in but the tiniest fraction of cases. Because of the inherent subjectivity of the trial judge's decisional process, his deliberate or unintentional disregard or misunderstanding of honest and trustworthy oral testimony is ordinarily hidden from the scrutiny of the upper court.

Since, however, the upper-court myth creates and perpetuates the illusory notion that upper courts can offset all the failings of the trial judges, the public puts too much reliance on, and gives too much kudos to, upper-court judges. Note the consequences: In states where judges are elected, the politicos, responsive to public opinion, usually nominate, for upper-court positions, lawyers of distinguished ability and integrity. But, as the public

---

1   I previously touched on this notion; see Reading III [of original text].

is not onto the far greater importance of the trial courts, the politicos often (not always) are much less careful about whom they nominate to sit on the trial-court bench. I do not mean that many elected trial judges are not men of competence, character and ability. I do mean that the public tends to give relatively little attention to their qualifications.

Yet the duties of trial judges demand far more ability than do those "higher" court judges. Concerned as the latter are primarily with the legal rules, knowledge of those rules and skill in dealing with them constitute the chief requisites for the performance of their task. Many lawyers possess such knowledge and skill, which can be acquired by an intelligent man through an education in a law school and a few years in practice. But neither in the law schools—as legal education goes today—nor elsewhere can a lawyer obtain any systematic training necessary to give him the peculiar skills a trial judge should have.

Writing of trial judges, Professor Morgan recently said: "Of course, no rules prescribed by legislation or judicial decision can create character or competence [in a trial judge]." "But," he continued, "it is equally true that no system of administering justice can be satisfactory if constructed on the hypothesis that the trial judge will be crooked or incompetent." Then he went on to say, "Inevitably some trial judges will be slippery, prejudiced or otherwise unfit for office." Please mark the word "inevitably." I grant the inevitability of some such misfortunes. But what are we doing to reduce them to a minimum? If the number of ill-equipped trial judges is larger than is inevitable, then we have negligently provided ourselves with a system of administering justice bound to be unsatisfactory to an extent that is not inevitable but evitable. I think we have been astonishingly careless in our haphazard method of educating and selecting men to serve as trial judges.

[...]

Dredd Scott v. Sandford

60 U.S. 393 (1857)

[60 U.S. 393,396] THIS case was brought up, by writ of error, from the Circuit Court of the United States for the district of Missouri.

Prior to the institution of the present suit, an action was brought by Scott for his freedom in the Circuit Court of St. Louis county, (State court,) where there was a verdict and judgment in his favor. On a writ of error to the Supreme Court of the State, the judgment below was reversed, and the case remanded to the Circuit Court, where it was continued to await the decision of the case now in question.

The declaration of Scott contained three counts; one, that Sandford had assaulted the plaintiff; one, that he had assaulted Harriet Scott, his wife; and one, that he had assaulted Eliza Scott and Lizzie Scott, his children,

Sandford appeared, and filed the following plea:

DRED SCOTT

v.

JOHN F. A. SANDFORD.

Plea to the Jurisdiction of the Court.

APRIL TERM, 1854.

And the said John F. A. Sandford, in his own proper person, comes and says that this court ought not to have or take further cognizance of the action aforesaid, because he says that said cause of action, and each and every of them, (if any such have accrued to the said Dred Scott,) accrued to the said Dred Scott out of the jurisdiction of this court, and exclusively within the jurisdiction of the courts of the State of Missouri, for that, to wit: the said plaintiff, Dred Scott, is not a citizen of the State of Missouri, as alleged in his declaration, because [60 U.S. 393,397] he is a negro of African descent; his ancestors were of pure African blood, and were brought into this country and sold as negro slaves, and this the said Sandford is ready to verify. Wherefore, he prays judgment whether this court can or will take further cognizance of the action aforesaid.

JOHN F. A. SANDFORD.

To this plea there was a demurrer in the usual form, which was argued in April, 1854, when the court gave judgment that the demurrer should be sustained.

In May, 1854, the defendant, in pursuance of an agreement between counsel, and with the leave of the court, pleaded in bar of the action:

1. Not guilty.
2. That the plaintiff was a negro slave, the lawful property of the defendant, and, as such, the defendant gently laid his hands upon him, and thereby had only restrained him, as the defendant had a right to do.
3. That with respect to the wife and daughters of the plaintiff, in the second and third counts of the declaration mentioned, the defendant had, as to them, only acted in the same manner, and in virtue of the same legal right.

In the first of these pleas, the plaintiff joined issue; and to the second and third, filed replications alleging that the defendant, of his own wrong and without the cause in his second and third pleas alleged, committed the trespasses, &c.

The counsel then filed the following agreed statement of facts, viz:

In the year 1834, the plaintiff was a negro slave belonging to Dr. Emerson, who was a surgeon in the army of the United States. In that year, 1834, said Dr. Emerson took the plaintiff from the State of Missouri to the military post at Rock Island, in the State of Illinois, and held him there as a slave until the month of April or May, 1836. At the time last mentioned, said Dr. Emerson removed the plaintiff from said military post at Rock Island to the military post at Fort Snelling, situate on the west bank of the Mississippi river, in the Territory known as Upper Louisiana, acquired by the United States of France, and situate north of the latitude of thirty-six degrees thirty minutes north, and north of the State of Missouri. Said Dr. Emerson held the plaintiff in slavery at said Fort Snelling, from said last-mentioned date until the year 1838.

In the year 1835, Harriet, who is named in the second count of the plaintiffs declaration, was the negro slave of Major Taliaferro, who belonged to the army of the United States. [60 U.S. 393,398] In that year, 1835, said Major Taliaferro took said Harriet to said Fort Snelling, a military post, situated as hereinbefore stated, and kept her there as a slave until the year 1836, and then sold and delivered her as a slave at said Fort Snelling unto the said Dr. Emerson hereinbefore named. Said Dr. Emerson held said Harriet in slavery at said Fort Snelling until the year 1838.

In the year 1836, the plaintiff and said Harriet at said Fort Snelling, with the consent of said Dr. Emerson, who then claimed to be their master and owner, intermarried, and took each other for husband and wife. Eliza and Lizzie, named in the third count of the plaintiffs declaration, are the fruit of that marriage. Eliza is about fourteen years old, and was born on board the steamboat Gipsey, north of the north line of the State of Missouri, and upon the river Mississippi. Lizzie is about seven years old, and was born in the State of Missouri, at the military post called Jefferson Barracks.

In the year 1838, said Dr. Emerson removed the plaintiff and said Harriet and their said daughter Eliza, from said Fort Snelling to the State of Missouri, where they have ever since resided.

Before the commencement of this suit, said Dr. Emerson sold and conveyed the plaintiff, said Harriet, Eliza, and Lizzie, to the defendant, as slaves, and the defendant has ever since claimed to hold them and each of them as slaves.

At the times mentioned in the plaintiffs declaration, the defendant, claiming to be owner as aforesaid, laid his hands upon said plaintiff, Harriet, Eliza, and Lizzie, and imprisoned them, doing in this respect, however, no more than what he might lawfully do if they were of right his slaves at such times.

Further proof may be given on the trial for either party.

It is agreed that Dred Scott brought suit for his freedom in the Circuit Court of St. Louis county; that there was a verdict and judgment in his favor; that on a writ, of error to the Supreme Court, the judgment below was reversed, and the same remanded to the Circuit Court, where it has been continued to await the decision of this case.

In May, 1854, the cause went before a jury, who found the following verdict, viz: 'As to the first issue joined in this case, we of the jury find the defendant not guilty; and as to the issue secondly above joined, we of the jury find that before and at the time when, &c., in the first count mentioned, the said Dred Scott was a negro slave, the lawful property of the defendant; and as to the issue thirdly above joined, we, the jury, find that before and at the time when, &c., in the second and third counts mentioned, the said Harriet, wife of [60 U.S. 393, 399] said Dred Scott, and Eliza and Lizzie, the daughters of the said Dred Scott, were negro slaves, the lawful property of the defendant.'

Whereupon, the court gave judgment for the defendant.

[...]

MR. CHIEF JUSTICE TANEY DELIVERED THE OPINION OF THE COURT.

This case has been twice argued. After the argument at the last term, differences of opinion were found to exist among the members of the court; and as the questions in controversy are of the highest importance, and the court was at that time much pressed by the ordinary business of the term, it was deemed advisable to continue the case, and direct a re-argument on some of the points, in order that we might have an opportunity of giving to the whole subject a more deliberate [60 U.S. 393,400] consideration. It has accordingly been again argued by counsel, and considered by the court; and I now proceed to deliver its opinion. There are two leading questions presented by the record: 1. Had the Circuit Court of the United States jurisdiction to hear and determine the case between these parties? And 2. If it had jurisdiction, is the judgment it has given erroneous or not? The plaintiff in error, who was also the plaintiff in the court below, was, with his wife and children, held as slaves by the defendant, in the State of Missouri; and he brought this action in the Circuit Court of the United States for that district, to assert the title of himself and his family to freedom. The declaration is in the form usually adopted in that State to try questions of this description, and contains the averment necessary to give the court jurisdiction; that he and the defendant are citizens of different States; that is, that he is a citizen of Missouri, and the defendant a citizen of New York. The defendant pleaded in abatement to the jurisdiction of the court, that the plaintiff was not a citizen of the State of Missouri, as alleged in his declaration, being a negro of African descent, whose ancestors were of pure African blood, and who were brought into this country and sold as slaves. To this plea the plaintiff demurred, and the defendant joined in demurrer. The court overruled the plea, and gave judgment that the defendant should answer over. And he thereupon put in sundry pleas in bar, upon which issues were joined; and at the trial the verdict and judgment were in his favor. Whereupon the plaintiff brought this writ of error. Before we speak of the pleas in bar, it will be proper to dispose of the questions which have arisen on the plea in abatement. That plea denies the right of the plaintiff to sue in a court of the United States, for the reasons therein stated. If the question raised by it is legally before us, and the court should be of opinion that the facts stated in it disqualify the plaintiff from becoming a citizen, in the sense in which that word is used in the Constitution of the United States, then the judgment of the Circuit Court is erroneous, and must be reversed. It is suggested, however, that this plea is not before us; and that as the judgment in the court below on this plea was in favor of the plaintiff, he does not seek to reverse it, or bring it before the court for revision by his writ of error; and also that the defendant waived this defence by pleading over, and thereby admitted the jurisdiction of the court. [60 U.S. 393,401] But, in making this objection, we think the peculiar and limited jurisdiction of courts of the United States has not been adverted to. This peculiar and limited jurisdiction has made it necessary, in these courts, to adopt different rules and principles of pleading, so far as jurisdiction is concerned, from those which regulate courts of common law in England, and in the different States of the Union which have adopted the common-law rules.

[…]

The question is simply this: Can a negro, whose ancestors were imported into this country, and sold as slaves, become a member of the political community formed and brought into existence by the Constitution of the United States, and as such become entitled to all the rights, and privileges, and immunities, guarantied by that instrument to the citizen? One of which rights is the privilege of suing in a court of the United States in the cases specified in the Constitution.

It will be observed, that the plea applies to that class of persons only whose ancestors were negroes of the African race, and imported into this country, and sold and held as slaves. The only matter in issue before the court, therefore, is, whether the descendants of such slaves, when they shall be emancipated, or who are born of parents who had become free before their birth, are citizens of a State, in the sense in which the word citizen is used in the Constitution of the United States. And this being the only matter in dispute on the pleadings, the court must be understood as speaking in this opinion of that class only, that is, of those persons who are the descendants of Africans who were imported into this country, and sold as slaves.

The situation of this population was altogether unlike that of the Indian race. The latter, it is true, formed no part of the colonial communities, and never amalgamated with them in social connections or in government. But although they were uncivilized, they were yet a free and independent people, associated together in nations or tribes, and governed by their own laws. Many of these political communities were situated in territories to which the white race claimed the ultimate [60 U.S. 393,404] right of dominion. But that claim was acknowledged to be subject to the right of the Indians to occupy it as long as they thought proper, and neither the English nor colonial Governments claimed or exercised any dominion over the tribe or nation by whom it was occupied, nor claimed the right to the possession of the territory, until the tribe or nation consented to cede it. These Indian Governments were regarded and treated as foreign Governments, as much so as if an ocean had separated the red man from the white; and their freedom has constantly been acknowledged, from the time of the first emigration to the English colonies to the present day, by the different Governments which succeeded each other. Treaties have been negotiated with them, and their alliance sought for in war; and the people who compose these Indian political communities have always been treated as foreigners not living under our Government. It is true that the course of events has brought the Indian tribes within the limits of the United States under subjection to the white race; and it has been found necessary, for their sake as well as our own, to regard them as in a state of pupilage, and to legislate to a certain extent over them and the territory they occupy. But they may, without doubt, like the subjects of any other foreign Government, be naturalized by the authority of Congress, and become citizens of a State, and of the United States; and if an individual should leave his nation or tribe, and take up his abode among the white population, he would be entitled to all the rights and privileges which would belong to an emigrant from any other foreign people.

We proceed to examine the case as presented by the pleadings.

The words 'people of the United States' and 'citizens' are synonymous terms, and mean the same thing. They both describe the political body who, according to our republican institutions, form the sovereignty, and who hold the power and conduct the Government through their representatives. They are what we familiarly call the 'sovereign people,' and every citizen is one of this people, and a constituent member of this sovereignty. The question before us is, whether the class of persons described in the plea in abatement compose a portion of this people, and are constituent members of this sovereignty? We think they are not, and that they are not included, and were not intended to be included, under the word 'citizens' in the Constitution, and can therefore claim none of the rights and privileges which that instrument provides for and secures to citizens of the United States. On the contrary, they were at that time considered as a subordinate [60 U.S. 393, 405] and inferior class of beings, who had been subjugated by the dominant race, and, whether emancipated or not, yet remained subject to their authority, and had no rights or privileges but such as those who held the power and the Government might choose to grant them.

It is not the province of the court to decide upon the justice or injustice, the policy or impolicy, of these laws. The decision of that question belonged to the political or lawmaking power; to those who formed the sovereignty and framed the Constitution. The duty of the court is, to interpret the instrument they have framed, with the best lights we can obtain on the subject, and to administer it as we find it, according to its true intent and meaning when it was adopted.

In discussing this question, we must not confound the rights of citizenship which a State may confer within its own limits, and the rights of citizenship as a member of the Union. It does not by any means follow, because he has all the rights and privileges of a citizen of a State, that he must be a citizen of the United States. He may have all of the rights and privileges of the citizen of a State, and yet not be entitled to the rights and privileges of a citizen in any other State. For, previous to the adoption of the Constitution of the United States, every State had the undoubted right to confer on whomsoever it pleased the character of citizen, and to endow him with all its rights. But this character of course was confined to the boundaries of the State, and gave him no rights or privileges in other States beyond those secured to him by the laws of nations and the comity of States. Nor have the several States surrendered the power of conferring these rights and privileges by adopting the Constitution of the United States. Each State may still confer them upon an alien, or any one it thinks proper, or upon any class or description of persons; yet he would not be a citizen in the sense in which that word is used in the Constitution of the United States, nor entitled to sue as such in one of its courts, nor to the privileges and immunities of a citizen in the other States. The rights which he would acquire would be restricted to the State which gave them. The Constitution has conferred on Congress the right to establish an uniform rule of naturalization, and this right is evidently exclusive, and has always been held by this court to be so. Consequently, no State, since the adoption of the Constitution, can by naturalizing an alien invest him with the rights and privileges secured to a citizen of a State under the Federal Government, although, so far as the State alone was concerned, he would undoubtedly be entitled to the rights of a citizen, and clothed with all the [60 U.S. 393,406] rights and immunities which the Constitution and laws of the State attached to that character.

It is very clear, therefore, that no State can, by any act or law of its own, passed since the adoption of the Constitution, introduce a new member into the political community created by the Constitution of the United States. It cannot make him a member of this community by making him a member of its own. And for the same reason it cannot introduce any person, or description of persons, who were not intended to be embraced in this new political family, which the Constitution brought into existence, but were intended to be excluded from it.

The question then arises, whether the provisions of the Constitution, in relation to the personal rights and privileges to which the citizen of a State should be entitled, embraced the negro African race, at that time in this country, or who might afterwards be imported, who had then or should afterwards be made free in any State; and to put it in the power of a single State to make him a citizen of the United States, and endue him with the full rights of citizenship in every other State without their consent? Does the Constitution of the United States act upon him whenever he shall be made free under the laws of a State, and raised there to the rank of a citizen, and immediately clothe him with all the privileges of a citizen in every other State, and in its own courts?

The court think the affirmative of these propositions cannot be maintained. And if it cannot, the plaintiff in error could not be a citizen of the State of Missouri, within the meaning of the Constitution of the United States, and, consequently, was not entitled to sue in its courts.

It is true, every person, and every class and description of persons, who were at the time of the adoption of the Constitution recognised as citizens in the several States, became also citizens of this new political body; but none other; it was formed by them, and for them and their posterity, but for no one else. And the personal rights and privileges guarantied to citizens of this new sovereignty were intended to embrace those only who were then members of the several State communities, or who should afterwards by birthright or otherwise become members, according to the provisions of the Constitution and the principles on which it was founded. It was the union of those who were at that time members of distinct and separate political communities into one political family, whose power, for certain specified purposes, was to extend over the whole territory of the United States. And it gave to each citizen rights and privileges outside of his State [60 U.S. 393,407] which he did not before possess, and placed him in every other State upon a perfect equality with its own citizens as to rights of person and rights of property; it made him a citizen of the United States.

It becomes necessary, therefore, to determine who were citizens of the several States when the Constitution was adopted. And in order to do this, we must recur to the Governments and institutions of the thirteen colonies, when they separated from Great Britain and formed new sovereignties, and took their places in the family of independent nations. We must inquire who, at that time, were recognised as the people or citizens of a State, whose rights and liberties had been outraged by the English Government; and who declared their independence, and assumed the powers of Government to defend their rights by force of arms.

In the opinion of the court, the legislation and histories of the times, and the language used in the Declaration of Independence, show, that neither the class of persons who had been imported as slaves, nor their descendants, whether they had become free or not, were then acknowledged as a part of the people, nor intended to be included in the general words used in that memorable instrument.

It is difficult at this day to realize the state of public opinion in relation to that unfortunate race, which prevailed in the civilized and enlightened portions of the world at the time of the Declaration of Independence, and when the Constitution of the United States was framed and adopted. But the public history of every European nation displays it in a manner too plain to be mistaken.

They had for more than a century before been regarded as beings of an inferior order, and altogether unfit to associate with the white race, either in social or political relations; and so far inferior, that they had no rights which the white man was bound to respect; and that the negro might justly and lawfully be reduced to slavery for his benefit. He was bought and sold, and treated as an ordinary article of merchandise and traffic, whenever a profit could be made by it. This opinion was at that time fixed and universal in the civilized portion of the white race. It was regarded as an axiom in morals as well as in politics, which no one thought of disputing, or supposed to be open to dispute; and men in every grade and position in society daily and habitually acted upon it in their private pursuits, as well as in matters of public concern, without doubting for a moment the correctness of this opinion.

And in no nation was this opinion more firmly fixed or more [60 U.S. 393,408] uniformly acted upon than by the English Government and English people. They not only seized them on the coast of Africa, and sold them or held them in slavery for their own use; but they took them as ordinary articles of merchandise to every country where they could make a profit on them, and were far more extensively engaged in this commerce than any other nation in the world.

The opinion thus entertained and acted upon in England was naturally impressed upon the colonies they founded on this side of the Atlantic. And, accordingly, a negro of the African race was regarded by them as an article of property, and held, and bought and sold as such, in every one of the thirteen colonies which united in the Declaration of Independence, and afterwards formed the Constitution of the United States. The slaves were more or less numerous in the different colonies, as slave labor was found more or less profitable. But no one seems to have doubted the correctness of the prevailing opinion of the time.

The legislation of the different colonies furnishes positive and indisputable proof of this fact.

[...]

The language of the Declaration of Independence is equally conclusive:

It begins by declaring that, 'when in the course of human events it becomes necessary for one people to dissolve the political bands which have connected them with another, and to [60 U.S. 393,410] assume among the powers of the earth the separate and equal station to which the laws of nature and nature's God entitle them, a decent respect for the opinions of mankind requires that they should declare the causes which impel them to the separation.'

It then proceeds to say: 'We hold these truths to be self-evident: that all men are created equal; that they are endowed by their Creator with certain unalienable rights; that among them is life, liberty, and the pursuit of happiness; that to secure these rights, Governments are instituted, deriving their just powers from the consent of the governed.'

The general words above quoted would seem to embrace the whole human family, and if they were used in a similar instrument at this day would be so understood. But it is too clear for dispute, that the enslaved African race were not intended to be included, and formed no part of the people who framed and adopted this declaration; for if the language, as understood in that day, would embrace them, the conduct of the distinguished men who framed the Declaration of Independence would have been utterly and flagrantly inconsistent with the principles they asserted; and instead of the sympathy of mankind, to which they so confidently appealed, they would have deserved and received universal rebuke and reprobation.

Yet the men who framed this declaration were great men-high in literary acquirements-high in their sense of honor, and incapable of asserting principles inconsistent with those on which they were acting. They perfectly understood the meaning of the language they used, and how it would be understood by others; and they knew that it would not in any part of the civilized world be supposed to embrace the negro race, which, by common consent, had been excluded from civilized Governments and the family of nations, and doomed to slavery. They spoke and acted according to the then established doctrines and principles, and in the ordinary language of the day, and no one misunderstood them. The unhappy black race were separated from the white by indelible marks, and laws long before established, and were never thought of or spoken of except as property, and when the claims of the owner or the profit of the trader were supposed to need protection.

This state of public opinion had undergone no change when the Constitution was adopted, as is equally evident from its provisions and language.

The brief preamble sets forth by whom it was formed, for what purposes, and for whose benefit and protection. It declares [60 U.S. 393,411] that it is formed by the people of the United States; that is to say, by those who were members of the different political communities in the several States; and its great object is declared to be to secure the blessings of liberty to themselves and their posterity. It speaks in general terms of the people of the United States, and of citizens of the several States, when it is providing for the exercise of the powers granted or the privileges secured to the citizen. It does not define what description of persons are intended to be included under these terms, or who shall be regarded as a citizen and one of the people. It uses them as terms so well understood, that no further description or definition was necessary.

But there are two clauses in the Constitution which point directly and specifically to the negro race as a separate class of persons, and show clearly that they were not regarded as a portion of the people or citizens of the Government then formed.

One of these clauses reserves to each of the thirteen States the right to import slaves until the year 1808, if it thinks proper. And the importation which it thus sanctions was unquestionably of persons of the race of which we are speaking, as the traffic in slaves in the United States had always been confined to them. And by the other provision the States pledge themselves to each other to maintain the right of property of the master, by delivering up to him any slave who may have escaped from his service, and be found within their respective territories. By the first above-mentioned clause, therefore, the right to purchase and hold this property is directly sanctioned and authorized for twenty years by the people who framed the Constitution. And by the second, they pledge themselves to maintain and uphold the right of the master in the manner specified, as long as the Government they then formed should endure. And these two provisions show, conclusively, that neither the description of persons therein referred to, nor their descendants, were embraced in any of the other provisions of the Constitution; for certainly these two clauses were not intended to confer on them or their posterity the blessings of liberty, or any of the personal rights so carefully provided for the citizen.

No one of that race had ever migrated to the United States voluntarily; all of them had been brought here as articles of merchandise. The number that had been emancipated at that time were but few in comparison with those held in slavery; and they were identified in the public mind with the race to which they belonged, and regarded as a part of the slave population rather than the free. It is obvious that they were not [60 U.S. 393,412] even in the minds of the framers of the Constitution when they were conferring special rights and privileges upon the citizens of a State in every other part of the Union.

Indeed, when we look to the condition of this race in the several States at the time, it is impossible to believe that these rights and privileges were intended to be extended to them.

It is very true, that in that portion of the Union where the labor of the negro race was found to be unsuited to the climate and unprofitable to the master, but few slaves were held at the time of the Declaration of Independence; and when the Constitution was adopted, it had entirely worn out in one of them, and measures had been taken for its gradual abolition in several others. But this change had not been produced by any change of opinion in relation to this race; but because it was discovered, from experience, that slave labor was unsuited to the climate and productions of these States: for some of the States, where it had ceased or nearly ceased to exist, were actively engaged in the slave trade, procuring cargoes on the coast of Africa, and transporting them for sale to those parts of the Union where their labor was found to be profitable, and suited to the climate and productions. And this traffic was openly carried on, and fortunes accumulated by it, without reproach from the people of the States where they resided. And it can hardly be supposed that, in the States where it was then countenanced in its worst form—that is, in the seizure and transportation—the people could have regarded those who were emancipated as entitled to equal rights with themselves.

[…]

The legislation of the States shows, in a manner not to be mistaken, the inferior and subject condition of that race at the time the Constitution was adopted, and long afterwards, throughout the thirteen States by which that instrument was framed; and it is hardly consistent with the respect due to these States, to suppose that they regarded at that time, as fellow-citizens and members of the sovereignty, a class of beings whom they had thus stigmatized; whom, as we are bound, out of respect to the State sovereignties, to assume they had deemed it just and necessary thus to stigmatize, and upon whom they had impressed such deep and enduring marks of inferiority and degradation; or, that when they met in convention to form the Constitution, they looked upon them as a portion of their constituents, or designed to include them in the provisions so carefully inserted for the security and protection of the liberties and rights of their citizens. It cannot be supposed that they intended to secure to them rights, and privileges, and rank, in the new political body throughout the Union, which every one of them denied within the limits of its own dominion. More especially, it cannot be believed that the large slaveholding States regarded them as included in the word citizens, or would have consented to a Constitution which might compel them to receive them in that character from another State. For if they were so received, and entitled to the privileges and immunities of citizens, it would exempt them from the operation of the special laws and from the police regulations which they considered to be necessary for their own safety. It would give to persons of the negro race, who were recognised as citizens in any one State of the Union, the right to enter every other State whenever they pleased, singly or in companies, without pass or passport, and without obstruction, to sojourn there as long as they pleased, to go where they pleased at every hour of the day or night without molestation, unless they committed some violation of law for which a white man would be punished; and it would give them the full liberty of speech in public and in private upon all subjects upon which its own citizens might speak; to hold public meetings upon political affairs, and to keep and carry arms wherever they went. And all of this would be done in the face of the subject race of the same color, both free and slaves, and inevitably producing discontent and insubordination among them, and endangering the peace and safety of the State.

It is impossible, it would seem, to believe that the great men of the slaveholding States, who took so large a share in framing the Constitution of the United States, and exercised so much influence in procuring its adoption, could have been so forgetful or regardless of their own safety and the safety of those who trusted and confided in them.

Besides, this want of foresight and care would have been utterly inconsistent with the caution displayed in providing for the admission of new members into this political family. For, when they gave to the citizens of each State the privileges and immunities of citizens in the several States, they at the same time took from the several States the power of naturalization, and confined that power exclusively to the Federal Government. No State was willing to permit another State to determine who should or should not be admitted as one of its citizens, and entitled to demand equal rights and privileges with their own people, within their own territories. The right of naturalization was therefore, with one accord, surrendered by the States, and confided to the Federal Government. And this power granted to Congress to establish an uniform rule of naturalization is, by the well-understood meaning of the word, confined to persons born in a foreign country, under a foreign Government. It is not a power to raise to the rank of a citizen any one born in the United States, who, from birth or parentage, by the laws of the country, belongs to an inferior and subordinate class. And when we find the States guarding themselves from the indiscreet or improper admission by other States of emigrants from other countries, by giving the power exclusively to Congress, we cannot fail to see that they could never have left with the States a much [60 U.S. 393,418] more important power-that is, the power of transforming into citizens a numerous class of persons, who in that character would be much more dangerous to the peace and safety of a large portion of the Union, than the few foreigners one of the States might improperly naturalize. The Constitution upon its adoption obviously took from the States all power by any subsequent legislation to introduce as a citizen into the political family of the United States any one, no matter where he was born, or what might be his character or condition; and it gave to Congress the power to confer this character upon those only who were born outside of the dominions of the United States. And no law of a State, therefore, passed since the Constitution was adopted, can give any right of citizenship outside of its own territory.

[...]

But it is said that a person may be a citizen, and entitled to [60 U.S. 393,422] that character, although he does not possess all the rights which may belong to other citizens; as, for example, the right to vote, or to hold particular offices; and that yet, when he goes into another State, he is entitled to be recognised there as a citizen, although the State may measure his rights by the rights which it allows to persons of a like character or class resident in the State, and refuse to him the full rights of citizenship.

This argument overlooks the language of the provision in the Constitution of which we are speaking.

Undoubtedly, a person may be a citizen, that is, a member of the community who form the sovereignty, although he exercises no share of the political power, and is incapacitated from holding particular offices. Women and minors, who form a part of the political family, cannot vote; and when a property qualification is required to vote or hold a particular office, those who have not the necessary qualification cannot vote or hold the office, yet they are citizens.

So, too, a person may be entitled to vote by the law of the State, who is not a citizen even of the State itself. And in some of the States of the Union foreigners not naturalized are allowed to vote. And the State may give the right to free negroes and mulattoes, but that does not make them citizens of the State, and still less of the United States. And the provision in the Constitution giving privileges and immunities in other States, does not apply to them.

Neither does it apply to a person who, being the citizen of a State, migrates to another State. For then he becomes subject to the laws of the State in which he lives, and he is no longer a citizen of the State from which he removed. And the State in which he resides may then, unquestionably, determine his status or condition, and place him among the class of persons who are not recognised as citizens, but belong to an inferior and subject race; and may deny him the privileges and immunities enjoyed by its citizens.

But so far as mere rights of person are concerned, the provision in question is confined to citizens of a State who are temporarily in another State without taking up their residence there. It gives them no political rights in the State, as to voting or holding office, or in any other respect. For a citizen of one State has no right to participate in the government of another. But if he ranks as a citizen in the State to which he belongs, within the meaning of the Constitution of the United States, then, whenever he goes into another State, the Constitution clothes him, as to the rights of person, will all the privileges and immunities which belong to citizens of the [60 U.S. 393, 423] State. And if persons of the African race are citizens of a State, and of the United States, they would be entitled to all of these privileges and immunities in every State, and the State could not restrict them; for they would hold these privileges and immunities under the paramount authority of the Federal Government, and its courts would be bound to maintain and enforce them, the Constitution and laws of the State to the contrary notwithstanding. And if the States could limit or restrict them, or place the party in an inferior grade, this clause of the Constitution would be unmeaning, and could have no operation; and would give no rights to the citizen when in another State. He would have none but what the State itself chose to allow him. This is evidently not the construction or meaning of the clause in question. It guaranties rights to the citizen, and the State cannot withhold them. And these rights are of a character and would lead to consequences which make it absolutely certain that the African race were not included under the name of citizens of a State, and were not in the contemplation of the framers of the Constitution when these privileges and immunities were provided for the protection of the citizen in other States.

No one, we presume, supposes that any change in public opinion or feeling, in relation to this unfortunate race, in the civilized nations of Europe or in this country, should induce the court to give to the words of the Constitution a more liberal construction in their favor than they were intended to bear when the instrument was framed and adopted. Such an argument would be altogether inadmissible in any tribunal called on to interpret it. If any of its provisions are deemed unjust, there is a mode prescribed in the instrument itself by which it may be amended; but while it remains unaltered, it must be construed now as it was understood at the time of its adoption. It is not only the same in words, but the same in meaning, and delegates the same powers to the Government, and reserves and secures the same rights and privileges to the citizen; and as long as it continues to exist in its present form, it speaks not only in the same words, but with the same meaning and intent with which it spoke when it came from the hands of its framers, and was voted on and adopted by the people of the United States. Any other rule of construction would abrogate the judicial character of this court, and make it the mere reflex of the popular opinion or passion of the day. This court was not created by the Constitution for such purposes. Higher and graver trusts have been confided to it, and it must not falter in the path of duty.

What the construction was at that time, we think can hardly admit of doubt. We have the language of the Declaration of Independence and of the Articles of Confederation, in addition to the plain words of the Constitution itself; we have the legislation of the different States, before, about the time, and since, the Constitution was adopted; we have the legislation of Congress, from the time of its adoption to a recent period; and we have the constant and uniform action of the Executive Department, all concurring together, and leading to the same result. And if anything in relation to the construction of the Constitution can be regarded as settled, it is that which we now give to the word 'citizen' and the word 'people.'

And upon a full and careful consideration of the subject, the court is of opinion, that, upon the facts stated in the plea in abatement, Dred Scott was not a citizen of Missouri within the meaning of the Constitution of the United States, and not entitled as such to sue in its courts; and, consequently, that the Circuit Court had no jurisdiction of the case, and that the judgment on the plea in abatement is erroneous.

Now, if the removal of which he speaks did not give them their freedom, then by his own admission he is still a slave; and whatever opinions may be entertained in favor of the citizenship of a free person of the African race, no one supposes that a slave is a citizen of the State or of the United States. If, therefore, the acts done by his owner did not make them free persons, he is still a slave, and certainly incapable of suing in the character of a citizen.

The principle of law is too well settled to be disputed, that a court can give no judgment for either party, where it has no jurisdiction; and if, upon the showing of Scott himself, it appeared that he was still a slave, the case ought to have been dismissed, and the judgment against him and in favor of the defendant for costs, is, like that on the plea in abatement, erroneous, and the suit ought to have been dismissed by the Circuit Court for want of jurisdiction in that court.

[…]

We proceed, therefore, to inquire whether the facts relied on by the plaintiff entitled him to his freedom. [60 U.S. 393,431] The case, as he himself states it, on the record brought here by his writ of error, is this:

The plaintiff was a negro slave, belonging to Dr. Emerson, who was a surgeon in the army of the United States. In the year 1834, he took the plaintiff from the State of Missouri to the military post at Rock Island, in the State of Illinois, and held him there as a slave until the month of April or May, 1836. At the time last mentioned, said Dr. Emerson removed the plaintiff from said military post at Rock Island to the military post at Fort Snelling, situate on the west bank of the Mississippi river, in the Territory known as Upper Louisiana, acquired by the United States of France, and situate north of the latitude of thirty-six degrees thirty minutes north, and north of the State of Missouri. Said Dr. Emerson held the plaintiff in slavery at said Fort Snelling, from said last-mentioned date until the year 1838.

In the year 1835, Harriet, who is named in the second count of the plaintiffs declaration, was the negro slave of Major Taliaferro, who belonged to the army of the United States. In that year, 1835, said Major Taliaferro took said Harriet to said Fort Snelling, a military post, situated as hereinbefore stated, and kept her there as a slave until the year 1836, and then sold and delivered her as a slave, at said Fort Snelling, unto the said Dr. Emerson hereinbefore named. Said Dr. Emerson held said Harriet in slavery at said Fort Snelling until the year 1838.

In the year 1836, the plaintiff and Harriet intermarried, at Fort Snelling, with the consent of Dr. Emerson, who then claimed to be their master and owner. Eliza and Lizzie, named in the third count of the plaintiffs declaration, are the fruit of that marriage. Eliza is about fourteen years old, and was born on board the steamboat Gipsey, north of the north line of the State of Missouri, and upon the river Mississippi. Lizzie is about seven years old, and was born in the State of Missouri, at the military post called Jefferson Barracks.

In the year 1838, said Dr. Emerson removed the plaintiff and said Harriet, and their said daughter Eliza, from said Fort Snelling to the State of Missouri, where they have ever since resided.

Before the commencement of this suit, said Dr. Emerson sold and conveyed the plaintiff, and Harriet, Eliza, and Lizzie, to the defendant, as slaves, and the defendant has ever since claimed to hold them, and each of them, as slaves.

In considering this part of the controversy, two questions arise: 1. Was he, together with his family, free in Missouri by reason of the stay in the territory of the United States hereinbefore [60 U.S. 393,432] mentioned? And 2. If they were not, is Scott himself free by reason of his removal to Rock Island, in the State of Illinois, as stated in the above admissions?

We proceed to examine the first question.

The act of Congress, upon which the plaintiff relies, declares that slavery and involuntary servitude, except as a punishment for crime, shall be forever prohibited in all that part of the territory ceded by France, under the name of Louisiana, which lies north of thirty-six degrees thirty minutes north latitude, and not included within the limits of Missouri. And the difficulty which meets us at the threshold of this part of the inquiry is, whether Congress was authorized to pass this law under any of the powers granted to it by the Constitution; for if the authority is not given by that instrument, it is the duty of this court to declare it void and inoperative, and incapable of conferring freedom upon any one who is held as a slave under the have of any one of the States.

The counsel for the plaintiff has laid much stress upon that article in the Constitution which confers on Congress the power 'to dispose of and make all needful rules and regulations respecting the territory or other property belonging to the United States;' but, in the judgment of the court, that provision has no bearing on the present controversy, and the power there given, whatever it may be, is confined, and was intended to be confined, to the territory which at that time belonged to, or was claimed by, the United States, and was within their boundaries as settled by the treaty with Great Britain, and can have no influence upon a territory afterwards acquired from a foreign Government. It was a special provision for a known and particular territory, and to meet a present emergency, and nothing more.

A brief summary of the history of the times, as well as the careful and measured terms in which the article is framed, will show the correctness of this proposition.

It will be remembered that, from the commencement of the Revolutionary war, serious difficulties existed between the States, in relation to the disposition of large and unsettled territories which were included in the chartered limits of some of the States. And some of the other States, and more especially Maryland, which had no unsettled lands, insisted that as the unoccupied lands, if wrested from Great Britain, would owe their preservation to the common purse and the common sword, the money arising from them ought to be applied in just proportion among the several States to pay the expenses of the war, and ought not to be appropriated to the use of the State in whose chartered limits they might happen [60 U.S. 393,433] to lie, to the exclusion of the other States, by whose combined efforts and common expense the territory was defended and preserved against the claim of the British Government.

These difficulties caused much uneasiness during the war, while the issue was in some degree doubtful, and the future boundaries of the United States yet to be defined by treaty, if we achieved our independence.

[...]

Now, as we have already said in an earlier part of this opinion, upon a different point, the right of property in a slave is distinctly and expressly affirmed in the Constitution. The right to traffic in it, like an ordinary article of merchandise and property, was guaranteed to the citizens of the United States, in every State that might desire it, for twenty years. And the Government in express terms is pledged to protect [60 U.S. 393,452] it in all future time, if the slave escapes from his owner. This is done in plain words-too plain to be misunderstood. And no word can be found in the Constitution which gives Congress a greater power over slave property, or which entitles property of that kind to less protection that property of any other description. The only power conferred is the power coupled with the duty of guarding and protecting the owner in his rights.

Upon these considerations, it is the opinion of the court that the act of Congress which prohibited a citizen from holding and owning property of this kind in the territory of the United States north of the line therein mentioned, is not warranted by the Constitution, and is therefore void; and that neither Dred Scott himself, nor any of his family, were made free by being carried into this territory; even if they had been carried there by the owner, with the intention of becoming a permanent resident.

We have so far examined the case, as it stands under the Constitution of the United States, and the powers thereby delegated to the Federal Government.

But there is another point in the case which depends on State power and State law. And it is contended, on the part of the plaintiff, that he is made free by being taken to Rock Island, in the State of Illinois, independently of his residence in the territory of the United States; and being so made free, he was not again reduced to a state of slavery by being brought back to Missouri.

[...]

As Scott was a slave when taken into the State of Illinois by his owner, and was there held as such, and brought back in that character, his status, as free or slave, depended on the laws of Missouri, and not of Illinois.

It has, however, been urged in the argument, that by the laws of Missouri he was free on his return. But whatever doubts or opinions may, at one time, have been entertained upon this subject, we are satisfied, upon a careful examination of all the cases decided in the State courts of Missouri referred to, that it is now firmly settled by the decisions of the highest court in the State, that Scott and his family upon their return were not free, but were, by the laws of Missouri, the property of the defendant; and that the Circuit Court of the United States had no jurisdiction, when, by the laws of the State, the plaintiff was a slave, and not a citizen.

Moreover, the plaintiff, it appears, brought a similar action against the defendant in the State court of Missouri, claiming the freedom of himself and his family upon the same grounds and the same evidence upon which hw relies in the case before the court. The case was carried before the Supreme Court of the State; was fully argued there; and that court decided that neither the plaintiff nor his family were entitled to freedom, and were still the slaves of the defendant; and reversed the judgment of the inferior State court, which had given a different decision. If the plaintiff supposed that this judgment of the Supreme Court of the State was erroneous, and that this court had jurisdiction to revise and reverse it, the only mode by which he could legally bring it before this court was by writ of error directed to the Supreme Court of the State, requiring it to transmit the record to this court. If this had been done, it is too plain for argument that the writ must have been dismissed for want of jurisdiction in this court.

[...]

Upon the whole, therefore, it is the judgment of this court, that it appears by the record before us that the plaintiff in error is not a citizen of Missouri, in the sense in which that word is used in the Constitution; and that the Circuit Court of the United States, for that reason, had no jurisdiction in the case, and could give no judgment in it. Its judgment for the defendant must, consequently, be reversed, and a mandate issued, directing the suit to be dismissed for want of jurisdiction.

MR. JUSTICE GRIER

...To this plea in abatement, a demurrer having been interposed on behalf of the plaintiff, it was sustained by the court. After the decision sustaining the demurrer, the defendant, in pursuance of a previous agreement between counsel, and with the leave of the court, pleaded in bar of the action: 1st, not guilty; 2dly, that the plaintiff was a negro slave, the lawful property of the defendant, and as such the defendant gently laid his hands upon him, and thereby had only restrained him, as the defendant had a right to do; 3dly, that with respect to the wife and daughters of the plaintiff, in the second and third counts of the declaration mentioned, the defendant had, as to them, only acted in the same manner, and in virtue of the same legal right.

Issues having been joined upon the above pleas in bar, the following statement, comprising all the evidence in the cause, was agreed upon and signed by the counsel of the respective parties, viz:

'In the year 1834, the plaintiff was a negro slave belonging to Doctor Emerson, who was a surgeon in the army of the United States. In that year, 1834, said Dr. Emerson took the plaintiff from the State of Missouri to the military post at Rock Island, in the State of Illinois, and held him there as a slave until the month of April or May, 1836. At the time last mentioned, said Dr. Emerson removed the plaintiff from said military post at Rock Island to the military post at Fort Snelling, situate on the west bank of the Mississippi river, in the Territory known as Upper Louisiana, acquired by the United States of France, and situate north of the latitude of thirty-six [60 U.S. 393,471] degrees thirty minutes north, and north of the State of Missouri. Said Dr. Emerson held the plaintiff in slavery at said Fort Snelling, from said last-mentioned date until the year 1838.

'In the year 1835, Harriet, who is named in the second count of the plaintiff's declaration, was the negro slave of Major Taliaferro, who belonged to the army of the United States. In that year, 1835, said Major Taliaferro took said Harriet to said Fort Snelling, a military post situated as hereinbefore stated, and kept her there as a slave until the year 1836, and then sold and delivered her as a slave at said Fort Snelling unto the said Dr. Emerson, hereinbefore named. Said Dr. Emerson held said Harriet in slavery at said Fort Snelling until the year 1838.

'In the year 1836, the plaintiff and said Harriet, at said Fort Snelling, with the consent of said Dr. Emerson, who then claimed to be their master and owner, intermarried, and took each other for husband and wife. Eliza and Lizzie, named in the -third count of the plaintiff's declaration, are the fruit of that marriage. Eliza is about fourteen years old, and was born on board the steamboat Gipsey, north of the north line of the State of Missouri, and upon the river Mississippi. Lizzie is about seven years old, and was born in the State of Missouri, at a military post called Jefferson barracks.

'In the year 1838, said Dr. Emerson removed the plaintiff and said Harriet, and their said daughter Eliza, from said Fort Snelling to the State of Missouri, where they have ever since resided.

'Before the commencement of this suit, said Dr. Emerson sold and conveyed the plaintiff, said Harriet, Eliza, and Lizzie, to the defendant, as slaves, and the defendant has ever since claimed to hold them and each of them as slaves.

[...]

MR. JUSTICE DANIEL

But with regard to slavery amongst the Romans, it is by no means true that emancipation, either during the republic or the empire, conferred, by the act itself, or implied, the status or the rights of citizenship.

The proud title of Roman citizen, with the immunities and rights incident thereto, and as contra-distinguished alike from the condition of conquered subjects or of the lower grades of native domestic residents, was maintained throughout the duration of the republic, and until a late period of the eastern empire, and at last was in effect destroyed less by an elevation of the inferior classes than by the degradation of the free, and the previous possessors of rights and immunities civil and political, to the indiscriminate abasement incident to absolute and simple despotism.

By the learned and elegant historian of the Decline and Fall of the Roman Empire, we are told that 'In the decline of the Roman empire, the proud distinctions of the republic were gradually abolished; and the reason or instinct of Justinian completed the simple form of an absolute monarchy. The emperor could not eradicate the popular reverence which always waits on the possession of hereditary wealth or the memory of famous ancestors. He delighted to honor with titles and emoluments his generals, magistrates, and senators, and his precarious indulgence communicated some rays of their glory to their wives and children. But in the eye of the law all Roman citizens were equal, and all subjects of the empire were citizens of Rome. That inestimable character was degraded to an obsolete and empty name. The voice of a Roman could no longer enact his laws, or create the annual ministers of his powers; his constitutional rights might have checked the arbitrary will of a master; and the bold adventurer from Germany or Arabia was admitted with equal favor to the civil and military command which the citizen alone had been once entitled to assume over the conquests of his fathers. The first Caesars had scrupulously guarded the distinction of ingenuous and servile birth, which was decided by the condition of the mother. The slaves who were liberated by a generous master immediately entered into the middle class of libertini or freedmen; but they could never be enfranchised from the duties of obedience and gratitude; whatever were the fruits of [60 U.S. 393,479] their industry, their patron and his family inherited the third part, or even the whole of their fortune, if they died without children and without a testament. Justinian respected the rights of patrons, but his indulgence removed the badge of disgrace from the two inferior orders of freedmen; whoever ceased to be a slave, obtained without reserve or delay the station of a citizen; and at length the dignity of an ingenuous birth was created or supposed by the omnipotence of the emperor.'

The above account of slavery and its modifications will be found in strictest conformity with the Institutes of Justinian. Thus, book 1st, title 3d, it is said: 'The first general division of persons in respect to their rights is into freemen and slaves.' The same title, sec. 4th: 'Slaves are born such, or become so. They are born such of bondwomen; they become so either by the law of nations, as by capture, or by the civil law.'

MR. JUSTICE MCLEAN

…An action of trespass was brought, which charges the defendant with an assault and imprisonment of the plaintiff, and also of Harriet Scott, his wife, Eliza and Lizzie, his two children, on the ground that they were his slaves, which was without right on his part, and against law.

The defendant filed a plea in abatement, 'that said causes of action, and each and every of them, if any such accrued to the said Dred Scott, accrued out of the jurisdiction of this court, and exclusively within the jurisdiction of the courts of the State of Missouri, for that to wit, said plaintiff, Dred Scott, is not a citizen of the State of Missouri, as alleged in his declaration, because he is a negro of African descent, his ancestors were of pure African blood, and were brought into this country and sold as negro slaves; and this the said Sandford is ready to verify; wherefore he prays judgment whether the court can or will take further cognizance of the action aforesaid.'

[…]

The decision on the demurrer was in favor of the plaintiff; and as the plaintiff prosecutes this writ of error, he does not complain of the decision on the demurrer. The defendant might have complained of this decision, as against him, and have prosecuted a writ of error, to reverse it. But as the case, under the instruction of the court to the jury, was decided in his favor, of course he had no ground of complaint.

But it is said, if the court, on looking at the record, shall clearly perceive that the Circuit Court had no jurisdiction, it is a ground for the dismissal of the case. This may be characterized as rather a sharp practice, and one which seldom, if ever, occurs. No case was cited in the argument as authority, and not a single case precisely in point is recollected in our reports. The pleadings do not show a want of jurisdiction. This want of jurisdiction can only be ascertained by a judgment on the demurrer to the special plea. No such case, it is believed, can be cited. But if this rule of practice is to be applied in this case, and the plaintiff in error is required to answer and maintain as well the points ruled in his favor, as to show the error of those ruled against him, he has more than an ordinary duty to perform. Under such circumstances, the want of jurisdiction in the Circuit Court must be so clear as not to admit of doubt. Now, the plea which raises the question of jurisdiction, in my judgment, is radically defective. The gravamen of the plea is this:

'That the plaintiff is a negro of African descent, his ancestors being of pure African blood, and were brought into this country, and sold as negro slaves.'

There is no averment in this plea which shows or conduces to show an inability in the plaintiff to sue in the Circuit Court. It does not allege that the plaintiff had his domicil in any other State, nor that he is not a free man in Missouri. He is averred to have had a negro ancestry, but this does not show that he is not a citizen of Missouri, within the meaning of the act of Congress authorizing him to sue in the Circuit Court. It has never been held necessary, to constitute a citizen within the act, that he should have the qualifications of an elector. Females and minors may sue in the Federal courts, and so may any individual who has a permanent domicil in the State under whose laws his rights are protected, and to which he owes allegiance.

Being born under our Constitution and laws, no naturalization is required, as one of foreign birth, to make him a citizen. The most general and appropriate definition of the term citizen is 'a freeman.' Being a freeman, and having his domicil in a State different from that of the defendant, he is a citizen within the act of Congress, and the courts of the Union are open to him.

It has often been held, that the jurisdiction, as regards parties, can only be exercised between citizens of different States and that a mere residence is not sufficient; but this has been said to distinguish a temporary from a permanent residence.

To constitute a good plea to the jurisdiction, it must negative those qualities and rights which enable an individual to sue in the Federal courts. This has not been done; and on this ground the plea was defective, and the demurrer was properly sustained. No implication can aid a plea in abatement or in bar; it must be complete in itself; the facts stated, if true, must abate or bar the right of the plaintiff to sue. This is not the character of the above plea. The facts stated, if admitted, are not inconsistent with other facts, which may be presumed, and which bring the plaintiff within the act of Congress.

The pleader has not the boldness to allege that the plaintiff is a slave, as that would assume against him the matter in controversy, and embrace the entire merits of the case in a plea to the jurisdiction. But beyond the facts set out in the plea, the court, to sustain it, must assume the plaintiff to be a slave, which is decisive on the merits. This is a short and an effectual mode of deciding the cause; but I am yet to learn that it is sanctioned by any known rule of pleading.

The defendant's counsel complain, that if the court take jurisdiction on the ground that the plaintiff is free, the assumption is against the right of the master. This argument is easily answered. In the first place, the plea does not show him to be a slave; it does not follow that a man is not free whose ancestors were slaves. The reports of the Supreme Court of Missouri show that this assumption has many exceptions; and there is no averment in the plea that the plaintiff is not within them.

By all the rules of pleading, this is a fatal defect in the plea. If there be doubt, what rule of construction has been established in the slave States? In Jacob v. Sharp, (Meigs's Rep., Tennessee, 114,) the court held, when there was doubt as to the constuction of a will which emancipated a slave, 'it must be construed to be subordinate to the higher and more important right of freedom.'

No injustice can result to the master, from an exercise of jurisdiction in this cause. Such a decision does not in any degree affect the merits of the case; it only enables the plaintiff to assert his claims to freedom before this tribunal. If the jurisdiction be ruled against him, on the ground that he is a slave, it is decisive of his fate.

It has been argued that, if a colored person be made a citizen of a State, he cannot sue in the Federal court. The Constitution declares that Federal jurisdiction 'may be exercised between citizens of different States,' and the same is provided [60 U.S. 393,533] in the act of 1789. The above argument is properly met by saying that the Constitution was intended to be a practical instrument; and where its language is too plain to be misunderstood, the argument ends.'

[...]

It is a power which belongs exclusively to Congress, as intimately connected with our Federal relations. A State may authorize foreigners to hold real estate within its jurisdiction, but it has no power to naturalize foreigners, and give them the rights of citizens. Such a right is opposed to the acts of Congress on the subject of naturalization, and subversive of the Federal powers. I regret that any countenance should be given from this bench to a practice like this in some of the States, which has no warrant in the Constitution.

In the argument, it was said that a colored citizen would not be an agreeable member of society. This is more a matter of taste than of law. Several of the States have admitted persons of color to the right of suffrage, and in this view have recognised them as citizens; and this has been done in the slave as well as the free States. On the question of citizenship, it must be admitted that we have not been very fastidious. Under the late treaty with Mexico, we have made citizens of all grades, combinations, and colors. The same was done in the admission of Louisiana and Florida. No one ever doubted, and no court ever held, that the people of these Territories did not become citizens under the treaty. They have exercised all the rights of citizens, without being naturalized under the acts of Congress.

There are several important principles involved in this case, which have been argued, and which may be considered under the following heads:

1. The locality of slavery, as settled by this court and the courts of the States. 2. The relation which the Federal Government bears to slavery in the States. 3. The power of Congress to establish Territorial Governments, and to prohibit the introduction of slavery therein. 4. The effect of taking slaves into a new State or Territory, and so holding them, where slavery is prohibited. 5. Whether the return of a slave under the control of his [60 U.S. 393, 534] master, after being entitled to his freedom, reduces him to his former condition.

6. Are the decisions of the Supreme Court of Missouri, on the questions before us, binding on this court, within the rule adopted.

In the course of my judicial duties, I have had occasion to consider and decide several of the above points.

1. As to the locality of slavery. The civil law throughout the Continent of Europe, it is believed, without an exception, is, that slavery can exist only within the territory where it is established; and that, if a slave escapes, or is carried beyond such territory, his mater cannot reclaim him, unless by virtue of some express stipulation. (Grotius, lib. 2, chap. 15, 5, 1; lib. 10, chap. 10, 2, 1; Wicqueposts Ambassador, lib. 1, p. 418; 4 Martin, 385; Case of the Creole in the House of Lords, 1842; 1 Phillimore on International Law, 316, 335.)

There is no nation in Europe which considers itself bound to return to his master a fugitive slave, under the civil law or the law of nations. On the contrary, the slave is held to be free where there is no treaty obligation, or compact in some other form, to return him to his master. The Roman law did now allow freedom to be sold. An ambassador or any other public functionary could not take a slave to France, Spain, or any other country of Europe, without emancipating him. A number of slaves escaped from a Florida plantation, and were received on board of ship by Admiral Cochrane; by the King's Bench, they were held to be free. (2 Barn. and Cres., 440.)

[…]

No case in England appears to have been more thoroughly examined than that of Somersett. The judgment pronounced by Lord Mansfield was the judgment of the Court of King's Bench. The cause was argued at great length, and with great ability, by Hargrave and others, who stood among the most eminent counsel in England. It was held under advisement from term to term, and a due sense of its importance was felt and expressed by the Bench.

In giving the opinion of the court, Lord Mansfield said:

> 'The state of slavery is of such a nature that it is incapable of being introduced on any reasons, moral or political, but only by positive law, which preserves its force long after the reasons, occasion, and time itself, from whence it was created, is erased from the memory; it is of a nature that nothing can be suffered to support it but positive law.'

[…]

I will now consider the relation which the Federal Government bears to slavery in the States:

Slavery is emphatically a State institution. In the ninth section of the first article of the Constitution, it is provided 'that the migration or importation of such persons as any of the States now existing shall think proper to admit, shall not be prohibited by the Congress prior to the year 1808, but a tax or duty may be imposed on such importation, not exceeding ten dollars for each person.'

In the Convention, it was proposed by a committee of eleven to limit the importation of slaves to the year 1800, when Mr. Pinckney moved to extend the time to the year 1808. This motion was carried-New Hampshire, Massachusetts, Connecticut, Maryland, North Carolina, South Carolina, and Georgia, voting in the affirmative; and New Jersey, Pennsylvania, and Virginia, in the negative. In opposition to the motion, Mr. Madison said: 'Twenty years will produce all the mischief that can be apprehended from the liberty to import slaves; so long a term will be more dishonorable to the American character than to say nothing about it in the Constitution.' (Madison Papers.)

The provision in regard to the slave trade shows clearly that Congress considered slavery a State institution, to be continued and regulated by its individual sovereignty; and to conciliate that interest, the slave trade was continued twenty years, not as a general measure, but for the 'benefit of such States as shall think proper to encourage it.'

[…]

The only connection which the Federal Government holds with slaves in a State, arises from that provision of the Constitution which declares that 'No person held to service or labor in one State, under the laws thereof, escaping into another, shall, in consequence of any law or regulation therein, be discharged from such service or labor, but shall be delivered up, on claim of the party to whom such service or labor may be due.'

This being a fundamental law of the Federal Government, it rests mainly for its execution, as has been held, on the judicial power of the Union; and so far as the rendition of fugitives from labor has become a subject of judicial action, the Federal obligation has been faithfully discharged.

In the formation of the Federal Constitution, care was taken to confer no power on the Federal Government to interfere with this institution in the States. In the provision respecting the slave trade, in fixing the ratio of representation, and providing for the reclamation of fugitives from labor, slaves were referred to as persons, and in no other respect are they considered in the Constitution.

We need not refer to the mercenary spirit which introduced the infamous traffic in slaves, to show the degradation of negro slavery in our country. This system was imposed upon our colonial settlements by the mother country, and it is due to truth to say that the commercial colonies and States were chiefly engaged in the traffic. But we know as a historical fact, that James Madison, that great and good man, a leading member in the Federal Convention, was solicitous to guard the language of that instrument so as not to convey the idea that there could be property in man.

I prefer the lights of Madison, Hamilton, and Jay, as a means of construing the Constitution in all its bearings, rather than to look behind that period, into a traffic which is now declared to be piracy, and punished with death by Christian nations. I do not like to draw the sources of our domestic relations from so dark a ground. Our independence was a great epoch in the history of freedom; and while I admit the Government was not made expecially for the colored race, yet many of them were citizens of the New England States, and exercised, the rights of suffrage when the Constitution was adopted, and it was not doubted by any intelligent person that its tendencies would greatly ameliorate their condition.

Many of the States, on the adoption of the Constitution, or [60 U.S. 393, 538] shortly afterward, took measures to abolish slavery within their respective jurisdictions; and it is a well-known fact that a belief was cherished by the leading men, South as well as North, that the institution of slavery would gradually decline, until it would become extinct. The increased value of slave labor, in the culture of cotton and sugar, prevented the realization of this expectation. Like all other communities and States, the South were influenced by what they considered to be their own interests.

But if we are to turn our attention to the dark ages of the world, why confine our view to colored slavery? On the same principles, white men were made slaves. All slavery has its origin in power, and is against right.

[…]

Now, if a slave abscond, he may be reclaimed; but if he accompany his master into a State or Territory where slavery is prohibited, such slave cannot be said to have left the service of his master where his services were legalized. And if slavery be limited to the range of the territorial laws, how can the slave be coerced to serve in a State or Territory, not only without the authority of law, but against its express provisions? What gives the master the right to control the will of his slave? The local law, which exists in some form. But where there is no such law, can the master control the will of the slave by force? Where no slavery exists, the presumption, without regard to color, is in favor of freedom. Under such a jurisdiction, may the colored man be levied on as the property of his master by a creditor? On the decease of the master, does the slave descend to his heirs as property? Can the master sell him? Any one or all of these acts may be done to the slave, where he is legally held to service. But where the law does not confer this power, it cannot be exercised.

Lord Mansfield held that a slave brought into England was free. Lord Stowell agreed with Lord Mansfield in this respect, and that the slave could not be coerced in England; but on her voluntary return to Antigua, the place of her slave domicil, her former status attached. The law of England did not prohibit slavery, but did not authorize it. The jurisdiction which prohibits slavery is much stronger in behalf of the slave within it, than where it only does not authorize it.

By virtue of what law is it, that a master may take his slave into free territory, and exact from him the duties of a slave? The law of the Territory does not sanction it. No authority can be claimed under the Constitution of the United States, or any law of Congress. Will it be said that the slave is taken as property, the same as other property which the master may own? To this I answer, that colored persons are made property by the law of the State, and no such power has been given to Congress. Does the master carry with him the law of the State from which he removes into the Territory? and does that enable him to coerce his slave in the Territory? Let us test this theory. If this may be done by a master from one slave State, it may be done by a master from every other slave State. This right is supposed to be connected with the person of the master, by virtue of the local law. Is it transferable? May it be negotiated, as a promissory note or bill of exchange? If it be assigned to a man from a free State, may he coerce the slave by virtue of it? What shall this thing be [60 U.S. 393,549] denominated? Is it personal or real property? Or is it an indefinable fragment of sovereignty, which every person carries with him from his late domicil? One thing is certain, that its origin has been very recent, and it is unknown to the laws of any civilized country.

A slave is brought to England from one of its islands, where slavery was introduced and maintained by the mother country. Although there is no law prohibiting slavery in England, yet there is no law authorizing it; and, for near a century, its courts have declared that the slave there is free from the coercion of the master. Lords Mansfield and Stowell agree upon this point, and there is no dissenting authority.

[…]

When Dred Scott, his wife and children, were removed from Fort Snelling to Missouri, in 1838, they were free, as the law was then settled, and continued for fourteen years afterwards, up to 1852, when the above decision was made. Prior to this, for nearly thirty years, as Chief Justice Gamble declares, the residence of a master with his slave in the State of Illinois, or in the Territory north of Missouri, where slavery was prohibited [60 U.S. 393, 555] by the act called the Missouri compromise, would manumit the slave as effectually as if he had executed a deed of emancipation; and that an officer of the army who takes his slave into that State or Territory, and holds him there as a slave, liberates him the same as any other citizen—and down to the above time it was settled by numerous and uniform decisions, and that on the return of the slave to Missouri, his former condition of slavery did not attach. Such was the settled law of Missouri until the decision of Scott and Emerson.

Plessy v. Ferguson

163 U.S. 537 (1896)

May 18, 1896. [163 U.S. 537, 538] This was a petition for writs of prohibition and certiorari originally filed in the supreme court of the state by Plessy, the plaintiff in error, against the Hon. John H. Ferguson, judge of the criminal district court for the parish of Orleans, and setting forth, in substance, the following facts:

That petitioner was a citizen of the United States and a resident of the state of Louisiana, of mixed descent, in the proportion of seven-eighths Caucasian and one-eighth African blood; that the mixture of colored blood was not discernible in him, and that he was entitled to every recognition, right, privilege, and immunity secured to the citizens of the United States of the white race by its constitution and laws; that on June 7, 1892, he engaged and paid for a first-class passage on the East Louisiana Railway, from New Orleans to Covington, in the same state, and thereupon entered a passenger train, and took possession of a vacant seat in a coach where passengers of the white race were accommodated; that such railroad company was incorporated by the laws of Louisiana as a common carrier, and was not authorized to distinguish between citizens according to their race, but, notwithstanding this, petitioner was required by the conductor, under penalty of ejection from said train and imprisonment, to vacate said coach, and occupy another seat, in a coach assigned by said company for persons not of the white race, and for no other reason than that petitioner was of the colored race; that, upon petitioner's refusal to comply with such order, he was, with the aid of a police officer, forcibly ejected from said coach, and hurried off to, and imprisoned in, the parish jail of [163 U.S. 537,539] New Orleans, and there held to answer a charge made by such officer to the effect that he was guilty of having criminally violated an act of the general assembly of the state, approved July 10, 1890, in such case made and provided.

The petitioner was subsequently brought before the recorder of the city for preliminary examination, and committed for trial to the criminal district court for the parish of Orleans, where an information was filed against him in the matter above set forth, for a violation of the above act, which act the petitioner affirmed to be null and void, because in conflict with the constitution of the United States; that petitioner interposed a plea to such information, based upon the unconstitutionality of the act of the general assembly, to which the district attorney, on behalf of the state, filed a demurrer; that, upon issue being joined upon such demurrer and plea, the court sustained the demurrer, overruled the plea, and ordered petitioner to plead over to the facts set forth in the information, and that, unless the judge of the said court be enjoined by a writ of prohibition from further proceeding in such case, the court will proceed to fine and sentence petitioner to imprisonment, and thus deprive him of his constitutional rights set forth in his said plea, notwithstanding the unconstitutionality of the act under which he was being prosecuted; that no appeal lay from such sentence, and petitioner was without relief or remedy except by writs of prohibition and certiorari. Copies of the information and other proceedings in the criminal district court were annexed to the petition as an exhibit.

Upon the filing of this petition, an order was issued upon the respondent to show cause why a writ of prohibition should not issue, and be made perpetual, and a further order that the record of the proceedings had in the criminal cause be certified and transmitted to the supreme court.

To this order the respondent made answer, transmitting a certified copy of the proceedings, asserting the constitutionality of the law, and averring that, instead of pleading or admitting that he belonged to the colored race, the said Plessy declined and refused, either by pleading or otherwise, to admit [163 U.S. 537, 540] that he was in any sense or in any proportion a colored man.

The case coming on for hearing before the supreme court, that court was of opinion that the law under which the prosecution was had was constitutional and denied the relief prayed for by the petitioner (Ex parte Plessy, 45 La. Ann. 80, 11 South. 948); whereupon petitioner prayed for a writ of error from this court, which was allowed by the chief justice of the supreme court of Louisiana.

[...]

MR. JUSTICE BROWN, AFTER STATING THE FACTS IN THE FOREGOING LANGUAGE, DELIVERED THE OPINION OF THE COURT.

This case turns upon the constitutionality of an act of the general assembly of the state of Louisiana, passed in 1890, providing for separate railway carriages for the white and colored races. Acts 1890, No. 111, p. 152.

The first section of the statute enacts 'that all railway companies carrying passengers in their coaches in this state, shall provide equal but separate accommodations for the white, and colored races, by providing two or more passenger coaches for each passenger train, or by dividing the passenger coaches by a partition so as to secure separate accommodations: provided, that this section shall not be construed to apply to street railroads. No person or persons shall be permitted to occupy seats in coaches, other than the ones assigned to them, on account of the race they belong to.'

By the second section it was enacted 'that the officers of such passenger trains shall have power and are hereby required [163 U.S. 537, 541] to assign each passenger to the coach or compartment used for the race to which such passenger belongs; any passenger insisting on going into a coach or compartment to which by race he does not belong, shall be liable to a fine of twenty-five dollars, or in lieu thereof to imprisonment for a period of not more than twenty days in the parish prison, and any officer of any railroad insisting on assigning a passenger to a coach or compartment other than the one set aside for the race to which said passenger belongs, shall be liable to a fine of twenty-five dollars, or in lieu thereof to imprisonment for a period of not more than twenty days in the parish prison; and should any passenger refuse to occupy the coach or compartment to which he or she is assigned by the officer of such railway, said officer shall have power to refuse to carry such passenger on his train, and for such refusal neither he nor the railway company which he represents shall be liable for damages in any of the courts of this state.'

The third section provides penalties for the refusal or neglect of the officers, directors, conductors, and employees of railway companies to comply with the act, with a proviso that 'nothing in this act shall be construed as applying to nurses attending children of the other race.' The fourth section is immaterial.

The information filed in the criminal district court charged, in substance, that Plessy, being a passenger between two stations within the state of Louisiana, was assigned by officers of the company to the coach used for the race to which he belonged, but he insisted upon going into a coach used by the race to which he did not belong. Neither in the information nor plea was his particular race or color averred.

The petition for the writ of prohibition averred that petitioner was seven-eights Caucasian and one-eighth African blood; that the mixture of colored blood was not discernible in him; and that he was entitled to every right, privilege, and immunity secured to citizens of the United States of the white race; and that, upon such theory, he took possession of a vacant seat in a coach where passengers of the white race were accommodated, and was ordered by the conductor to vacate [163 U.S. 537, 542] said coach, and take a seat in another, assigned to persons of the colored race, and, having refused to comply with such demand, he was forcibly ejected, with the aid of a police officer, and imprisoned in the parish jail to answer a charge of having violated the above act.

The constitutionality of this act is attacked upon the ground that it conflicts both with the thirteenth amendment of the constitution, abolishing slavery, and the fourteenth amendment, which prohibits certain restrictive legislation on the part of the states.

1. That it does not conflict with the thirteenth amendment, which abolished slavery and involuntary servitude, except a punishment for crime, is too clear for argument. Slavery implies involuntary servitude,—a state of bondage; the ownership of mankind as a chattel, or, at least, the control of the labor and services of one man for the benefit of another, and the absence of a legal right to the disposal of his own person, property, and services. This amendment was said in the Slaughter-House Cases, 16 Wall. 36, to have been intended primarily to abolish slavery, as it had been previously known in this country, and that it equally forbade Mexican peonage or the Chinese coolie trade, when they amounted to slavery or involuntary servitude, and that the use of the word 'servitude' was intended to prohibit the use of all forms of involuntary slavery, of whatever class or name. It was intimated, however, in that case, that this amendment was regarded by the statesmen of that day as insufficient to protect the colored race from certain laws which had been enacted in the Southern states, imposing upon the colored race onerous disabilities and burdens, and curtailing their rights in the pursuit of life, liberty, and property to such an extent that their freedom was of little value; and that the fourteenth amendment was devised to meet this exigency.

So, too, in the Civil Rights Cases, 109 U.S. 3, 3 Sup. Ct. 18, it was said that the act of a mere individual, the owner of an inn, a public conveyance or place of amusement, refusing accommodations to colored people, cannot be justly regarded as imposing any badge of slavery or servitude upon the applicant, but [163 U.S. 537,543] only as involving an ordinary civil injury, properly cognizable by the laws of the state, and presumably subject to redress by those laws until the contrary appears. 'It would be running the slavery question into the ground,' said Mr. Justice Bradley, 'to make it apply to every act of discrimination which a person may see fit to make as to the guests he will entertain, or as to the people he will take into his coach or cab or car, or admit to his concert or theater, or deal with in other matters of intercourse or business.'

A statute which implies merely a legal distinction between the white and colored races—a distinction which is founded in the color of the two races, and which must always exist so long as white men are distinguished from the other race by color-has no tendency to destroy the legal equality of the two races, or re-establish a state of involuntary servitude. Indeed, we do not understand that the thirteenth amendment is strenuously relied upon by the plaintiff in error in this connection.

2. By the fourteenth amendment, all persons born or naturalized in the United States, and subject to the jurisdiction thereof, are made citizens of the United States and of the state wherein they reside; and the states are forbidden from making or enforcing any law which shall abridge the privileges or immunities of citizens of the United States, or shall deprive any person of life, liberty, or property without due process of law, or deny to any person within their jurisdiction the equal protection of the laws.

The proper construction of this amendment was first called to the attention of this court in the Slaughter-House Cases, 16 Wall. 36, which involved, however, not a question of race, but one of exclusive privileges. The case did not call for any expression of opinion as to the exact rights it was intended to secure to the colored race, but it was said generally that its main purpose was to establish the citizenship of the negro, to give definitions of citizenship of the United States and of the states, and to protect from the hostile legislation of the states the privileges and immunities of citizens of the United States, as distinguished from those of citizens of the states. [163 U.S. 537, 544] The object of the amendment was undoubtedly to enforce the absolute equality of the two races before the law, but, in the nature of things, it could not have been intended to abolish distinctions based upon color, or to enforce social, as distinguished from political, equality, or a commingling of the two races upon terms unsatisfactory to either. Laws permitting, and even requiring, their separation, in places where they are liable to be brought into contact, do not necessarily imply the inferiority of either race to the other, and have been generally, if not universally, recognized as within the competency of the state legislatures in the exercise of their police power. The most common instance of this is connected with the establishment of separate schools for white and colored children, which have been held to be a valid exercise of the legislative power even by courts of states where the political rights of the colored race have been longest and most earnestly enforced.

One of the earliest of these cases is that of Roberts v. City of Boston, 5 Cush. 198, in which the supreme judicial court of Massachusetts held that the general school committee of Boston had power to make provision for the instruction of colored children in separate schools established exclusively for them, and to prohibit their attendance upon the other schools. 'The great principle,' said Chief Justice Shaw, 'advanced by the learned and eloquent advocate for the plaintiff [Mr. Charles Sumner], is that, by the constitution and laws of Massachusetts, all persons, without distinction of age or sex, birth or color, origin or condition, are equal before the law. ... But, when this great principle comes to be applied to the actual and various conditions of persons in society, it will not warrant the assertion that men and women are legally clothed with the same civil and political powers, and that children and adults are legally to have the same functions and be subject to the same treatment; but only that the rights of all, as they are settled and regulated by law, are equally entitled to the paternal consideration and protection of the law for their maintenance and security.' It was held that the powers of the committee extended to the establishment [163 U.S. 537,545] of separate schools for children of different ages, sexes and colors, and that they might also establish special schools for poor and neglected children, who have become too old to attend the primary school, and yet have not acquired the rudiments of learning, to enable them to enter the ordinary schools. Similar laws have been enacted by congress under its general power of legislation over the District of Columbia (sections 281–283, 310, 319, Rev. St. D. C.), as well as by the legislatures of many of the states, and have been generally, if not uniformly, sustained by the courts. State v. McCann, 21 Ohio St. 210; Lehew v. Bmmmell (Mo. Sup.) 15 S. W. 765; Ward v. Flood, 48 Cal. 36; Bertonneau v. Directors of City Schools, 3 Woods, 177, Fed. Cas. No. 1,361; People v. Gallagher, 93 N. Y. 438; Cory v. Carter, 48 Ind. 337; Dawson v. Lee, 83 Ky. 49.

Laws forbidding the intermarriage of the two races may be said in a technical sense to interfere with the freedom of contract, and yet have been universally recognized as within the police power of the state. State v. Gibson, 36 Ind. 389.

The distinction between laws interfering with the political equality of the negro and those requiring the separation of the two races in schools, theaters, and railway carriages has been frequently drawn by this court. Thus, in Strauder v. West Virginia, 100 U.S. 303, it was held that a law of West Virginia limiting to white male persons 21 years of age, and citizens of the state, the right to sit upon juries, was a discrimination which implied a legal inferiority in civil society, which lessened the security of the right of the colored race, and was a step towards reducing them to a condition of servility. Indeed, the right of a colored man that, in the selection of jurors to pass upon his life, liberty, and property, there shall be no exclusion of his race, and no discrimination against them because of color, has been asserted in a number of cases. Virginia v. Rivers, 100 U.S. 313: Neal v. Delaware, 103 U.S. 370: ush v. Com., 107 U.S. 110.1 Sup. Ct. 625; Gibson v. Mississippi, 162 U.S. 565 , 16 Sup. Ct. 904. So, where the laws of a particular locality or the charter of a particular railway corporation has provided that no person shall be excluded from the cars on account of [163 U.S. 537, 546] color, we have held that this meant that persons of color should travel in the same car as white ones, and that the enactment was not satisfied by the company providing cars assigned exclusively to people of color, though they were as good as those which they assigned exclusively to white persons. Railroad Co. v. Brown, 17 Wall. 445.

Upon the other hand, where a statute of Louisiana required those engaged in the transportation of passengers among the states to give to all persons traveling within that state, upon vessels employed in that business, equal rights and privileges in all parts of the vessel, without distinction on account of race or color, and subjected to an action for damages the owner of such a vessel who excluded colored passengers on account of their color from the cabin set aside by him for the use of whites, it was held to be, so far as it applied to interstate commerce, unconstitutional and void. Hall v. De Cuir, 95 U.S. 485. The court in this case, however, expressly disclaimed that it had anything whatever to do with the statute as a regulation of internal commerce, or affecting anything else than commerce among the states.

In the Civil Rights Cases, 109 U.S. 3, 3 Sup. Ct. 18, it was held that an act of congress entitling all persons within the jurisdiction of the United States to the full and equal enjoyment of the accommodations, advantages, facilities, and privileges of inns, public conveyances, on land or water, theaters, and other places of public amusement, and made applicable to citizens of every race and color, regardless of any previous condition of servitude, was unconstitutional and void, upon the ground that the fourteenth amendment was prohibitory upon the states only, and the legislation authorized to be adopted by congress for enforcing it was not direct legislation on matters respecting which the states were prohibited from making or enforcing certain laws, or doing certain acts, but was corrective legislation, such as might be necessary or proper for counter-acting and redressing the effect of such laws or acts. In delivering the opinion of the court, Mr. Justice Bradley observed that the fourteenth amendment 'does not invest congress with power to legislate upon subjects that are within the [163

U.S. 537, 547] domain of state legislation, but to provide modes of relief against state legislation or state action of the kind referred to. It does not authorize congress to create a code of municipal law for the regulation of private rights, but to provide modes of redress against the operation of state laws, and the action of state officers, executive or judicial, when these are subversive of the fundamental rights specified in the amendment. Positive rights and privileges are undoubtedly secured by the fourteenth amendment; but they are secured by way of prohibition against state laws and state proceedings affecting those rights and privileges, and by power given to congress to legislate for the purpose of carrying such prohibition into effect; and such legislation must necessarily be predicated upon such supposed state laws or state proceedings, and be directed to the correction of their operation and effect.'

Much nearer, and, indeed, almost directly in point, is the case of the Louisville, N. O. & T. Ry. Co. v. State, 133 U.S. 587, 10 Sup. Ct. 348, wherein the railway company was indicted for a violation of a statute of Mississippi, enacting that all railroads carrying passengers should provide equal, but separate, accommodations for the white and colored races, by providing two or more passenger cars for each passenger train, or by dividing the passenger cars by a partition, so as to secure separate accommodations. The case was presented in a different aspect from the one under consideration, inasmuch as it was an indictment against the railway company for failing to provide the separate accommodations, but the question considered was the constitutionality of the law. In that case, the supreme court of Mississippi (66 Miss. 662, 6 South. 203) had held that the statute applied solely to commerce within the state, and, that being the construction of the state statute by its highest court, was accepted as conclusive. 'If it be a matter,' said the court (page 591, 133 U. S., and page 348, 10 Sup. Ct.), 'respecting commerce wholly within a state, and not interfering with commerce between the states, then, obviously, there is no violation of the commerce clause of the federal constitution. ... No question arises under this section as to the power of the state to separate in different compartments interstate passengers [163 U.S. 537, 548], or affect, in any manner, the privileges and rights of such passengers. All that we can consider is whether the state has the power to require that railroad trains within her limits shall have separate accommodations for the two races. That affecting only commerce within the state is no invasion of the power given to congress by the commerce clause.'

A like course of reasoning applies to the case under consideration, since the supreme court of Louisiana, in the case of State v. Judge, 44 La. Ann. 770, 11 South. 74, held that the statute in question did not apply to interstate passengers, but was confined in its application to passengers traveling exclusively within the borders of the state.

[…]

While we think the enforced separation of the races, as applied to the internal commerce of the state, neither abridges the privileges or immunities of the colored man, deprives him of his property without due process of law, nor denies him the equal protection of the laws, within the meaning of the fourteenth amendment, we are not prepared to say that the conductor, in assigning passengers to the coaches according to their race does not act at his peril, or that the provision of the second section of the act that denies to the passenger compensation [163 U.S. 537, 549] in damages for a refusal to receive him into the coach in which he properly belongs is a valid exercise of the legislative power. Indeed, we understand it to be conceded by the state's attorney that such part of the act as exempts from liability the railway company and its officers is unconstitutional. The power to assign to a particular coach obviously implies the power to determine to which race the passenger belongs, as well as the power to determine who, under the laws of the particular state, is to be deemed a white, and who a colored, person. This question, though indicated in the brief of the plaintiff in error, does not properly arise upon the record in this case, since the only issue made is as to the unconstitutionality of the act, so far as it requires the railway to provide separate accommodations, and the conductor to assign passengers according to their race.

It is claimed by the plaintiff in error that, in an mixed community, the reputation of belonging to the dominant race, in this instance the white race, is 'property,' in the same sense that a right of action or of inheritance is property. Conceding this to be so, for the purposes of this case, we are unable to see how this statute deprives him of, or in any way affects his right to, such property. If he be a white man, and assigned to a colored coach, he may have his action for damages against the company for being deprived of his so-called 'property.' Upon the other hand, if he be a colored man, and be so assigned, he has been deprived of no property, since he is not lawfully entitled to the reputation of being a white man.

In this connection, it is also suggested by the learned counsel for the plaintiff in error that the same argument that will justify the state legislature in requiring railways to provide separate accommodations for the two races will also authorize them to require separate cars to be provided for people whose hair is of a certain color, or who are aliens, or who belong to certain nationalities, or to enact laws requiring colored people to walk upon one side of the street, and white people upon the other, or requiring white men's houses to be painted white, and colored men's black, or their vehicles or business signs to be of different colors, upon the theory that one side [163 U.S. 537, 550] of the street is as good as the other, or that a house or vehicle of one color is as good as one of another color. The reply to all this is that every exercise of the police power must be reasonable, and extend only to such laws as are enacted in good faith for the promotion of the public good, and not for the annoyance or oppression of a particular class. Thus, in Yick Wo v. Hopkins, 118 U.S. 356, 6 Sup. Ct. 1064, it was held by this court that a municipal ordinance of the city of San Francisco, to regulate the carrying on of public laundries within the limits of the municipality, violated the provisions of the constitution of the United States, if it conferred upon the municipal authorities arbitrary power, at their own will, and without regard to discretion, in the legal sense of the term, to give or withhold consent as to persons or places, without regard to the competency of the persons applying or the propriety of the places selected for the carrying on of the business. It was held to be a covert attempt on the part of the municipality to make an arbitrary and unjust discrimination against the Chinese race. While this was the case of a municipal ordinance, a like principle has been held to apply to acts of a state legislature passed in the exercise of the police power. Railroad Co. v. Husen, 95 U.S. 465: Louisville & N. R. Co. v. Kentucky, 161 U.S. 677, 16 Sup. Ct. 714, and cases cited on page 700, 161 U. S., and page 714, 16 Sup. Ct.; Daggett v. Hudson, 43 Ohio St. 548, 3 N. E. 538; Capen v. Foster, 12 Pick. 485; State v. Baker, 38 Wis. 71; Monroe v. Collins, 17 Ohio St. 665; Hulseman v. Rems, 41 Pa. St. 396; Osman v. Riley, 15 Cal. 48.

So far, then, as a conflict with the fourteenth amendment is concerned, the case reduces itself to the question whether the statute of Louisiana is a reasonable regulation, and with respect to this there must necessarily be a large discretion on the part of the legislature. In determining the question of reasonableness, it is at liberty to act with reference to the established usages, customs, and traditions of the people, and with a view to the promotion of their comfort, and the preservation of the public peace and good order. Gauged by this standard, we cannot say that a law which authorizes or even requires the separation of the two races in public conveyances [163 U.S. 537, 551] is unreasonable, or more obnoxious to the fourteenth amendment than the acts of congress requiring separate schools for colored children in the District of Columbia, the constitutionality of which does not seem to have been questioned, or the corresponding acts of state legislatures.

We consider the underlying fallacy of the plaintiff's argument to consist in the assumption that the enforced separation of the two races stamps the colored race with a badge of inferiority. If this be so, it is not by reason of anything found in the act, but solely because the colored race chooses to put that construction upon it. The argument necessarily assumes that if, as has been more than once the case, and is not unlikely to be so again, the colored race should become the dominant power in the state legislature, and should enact a law in precisely similar terms, it would thereby relegate the white race to an inferior position. We imagine that the white race, at least, would not acquiesce in this assumption. The argument also assumes that social prejudices may be overcome by legislation, and that equal rights cannot be secured to the negro except by an enforced commingling of the two races. We cannot accept this proposition. If the two races are to meet upon terms of social equality, it must be the result of natural affinities, a mutual appreciation of each other's merits, and a voluntary consent of individuals. As was said by the court of appeals of New York in People v. Gallagher, 93 N. Y. 438, 448: 'This end can neither be accomplished nor promoted by laws which conflict with the general sentiment of the community upon whom they are designed to operate. When the government, therefore, has secured to each of its citizens equal rights before the law, and equal opportunities for improvement and progress, it has accomplished the end for which it was organized, and performed all of the functions respecting social advantages with which it is endowed.' Legislation is powerless to eradicate racial instincts, or to abolish distinctions based upon physical differences, and the attempt to do so can only result in accentuating the difficulties of the present situation. If the civil and political rights of both races be equal, one cannot be inferior to the other civilly [163 U.S. 537, 552] or politically. If one race be inferior to the other socially, the constitution of the United States cannot put them upon the same plane.

It is true that the question of the proportion of colored blood necessary to constitute a colored person, as distinguished from a white person, is one upon which there is a difference of opinion in the different states; some holding that any visible admixture of black blood stamps the person as belonging to the colored race (State v. Chavers, 5 Jones [N. C.] 1); others, that it depends upon the preponderance of blood (Gray v. State, 4 Ohio, 354; Monroe v. Collins, 17 Ohio St. 665); and still others, that the predominance of white blood must only be in the proportion of three-fourths (People v. Dean, 14 Mich. 406; Jones v. Com., 80 Va. 544). But these are questions to be determined under the laws of each state, and are not properly put in issue in this case. Under the allegations of his petition, it may undoubtedly become a question of importance whether, under the laws of Louisiana, the petitioner belongs to the white or colored race.

The judgment of the court below is therefore affirmed.

Mr. Justice BREWER did not hear the argument or participate in the decision of this case.

MR. JUSTICE HARLAN DISSENTING.

By the Louisiana statute the validity of which is here involved, all railway companies (other than street-railroad companies) carry passengers in that state are required to have separate but equal accommodations for white and colored persons, 'by providing two or more passenger coaches for each passenger train, or by dividing the passenger coaches by a partition so as to secure separate accommodations.' Under this statute, no colored person is permitted to occupy a seat in a coach assigned to white persons; nor any white person to occupy a seat in a coach assigned to colored persons. The managers of the railroad are not allowed to exercise any discretion in the premises, but are required to assign each passenger to some coach or compartment set apart for the exclusive use of is race. If a passenger insists upon going into a coach or compartment not set apart for persons of his race, [163 U.S. 537, 553] he is subject to be fined, or to be imprisoned in the parish jail. Penalties are prescribed for the refusal or neglect of the officers, directors, conductors, and employees of railroad companies to comply with the provisions of the act.

Only 'nurses attending children of the other race' are excepted from the operation of the statute. No exception is made of colored attendants traveling with adults. A white man is not permitted to have his colored servant with him in the same coach, even if his condition of health requires the constant personal assistance of such servant. If a colored maid insists upon riding in the same coach with a white woman whom she has been employed to serve, and who may need her personal attention while traveling, she is subject to be fined or imprisoned for such an exhibition of zeal in the discharge of duty.

While there may be in Louisiana persons of different races who are not citizens of the United States, the words in the act 'white and colored races' necessarily include all citizens of the United States of both races residing in that state. So that we have before us a state enactment that compels, under penalties, the separation of the two races in railroad passenger coaches, and makes it a crime for a citizen of either race to enter a coach that has been assigned to citizens of the other race.

Thus, the state regulates the use of a public highway by citizens of the United States solely upon the basis of race.

However apparent the injustice of such legislation may be, we have only to consider whether it is consistent with the constitution of the United States.

That a railroad is a public highway, and that the corporation which owns or operates it is in the exercise of public functions, is not, at this day, to be disputed. Mr. Justice Nelson, speaking for this court in New Jersey Steam Nav. Co. v. Merchants' Bank, 6 How. 344, 382, said that a common carrier was in the exercise 'of a sort of public office, and has public duties to perform, from which he should not be permitted to exonerate himself without the assent of the parties concerned.' Mr. Justice Strong, delivering the judgment of [163 U.S. 537,554] this court in Olcott v. Supervisors, 16 Wall. 678, 694, said: 'That railroads, though constructed by private corporations, and owned by them, are public highways, has been the doctrine of nearly all the courts ever since such conveniences for passage and transportation have had any existence. Very early the question arose whether a state's right of eminent domain could be exercised by a private corporation created for the purpose of constructing a railroad. Clearly, it could not, unless taking land for such a purpose by such an agency is taking land for public use. The right of eminent domain nowhere justifies taking property for a private use. Yet it is a doctrine universally accepted that a state legislature may authorize a private corporation to take land for the construction of such a road, making compensation to the owner. What else does this doctrine mean if not that building a railroad, though it be built by a private corporation, is an act done for a public use?' So, in Township of Pine Grove v. Talcott, 19 Wall. 666, 676: 'Though the corporation [a railroad company] was private, its work was public, as much so as if it were to be constructed by the state.' So, in Inhabitants of Worcester v. Western R. Corp., 4 Mete. (Mass.) 564: 'The establishment of that great thoroughfare is regarded as a public work, established by public authority, intended for the public use and benefit, the use of which is secured to the whole community, and constitutes, therefore, like a canal, turnpike, or highway, a public easement.' 'It is true that the real and personal property, necessary to the establishment and management of the railroad, is vested in the corporation; but it is in trust for the public.'

In respect of civil rights, common to all citizens, the constitution of the United States does not, I think, permit any public authority to know the race of those entitled to be protected in the enjoyment of such rights. Every true man has pride of race, and under appropriate circumstances, when the rights of others, his equals before the law, are not to be affected, it is his privilege to express such pride and to take such action based upon it as to him seems proper. But I deny that any legislative body or judicial tribunal may have regard to the [163 U.S. 537, 555] race of citizens when the civil rights of those citizens are involved. Indeed, such legislation as that here in question is inconsistent not only with that equality of rights which pertains to citizenship, national and state, but with the personal liberty enjoyed by every one within the United States.

The thirteenth amendment does not permit the withholding or the deprivation of any right necessarily inhering in freedom. It not only struck down the institution of slavery as previously existing in the United States, but it prevents the imposition of any burdens or disabilities that constitute badges of slavery or servitude. It decreed universal civil freedom in this country. This court has so adjudged. But, that amendment having been found inadequate to the protection of the rights of those who had been in slavery, it was followed by the fourteenth amendment, which added greatly to the dignity and glory of American citizenship, and to the security of personal liberty, by declaring that 'all persons born or naturalized in the United States, and subject to the jurisdiction thereof, are citizens of the United States and of the state wherein they reside,' and that 'no state shall make or enforce any law which shall abridge the privileges or immunities of citizens of the United States; nor shall any state deprive any person of life, liberty or property without due process of law, nor deny to any person within its jurisdiction the equal protection of the laws.' These two amendments, if enforced according to their true intent and meaning, will protect all the civil rights that pertain to freedom and citizenship. Finally, and to the end that no citizen should be denied, on account of his race, the privilege of participating in the political control of his country, it was declared by the fifteenth amendment that 'the right of citizens of the United States to vote shall not be denied or abridged by the United States or by any state on account of race, color or previous condition of servitude.'

These notable additions to the fundamental law were welcomed by the friends of liberty throughout the world. They removed the race line from our governmental systems. They had, as this court has said, a common purpose, namely, to secure 'to a race recently emancipated, a race that through [163 U.S. 537, 556] many generations have been held in slavery, all the civil rights that the superior race enjoy.' They declared, in legal effect, this court has further said, 'that the law in the states shall be the same for the black as for the white; that all persons, whether colored or white, shall stand equal before the laws of the states; and in regard to the colored race, for whose protection the amendment was primarily designed, that no discrimination shall be made against them by law because of their color.' We also said: The words of the amendment, it is true, are prohibitory, but they contain a necessary implication of a positive immunity or right, most valuable to the colored race,—the right to exemption from unfriendly legislation against them distinctively as colored; exemption from legal discriminations, implying inferiority in civil society, lessening the security of their enjoyment of the rights which others enjoy; and discriminations which are steps towards reducing them to the condition of a subject race.' It was, consequently, adjudged that a state law that excluded citizens of the colored race from juries, because of their race, however well qualified in other respects to discharge the duties of jurymen, was repugnant to the fourteenth amendment.

[...]

At the present term, referring to the previous adjudications, this court declared that 'underlying all of those decisions is the principle that the constitution of the United States, in its present form, forbids, so far as civil and political rights are concerned, discrimination by the general government or the states against any citizen because of his race. All citizens are equal before the law.' Gibson v. State, 162 U.S. 565 , 16 Sup. Ct. 904.

The decisions referred to show the scope of the recent amendments of the constitution. They also show that it is not within the power of a state to prohibit colored citizens, because of their race, from participating as jurors in the administration of justice.

It was said in argument that the statute of Louisiana does [163 U.S. 537, 557] not discriminate against either race, but prescribes a rule applicable alike to white and colored citizens. But this argument does not meet the difficulty. Every one knows that the statute in question had its origin in the purpose, not so much to exclude white persons from railroad cars occupied by blacks, as to exclude colored people from coaches occupied by or assigned to white persons. Railroad corporations of Louisiana did not make discrimination among whites in the matter of commodation for travelers. The thing to accomplish was, under the guise of giving equal accommodation for whites and blacks, to compel the latter to keep to themselves while traveling in railroad passenger coaches. No one would be so wanting in candor as to assert the contrary. The fundamental objection, therefore, to the statute, is that it interferes with the personal freedom of citizens. 'Personal liberty,' it has been well said, 'consists in the power of locomotion, of changing situation, or removing one's person to whatsoever places one's own inclination may direct, without imprisonment or restraint, unless by due course of law.' 1 Bl. Comm. *134. If a white man and a black man choose to occupy the same public conveyance on a public highway, it is their right to do so; and no government, proceeding alone on grounds of race, can prevent it without infringing the personal liberty of each.

It is one thing for railroad carriers to furnish, or to be required by law to furnish, equal accommodations for all whom they are under a legal duty to carry. It is quite another thing for government to forbid citizens of the white and black races from traveling in the same public conveyance, and to punish officers of railroad companies for permitting persons of the two races to occupy the same passenger coach. If a state can prescribe, as a rule of civil conduct, that whites and blacks shall not travel as passengers in the same railroad coach, why may it not so regulate the use of the streets of its cities and towns as to compel white citizens to keep on one side of a street, and black citizens to keep on the other? Why may it not, upon like grounds, punish whites and blacks who ride together in street cars or in open vehicles on a public road [163 U.S. 537, 558] or street? Why may it not require sheriffs to assign whites to one side of a court room, and blacks to the other? And why may it not also prohibit the commingling of the two races in the galleries of legislative halls or in public assemblages convened for the consideration of the political questions of the day? Further, if this statute of Louisiana is consistent with the personal liberty of citizens, why may not the state require the separation in railroad coaches of native and naturalized citizens of the United States, or of Protestants and Roman Catholics?

The answer given at the argument to these questions was that regulations of the kind they suggest would be unreasonable, and could not, therefore, stand before the law. Is it meant that the determination of questions of legislative power depends upon the inquiry whether the statute whose validity is questioned is, in the judgment of the courts, a reasonable one, taking all the circumstances into consideration? A statute may be unreasonable merely because a sound public policy forbade its enactment. But I do not understand that the courts have anything to do with the policy or expediency of legislation. A statute may be valid, and yet, upon grounds of public policy, may well be characterized as unreasonable. Mr. Sedgwick correctly states the rule when he says that, the legislative intention being clearly ascertained, 'the courts have no other duty to perform than to execute the legislative will, without any regard to their views as to the wisdom or justice of the particular enactment.' Sedg. St. & Const. Law, 324. There is a dangerous tendency in these latter days to enlarge the functions of the courts, by means of judicial interference with the will of the people as expressed by the legislature. Our institutions have the distinguishing characteristic that the three departments of government are coordinate and separate. Each much keep within the limits defined by the constitution. And the courts best discharge their duty by executing the will of the law-making power, constitutionally expressed, leaving the results of legislation to be dealt with by the people through their representatives. Statutes must always have a reasonable construction. Sometimes they are to be construed strictly, sometimes literally, in order to carry out the legislative [163 U.S. 537, 559] will. But, however construed, the intent of the legislature is to be respected if the particular statute in question is valid, although the courts, looking at the public interests, may conceive the statute to be both unreasonable and impolitic. If the power exists to enact a statute, that ends the matter so far as the courts are concerned. The adjudged cases in which statutes have been held to be void, because unreasonable, are those in which the means employed by the legislature were not at all germane to the end to which the legislature was competent.

The white race deems itself to be the dominant race in this country. And so it is, in prestige, in achievements, in education, in wealth, and in power. So, I doubt not, it will continue to be for all time, if it remains true to its great heritage, and holds fast to the principles of constitutional liberty. But in view of the constitution, in the eye of the law, there is in this country no superior, dominant, ruling class of citizens. There is no caste here. Our constitution is color-blind, and neither knows nor tolerates classes among citizens. In respect of civil rights, all citizens are equal before the law. The humblest is the peer of the most powerful. The law regards man as man, and takes no account of his surroundings or of his color when his civil rights as guaranteed by the spreme law of the land are involved. It is therefore to be regretted that this high tribunal, the final expositor of the fundamental law of the land, has reached the conclusion that it is competent for a state to regulate the enjoyment by citizens of their civil rights solely upon the basis of race.

In my opinion, the judgment this day rendered will, in time, prove to be quite as pernicious as the decision made by this tribunal in the Dred Scott Case.

It was adjudged in that case that the descendants of Africans who were imported into this country, and sold as slaves, were not included nor intended to be included under the word 'citizens' in the constitution, and could not claim any of the rights and privileges which that instrument provided for and secured to citizens of the United States; that, at time of the adoption of the constitution, they were 'considered as a subordinate and inferior class of beings, who had been subjugated by the dominant [163 U.S. 537, 560] race, and, whether emancipated or not, yet remained subject to their authority, and had no rights or privileges but such as those who held the power and the government might choose to grant them.' 17 How. 393, 404. The recent amendments of the constitution, it was supposed, had eradicated these principles from our institutions. But it seems that we have yet, in some of the states, a dominant race,—a superior class of citizens,—which assumes to regulate the enjoyment of civil rights, common to all citizens, upon the basis of race. The present decision, it may well be apprehended, will not only stimulate aggressions, more or less brutal and irritating, upon the admitted rights of colored citizens, but will encourage the belief that it is possible, by means of state enactments, to defeat the beneficent purposes which the people of the United States had in view when they adopted the recent amendments of the constitution, by one of which the blacks of this country were made citizens of the United States and of the states in which they respectively reside, and whose privileges and immunities, as citizens, the states are forbidden to abridge. Sixty millions of whites are in no danger from the presence here of eight millions of blacks. The destinies of the two races, in this country, are indissolubly linked together, and the interests of both require that the common government of all shall not permit the seeds of race hate to be planted under the sanction of law. What can more certainly arouse race hate, what more certainly create and perpetuate a feeling of distrust between these races, than state enactments which, in fact, proceed on the ground that colored citizens are so inferior and degraded that they cannot be allowed to sit in public coaches occupied by white citizens? That, as all will admit, is the real meaning of such legislation as was enacted in Louisiana.

The sure guaranty of the peace and security of each race is the clear, distinct, unconditional recognition by our governments, national and state, of every right that inheres in civil freedom, and of the equality before the law of all citizens of the United States, without regard to race. State enactments regulating the enjoyment of civil rights upon the basis of race, and cunningly devised to defeat legitimate results of the [163 U.S. 537, 561] war, under the pretense of recognizing equality of rights, can have no other result than to render permanent peace impossible, and to keep alive a conflict of races, the continuance of which must do harm to all concerned. This question is not met by the suggestion that social equality cannot exist between the white and black races in this country. That argument, if it can be properly regarded as one, is scarcely worthy of consideration; for social equality no more exists between two races when traveling in a passenger coach or a public highway than when members of the same races sit by each other in a street car or in the jury box, or stand or sit with each other in a political assembly, or when they use in common the streets of a city or town, or when they are in the same room for the purpose of having their names placed on the registry of voters, or when they approach the ballot box in order to exercise the high privilege of voting.

There is a race so different from our own that we do not permit those belonging to it to become citizens of the United States. Persons belonging to it are, with few exceptions, absolutely excluded from our country. I allude to the Chinese race. But, by the statute in question, a Chinaman can ride in the same passenger coach with white citizens of the United States, while citizens of the black race in Louisiana, many of whom, perhaps, risked their lives for the preservation of the Union, who are entitled, by law, to participate in the political control of the state and nation, who are not excluded, by law or by reason of their race, from public stations of any kind, and who have all the legal rights that belong to white citizens, are yet declared to be criminals, liable to imprisonment, if they ride in a public coach occupied by citizens of the white race. It is scarcely just to say that a colored citizen should not object to occupying a public coach assigned to his own race. He does not object, nor, perhaps, would he object to separate coaches for his race if his rights under the law were recognized. But he does object, and he ought never to cease objecting, that citizens of the white and black races can be adjudged criminals because they sit, or claim the right to sit, in the same public coach on a public highway. [163 U.S. 537, 562] The arbitrary separation of citizens, on the basis of race, while they are on a public highway, is a badge of servitude wholly inconsistent with the civil freedom and the equality before the law established by the constitution. It cannot be justified upon any legal grounds.

If evils will result from the commingling of the two races upon public highways established for the benefit of all, they will be infinitely less than those that will surely come from state legislation regulating the enjoyment of civil rights upon the basis of race. We boast of the freedom enjoyed by our people above all other peoples. But it is difficult to reconcile that boast with a state of the law which, practically, puts the brand of servitude and degradation upon a large class of our fellow citizens,—our equals before the law. The thin disguise of 'equal' accommodations for passengers in railroad coaches will not mislead any one, nor atone for the wrong this day done.

The result of the whole matter is that while this court has frequently adjudged, and at the present term has recognized the doctrine, that a state cannot, consistently with the constitution of the United States, prevent white and black citizens, having the required qualifications for jury service, from sitting in the same jury box, it is now solemnly held that a state may prohibit white and black citizens from sitting in the same passenger coach on a public highway, or may require that they be separated by a 'partition' when in the same passenger coach. May it not now be reasonably expected that astute men of the dominant race, who affect to be disturbed at the possibility that the integrity of the white race may be corrupted, or that its supremacy will be imperiled, by contact on public highways with black people, will endeavor to procure statutes requiring white and black jurors to be separated in the jury box by a 'partition,' and that, upon retiring from the court room to consult as to their verdict, such partition, if it be a movable one, shall be taken to their consultation room, and set up in such way as to prevent black jurors from coming too close to their brother jurors of the white race. If the 'partition' used in the court room happens to be stationary, provision could be made for screens with openings through [163 U.S. 537, 563] which jurors of the two races could confer as to their verdict without coming into personal contact with each other. I cannot see but that, according to the principles this day announced, such state legislation, although conceived in hostility to, and enacted for the purpose of humiliating, citizens of the United States of a particular race, would be held to be consistent with the constitution.

I do not deem it necessary to review the decisions of state courts to which reference was made in argument. Some, and the most important, of them, are wholly inapplicable, because rendered prior to the adoption of the last amendments of the constitution, when colored people had very few rights which the dominant race felt obliged to respect, Others were made at a time when public opinion, in many localities, was dominated by the institution of slavery; when it would not have been safe to do justice to the black man; and when, so far as the rights of blacks were concerned, race prejudice was, practically, the supreme law of the land. Those decisions cannot be guides in the era introduced by the recent amendments of the supreme law, which established universal civil freedom, gave citizenship to all born or naturalized in the United States, and residing ere, obliterated the race line from our systems of governments, national and state, and placed our free institutions upon the broad and sure foundation of the equality of all men before the law.

I am of opinion that the state of Louisiana is inconsistent with the personal liberty of citizens, white and black, in that state, and hostile to both the spirit and letter of the constitution of the United States. If laws of like character should be enacted in the several states of the Union, the effect would be in the highest degree mischievous. Slavery, as an institution tolerated by law, would, it is true, have disappeared from our country; but there would remain a power in the states, by sinister legislation, to interfere with the full enjoyment of the blessings of freedom, to regulate civil rights, common to all citizens, upon the basis of race, and to place in a condition of legal inferiority a large body of American citizens, now constituting a part of the political community, called the [163 U.S. 537, 564] 'People of the United States,' for whom, and by whom through representatives, our government is administered. Such a system is inconsistent with the guaranty given by the constitution to each state of a republican form of government, and may be stricken down by congressional action, or by the courts in the discharge of their solemn duty to maintain the supreme law of the land, anything in the constitution or laws of any state to the contrary notwithstanding.

For the reason stated, I am constrained to withhold my assent from the opinion and judgment of the majority.

Brown v. Board of Education of Topeka

347 U.S. 483 (1954)

Segregation of white and Negro children in the public schools of a State solely on the basis of race, pursuant to state laws permitting or requiring such segregation, denies to Negro children the equal protection of the laws guaranteed by the Fourteenth Amendment—even though the physical facilities and other "tangible" factors of white and Negro schools may be equal. [...]

a. The history of the Fourteenth Amendment is inconclusive as to its intended effect on public education. [...]

b. The question presented in these cases must be determined, not on the basis of conditions existing when the Fourteenth Amendment was adopted, but in the light of the full development of public education and its present place in American life throughout the Nation. [...]

c. Where a State has undertaken to provide an opportunity for an education in its public schools, such an opportunity is a right which must be made available to all on equal terms. [...]

d. Segregation of children in public schools solely on the basis of race deprives children of the minority group of equal educational opportunities, even though the physical facilities and other "tangible" factors may be equal. Pp. [...]

e. The "separate but equal" doctrine adopted in Plessy v. Ferguson, 163 U.S. 537, has no place in the field of public education. [...] [347 U.S. 483, 484]

f. The cases are restored to the docket for further argument on specified questions relating to the forms of the decrees. [...]

[...]

MR. CHIEF JUSTICE WARREN DELIVERED THE OPINION OF THE COURT.

These cases come to us from the States of Kansas, South Carolina, Virginia, and Delaware. They are premised on different facts and different local conditions, but a common legal question justifies their consideration together in this consolidated opinion.[1] [347 U.S. 483, 487]

In each of the cases, minors of the Negro race, through their legal representatives, seek the aid of the courts in obtaining admission to the public schools of their community on a nonsegregated basis. In each instance, [347 U.S. 483, 488] they had been denied admission to schools attended by white children under laws requiring or permitting segregation according to race. This segregation was alleged to deprive the plaintiffs of the equal protection of the laws under the Fourteenth Amendment. In each of the cases other than the Delaware case, a three-judge federal district court denied relief to the plaintiffs on the so-called "separate but equal" doctrine announced by this Court in Plessy v. Ferguson, 163 U.S. 537. Under that doctrine, equality of treatment is accorded when the races are provided substantially equal facilities, even though these facilities be separate. In the Delaware case, the Supreme Court of Delaware adhered to that doctrine, but ordered that the plaintiffs be admitted to the white schools because of their superiority to the Negro schools.

The plaintiffs contend that segregated public schools are not "equal" and cannot be made "equal," and that hence they are deprived of the equal protection of the laws. Because of the obvious importance

---

1   In the Kansas case, Brown v. Board of Education, the plaintiffs are Negro children of elementary school age residing in Topeka. They brought this action in the United States District Court for the District of Kansas to enjoin enforcement of a Kansas statute which permits, but does not require, cities of more than 15,000 population to maintain separate school facilities for Negro and white students. Kan. Gen. Stat. 72-1724 (1949). Pursuant to that authority, the Topeka Board of Education elected to establish segregated elementary schools. Other public schools in the community, however, are operated on a nonsegregated basis. The three-judge District Court, convened under 28 U.S.C. 2281 and 2284, found that segregation in public education has a detrimental effect upon Negro children, but denied relief on the ground that the Negro and white schools were substantially equal with respect to buildings, transportation, curricula, and educational qualifications of teachers. 98 F. Supp. 797. The case is here on direct appeal under 28 U.S.C. 1253. In the South Carolina case, Briggs v. Elliott, the plaintiffs are Negro children of both elementary and high school age residing in Clarendon County. They brought this action in the United States District Court for the Eastern District of South Carolina to enjoin enforcement of provisions in the state constitution and statutory code which require the segregation of Negroes and whites in public schools. S. C. Const., Art. XI, 7; S. C. Code 5377 (1942). The three-judge District Court, convened under 28 U.S.C. 2281 and 2284, denied the requested relief. The court found that the Negro schools were inferior to the white schools and ordered the defendants to begin immediately to equalize the facilities. But the court sustained the validity of the contested provisions and denied the plaintiffs admission [347 U.S. 483,487] to the white schools during the equalization program. 98 F. Supp. 529. This Court vacated the District Court's judgment and remanded the case for the purpose of obtaining the court's views on a report filed by the defendants concerning the progress made in the equalization program. 342 U.S. 350 . On remand, the District Court found that substantial equality had been achieved except for buildings and that the defendants were proceeding to rectify this inequality as well. 103 F. Supp. 920. The case is again here on direct appeal under 28 U.S.C. 1253. In the Virginia case, Davis v. County School Board, the plaintiffs are Negro children of high school age residing in Prince Edward county. They brought this action in the United States District Court for the Eastern District of Virginia to enjoin enforcement of provisions in the state constitution and statutory code which require the segregation of Negroes and whites in public schools. Va. Const., 140; Va. Code 22-221 (1950). The three-judge District Court, convened under 28 U.S.C. 2281 and 2284, denied the requested relief. The court found the Negro school inferior in physical plant, curricula, and transportation, and ordered the defendants forthwith to provide substantially equal curricula and transportation and to "proceed with all reasonable diligence and dispatch to remove" the inequality in physical plant. But, as in the South Carolina case, the court sustained the validity of the contested provisions and denied the plaintiffs admission to the white schools during the equalization program. 103 F. Supp. 337. The case is here on direct appeal under 28 U.S.C. 1253. In the Delaware case, Gebhart v. Belton, the plaintiffs are Negro children of both elementary and high school age residing in New Castle County. They brought this action in the Delaware Court of Chancery to enjoin enforcement of provisions in the state constitution and statutory code which require the segregation of Negroes and whites in public schools. Del. Const., Art. X, 2; Del. Rev. Code 2631 (1935). The Chancellor gave judgment for the plaintiffs and ordered their immediate admission to schools previously attended only by white children, on the ground that the Negro schools were inferior with respect to teacher training, pupil-teacher ratio, extracurricular activities, physical plant, and time and distance involved [347 U.S. 483,488] in travel. 87 A. 2d 862. The Chancellor also found that segregation itself results in an inferior education for Negro children (see note 10, infra), but did not rest his decision on that ground. Id., at 865. The Chancellor's decree was affirmed by the Supreme Court of Delaware, which intimated, however, that the defendants might be able to obtain a modification of the decree after equalization of the Negro and white schools had been accomplished. 91 A. 2d 137, 152. The defendants, contending only that the Delaware courts had erred in ordering the immediate admission of the Negro plaintiffs to the white schools, applied to this Court for certiorari. The writ was granted, 344 U.S. 891 . The plaintiffs, who were successful below, did not submit a cross-petition.

of the question presented, the Court took jurisdiction. [2] Argument was heard in the 1952 Term, and reargument was heard this Term on certain questions propounded by the Court. [3] [347 U.S. 483, 489]

Reargument was largely devoted to the circumstances surrounding the adoption of the Fourteenth Amendment in 1868. It covered exhaustively consideration of the Amendment in Congress, ratification by the states, then existing practices in racial segregation, and the views of proponents and opponents of the Amendment. This discussion and our own investigation convince us that, although these sources cast some light, it is not enough to resolve the problem with which we are faced. At best, they are inconclusive. The most avid proponents of the post-War Amendments undoubtedly intended them to remove all legal distinctions among "all persons born or naturalized in the United States." Their opponents, just as certainly, were antagonistic to both the letter and the spirit of the Amendments and wished them to have the most limited effect. What others in Congress and the state legislatures had in mind cannot be determined with any degree of certainty.

An additional reason for the inconclusive nature of the Amendment's history, with respect to segregated schools, is the status of public education at that time. [4] In the South, the movement toward free common schools, supported [347 U.S. 483,490] by general taxation, had not yet taken hold. Education of white children was largely in the hands of private groups. Education of Negroes was almost nonexistent, and practically all of the race were illiterate. In fact, any education of Negroes was forbidden by law in some states. Today, in contrast, many Negroes have achieved outstanding success in the arts and sciences as well as in the business and professional world. It is true that public school education at the time of the Amendment had advanced further in the North, but the effect of the Amendment on Northern States was generally ignored in the congressional debates. Even in the North, the conditions of public education did not approximate those existing today. The curriculum was usually rudimentary; ungraded schools were common in rural areas; the school term was but three months a year in many states; and compulsory school attendance was virtually unknown. As a consequence, it is not surprising that there should be so little in the history of the Fourteenth Amendment relating to its intended effect on public education.

In the first cases in this Court construing the Fourteenth Amendment, decided shortly after its adoption, the Court interpreted it as proscribing all state-imposed discriminations against the Negro race. [5] The doctrine of [347 U.S. 483, 491] "separate but equal" did not make its appearance in this

---

2   344 U.S. 1. 141, 891.

3   345 U.S. 972. The Attorney General of the United States participated both Terms as amicus curiae.

4   For a general study of the development of public education prior to the Amendment, see Butts and Cremin, A History of Education in American Culture (1953), Pts. I, II; Cubberley, Public Education in the United States (1934 ed.), cc. II–XII. School practices current at the time of the adoption of the Fourteenth Amendment are described in Butts and Cremin, supra, at 269–275; Cubberley, supra, at 288–339, 408–431; Knight, Public Education in the South (1922), cc. VIII, IX. See also H. Ex. Doc. No. 315, 41st Cong., 2d Sess. (1871). Although the demand for free public schools followed substantially the same pattern in both the North and the South, the development in the South did not begin to gain momentum until about 1850, some twenty years after that in the North. The reasons for the somewhat slower development in the South (e. g., the rural character of the South and the different regional attitudes toward state assistance) are well explained in Cubberley, supra, at 408–423. In the country as a whole, but particularly in the South, the War [347 U.S. 483, 490] virtually stopped all progress in public education. Id., at 427–428. The low status of Negro education in all sections of the country, both before and immediately after the War, is described in Beale, A History of Freedom of Teaching in American Schools (1941), 112–132, 175–195. Compulsory school attendance laws were not generally adopted until after the ratification of the Fourteenth Amendment, and it was not until 1918 that such laws were in force in all the states. Cubberley, supra, at 563–565.

5   Slaughter-House Cases, 16 Wall. 36, 67–72 (1873); Strauder v. West Virginia, 100 U.S. 303, 307–308 (1880): "It ordains that no State shall deprive any person of life, liberty, or property, without due process of law, or deny to any person within its jurisdiction the equal protection of the laws. What is this but [347 U.S. 483, 491] declaring that the law in the States shall be the same for the black as for the white; that all persons, whether colored or white, shall stand equal before the laws of the States, and, in regard to the colored race, for whose protection the amendment was primarily designed, that no discrimination shall be made against them by law because of their color? The words of the amendment, it is true, are prohibitory, but they contain a necessary implication of a positive immunity, or right, most valuable to the colored race,—the right to

Court until 1896 in the case of Plessy v. Ferguson, supra, involving not education but transportation.[6] American courts have since labored with the doctrine for over half a century. In this Court, there have been six cases involving the "separate but equal" doctrine in the field of public education.[7] In Cumming v. County Board of Education, 175 U.S. 528. and Gong Lum v. Rice, 275 U.S. 78, the validity of the doctrine itself was not challenged.[8] In more recent cases, all on the graduate school [347 U.S. 483, 492] level, inequality was found in that specific benefits enjoyed by white students were denied to Negro students of the same educational qualifications. Missouri ex rel. Gaines v. Canada, 305 U.S. 337; Sipuel v. Oklahoma, 332 U.S. 631; Sweatt v. Painter, 339 U.S. 629; McLaurin v. Oklahoma State Regents, 339 U.S. 637. In none of these cases was it necessary to re-examine the doctrine to grant relief to the Negro plaintiff. And in Sweatt v. Painter, supra, the Court expressly reserved decision on the question whether Plessy v. Ferguson should be held inapplicable to public education.

In the instant cases, that question is directly presented. Here, unlike Sweatt v. Painter, there are findings below that the Negro and white schools involved have been equalized, or are being equalized, with respect to buildings, curricula, qualifications and salaries of teachers, and other "tangible" factors.[9] Our decision, therefore, cannot turn on merely a comparison of these tangible factors in the Negro and white schools involved in each of the cases. We must look instead to the effect of segregation itself on public education.

In approaching this problem, we cannot turn the clock back to 1868 when the Amendment was adopted, or even to 1896 when Plessy v. Ferguson was written. We must consider public education in the light of its full development and its present place in American life throughout [347 U.S. 483, 493] the Nation. Only in this way can it be determined if segregation in public schools deprives these plaintiffs of the equal protection of the laws.

Today, education is perhaps the most important function of state and local governments. Compulsory school attendance laws and the great expenditures for education both demonstrate our recognition of the importance of education to our democratic society. It is required in the performance of our most basic public responsibilities, even service in the armed forces. It is the very foundation of good citizenship. Today it is a principal instrument in awakening the child to cultural values, in preparing him for later professional training, and in helping him to adjust normally to his environment. In these days, it is doubtful that any child may reasonably be expected to succeed in life if he is denied the

---

exemption from unfriendly legislation against them distinctively as colored,—exemption from legal discriminations, implying inferiority in civil society, lessening the security of their enjoyment of the rights which others enjoy, and discriminations which are steps towards reducing them to the condition of a subject race." See also Virginia v. Rives, 100 U.S. 313. 318 (1880): Ex parte Virginia, 100 U.S. 339.344–345 (1880).

6   The doctrine apparently originated in Roberts v. City of Boston, 59 Mass. 198, 206 (1850), upholding school segregation against attack as being violative of a state constitutional guarantee of equality. Segregation in Boston public schools was eliminated in 1855. Mass. Acts 1855, c. 256. But elsewhere in the North segregation in public education has persisted in some communities until recent years. It is apparent that such segregation has long been a nationwide problem, not merely one of sectional concern.

7   See also Berea College v. Kentucky, 211 U.S. 45 (1908).

8   In the Cumming case, Negro taxpayers sought an injunction requiring the defendant school board to discontinue the operation of a high school for white children until the board resumed operation of a high school for Negro children. Similarly, in the Gong Lum case, the plaintiff, a child of Chinese descent, contended only that state authorities had misapplied the doctrine by classifying him with Negro children and requiring him to attend a Negro school.

9   In the Kansas case, the court below found substantial equality as to all such factors. 98 F. Supp. 797, 798. In the South Carolina case, the court below found that the defendants were proceeding "promptly and in good faith to comply with the court's decree." 103 F. Supp. 920, 921. In the Virginia case, the court below noted that the equalization program was already "afoot and progressing" (103 F. Supp. 337, 341); since then, we have been advised, in the Virginia Attorney General's brief on reargument, that the program has now been completed. In the Delaware case, the court below similarly noted that the state's equalization program was well under way. 91 A. 2d 137, 149.

opportunity of an education. Such an opportunity, where the state has undertaken to provide it, is a right which must be made available to all on equal terms.

We come then to the question presented: Does segregation of children in public schools solely on the basis of race, even though the physical facilities and other "tangible" factors may be equal, deprive the children of the minority group of equal educational opportunities? We believe that it does.

In Sweatt v. Painter, supra, in finding that a segregated law school for Negroes could not provide them equal educational opportunities, this Court relied in large part on "those qualities which are incapable of objective measurement but which make for greatness in a law school." In McLaurin v. Oklahoma State Regents, supra, the Court, in requiring that a Negro admitted to a white graduate school be treated like all other students, again resorted to intangible considerations: "... his ability to study, to engage in discussions and exchange views with other students, and, in general, to learn his profession." [347 U.S. 483, 494] Such considerations apply with added force to children in grade and high schools. To separate them from others of similar age and qualifications solely because of their race generates a feeling of inferiority as to their status in the community that may affect their hearts and minds in a way unlikely ever to be undone. The effect of this separation on their educational opportunities was well stated by a finding in the Kansas case by a court which nevertheless felt compelled to rule against the Negro plaintiffs:

> "Segregation of white and colored children in public schools has a detrimental effect upon the colored children. The impact is greater when it has the sanction of the law; for the policy of separating the races is usually interpreted as denoting the inferiority of the negro group. A sense of inferiority affects the motivation of a child to learn. Segregation with the sanction of law, therefore, has a tendency to [retard] the educational and mental development of negro children and to deprive them of some of the benefits they would receive in a racial[ly] integrated school system."[10]

Whatever may have been the extent of psychological knowledge at the time of Plessy v. Ferguson, this finding is amply supported by modem authority.[11] Any language [347 U.S. 483, 495] in Plessy v. Ferguson contrary to this finding is rejected.

We conclude that in the field of public education the doctrine of "separate but equal" has no place. Separate educational facilities are inherently unequal. Therefore, we hold that the plaintiffs and others similarly situated for whom the actions have been brought are, by reason of the segregation complained of, deprived of the equal protection of the laws guaranteed by the Fourteenth Amendment. This disposition makes unnecessary any discussion whether such segregation also violates the Due Process Clause of the Fourteenth Amendment.[12]

---

10 A similar finding was made in the Delaware case: "I conclude from the testimony that in our Delaware society, State-imposed segregation in education itself results in the Negro children, as a class, receiving educational opportunities which are substantially inferior to those available to white children otherwise similarly situated." 87 A. 2d 862, 865.

11 K. B. Clark, Effect of Prejudice and Discrimination on Personality Development (Midcentury White House Conference on Children and Youth, 1950); Witmer and Kotinsky, Personality in the Making (1952), c. VI; Deutscher and Chein, The Psychological Effects of Enforced Segregation: A Survey of Social Science Opinion, 26 J. Psychol. 259 (1948); Chein, What are the Psychological Effects of [347 U.S. 483, 495] Segregation Under Conditions of Equal Facilities?, 3 Int. J. Opinion and Attitude Res. 229 (1949); Brameld, Educational Costs, in Discrimination and National Welfare (MacIver, ed., (1949), 44–48; Frazier, The Negro in the United States (1949), 674–681. And see generally Myrdal, An American Dilemma (1944).

12 See Bolling v. Sharpe, post, p. 497, concerning the Due Process Clause of the Fifth Amendment.

Because these are class actions, because of the wide applicability of this decision, and because of the great variety of local conditions, the formulation of decrees in these cases presents problems of considerable complexity. On reargument, the consideration of appropriate relief was necessarily subordinated to the primary question—the constitutionality of segregation in public education. We have now announced that such segregation is a denial of the equal protection of the laws. In order that we may have the full assistance of the parties in formulating decrees, the cases will be restored to the docket, and the parties are requested to present further argument on Questions 4 and 5 previously propounded by the Court for the reargument this Term.[13] The Attorney General [347 U.S. 483, 496] of the United States is again invited to participate. The Attorneys General of the states requiring or permitting segregation in public education will also be permitted to appear as amici curiae upon request to do so by September 15, 1954, and submission of briefs by October 1, 1954.[14]

---

13 "4. Assuming it is decided that segregation in public schools violates the Fourteenth Amendment "(a) would a decree necessarily follow providing that, within the [347 U.S. 483, 496] limits set by normal geographic school districting, Negro children should forthwith be admitted to schools of their choice, or "(b) may this Court, in the exercise of its equity powers, permit an effective gradual adjustment to be brought about from existing segregated systems to a system not based on color distinctions? "5. On the assumption on which questions 4 (a) and (b) are based, and assuming further that this Court will exercise its equity powers to the end described in question 4 (b), "(a) should this Court formulate detailed decrees in these cases; "(b) if so, what specific issues should the decrees reach; "(c) should this Court appoint a special master to hear evidence with a view to recommending specific terms for such decrees; "(d) should this Court remand to the courts of first instance with directions to frame decrees in these cases, and if so what general directions should the decrees of this Court include and what procedures should the courts of first instance follow in arriving at the specific terms of more detailed decrees?"

14 See Rule 42, Revised Rules of this Court (effective July 1, 1954). [347 U.S. 483, 497]

Two Models of the Criminal Process

Hervert L. Packer

Values and the Criminal Process

WHY BUILD MODELS?

People who commit crimes appear to share the prevalent impression that punishment is an unpleasantness that is best avoided. They ordinarily take care to avoid being caught. If arrested, they ordinarily deny their guilt and otherwise try not to cooperate with the police. If brought to trial, they do whatever their resources permit to resist being convicted. And, even after they have been convicted and sent to prison, their efforts to secure their freedom do not cease. It is a struggle from start to finish. This struggle is often referred to as the criminal process, a compendious term that stands for all the complexes of activity that operate to bring the substantive law of crime to bear (or to avoid bringing it to bear) on persons who are suspected of having committed crimes. It can be described, but only partially and inadequately, by referring to the rules of law that govern the apprehension, screening, and trial of persons suspected of crime. It consists at least as importantly of patterns of official activity that correspond only in the roughest kind of way to the prescriptions of procedural rules. As a result of recent emphasis on empirical research into the administration of criminal justice, we are just beginning to be aware how very rough the correspondence is.[1]

---

[1] See, *e.g.*, Goldstein, *Police Discretion Not To Invoke the Criminal Process: Low-Visibility Decisions in the Administration of Criminal Justice, 69* Yale L.J. 543 (1960) ; LaFave, *Detention for Investigation by the Police: An Analysis of Current Practices, 1962* Wash. U.L.Q. 331. Both articles are based to some extent on material gathered in the American Bar Foundation Survey of the Administration of Criminal Justice in the United States.

Hervert L. Packer, "Two Models of the Criminal Process," *University of Pennsylvania Law Review*, vol. 113, no. 1, pp. 2-3, 5-19, 22-23. Copyright © 1964 by University of Pennsylvania Law School. Reprinted with permission.

At the same time, and perhaps in part as a result of this new accretion of knowledge, some of our lawmaking institutions—and particularly the Supreme Court of the United States—have begun to add measurably to the prescriptions of law that are meant to govern the operation of the criminal process. This accretion has become, in the last few years, exponential in extent and velocity. We are faced with an interesting paradox: the more we learn about the Is of the criminal process, the more we are instructed about its Ought and the greater the gulf between Is and Ought appears to become. We learn that very few people get adequate legal representation in the criminal process; we are simultaneously told that the Constitution requires people to be afforded adequate legal representation in the criminal process.[2] We learn that coercion is often used to extract confessions from suspected criminals; we are then told that convictions based on coerced confessions may not be permitted to stand.[3] We discover that the police in gathering evidence often use methods that violate the norms of privacy protected by the fourth amendment; we are told that evidence so obtained must be excluded from the criminal trial.[4] But these prescriptions about how the process ought to operate do not automatically become part of the patterns of official behavior in the criminal process. Is and Ought share an increasingly uneasy coexistence. Doubts are stirred about the kind of criminal process we want to have.

The kind of criminal process we have is an important determinant of the kind of behavior content that the criminal law ought rationally to comprise. Logically, the substantive question may appear to be anterior: decide what kinds of conduct one wants to reach through the criminal process, and then decide what kind of process is best calculated to deal with those kinds of conduct. It has not worked that way. On the whole, the process has been at least as much a Given as the content of the criminal law. But it is far from being a Given in any rigid sense.

[…]

One way to do this kind of job is to abstract from reality, to build a model. In a sense that is what an examination of the constitutional and statutory provisions that govern the operation of the criminal process would produce. This, in effect, is the way analysis of the legal system has traditionally proceeded. The method has considerable utility as an index of current value choices; but it produces a model that will not tell us very much about some important problems that the system encounters and that will only fortuitously tell us anything useful about how the system actually operates. On the other hand, the kind of model that might emerge from an attempt to cut loose from the law on the books and to describe, as accurately as possible, what actually goes on in the real-life world of the criminal process would so subordinate the inquiry to the tyranny of the actual that the existence of competing value choices would be obscured. The kind of criminal process we have depends importantly on certain value choices that are reflected, explicitly or implicitly, in its habitual functioning. The kind of model we need is one that permits us to recognize explicitly the value choices that underlie the details of the criminal process. In a word, what we need is a *normative* model, or rather two models, to let us perceive the normative antinomy that runs deep in the life of the criminal law. These models may not be labelled Good and Bad, and I hope they will not be taken in that sense. Rather, they represent an attempt to abstract two separate value systems that compete for attention in the operation of the criminal process. Neither is presented as either corresponding to reality or as representing what the criminal process ought to be. The two models merely afford a convenient way to talk about the operation of a process whose day-to-day functioning involves a constant series of minute adjustments

---

2   Gideon v. Wainwright, 372 U.S. 335 (1963).

3   *E.g.*, Haynes v. Washington, 373 U.S. 503 (1963); Escobedo v. Illinois, 378 U.S. 478 (1964).

4   Mapp v. Ohio, 367 U.S. 643 (1961).

between the competing demands of two value systems and whose normative future likewise involves a series of resolutions, of greater or lesser magnitude, of the tensions between mutually exclusive claims.

I call these two models the Due Process Model and the Crime Control Model.

[...]

There is a risk in an enterprise of this sort that is latent in any attempt to polarize. It is, simply, that values are too various to be pinned down to yes or no answers. When we polarize, we distort. The models are, in a sense, distortions. The attempt here is only to clarify the terms of discussion by isolating the assumptions that underlie competing policy claims and examining the conclusions to which those claims, if fully accepted, would lead. This Article does not make value choices, but only describes what are thought to be their consequences.

VALUES UNDERLYING THE MODELS

In this section we shall develop two competing systems of values, the tension between which accounts for the intense activity now observable in the development of the criminal process. The models we are about to examine attempt to give operational content to these conflicting schemes of values. Like the values underlying them, the models are polarities. Just as the models are not to be taken as describing real-world situations, so the values that underlie them are not to be regarded as expressing the values held by any one person. The values are presented here as an aid to analysis, not as a program for action.

SOME COMMON GROUND

One qualification needs to be made to the assertion of polarity in the two models. While it would be possible to construct models that exist in an institutional vacuum, it would not serve our purposes to do so. We are not postulating a criminal process that operates in any kind of society at all, but rather one that operates within the framework of contemporary American society. This leaves plenty of room for polarization, but it does require the observance of some limits. A model of the criminal process that left out of account relatively stable and enduring features of the American legal system would not have much relevance to our central task. For convenience, these elements of stability and continuity can be roughly equated with minimal agreed limits expressed in the Constitution of the United States and, more importantly, with unarticulated assumptions that can be perceived to underlie those limits. Of course, it is true that the Constitution is constantly appealed to by proponents and opponents of many measures that affect the criminal process. And only the naive would deny that there are few conclusive positions that can be reached by appeal to the Constitution. Yet assumptions do exist about the criminal process that are widely shared and that may be viewed as common ground for the operation of any model of the criminal process. Our first task is to clarify these assumptions.

First, there is the assumption implicit in the ex post facto clause of the Constitution[5] that the function of defining conduct that may be treated as criminal is separate from and anterior to the process of identifying and dealing with persons as criminals. How wide or narrow the definition of criminal conduct must be is an important question of policy that yields highly variant results depending on the values held by those making the relevant decisions.[6] But that there must be a means of definition that

---

5   U.S. Const, art. 1, § 9.
6   See Note, *The Void-for-Vagueness Doctrine in the Supreme Court*, 109 U. Pa. L. Rev. 67 (1960).

is in some sense separate from and anterior to the operation of the process is clear. If that were not so, our efforts to deal with the phenomenon of organized crime would appear ludicrous indeed (which is not to say that we have by any means exhausted the potentialities for dealing with that problem within the limits of this basic assumption).

A related assumption that limits the area of controversy is that the criminal process ordinarily ought to be invoked by those charged with the responsibility for doing so when it appears that a crime has been committed and that there is a reasonable prospect of apprehending and convicting its per-petrator. Although the area of police and prosecutorial discretion not to invoke the criminal process is demonstrably broad, it is common ground that these officials have no general dispensing power. If the legislature has decided that certain conduct is to be treated as criminal, the decision-makers at every level of the criminal process are expected to accept that basic decision as a premise for action. The controversial nature of the occasional case in which that is not the role played by the relevant decision-makers only serves to highlight the strength with which the premise holds.[7] This assumption may be viewed as the other side of the ex post facto coin. Just as conduct that is not proscribed as criminal may not be dealt with in the criminal process, so must conduct that has been denominated as criminal be so treated by the participants in the process.[8]

Next, there is the assumption that there are limits to the powers of government to investigate and apprehend persons suspected of committing crimes. I do not refer to the controversy (settled recently, at least in broad outline) as to whether the fourth amendment's prohibitions against unreasonable searches and seizures applies to the states with equal force as to the federal government.[9] Rather, I refer to the general assumption that there is a degree of scrutiny and a degree of control that have to be exercised with respect to the activities of law enforcement officers, that the security and privacy of the individual may not be invaded at will. It is possible to imagine a society in which not even lip service is paid to this assumption. Nazi Germany approached but never quite reached this position. But no one in our society would maintain that every individual may be taken into custody at any time and held without any limitation of time during the process of investigating his possible commission of crimes, or that there should be no form of redress for violation of at least some standards for official investigative conduct. Although this assumption may not appear to have much in the way of positive content, its absence would render moot some of our most hotly controverted problems. If there were not general agreement that there must be some limits on police power to detain and investigate, the very controversial provisions of the Uniform Arrest Act,[10] permitting the police to detain for ques-tioning for a short period even though they do not have grounds for making an arrest, would be a magnanimous concession by the all-powerful state rather than, as it is now perceived, a substantial expansion of police power.

Finally, there is a complex of assumptions embraced within terms like "the adversary system," "procedural due process," "notice and an opportunity to be heard," "day in court," and the like. Common to them all is the notion that the alleged criminal is not merely an object to be acted upon, but an independent entity in the process who may, if he so desires, force the operators of the process to demonstrate to an independent authority (judge and jury) that he is guilty of the charges against him. It is a minimal asumption. It speaks in terms of "may," not "must." It permits but does not require the accused, acting by himself or through his own agent, to play an active role in the process; by virtue

---

7   *E.g.,* Poe v. Ullrnan, 367 U.S. 497 (1961).

8   Hall, General Principles of Criminal Law 382–87 (2d ed. 1960).

9   Mapp v. Ohio, 367 U.S. 643 (1961); Ker v. California, 374 U.S. 23 (1963).

10   See pp. 28–29 *infra.*

of that fact, the process becomes or has the capacity to become a contest between, if not equals, at least independent actors. Now, as we shall see, much of the space between the two models is occupied by stronger or weaker notions of how this contest is to be arranged, how often it is to be played, and by what rules. The Crime Control Model tends to deemphasize this adversary aspect of the process; the Due Process Model tends to make it central. The common ground, and it is an important one, is that the process has, for everyone subjected to it, at least the potentiality of becoming to some extent an adversary struggle.

[…]

CRIME CONTROL VALUES

The value system that underlies the Crime Control Model is based on the proposition that the repression of criminal conduct is by far the most important function to be performed by the criminal process. The failure of law enforcement to bring criminal conduct under tight control is viewed as leading to the breakdown of public order and thence to the disappearance of an important condition of human freedom. If the laws go unenforced, which is to say, if it is perceived that there is a high percentage of failure to apprehend and convict in the criminal process, a general disregard for legal controls tends to develop. The law-abiding citizen then becomes the victim of all sorts of unjustifiable invasions of his interests. His security of person and property is sharply diminished and, therefore, so is his liberty to function as a member of society. The claim ultimately is that the criminal process is a positive guarantor of social freedom.[11] In order to achieve this high purpose, the Crime Control Model requires that primary attention be paid to the efficiency with which the criminal process operates to screen suspects, determine guilt, and secure appropriate dispositions of persons convicted of crime.

Efficiency of operation is not, of course, a criterion that can be applied in a vacuum. By "efficiency" we mean the system's capacity to apprehend, try, convict, and dispose of a high proportion of criminal offenders whose offenses become known. In a society in which only the grossest forms of antisocial behavior were made criminal and in which the crime rate was exceedingly low, the criminal process might require many more man-hours of police, prosecutorial, and judicial time per case than ours does, and still operate with tolerable efficiency. On the other hand, a society that was prepared to increase substantially the resources devoted to the suppression of crime might cope with a rising crime rate without sacrifice of efficiency while continuing to maintain an elaborate and time-consuming set of criminal processes. However, neither of these hypotheses corresponds with social reality in this country. We use the criminal sanction to cover an increasingly wide spectrum of behavior thought to be antisocial, and the amount of crime is very large indeed. At the same time, while precise measures are not available, it does not appear that we are disposed in the public sector of the economy to increase very drastically the quantity, much less the quality, of the resources devoted to the suppression of criminal activity through the operation of the criminal process. These factors have an important bearing on the criteria of efficiency and, therefore, on the nature of the Crime Control Model.

The model, in order to operate successfully, must produce a high rate of apprehension and conviction and must do so in a context where the magnitudes being dealt with are very large, and the resources for dealing with them are very limited. There must then be a premium on speed and finality. Speed, in turn, depends on informality and on uniformity; finality depends on minimizing the occasions for challenge. The process must not be cluttered with ceremonious rituals that do not advance the progress of a case. Facts can be established more quickly through interrogation in a police station

---

11   For a representative statement see Barrett, *supra* note 2, at 11–16.

than through the formal process of examination and cross-examination in a court; it follows that extra judicial processes should be preferred to judicial processes, informal to formal operations. Informality is not enough; there must also be uniformity. Routine stereotyped procedures are essential if large numbers are being handled. The model that will operate successfully on these presuppositions must be an administrative, almost a managerial, model. The image that comes to mind is an assembly line or a conveyor belt down which moves an endless stream of cases, never stopping, carrying the cases to workers who stand at fixed stations and who perform on each case as it comes by the same small but essential operation that brings it one step closer to being a finished product, or, to exchange the metaphor for the reality, a closed file.

The criminal process, on this model, is seen as a screening process in which each successive stage—prearrest investigation, arrest, post-arrest investigation, preparation for trial, trial or entry of plea, conviction, and disposition—involves a series of routinized operations whose success is gauged primarily by their tendency to pass the case along to a successful conclusion.

What is a successful conclusion? One that throws off at an early stage those cases in which it appears unlikely that the person apprehended is an offender and then secures, as expeditiously as possible, the conviction of the rest with a minimum of occasions for challenge, let alone postaudit. By the application of administrative expertness, primarily that of the police and prosecutors, an early determination of probable innocence or guilt emerges. The probably innocent are screened out. The probably guilty are passed quickly through the remaining stages of the process. The key to the operation of the model as to those who are not screened out is what I shall call a presumption of guilt. The concept requires some explanation, since it may appear startling to assert that what appears to be the precise converse of our generally accepted ideology of a presumption of innocence can be an essential element of a model that does correspond in some regards to the real-life operation of the criminal process.

The presumption of guilt allows the Crime Control Model to deal efficiently with large numbers. The supposition is that the screening processes operated by police and prosecutors are reliable indicators of probable guilt. Once a man has been investigated without being found to be probably innocent, or, to put it differently, once a determination has been made that there is enough evidence of guilt so that he should be held for further action rather than released from the process, then all subsequent activity directed toward him is based on the view that he is probably guilty. The precise point at which this occurs will vary from case to case; in many cases it will occur as soon as the suspect is arrested or even before, if the evidence of probable guilt that has come to the attention of the authorities is sufficiently strong. But in any case, the presumption of guilt will begin to operate well before the "suspect" becomes a "defendant."

[…]

The presumption of innocence is a direction to officials how they are to proceed, not a prediction of outcome. The presumption of guilt, however, is basically a prediction of outcome. The presumption of innocence is really a direction to the authorities to ignore the presumption of guilt in their treatment of the suspect. It tells them, in effect, to close their eyes to what will frequently seem to be factual probabilities. The reasons why it tells them that are among the animating presuppositions of the Due Process Model, and we will come to them shortly. It is enough to note at this point that the presumption of guilt is descriptive and factual; the presumption of innocence is normative and legal. The pure Crime Control Model finds unacceptable the presumption of innocence although, as we shall see, its real-life emanations are brought into uneasy compromise with the dictates of this dominant ideological position. For this model the presumption of guilt assures the dominant goal of repressing crime through highly summary processes without any great loss of efficiency (as previously defined), for in the run of cases, the preliminary screening processes operated by the police and the prosecuting officials contain adequate guarantees of reliable factfinding. Indeed, the position is a stronger one. It is that subsequent processes, particularly of a formal adjudicatory nature, are unlikely to produce as reliable factfinding as the expert administrative process that precedes them. The criminal process thus must put special weight on the quality of administrative factfinding. It becomes important, then, to place as few restrictions as possible on the character of the administrative factfinding processes and to limit restrictions to those that enhance reliability, excluding those designed for other purposes. As we shall see, the desire to avoid restrictions on administrative factfinding is a consistent theme in the development of the Crime Control Model.

For this model the early administrative factfinding stages are centrally vital. The complementary proposition is that the subsequent stages are relatively unimportant and should be truncated as much as possible. This, too, produces tensions with presently dominant ideology. The pure Crime Control Model has very little use for many conspicuous features of the adjudicative process and in real life works a number of ingenious compromises with it. Even in the pure model, however, there have to be devices for dealing with the suspect after the preliminary screening process has resulted in a determination of probable guilt. The focal device, as we shall see, is the plea of guilty; through its use adjudicative factfinding is reduced to a minimum. It might be said of the Crime Control Model that, reduced to its barest essentials and when operating at its most successful pitch, it consists of two elements: (a) an administrative factfinding process leading to exoneration of the suspect, or to (b) the entry of a plea of guilty.

DUE PROCESS VALUES

If the Crime Control Model resembles an assembly line, the Due Process Model looks very much like an obstacle course. Each of its successive stages is designed to present formidable impediments to carrying the accused any further along in the process. Its ideology is not the converse of that underlying the Crime Control Model. It does not deny the social desirability of repressing crime, although its critics have been known to claim so. Its ideology is composed of a complex of ideas, some of them based on judgments about the efficacy of crime control devices. The ideology of due process is far more deeply impressed on the formal structure of the law than is the ideology of crime control; yet, an accurate tracing of the strands of which it is made is strangely difficult.[12] What follows is only an attempt at an approximation.

The Due Process Model encounters its rival on the Crime Control Model's own ground in respect to the reliability of factfinding processes. The Crime Control Model, as we have suggested in a preliminary way, places heavy reliance on the ability of investigative and prosecutorial officers, acting in an informal setting in which their distinctive skills are given full sway, to elicit and reconstruct a tolerably accurate account of what actually took place in an alleged criminal event. The Due Process Model rejects this premise and substitutes for it a view of informal, nonadjudicative factfinding that stresses the possibility of error: people are notoriously poor observers of disturbing events—the more emotion-arousing the context, the greater the possibility that recollection will be incorrect; confessions and admissions by persons in police custody may be induced by physical or psychological coercion, so that the police end up hearing what the suspect thinks they want to hear

---

12   For a perceptive account dealing with a wider spectrum of problems than those posed by the criminal process, see Kadish, *Methodology and Criteria in Due Process Adjudication—A Survey and Criticism*, 66 Yale L.J. 319 (1957).

rather than the truth; witnesses may be animated by a bias or interest that no one would trouble to discover except one specially charged with protecting the interests of the accused—which the police are not. Considerations of this kind all lead to the rejection of informal factfinding processes as definitive of factual guilt and to the insistence on formal, adjudicative, adversary factfinding processes in which the factual case against the accused is publicly heard by an impartial tribunal and is evaluated only after the accused has had a full opportunity to discredit the case against him. Even then the distrust of factfinding processes that animates the Due Process Model is not dissipated. The possibilities of human error being what they are, further scrutiny is necessary, or at least must be available, lest in the heat of battle facts have been overlooked or suppressed. How far this subsequent scrutiny must be available is hotly controverted today; in the pure Due Process Model the answer would be: at least as long as there is an allegation of factual error that has not received an adjudicative hearing in a factfinding context. The demand for finality is thus very low in the Due Process Model.

This strand of due process ideology is not enough to sustain the model. If all that were at issue between the two models was a series of questions about the reliability of factfinding processes, we would have but one model of the criminal process, the nature of whose constituent elements would pose questions of fact, not of value. Even if the discussion is confined for the moment to the question of reliability, it is apparent that more is at stake than simply an evaluation of what kinds of factfinding processes, alone or in combination, are likely to produce the most nearly reliable results. The stumbling-block is this: how much reliability is compatible with efficiency? Granted that informal factfinding will make some mistakes that will be remedied if backed up by adjudicative factfinding, the desirability of providing this backup is not affirmed or negated by factual demonstrations or predictions that the increase in reliability will be x percent or x plus n percent. It still remains to ask how much weight is to be given to the competing demands of reliability (a high degree of probability in each case that factual guilt has been accurately determined) and efficiency (a process that deals expeditiously with the large numbers of cases that it ingests). Just as the Crime Control Model is more optimistic about the unlikelihood of error in a significant number of cases, it is also more lenient in establishing a tolerable level of error. The Due Process Model insists on the prevention and elimination of mistakes to the extent possible; the Crime Control Model accepts the probability of mistakes up to the level at which they interfere with the goal of repressing crime, either because too many guilty people are escaping or, more subtly, because general awareness of the unreliability of the process leads to a decrease in the deterrent efficacy of the criminal law. On this view reliability and efficiency are not polar opposites but rather complementary characteristics. The system is reliable *because* efficient; reliability becomes a matter of independent concern only when it becomes so attenuated as to impair efficiency. All of this the Due Process Model rejects. If efficiency suggests shortcuts around reliability, those demands must be rejected. The aim of the process is at least as much to protect the factually innocent as it is to convict the factually guilty. It somewhat resembles quality control in industrial technology: tolerable deviation from standard varies with the importance of conformity to standard in the destined use of the product. The Due Process Model resembles a factory that has to devote a substantial part of its input to quality control. This necessarily reduces quantitative output.

This is only the beginning of the ideological difference between the two models. The Due Process Model could disclaim any attempt to provide enhanced reliability for the factfinding process and still produce a set of institutions and processes that would differ sharply from those posited by the demands of the Crime Control Model. Indeed, it may not be too great an oversimplification to assert that in point of historical development the doctrinal pressures that have emanated from the demands of the Due Process Model have tended to evolve from an original matrix of concern with the maximization of reliability into something quite different and more far-reaching.[13] This complex of values can be symbolized although not adequately described by the concept of the primacy of the individual and the complementary concept of limitation on official power.

The combination of stigma and loss of liberty that is embodied in the end result of the criminal process is viewed as being the heaviest deprivation that government can inflict on the individual. Furthermore, the processes that culminate in these highly afflictive sanctions are in themselves coercive, restricting, and demeaning. Power is always subject to abuse, sometimes subtle, other times, as in the criminal process, open and ugly. Precisely because of its potency in subjecting the individual to the coercive power of the state, the criminal process must, on this model, be subjected to controls and safeguards that prevent it from operating with maximal efficiency. According to this ideology, maximal efficiency means maximal tyranny. And, while no one would assert that minimal efficiency means minimal tyranny, the proponents of the Due Process Model would accept with considerable equanimity a substantial diminution in the efficiency with which the criminal process operates in the interest of preventing official oppression of the individual.

The most modest-seeming but potentially far-reaching mechanism by which the Due Process Model implements these antiauthoritarian values is the doctrine of legal guilt. According to this doctrine, an individual is not to be held guilty of crime merely on a showing that in all probability, based upon reliable evidence, he did factually what he is said to have done. Instead, he is to be held guilty if and only if these factual determinations are made in procedurally regular fashion and by authorities acting within competences duly allocated to them. Furthermore, he is not to be held guilty, even though the factual determination is or might be adverse to him, if various rules designed to safeguard the integrity of the process are not given effect: the tribunal that convicts him must have the power to deal with his kind of case ("jurisdiction") and must be geographically appropriate ("venue"); too long a time must not have elapsed since the offense was committed ("statute of limitations"); he must not have been previously convicted or acquitted of the same or a substantially similar offense ("double jeopardy") ; he must not fall within a category of persons, such as children or the insane, who are legally immune to conviction ("criminal responsibility") ; and so on. None of these requirements has anything to do with the factual question of whether he did or did not engage in the conduct that is charged as the offense against him; yet favorable answers to any of them will mean that he is legally innocent. Wherever the competence to make adequate factual determinations lies, it is apparent that only a tribunal that is aware of these guilt-defeating doctrines and is willing to apply them can be viewed as competent to make determinations of legal guilt. The police and the prosecutors are ruled out by lack of capacity in the first instance and by lack of assurance of willingness in the second. Only an impartial tribunal can be trusted to make determinations of legal as opposed to factual guilt.

[…]

Beyond the question of predictability this model posits a functional reason for observing the presumption of innocence: by forcing the state to prove its case against the accused in an adjudicative context, the presumption of innocence serves to force into play all the qualifying and disabling doctrines that limit the use of the criminal sanction against the individual, thereby enhancing his

---

13 It is instructive to compare, for example, the emphasis on diminished reliability in early coerced confession cases like Brown v. Mississippi, 297 U.S. 278 (1936), with the subsequent development of a rationale that stresses the assertedly limited roles assigned to the state and the accused in an adversary system, *e.g.*, Rogers v. Richmond, 365 U.S. 534 (1961).

opportunity to secure a favorable outcome. In this sense the presumption of innocence may be seen to operate as a kind of self-fulfilling prophecy. By opening up a procedural situation that permits the successful assertion of defenses that have nothing to do with factual guilt, it vindicates the proposition that the factually guilty may nonetheless be legally innocent and should therefore be given a chance to qualify for that kind of treatment.

The possibility of legal innocence is expanded enormously when the criminal process is viewed as the appropriate forum for correcting its own abuses. This notion may well account for a greater amount of the distance between the two models than any other. In theory the Crime Control Model can tolerate rules that forbid illegal arrests, unreasonable searches, coercive interrogations, and the like if their enforcement is left primarily to managerial sanctions internally imposed. What it cannot tolerate is the vindication of those rules in the criminal process itself through the exclusion of evidence illegally obtained or through the reversal of convictions in cases where the criminal process has breached the rules laid down for its observance. The availability of these corrective devices fatally impairs the efficiency of the process. The Due Process Model, while it may in the first instance be addressed to the maintenance of reliable factfinding techniques, comes eventually to incorporate prophylactic and deterrent rules that result in the release of the factually guilty even in cases in which blotting out the illegality would still leave an adjudicative factfinder convinced of the accused's guilt.[14]

Another strand in the complex of attitudes that underlies the Due Process Model is the idea—itself a shorthand statement for a complex of attitudes—of equality. This notion has only recently emerged as an explicit basis for pressing the demands of the Due Process Model, but it appears to represent, at least in its potential, a most powerful norm for influencing official conduct. Stated most starkly, the ideal of equality holds that "there can be no equal justice where the kind of trial a man gets depends on the amount of money he has,"[15]

The factual predicate underlying this assertion is that there are gross inequalities in the financial means of criminal defendants as a class, that in an adversary system of criminal justice, an effective defense is largely a function of the resources that can be mustered on behalf of the accused, and that a very large proportion of criminal defendants are, operationally speaking, "indigent"[16] in terms of their ability to finance an effective defense. This factual premise has been strongly reinforced by recent studies that in turn have been both a cause and an effect of an increasing emphasis upon norms for the criminal process based on the premise.

The norms derived from the premise do not take the form of an insistence upon governmental responsibility to provide literally equal opportunities for all criminal defendants to challenge the process. Rather, they take as their point of departure the notion that the criminal process, initiated as it is by government and containing as it does the likelihood of severe deprivations at the hands of government, imposes some kind of public obligation to ensure that financial inability does not destroy the capacity of an accused to assert what may be meritorious challenges to the processes being invoked against him.[17]

---

14 This tendency, seen most starkly in the exclusionary rule for illegally seized evidence, Mapp v. Ohio, 367 U.S. 643 (1961), is also involved in the rejection of the "special circumstances" approach to testing the deprivation of counsel, Gideon v. Wainwright, 372 U.S. 335 (1963), and in the apparently similar trend in confession cases, Mallory v. United States, 354 U.S. 449 (1957) ; Escobedo v. Illinois, 378 U.S. 478 (1964).

15 Griffin v. Illinois, 351 U.S. 12, 19 (1956).

16 The vacuity of the concept of indigence is exposed in Att'y Gen. Comm, on Poverty and the Administration of Federal Criminal Justice, Report 7–8, 40–41 (1963) [hereinafter cited as Att'y Gen. Rep.].

17 E.g., id. at 8–11.

The demands made by a norm of this kind are likely by its very nature to be quite sweeping. Although its imperatives may be initially limited to determining whether in a particular case the accused was injured or prejudiced by his relative inability to make an appropriate challenge, the norm of equality very quickly moves to another level on which the demand is that the process in general be adapted to minimize discriminations rather than that a mere series of *post hoc* determinations of discrimination be made or makeable.

It should be observed that the impact of the equality norm will vary greatly depending upon the point in time at which it is introduced into a model of the criminal process. If one were starting from scratch to decide how the process ought to work, the norm of equality would have nothing very important to say on such questions as, for example, whether an accused should have the effective assistance of counsel in deciding whether to enter a plea of guilty. One could decide, on quite independent considerations, that it is or is not a good thing to afford that facility to the generality of persons accused of crime. But the impact of the equality norm becomes far greater when it is brought to bear on a process whose contours have already been shaped. If our model of the criminal process affords defendants who are in a financial position to consult a lawyer before entering a plea the right to do so, then the equality norm exerts powerful pressure to provide such an opportunity to all defendants and to regard the failure to do so as a malfunctioning of the process from whose consequences the accused is entitled to be relieved. In a sense that has been the role of the equality norm in affecting the real-world criminal process. It has made its appearance on the scene comparatively late[18] and has therefore encountered a situation in which, in terms of the system as it operates, the relative financial inability of most persons accused of crime sharply distinguishes their treatment from the small minority of the financially capable. For that reason its impact has already been substantial and may be expected to be even more so in the future.

[...]

One last introductory note. What assumptions do we make about the sources of authority to shape the real-world operations of the criminal process? What agencies of government have the power to pick and choose between their competing demands? Once again, the limiting features of the American context come into play. Ours is not a system of legislative supremacy. The distinctively American institution of judicial review exercises a limiting and, ultimately, a shaping influence on the criminal process. Because the Crime Control Model is basically an affirmative model, emphasizing at every turn the existence and exercise of official power, its validating authority is ultimately legislative (although proximately administrative). Because the Due Process Model is basically a negative model, asserting limits on the nature of official power and on the modes of its exercise, its validating authority is judicial and requires an appeal to supra-legislative law, to the law of the Constitution. To the extent that tensions between the two models are resolved by deference to the Due Process Model, the authoritative force at work is the judicial power, working in the distinctively judicial mode of invoking the sanction of nullity. That is at once the strength and the weakness of the Due Process Model: its strength because in our system the appeal to the Constitution provides the last and the overriding word; its weakness because saying no in specific cases is an exercise in futility unless there is a general willingness on the part of the officials who operate the process to apply negative prescriptions across the board. It is no accident that statements reinforcing the Due Process Model come from the courts while at the same time facts denying it are established by the police and prosecutors.

---

18   Griffin v. Illinois, 351 U.S. 12 (1956), is generally regarded as being the first decision of the Supreme Court explicitly and exclusively grounded on the equality norm.

DISCUSSION QUESTIONS

1. Explain why two judges who have a similar upbringing can hear the same case and rule differently.

2. Is it possible to have a truly fair trial in America? Why or why not?

3. With the progression of time in the United States, how has the Supreme Court's idea of African Americans changed? How does this demonstrate that courts are a reflection of local community attitudes, values, and norms?

4. From a realist perspective, how would one explain the decision in *Brown v. Board of Education*?

5. What was the effect of *Scott v. Sandford*? *Plessy v. Ferguson*? *Brown v. Board of Education*?

6. What impact does the upper court myth have on the lower courts?

7. On the continuum of crime control and due process, where do you think trial courts fall?

8. Why might a police officer support the crime control model over the due process model?

9. Why does the crime control model support the notion of guilty until proven innocent? What are the implications of this?

10. Does a jury help ensure that similarly situated offenders get similar sentences?

TRIAL COURTS AS ORGANIZATIONS

Introduction

Based in legal realism is the notion that trial courts operate as organizations. In this respect, the courts have administrative and bureaucratic concerns similar to any other organization—be it a university or even a retail store. These concerns influence the operation of the criminal court system, including its actors, and ultimately affect case processing. As mentioned and emphasized in this section's readings, a vast majority of cases are resolved through a plea of guilty. The organizational nature of the courts provides an explanation for this phenomenon.

The Not So Adversarial Court System

Criminal justice dramas on television often portray a very adversarial court process in which attorneys battle with each other in representation of their respective clients. The truth is that most justice is not achieved in an adversarial manner. In the majority of circumstances, the criminal process in the trial courts leans toward cooperation and collaboration among attorneys, even those traditionally thought to be on opposing sides. Jerome Skolnick, in the reading "Social Control in the Adversary System," puts this eloquently when he states, "administrative requirements characterizing the American administration of criminal justice make for a reciprocal relationship between prosecutor and defense attorney that strains toward cooperation." He presents a field work study of public defenders and prosecutors to further understand their tendency to cooperate.

Abraham Blumberg, in "The Practice of Law as Confidence Game: Organizational Cooptation of a Profession," explains this cooperative nature further using the defense attorney as an example. He identifies defense attorneys as double agents, working for the court and for the accused. While they are expected to be an adversary to the prosecutor for purposes of the client, it is often an image that is portrayed and not necessarily a reality. As Blumberg notes, defense attorneys typically have close relationships with both prosecutors and judges, which should not be surprising considering they work together on a daily basis. As colleagues within the system, defense attorneys have a greater obligation to these colleagues and the overall functioning of the courthouse then they do to their clients.

Why Cooperate?

It is argued that the source of this cooperation stems largely from the organizational obligations of the court system. Grounded in the original work of Skolnick and Blumberg, in "Criminal Trial Courts as Organizational Systems," Christi Metcalfe details how these organizational obligations alter case processing. Metcalfe identifies key organizational goals, including the need to (a) efficiently process cases and (b) reduce uncertainties regarding the outcome of the case. She explains how these goals lend themselves toward a system of negotiation and bargaining, resulting in a high rate of cases resolved through a guilty plea. Guilty pleas quicken the pace of case processing and reduce many of the uncertainties posed by a trial, including how a jury will react to a case and what a judge will decide as an appropriate sentence.

This type of system is best facilitated through cooptation, cooperation, and coordination among the attorneys and actors in the courthouse. They assimilate to each other's needs, they focus on the benefits of cooperation, and they coordinate their efforts for the achievement of the court's organizational goals. As Skolnick states, "it is believed that the more smoothly the actors within it work together, the more likely will the institution achieve its aims." Teamwork becomes essential to the proper functioning of the courthouse, thereby contributing to a less adversarial system. Skolnick explains the administrative concerns of prosecutors and how prosecutors depend on defense attorneys who are experienced and understand the system to make achievement of the organizational goals easier. Metcalfe also calls attention to the fact that experienced attorneys who are more familiar to the system and its administrative priorities can facilitate cooperation.

Often, the focus on these organizational goals comes at the expense of due process ideals. Blumberg presents it as a conflict between processing large caseloads on one side and the ideological requirements of due process on the other side. This conflict resembles the distinction between the crime control and due process models discussed in Section 1. The organizational goals are often so demanding, that the actors tend to abandon some of these ideological values, like due process, for the purpose of fulfilling the organizational obligations. In this way, the system becomes more crime control oriented. The court organization, itself, can be a significant factor that alters or affects case outcomes, particularly when it comes to how the case is resolved, also referred to as the mode of disposition.

Skolnick points to a concern regarding the focus on the organizational goals and the resulting cooperation among attorneys. He recognizes that "there is always a tipping point where cooperation may shade off into collusion, thereby subverting the ethical basis of the system." This sentiment largely depends on the extent to which the system's adaptations to its bureaucratic concerns have compromised due process. Has the system become too coercive? Is a system heavily reliant on guilty pleas a system without due process? Is plea bargaining fraught with injustices? Or is plea bargaining just a routinized version of due process that should be valued for its flexibility?

The Influence of Outsiders

Both Blumberg and Metcalfe recognize that the court is a closed community and outsiders to this community can present contingencies and constraints on the court that affect the plea driven system in place. These outsiders include, but are not limited to, the defendants, victims, police, legislature, appellate courts, and media. The court is dependent, to a certain extent, on each of these outsiders to function and coordinates with these outsiders accordingly. This coordination and agreement between the court and its environment is referred to as domain consensus. However, these outsiders can disrupt the ongoing internal operations of the court as well, especially because they often impose the ideological goals of due process and justice on the court. For this reason, the court attempts to operate in a low visibility arena, where it does not draw too much attention to itself and can maintain its normal functioning.

In "It's Not the Old Ball Game: Three Strikes and the Courtroom Workgroup," John Harris and Paul Jesilow demonstrate how outsiders can disrupt norms in case processing. They focus specifically on the influence of Three Strikes Laws instituted by the California legislature on the operations of the courtroom workgroup. Interviews and surveys with judges, prosecutors, and defense attorneys reveal that Three Strikes disrupted plea bargaining in California such that pleas became less likely when defendants already had prior strikes. In this way, the law altered the dynamic of courtroom relationships and disrupted the mechanisms put in place for the efficient processing of cases. Similar disruptions can be seen in the context of other environmental pressures, such as sentencing guidelines, reductions in the court's operating budget, increased support for "get tough" policies, and media attention to a high profile case, just to name a few.

Skolnick also calls attention to the public relations role of prosecutors, meaning that prosecutors alter their behavior in response to their communities. In light of public opinion, prosecutors are concerned about maintaining a "respectable record," as well as "a reputation for utter credibility, inevitable truth, almost of invincibility." Prosecutors want to be seen by the community as the people ensuring their safety by keeping criminals off the streets. Therefore, prosecutors alter their behavior in accordance with these responsibilities to the public. In addition to the administrative concerns discussed above, this public relations role actually leads to greater cooperation with defense attorneys and would presumably increase the occurrence of plea bargains.

Recently, plea bargaining practices have come under increased scrutiny by the Supreme Court. In *Missouri v. Frye,* the Court decided that defense attorneys are required to communicate plea offers to the defendant, and not doing so is a violation of the Sixth Amendment. In *Lafler v. Cooper,* the court held that there are protections for defendants who reject a favorable plea bargain when a defense attorney inappropriately advises them to reject it. The legal rules established in these cases can affect the plea process in criminal courts. The two cases seem to be calling for increased guidelines and formalities around plea bargaining, which would likely impede the efficiency of the process and ultimately impact the functioning of the court organization.

Social Control in the Adversary System

Jerome H. Skolnick

To understand the social control problem of the adversary system, we begin with what is admittedly a conceptual oversimplification—that social organizations are based upon norms of either conflict or cooperation. The family, the university, the industrial enterprise are institutions predicated upon the idea of cooperation. It is believed that the more smoothly the actors within it work together, the more likely will the institution achieve its aims. For such institutions, the key problem of social control is to find means for countering forces that precipitate conflict.

There are, however, institutions experiencing just the opposite problem. The most striking example of an institution based upon conflict is the *sporting event.* Not only are most sporting events zero-sum games in which one player must lose and the other win; even more fundamental is the condition that each player try to win. Should a fight be "fixed," it might be that the outcome would be the same as if the fight had not been fixed. Underlying the sporting event, however, is the principle of conflict. Within the ethic of the institution it is understood that each fighter will attempt to throw his best punches, that each will strain to achieve victory. Otherwise, the fight is not considered genuine. *Procedure* is as important as *outcome.*

As a procedural matter, the adversary system may similarly be viewed as resting upon an assumption of genuine conflict. As the Allen report (1963) states:

The adversary system is the institution devised by our legal order for the proper reconciliation of public and private interests in the crucial areas of penal regulation. As such, it makes essential and invaluable contributions to the maintenance of the free society. The essence of the adversary system is *challenge.* The survival of our system of criminal justice and the value which it advances depends upon a constant, searching, and creative questioning of official decisions and assertions of authority at all stages of the process.

Jerome H. Skolnick, "Social Control in the Adversary System," The Journal of Conflict Resolution, vol. 11, no. 1, pp. 52-55, 57-59, 68-70. Copyright © 1967 by SAGE Publications. Reprinted with permission.

The proper performance of the defense function is thus as vital to the health of the system as the performance of the prosecuting and adjudicatory functions [pp. 10–11, italics added].

The introduction of this quotation should not be taken to mean that the adversary system is the only, or even the best, system possible "for reconciling public and private interests in the crucial areas of penal regulation." All it is intended to suggest is that, as a procedural matter, there seems to be a fundamental norm of challenge underlying the system. It is therefore like the sporting event in that it presupposes an underlying ethic of genuine conflict. Furthermore, as in all institutions based on conflict, there is a perception of "deviance" when actors who are supposed to be genuinely antagonistic begin to cooperate. Adam Smith expresses a social control problem of the free enterprise economy as follows:

People of the same trade seldom meet together even for merriment and diversion, but the conversation ends in a conspiracy against the public, or on some contrivance to raise prices. It is impossible indeed to prevent such meetings by any law which either could be executed, or would be consistent with liberty and justice. But though the law cannot hinder people of the same trade from sometimes assembling together, it ought to do nothing to facilitate such assemblies, much less to render them necessary [Smith, 1776, p. 116].

Just as it is sometimes argued that monopolies are more economic than free enterprise, the aims of truth and justice may be considered better achieved through the institution of the interrogating magistrate. From the point of view of the sociological analyst of the system, however, the argument is relevant mainly insofar as it provides a resource for actors in the system who deviate from die norm of adversariness, that is, it gives them a justification for "deviant behavior." It may even be that all conflict systems are unnecessary, but that is not the point. The point is that all conflict systems share a similar problem of social control; that problem is conflict maintenance, or the control of tendencies toward cooperation.

The purpose of this paper is to describe and analyze outstanding features of the adversary system, as observed in operation, that are relevant to the social control problem of conflict maintenance in the adversary system. Thus, the paper is concerned with actual deviation from the adversary model and the conditions and principles accounting for such deviation. The first section will principally examine pressures on the prosecutor to reduce conflict. The second section will examine prosecutor—defense attorney relations, with the issue of "deviance" from conflict norms as its principal subject. Finally, the paper will analyze the conflict model for varying categories of defense attorney. The principal theme of the paper is that administrative requirements characterizing the American administration of criminal justice make for a reciprocal relationship between prosecutor and defense attorney that strains toward cooperation; that this relationship is based upon interests wider than those of the parties they represent, the State and the accused; that the public defender, as an institution, does not significantly differ from other "cooperative" defense attorneys; and that the dilemma of the adversary system arises from the fact that such tendencies toward "cooperation"— under existing conditions—do not demonstrably impede the quality of representation.

Source of Data and Method

Data are based upon a study of one California county, which shall be called La Loma. La Loma County has a population of approximately one million, and is dominated by one city, which shall be called Westville. Westville's population is nearly 400,000, approximately 30 percent of whom are nonwhite.

Two criminal trial courts operate at the felony level. There are seven municipal courts and a traffic court in Westville, two municipal courts in Elmwood, and another municipal court serving the western part of the county. Municipal courts hold preliminary hearings and misdemeanor trials. Both levels of court were studied, but most of the data in this paper derive from observations relating to the felony courts. In the fiscal year 1961–62 there were 1,893 felony cases in the county, with Westville accounting for more than 60 percent. Of all felony cases, 61 percent were handled by the public defender's office.

The research method is described in greater detail elsewhere (Skolnick, 1966, pp. 23–41). Mainly, it was participant observation in a face-to-face professional community of about 100 attorneys and judges. The principal investigator spent three months in the office of the public defender (who had a staff of fifteen), four months in the office of the prosecutor (who had a staff of forty), and six months in the police department (about 700 men) over an eighteen-month period commencing in the summer of 1962. Attorneys and police usually were aware of the investigator's true identity, while defendants were not. In studying public defenders, for example, the investigator would select one who was not scheduled for trial and follow him on his daily round of interview and negotiation, since the main subject of interest was the system of justice without trial.

The Guilty Plea

The question of the actual operation of the adversary system—the "proper performance" of both defense and prosecutorial roles—is raised generally by the fact that most criminal cases, contrary to popular notions of the administration of criminal law portrayed in mass media, do not go to trial. The overwhelming majority of criminal cases are settled by the accused's plea of guilty. In the federal courts, pleas of *nolo contendere* and guilty pleas accounted for 79 percent of the dispositions of all criminal cases between 1957 and 1962, and approximately another 10 percent should be added in describing the number of convictions obtained. In general, the state courts trail by about 10 percent (see Vetri, 1964).

[…]

The Prosecutorial Role and Prosecutor Discretion

In law and in practice, the prosecutor enjoys wide discretion,[1] especially in the details of charging the defendant. A simple view of the prosecutor's role would principally emphasize the prosecutor's responsibility to argue the case for the state. In fact, however, the responsibilities of the prosecutor were observed to be more extensive and complex, taking into account administrative concerns as well as the task of prosecution.

---

1   Relevant materials are summarized in Paulsen and Kadish (1962, pp. 965–69).

Most organizations within a bureaucracy seek to expand their authority; the prosecutor is also interested in expansive authority, but he already has it; thus his greatest concern is with maintaining his present latitude, that is, with avoiding action that might limit his future enjoyment of present discretionary power. He is, therefore, interested in making a favorable impression on a diffuse public—including courts, political authorities, and the man in the street. His specific task is to strike a balance between those cases which, for a variety of reasons—usually related to public interest—he cannot deal out; and those which, in deference to his administrative responsibilities, he needs to settle before trial. In brief, he is required to keep the calendar moving, at the same time not appearing to be "giving anything away" to the defense.

If criminal procedure were to be analyzed through statutes and cases alone, the pervading importance of administrative concerns would hardly be apparent. Viewing the system in action, however, it becomes clear that system norms can be inferred from sanctions within the system itself, with the values of the system expressed through its penalties. In the system studied there were strong informal controls to enhance the smooth *functioning* of the system itself. Thus an assertion regarding the pertinence of administrative concerns is evidenced by the weight of the sanctions favoring administration.

Judges, for example, typically exhibit a strong interest in calendar movement. The criminal court judge who allows his calendar to lag will in turn be cautioned by his presiding judge. Judges observed and interviewed made clear their potent interest in maintaining the administrative security of the courts. Similarly, in each of the two felony courts studied, the prosecutor's office maintained a calendar man, a legal-administrative "quarterback" who, in consultation with the trial lawyers in the district attorney's office, was responsible for making tactical decisions regarding the development of cases assigned to his court. It rarely happens that pleas of guilty are turned down, and judges tend to be especially unhappy with calendar men who "overcharge," that is, who, out of zeal or inexperience—the two are often associated— charge the defendant with potential sanctions severe enough to discourage pleas of guilty. One judge, when asked what he would do in such a situation, replied.

I would talk to him and try to teach him how I wanted him to conduct himself in my court [And if that didn't work?] I often have occasion to see the district attorney—that is—on social occasions. If I am running the criminal department, he might ask me how things are going, and I'd suggest to him that the deputy he has in there isn't doing a very good job, and that I think he ought to be replaced. Usually, when I make such a judgment, the district attorney will go along with me.

The importance of the calendar man's job is suggested first by the fact that the overwhelming majority of criminal cases are settled by the accused's plea of guilty (exceeding 80 percent in the county studied). Among those in the system, it is generally believed that if the trial model were to become the routine mechanism for settling issues of criminality, the system would conceivably break down from overuse—there would be too many cases for too few courts.

[…]

Finally, and also connected to public relations, is the prosecutor's interest in non-defeat. In the county studied, the prosecutor's office cared less about winning than about *not losing*, This norm is so intrinsic to the rationale of the prosecutor's office that one does not often hear it articulated. Nevertheless it is very powerful. It cannot be attributed to such a simple and obvious fact as the periodic requirement of reelection. Indeed, reelection seemed to be taken for granted, and an observer would be hard put to relate prosecutorial decisions directly to electoral requirements. Not only does the prosecutor desire to maintain a respectable record, but more than that, he seeks to maintain, insofar as possible, a reputation for utter credibility, inevitable truth, almost of invincibility.

The role of the prosecutor in an adversary system is accusatorial. He brings a charge, and the merit of the accusation is weighed by judge and jury. He is expected, however, before bringing the charge, to weigh its merits, including statements of fact. Thus, when a prosecutor brings a charge, he has himself made an investigation. It is as if the prosecutor were addressing the community as follows: "I have investigated, I have charged, I have found the man guilty; so should you." That the defendant is represented by counsel, that counsel has usually discussed the case with the prosecutor, tends to reinforce the prosecutor's confidence in the merits of his accusations. The adversary system is not, as it is frequently presented, a model of charge by complainant and defense by accused. Rather, the complainant's charge is considered by the prosecutor, the defense attorney usually discusses its merits, and the prosecutor comes to a decision to present the accusation, to act as attorney for the complainant. When the prosecutor makes such a decision to accuse, he does not care to be "reversed" in his judgment. His conception of esteem is recognition as a quasi-magisterial functionary. Such a status implies credibility, not only as to the prosecutor's belief in his own assertions, but also as to his capacity to assess the assertions of others before making his own.

The advantages of preserving such a magisterial posture are obvious for the routine functioning of the office, if the image can be maintained. If there is a presumption of innocence aiding the accused, when the prosecutor achieves a quasi-magisterial acceptance, he enjoys the countervailing advantage of a presumption of administrative regularity. Nothing can be more destructive to this posture, however, than a series of defeats in the courtroom. Credibility leads to victory, victory to the quasi-magisterial status, and quasi-magisterial status to enhanced credibility, all of which eases the task of the prosecutor.

In this context, prosecutor discretion itself puts certain pressures on the prosecutor. He is not only allotted the task of representing the interests of the state in the particular case but, given his discretion, he is also expected to play an administrative and public relations role. If prosecutors were selected from a community of lawyers, to represent the state in the individual case, the office itself would not have the administrative concerns or the public-relational concerns that presently characterize it. Most important, perhaps, there would be little need to enhance the status of the *office* itself. Thus the very structure of the prosecutor's office, and the tasks that are allotted to it, tend to create a social control problem for the adversary system. The prosecutor must attempt to "work with" defense attorneys to achieve goals wider than those ordinarily contemplated by a "squaring off" between two individual contestants, the state and the accused.

The Calendar Man and the Defense Community

If, as suggested, the calendar man not only is responsible for the conviction of the accused but also bears a heavy administrative responsibility for court functioning, he must elicit the cooperation of defense attorneys. From the point of view of the prosecutor, however, the idea of "prosecutor-defense attorney relations" is an oversimplified conception. He does not view a defense attorney solely in terms of his formal role as legal representative of an accused, but rather in light of the attorney's history of relations with the prosecutor's office and his position in the defense attorney community. Or, from the vantage point of the defendant, the strength of his defense depends in part upon the actual "facts" of his case, in part on how the defense is presented to the prosecution, and in part on who his defense attorney is. Principally, the prosecutor views the defense attorney in terms of the latter's "reasonableness," that is, the attorney's ability to discern a generous offer of settlement, and to be willing to encourage his client to accept such an offer. Prosecutorial discretion thus creates the fundamental conditions for the reduction of conflict.

From the vantage point of the prosecutor's office studied, there were at least four categories of defense attorney. One category comprised defense attorneys who tried relatively few criminal cases. These attorneys had variable relations with the prosecutor. One might think that, because of the inexperience of such attorneys, the prosecutor's office would prefer to deal with them. On the contrary, the more inexperienced the defense attorney, the more likely he was to pose an *administrative* problem for the prosecutor's office. Since the prosecutor is concerned not merely with convictions but with administrative efficiency, he tends to prefer to deal with attorneys who "know their business." To be sure, the prosecutor has an advantage over the inexperienced attorney in court trial, but that is relatively unimportant. Court trials waste time and money. Furthermore, in dealing with an inexperienced defense attorney the prosecutor is often faced with a man who, because of his own lack of knowledge, will be unnecessarily mistrustful of collaboration, even though in such cases the prosecutor may lean over backward to give the neophyte a fair shake. Experienced attorneys who maintain a general practice frequently forward criminal cases to experienced defense attorneys, believing that they serve their clients more advantageously.

There was also a group of defense attorneys who maintained both a small but active criminal practice and rather hostile relations with the prosecutor's office. Most defense attorneys and members of the prosecutor's office regarded them as "gamblers." They might occasionally gain an acquittal for their clients in cases where a "cooperative" defense attorney would have advised a plea of guilty. At the same time, the practices of such attorneys exemplified the dangers of adversariness for the rest of the criminal law community. In order to make it in the interest of the clients of other defense attorneys to plead their clients guilty, the district attorney had to demonstrate the negative consequences of adversariness through his victories over adversarially-oriented defense attorneys. Thus such attorneys tended to "win big" or "lose big," and the more successful defense attorneys preferred to avoid such tactics. Had the entire defense community united to frustrate the operations of the district attorney's office, they might have succeeded in changing the power structure of the system. As it was, however, the highly adversarial attorneys succeeded mainly in demonstrating the negative consequences of an adversarial posture, thereby unintentionally contributing to the power position of the prosecutor.

From the point of view of the prosecutor's office, greatest concern is with defense attorneys who represent the most numerous defendants, and also those who represent defendants in the most important cases. From this viewpoint the most important defense attorney is the public defender, whose office represented more than 60 percent of the accused felons in the county studied. The prosecutor also perceived a "group" of five or six "successful" criminal lawyers, with whom he had close and continuing relations. Still, because of the volume of cases that he handled, the public defender (PD) was the most important defense "agency" in the community.

[…]

The problem of the adversary system is maintaining the ethic of individuality and challenge in a system where the professionals will see greater advantage in cooperativeness than in conflict. That the prosecutor has his concerns for administrative efficiency and public relations creates a situation for the defense attorney— whether private or public—in which he must take account of the prosecutor's capacity to offer his client a less punitive outcome than he might receive if he were to challenge the state. Most defense attorneys strongly defend the system on pragmatic grounds. "The trial," said one cooperative defense attorney, "is a situation where reasonable minds cannot agree. Not only does it cost money to run a trial, but trials often get defendants into trouble." The attorney explained that the defendant will be harmed when he takes the stand and appears to lie, especially when his testimony tends to impugn the reputation of otherwise seemingly innocent people—as, for example, in the rape case where the defendant alleges that the girl invited his attentions. Similarly, if the crime involved . . . . physical assault, the trial may reveal details of brutality.

Regression toward cooperation, is, however, a general propensity found in all conflict situations. As Schelling says (1960, pp. 4–5), "Pure conflict, in which the interests of two antagonists are completely opposed, is a special case; it would arise in a war of complete extermination, otherwise not even in war. For this reason, 'winning' in a conflict does not have a strictly competitive meaning; it is not winning relative to one's adversary. It means gaining relative to one's own value system; and this may be done by bargaining, by mutual accommodation, and by the avoidance of mutually damaging behavior." It is only when the maintenance of conflict is itself a value, *as a procedural ethic,* that tendencies toward cooperation become a social control problem for the system advocating the ethic. In such a system there is always a tipping point where cooperation may shade off into collusion, thereby subverting the ethical basis of the system.

[...]

REFERENCES

Allen, Francis A. (chairman). *Poverty and the Administration of Federal Criminal Justice.* Report of the Attorney General's Committee. Washington, D.C.: Government Printing Office, 1963.

Ares, C. E., A. Rankin, and H. J. Sturz. "The Manhattan Bail Project; An Interim Report on the Use of Pre-Trial Parole," *NYU Law Review,* 38 (1963), 67.

Foote, C. "Compelling Appearances in Court—Administration of Bail in Philadelphia," *University of Pennsylvania Law Review,* 102 (1954), 1031–79.

———. "A Study of the Administration of Bail in New York City," *University of Pennsylvania Law Review,* 106 (1958), 693.

Fuller, L. "The Adversary System." In: H. Berman (ed.), *Talks on American Law.* New York: Vintage Books, 1961.

———. "Collective Bargaining and the Arbitrator," *Wisconsin Law Review,* 3 (Jan. 1963), 18–19.

Gallo, P. S., Jr., and C. G. McClintock. "Cooperative and Competitive Behavior in Mixed-Motive Games," *Journal of Conflict Resolution,* 9, 1 (March 1965), 68–77.

Golde, S. P. 'Interviewing Clients: Initial Steps." In: *California Criminal Law Practice,* California Continuing Education of the Bar, 1964.

McDonald, D. *The Law: Interviews with Edward Bennett Williams and Bethuel M. Webster.* Santa Barbara, Calif.: Center for the Study of Democratic Institutions, 1962.

Paulsen, M. G., and S. H. Kadish. *Criminal Law and Its Processes.* Boston: Little, Brown, 1962.

Schelling, T. C. *The Strategy of Conflict.* Cambridge, Mass,: Harvard University Press, 1960.

Skolnick, J. *Justice Without Trial: Law Enforcement in Democratic Society.* New York: Wiley, 1966.

Smith, A. *An Inquiry into the Nature and Causes of the Wealth of Nations.* (McCulloek edn.) London: Ward, Lock Bowden, 1776.

Sudnow, D. "Normal Crimes: Sociological Features of the Penal Code in a Public Defender Office," *Social Problems,* 12 (1965).

Vetri, D. R. "Note: Guilty Plea Bargaining: Compromises by Prosecutors to Secure Guilty Pleas," *University of Pennsylvania Law Review,* 112 (1964), 865–95.

The Practice of Law as a Confidence Game

Organizational Co-Optation of a Profession

Abraham S. Blumberg

reading 2.2

The overwhelming majority of convictions in criminal cases (usually over 90 per cent) are not the product of a combative, trial-by-jury process at all, but instead merely involve the sentencing of the individual after a negotiated, bargained-for plea of guilty has been entered.[1] Although more recently the overzealous role of police and prosecutors in producing pretrial confessions and admissions has achieved a good deal of notoriety, scant attention has been paid to the organizational structure and personnel of the criminal court itself. Indeed, the extremely high conviction rate produced without die features of an adversary trial in our courts would tend to suggest that the "trial" becomes a perfunctory reiteration and validation of the pretrial interrogation and investigation.[2]

The institutional setting of die court defines a role for the defense counsel in a criminal case radically different from the one traditionally depicted.[3] Sociologists and others have

---

1   F. J. Davis et al., Society and the Law: New Meanings for an Old Profession 301 (1962); L. Orfield, Criminal Procedure from Arrest to Appeal 297 (1947).

D. J. Newman, *Pleading Guilty for Considerations: A Study of Bargain Justice*, 46 J. Crim. L. C. & P.S. 780–90 (1954). Newman's data covered only one year, 1954, in a midwestern community, however, it is in general confirmed by my own data drawn from a far more populous area, and from what is one of the major criminal courts in the country, for a period of fifteen years from 1950 to 1964 inclusive. The English experience tends also to confirm American data, see N. Walker, Crime and Punishment in Britain: An Analysis of the Penal System (1965). See also D. J. Newman, Conviction: The Determination of Guilt or Innocence Without Trial (1966), for a comprehensive legalistic study of the guilty plea sponsored by the American Bar Foundation. The criminal court as a social system, an analysis of "bargaining" and its functions in the criminal court's organizational structure, are examined in my forthcoming book, The Criminal Court: A Sociological Perspective, to be published by Quadrangle Books, Chicago.

2   G. Feifer, Justice in Moscow (1965). The Soviet trial has been termed "an appeal from the pretrial investigation" and Feifer notes that the Soviet "trial" is simply a recapitulation of the data collected by the pretrial investigator. The notions of a trial being a "tabula rasa" and presumptions of innocence are wholly alien to Soviet notions of justice. ... "the closer the investigation resembles the finished script, the better ..." *Id.* at 86.

3   For a concise statement of the constitutional and economic aspects of the right to legal assistance, see M. G. Paulsen, Equal Justice for the Poor Man (1964); for a brief traditional description of the legal profession see P. A. Freund, *The Legal Profession*,

focused their attention on the deprivations and social disabilities of such variables as race, ethnicity, and social class as being the source of an accused person's defeat in a criminal court. Largely over-looked is the variable of the court organization itself, which possesses a thrust, purpose, and direction of its own. It is grounded in pragmatic values, bureaucratic priorities, and administrative instruments. These exalt maximum production and the particularistic career designs of organizational incumbents, whose occupational and career commitments tend to generate a set of priorities. These priorities exert a higher claim than the stated ideological goals of "due process of law," and are often inconsistent with them.

Organizational goals and discipline impose a set of demands and conditions of practice on the respective professions in the criminal court, to which they respond by abandoning their ideological and professional commitments to the accused client, in the service of these higher claims of the court organization. All court personnel, including the accused's own lawyer, tend to be coopted to become agent-mediators[4] who help the accused redefine his situation and restructure his perceptions con-comitant with a plea of guilty.

Of all the occupational roles in the court the only private individual who is officially recognized as having a special status and concomitant obligations is the lawyer. His legal status is that of "an officer of the court" and he is held to a standard of ethical performance and duty to his client as well as to the court. This obligation is thought to be far higher than that expected of ordinary individuals occu-pying the various occupational statuses in the court community. However, lawyers, whether privately retained or of the legal-aid, public defender variety, have close and continuing relations with the pros-ecuting office and the court itself through discreet relations with the judges via their law secretaries or "confidential" assistants. Indeed, lines of communication, influence and contact with those offices, as well as with the Office of the Clerk of the court, Probation Division, and with the press, are essential to present and prospective requirements of criminal law practice. Similarly, the subtle involvement of the press and other mass media in the court's organizational network is not readily discernible to the casual observer. Accused persons come and go in the court system schema, but the structure and its occupational incumbents remain to carry on their respective career, occupational and organizational enterprises. The individual stridencies, tensions, and conflicts a given accused person's case may present to all the participants are overcome, because the formal and informal relations of all the groups in the court setting require it. The probability of continued future relations and interaction must be preserved at all costs.

This is particularly true of the "lawyer regulars" i.e., those defense lawyers, who by virtue of their continuous appearances in behalf of defendants, tend to represent the bulk of a criminal court's non-indigent case workload, and those lawyers who are not "regulars," who appear almost casually in behalf of an occasional client. Some of the "lawyer regulars" are highly visible as one moves about the major urban centers of the nation, their offices line the back streets of the courthouses, at times shar-ing space with bondsmen. Their political "visibility" in terms of local club house ties, reaching into the judge's chambers and prosecutor's office, are also deemed essential to successful practitioners. Previous research has indicated that the "lawyer regulars" make no effort to conceal their dependence upon police, bondsmen, jail personnel. Nor do they conceal the necessity for maintaining intimate relations with all levels of personnel in the court setting as a means of obtaining, maintaining, and

---

Daedalus 689–700(1963).

4   I use the concept in the general sense that Erving Goffman employed it in his Asylums: Essays on the Social Situation of Mental Patients and Other Inmates (1961).

building their practice. These informal relations are the *sine qua non* not only of retaining a practice, but also in the negotiation of pleas and sentences.[5]

The client, then, is a secondary figure in the court system as in certain other bureaucratic settings.[6] He becomes a means to other ends of the organization's incumbents. He may present doubts, contingencies, and pressures which challenge existing informal arrangements or disrupt them; but these tend to be resolved in favor of the continuance of the organization and its relations as before. There is a greater community of interest among all the principal organizational structures and their incumbents than exists elsewhere in other settings. The accused's lawyer has far greater professional, economic, intellectual and other ties to the various elements of the court system than he does to his own client. In short, the court is a closed community.

This is more than just the case of the usual "secrets" of bureaucracy which are fanatically defended from an outside view. Even all elements of the press are zealously determined to report on that which will not offend the board of judges, the prosecutor, probation, legal-aid, or other officials, in return for privileges and courtesies granted in the past and to be granted in the future. Rather than any view of the matter in terms of some variation of a "conspiracy" hypothesis, the simple explanation is one of an ongoing system handling delicate tensions, managing the trauma produced by law enforcement and administration, and requiring almost pathological distrust of "outsiders" bordering on group paranoia.

The hostile attitude toward "outsiders" is in large measure engendered by a defensiveness itself produced by the inherent deficiencies of assembly line justice, so characteristic of our major criminal courts. Intolerably large caseloads of defendants which must be disposed of in an organizational context of limited resources and personnel, potentially subject the participants in the court community to harsh scrutiny from appellate courts, and other public and private sources of condemnation. As a consequence, an almost irreconcilable conflict is posed in terms of intense pressures to process large numbers of cases on the one hand, and the stringent ideological and legal requirements of "due process of law," on the other hand. A rather tenuous resolution of the dilemma has emerged in the shape of a large variety of bureaucratically ordained and controlled "work crimes," short cuts, deviations, and outright rule violations adopted as court practice in order to meet production norms. Fearfully anticipating criticism on ethical as well as legal grounds, all the significant participants in the court's social structure are bound into an organized system of complicity. This consists of a work arrangement in which the patterned, covert, informal breaches, and evasions of "due process" are institutionalized, but are, nevertheless, denied to exist.

These institutionalized evasions will be found to occur to some degree, in all criminal courts. Their nature, scope and complexity are largely determined by the size of the court, and the character of the community in which it is located, *e.g.,* whether it is a large, urban institution, or a relatively small rural county court. In addition, idiosyncratic, local conditions may contribute to a unique flavor in the character and quality of the criminal law's administration in a particular community. However, in most instances a variety of stratagems are employed—some subtle, some crude, in effectively disposing

5   A. L. Wood, *Informal Relations in the Practice of Criminal Law*, 62 Am. J. Soc. 48–55 (1956); J. E. Carlin, Lawyers on Their Own 105–09 (1962); R. Goldfarb, Ransom—A Critique of the American Bail System 114–15 (1965). In connection with relatively recent data as to recruitment to the legal profession, and variables involved in the type of practice engaged in, will be found in J. Ladinsky, *Careers of Lawyers, Law Practice, and Legal Institutions*, 28 am. Soc. Rev. 47–54 (1963). See also S. Warkov & J. Zelan, Lawyers in the Making (1965).

6   There is a real question to be raised as to whether in certain organizational settings, a complete reversal of the bureaucratic-ideal has not occurred. That is, it would seem, in some instances the organization appears to exist to serve the needs of its various occupational incumbents, rather than its clients. A. Etzioni, Modern Organizations 94–104 (1964).

of what are often too large caseloads. A wide variety of coercive devices are employed against an accused-client, couched in a depersonalized, instrumental, bureaucratic version of due process of law, and which are in reality a perfunctory obeisance to the ideology of due process. These include some very explicit pressures which are exerted in some measure by all court personnel, including judges, to plead guilty and avoid trial. In many instances the sanction of a potentially harsh sentence is utilized as the visible alternative to pleading guilty, in the case of recalcitrants. Probation and psychiatric reports are "tailored" to organizational needs, or are at least responsive to the court organization's requirements for the refurbishment of a defendant's social biography, consonant with his new status. A resourceful judge can, through his subtle domination of the proceedings, impose his will on the final outcome of a trial. Stenographers and clerks, in their function as record keepers, are on occasion pressed into service in support of a judicial need to "rewrite" the record of a courtroom event. Bail practices are usually employed for purposes other than simply assuring a defendant's presence on the date of a hearing in connection with his case. Too often, the discretionary power as to bail is part of the arsenal of weapons available to collapse the resistance of an accused person. The foregoing is a most cursory examination of some of the more prominent "short cuts" available to any court organization. There are numerous other procedural strategies constituting due process deviations, which tend to become the work style artifacts of a court's personnel. Thus, only court "regulars" who are "bound in" are really accepted; others are treated routinely and in almost a coldly correct manner.

The defense attorneys, therefore, whether of the legal-aid, public defender variety, or privately retained, although operating in terms of pressures specific to their respective role and organizational obligations, ultimately are concerned with strategies which tend to lead to a plea. It is the rational, impersonal elements involving economies of time, labor, expense and a superior commitment of the defense counsel to these rationalistic values of maximum production[7] of court organization that prevail, in his relationship with a client. The lawyer "regulars" are frequently former staff members of the prosecutor's office and utilize the prestige, know-how and contacts of their former affiliation as part of their stock in trade. Close and continuing relations between the lawyer "regular" and his former colleagues in the prosecutor's office generally overshadow the relationship between die regular and his client. The continuing colleagueship of supposedly adversary counsel rests on real professional and organizational needs of a *quid pro quo,* which goes beyond the limits of an accommodation or *modus vivendi* one might ordinarily expect under the circumstances of an otherwise seemingly adversary relationship. Indeed, the adversary features which are manifest are for the most part muted and exist even in their attenuated form largely for external consumption. The principals, lawyer and assistant district attorney, rely upon one another's cooperation for their continued professional existence, and so the bargaining between them tends usually to be "reasonable" rather than fierce.

[…]

---

7 Three relatively recent items reported in the New York Times, tend to underscore this point as it has manifested itself in one of the major criminal courts. In one instance the Bronx County Bar Association condemned "mass assembly-line justice," which "was rushing defendants into pleas of guilty and into convictions, in violation of their legal rights." N.Y. Times, March 10, 1965, p. 51. Another item, appearing somewhat later that year reports a judge criticizing his own court system (the New York Criminal Court), that "pressure to set statistical records in disposing of cases had hurt the administration of justice." N.Y. Times, Nov. 4, 1965, p. 49. A third, and most unusual recent public discussion in the press was a statement by a leading New York appellate judge decrying "instant justice" which is employed to reduce court calendar congestion "… converting our courthouses into counting houses …, as in most big cities where the volume of business tends to overpower court facilities." N.Y. Times, Feb. 5, 1966, p. 58.

DEFENSE LAWYER AS DOUBLE AGENT

The lawyer has often been accused of stirring up unnecessary litigation, especially in the field of negligence. He is said to acquire a vested interest in a cause of action or claim which was initially his client's. The strong incentive of possible fee motivates the lawyer to promote litigation which would otherwise never have developed. However, the criminal lawyer develops a vested interest of an entirely different nature in his client's case: to limit its scope and duration rather than do battle. Only in this way can a case be "profitable." Thus, he enlists the aid of relatives not only to assure payment of his fee, but he will also rely on these persons to help him in his agent-mediator role of convincing the accused to plead guilty, and ultimately to help in "cooling out" the accused if necessary.

It is at this point that an accused-defendant may experience his first sense of "betrayal." While he had perhaps perceived the police and prosecutor to be adversaries, or possibly even the judge, the accused is wholly unprepared for his counsel's role performance as an agent-mediator. In the same vein, it is even less likely to occur to an accused that members of his own family or other kin may become agents, albeit at the behest and urging of other agents or mediators, acting on the principle that they are in reality helping an accused negotiate the best possible plea arrangement under the circumstances. Usually, it will be the lawyer who will activate next of kin in this role, his ostensible motive being to arrange for his fee. But soon latent and unstated motives will assert themselves, with entreaties by counsel to the accused's next of kin, to appeal to the accused to "help himself" by pleading. *Gemein-schaft* sentiments are to this extent exploited by a defense lawyer (or even at times by a district attorney) to achieve specific secular ends, that is, of concluding a particular matter with all possible dispatch.

The fee is often collected in stages, each installment usually payable prior to a necessary court appearance required during the course of an accused's career journey. At each stage, in his interviews and communications with the accused, or in addition, with members of his family, if they are helping with the fee payment, the lawyer employs an air of professional confidence and "inside-dopesterism" in order to assuage anxieties on all sides. He makes the necessary bland assurances, and in effect manipulates his client, who is usually willing to do and say the things, true or not, which will help his attorney extricate him. Since the dimensions of what he is essentially selling, organizational influence and expertise, are not technically and precisely measurable, the lawyer can make extravagant claims of influence and secret knowledge with impunity. Thus, lawyers frequently claim to have inside knowledge in connection with information in the hands of the D.A., police, probation officials or to have access to these functionaries. Factually, they often do, and need only to exaggerate the nature of their relationships with them to obtain the desired effective impression upon the client. But, as in the genuine confidence game, the victim who has participated is loathe to do anything which will upset the lesser plea which his lawyer has "conned" him into accepting.[8]

In effect, in his role as double agent, the criminal lawyer performs an extremely vital and delicate mission for the court organization and the accused. Both principals are anxious to terminate the

---

8   The question has never been raised as to whether "bargain justice," "copping a plea," or justice by negotiation is a constitutional process. Although it has become the most central aspect of the process of criminal law administration, it has received virtually no close scrutiny by the appellate courts. As a consequence, it is relatively free of legal control and supervision. But, apart from any questions of the legality of bargaining, in terms of the pressures and devices that are employed which tend to violate due process of law, there remain ethical and practical questions. The system of bargain-counter justice is like the proverbial iceberg, much of its danger is concealed in secret negotiations and its least alarming feature, the final plea, being the one presented to public view. See A. S. Trebach, The Rationing of Justice 74–94 (1964); Note, *Guilty Plea Bargaining: Compromises by Prosecutors to Secure Guilty Pleas*, 112 U. Pa. L. Rev. 865–95 (1964).

litigation with a minimum of expense and damage to each other. There is no other personage or role incumbent in the total court structure more strategically located, who by training and in terms of his own requirements, is more ideally suited to do so than the lawyer. In recognition of this, judges will cooperate with attorneys in many important ways. For example, they will adjourn the case of an accused in jail awaiting plea or sentence if the attorney requests such action. While explicitly this may be done for some innocuous and seemingly valid reason, the tacit purpose is that pressure is being applied by the attorney for the collection of his fee, which he knows will probably not be forthcoming if the case is concluded. Judges are aware of this tactic on the part of lawyers, who, by requesting an adjournment, keep an accused incarcerated awhile longer as a not too subtle method of dunning a client for payment. However, the judges will go along with this, on the ground that important ends are being served. Often, the only end served is to protect a lawyer's fee.

The judge will help an accused's lawyer in still another way. He will lend the official aura of his office and courtroom so that a lawyer can stage manage an impression of an "all out" performance for the accused in justification of his fee. The judge and other court personnel will serve as a backdrop for a scene charged with dramatic fire, in which the accused's lawyer makes a stirring appeal in his behalf. With a show of restrained passion, the lawyer will intone the virtues of the accused and recite the social deprivations which have reduced him to his present state. The speech varies somewhat, depending on whether the accused has been convicted after trial or has pleaded guilty. In the main, however, the incongruity, superficiality, and ritualistic character of the total performance is underscored by a visibly impassive, almost bored reaction on the part of the judge and other members of the court retinue.

Afterward, there is a hearty exchange of pleasantries between the lawyer and district attorney, wholly out of context in terms of the supposed adversary nature of the preceding events. The fiery passion in defense of his client is gone, and the lawyers for both sides resume their offstage relations, chatting amiably and perhaps including the judge in their restrained banter. No other aspect of their visible conduct so effectively serves to put even a casual observer on notice, that these individuals have claims upon each other. These seemingly innocuous actions are indicative of continuing organizational and informal relations, which, in their intricacy and depth, range far beyond any priorities or claims a particular defendant may have.[9]

Criminal law practice is a unique form of private law practice since it really only appears to be private practice.[10] Actually it is bureaucratic practice, because of the legal practitioner's enmeshment in the authority, discipline, and perspectives of the court organization. Private practice, supposedly, in a professional sense, involves the maintenance of an organized, disciplined body of knowledge and learning; the individual practitioners are imbued with a spirit of autonomy and service, the earning of a livelihood being incidental In the sense that the lawyer in the criminal court serves as a double

---

9   For a conventional summary statement of some of the inevitable conflicting loyalties encountered in the practice of law, see E. E. Cheatham, Cases and Materials on the Legal Profession 70–79 (2d ed. 1955).

10   Some lawyers at either end of the continuum of law practice appear to have grave doubts as to whether it is indeed a profession at all. J. E. Carlin, *op. cit. supra* note 11, at 192; E. O. Smigel *supra*, note 16, at 304–305. Increasingly, it is perceived as a business with widespread evasion of the Canons of Ethics, duplicity and chicanery being practiced in an effort to get and keep business. The poet, Carl Sandburg, epitomized this notion in the following vignette: "Have you a criminal lawyer in this burg?" "We think so but we haven't been able to prove it on him." C. Sandburg, The People, Yes 154 (1936).

   Thus, while there is a considerable amount of dishonesty present in law practice involving fee splitting, thefts from clients, influence peddling, firing, questionable use of favors and gifts to obtain business or influence others, this sort of activity is most often attributed to the "solo," private practice lawyer. See A. L. Wood, *Professional Ethics Among Criminal Lawyers*, Social Problems 70–83 (1959). However, to some degree, large scale "downtown" elite firms also engage in these dubious activities. The difference is that the latter firms enjoy a good deal of immunity from these harsh charges because of their institutional and organizational advantages, in terms of near monopoly over more desirable types of practice, as well as exerting great influence in the political, economic and professional realms of power.

agent, serving higher organizational rather than professional ends, he may be deemed to be engaged in bureaucratic rather than private practice. To some extent the lawyer-client "confidence game," in addition to its other functions, serves to conceal this fact.

Courts, like many other modem large-scale organizations possess a monstrous appetite for the cooptation of entire professional groups as well as individuals.[11] Almost all those who come within the ambit of organizational authority, find that their definitions, perceptions and values have been refurbished, largely in terms favorable to the particular organization and its goals. As a result, recent Supreme Court decisions may have a long range effect which is radically different from that intended or anticipated. The more libertarian rules will tend to produce the rather ironic end result of augmenting the *existing* organizational arrangements, enriching court organizations with more personnel and elaborate structure, which in turn will maximize organizational goals of "efficiency" and production. Thus, many defendants will find that courts will possess an even more sophisticated apparatus for processing them toward a guilty plea.

---

11 Some of the resources which have become on integral part of our courts, *e.g.*, psychiatry, social work and probation, were originally intended as part of an ameliorative, therapeutic effort to individualize offenders. However, there is some evidence that a quite different result obtains, than the one originally intended. The ameliorative instruments have been coopted by the court in order to more "efficiently" deal with a court's caseload, often to the legal disadvantage of an accused person. See F. A. Allen, The Borderland of Criminal Justice (1964); T. S. Szasz, Law, Liberty and Psychiatry (1963) and also Szasz's most recent, Psychiatric Justice (1965); L. Diana, *The Rights of Juvenile Delinquents: An Appraisal of Juvenile Court Procedures*, 47 J. Crim. L. C. & P.S. 561–69 (1957).

Criminal Courts as Organizational Systems

Christi Metcalfe

Introduction

About ninety-five percent of felony cases that come before the criminal courts are resolved by pleas of guilt or no contest (Johnson et al. 2014). Despite this recurrent phenomenon, most studies of courtroom behavior are designed to predict sentence severity, with sentencing being a phase in the process that occurs after the decision to plea. Because the decision to plea impacts the sentence received, pleading guilty is a commonality that must be explained in order to better understand criminal trial courts and sentencing. While factors of the defendant and case may explain part of this decision, the impact of the internal and external environments of the court, including its bureaucratic concerns, should also be taken into account. The court, just like any business, functions in an environment characterized by goals, uncertainties, and limited resources while trying to manage cases—all of which can impact the mode of disposition. A comprehensive or integrated theoretical model grounded in the work of Parsons (1961, 1969) and Thompson (1967) is proposed as a basis for providing compelling explanations of the empirical research on court practices that incorporates the decision to prosecute and sentencing, as well as the plea process. The theoretical model highlights the impact of the bureaucratic operations of the criminal court.

A COMPREHENSIVE MODEL OF COURTS AS ORGANIZATIONS

An organization can be seen as an "arrangement of personnel for facilitating the accomplishment of some agreed upon purpose through the allocation of functions and responsibilities" (Selznick 1948, p. 25). The model proposes that any criminal trial court, at the most basic level, functions as an organization with various actors, including court administrators, court clerks, secretaries, judges, prosecutors, and defense attorneys, who perform specific roles within the court organization as a means of working toward agreed-upon goals and priorities. These goals are typically set by the *bureaucracy* of the court, or the court administration, who oversees operations of the courthouse to keep it functioning (Thompson, 1967). The most important goals are those involving the major operating policies and the daily decisions about individuals working within the organization (Perrow 1961). In this context, the main focus of the court's bureaucracy is the caseload that comes to the court. Court administrators (including clerks and secretaries) stress the need for efficiency in case processing to properly manage the burden of large caseloads. Essentially, the courts' heavy caseloads create demands on judges, prosecutors, and defense attorneys to bring these cases to a quick resolution.

Theoretically, it can be argued that there are ideologically based goals and organizationally based goals within the court (Eisenstein and Jacob 1977). The ideologically based goals are oriented toward justice, due process, and fairness—the traditionally understood beacons of the court system. These ideological goals largely represent the *culture* or customs of the courthouse. To a certain degree, each of the actors is influenced by these integral values of the criminal justice process. Judges are often seen as the representatives of justice within the court system, ensuring that due process rights are respected and that defendants are treated fairly (Cole 1976; Pollitz Worden 1995). Prosecutors serve as advocates for the people and victims, and carry out the rules or laws established by the legislature with respect to court procedures and behavior (Jacob, 1970). Defense attorneys work to uphold defendants' due process rights and give them a voice throughout the process (Casper 1970; Cole 1970).

Despite these cultural values of due process, justice, and fairness, it is argued that the burden of the bureaucracy creates an environment in which the members of the courtroom workgroup, including judges, prosecutors, and defense attorneys, sacrifice these ideological and professional commitments for the organizational obligations (Blumberg 1967). These obligations are manifested in the court's organizational goals, where the focus becomes expeditious and efficient case processing above all else. To make the process more efficient, the court also tries to eliminate uncertainties within case processing that can delay the resolution of cases and create backlogs in the system.

The courtroom workgroup relies on various *technologies* or techniques, including adversarial proceedings (i.e., trials) and negotiations or bargaining, in an attempt to achieve these goals (Eisenstein and Jacob 1977). Specifically, the courtroom workgroup must balance these work techniques to adapt to the organizational goals while still maintaining the cultural values of due process, justice, and fairness, even though the both often contradict each other. In working towards the shared values and goals of the court organization, cooperation and collaboration actually become the norm in what would otherwise be an adversarial setting (Cole 1970; Eistenstein and Jacob 1977; Skolnick 1967). Since the main goal of the bureaucracy is a high rate of apprehension, there is a greater need to focus on speed and finality, or efficiency and uncertainty reduction, which is dependent on an informal and cooperative system of justice (Packer 1968). The result is the resolution of large caseloads through short cuts, deviations, rule violations, and coercive devices in the form of pressures to plead guilty and avoid trial (Blumberg 1967).

Figure 2.3.1. The Court Organization

Figure 2.3.1 provides a visual of criminal trial courts in the context just discussed. As the figure demonstrates, the court organization is an integration of a *bureaucracy* (i.e., administration), *culture* (i.e., norms and customs), and *technology* (i.e., process for resolving cases). The bureaucracy promotes *goal attainment*, specifically as it pertains to increasing the efficiency of case processing and reducing any uncertainties in the process. The culture of the court is best reflected in the values of justice, due process, and fairness, which the court strives to *maintain* and portray (hence the designation "*pattern maintenance*"). Finally, the court possesses a core technology system where cases are resolved by judges, prosecutors, and defense attorneys through various strategies and techniques. In processing cases, the courtroom workgroup must *adapt* to maintain the values of the court organization while also trying to achieve the goals set by the bureaucracy. Trials best represent the court's values, while plea bargains best achieve the bureaucratic goals. With so many cases resulting in a plea, the balance appears to be tipped toward the organizational demands.

INFLUENCES ON THE COURT ORGANIZATION

Within the courthouse, the organizational goals of efficiency and uncertainty reduction are undermined most by (1) trials, (2) insufficient case information, and (3) unfamiliar or inexperienced actors (Albonetti, 1986, 1987, 1991; Eisenstein and Jacob 1977; Galanter, 1974; Skolnick, 1967). In a trial, the court is to render decisions for specific disputes in order to bring settlement to a case (Frank 1950). Trials pose uncertainties because of the unknown nature of the decision, which stems from the uncertainty of the legal rules to be applied to the facts of the case and external factors, such as political expectations, pressures from victims, and juries (Albonetti 1986, 1987, 1991, 1999; Burstein 1979; Frank 1950). For instance, in many circumstances, attorneys cannot accurately predict how juries and judges will perceive particular defendants, meaning attorneys lose control over the criminalization process when cases go to trial (Albonetti, 1986). During a trial, the outcome represents a compromise between the legal policies or principles related to the case, as well as external pressures and subjective leanings of those involved, resulting in uncertain outcomes (Frank 1950). Plea bargaining, which avoids the necessity of a trial, adds rationality to the system and eliminates these uncertainties trials introduce. Defense attorneys can present specific outcomes to their clients, which they can expect if they plead guilty. In a trial, defense attorneys cannot adequately advise their clients of the outcome— because it is unknown and can be influenced by numerous factors during the trial—and prosecutors cannot guarantee that the decision will be in favor of the government and/or the victim. In relying on plea deals to reduce uncertainties in the outcome, case processing can continue to run efficiently.

Further uncertainties are introduced when there is limited information relevant to the case. Albonetti (1986) suggests that particular factors within case files can lead to more predictable outcomes, including the amount of evidence, presence of multiple witnesses, credibility of victims, use of a weapon, prior record, and arrest at the scene of the alleged crime. Cases lacking information in these areas can add uncertainties to the process such that the outcome becomes questionable. Plea deals are a useful tool in this circumstance for reducing uncertainties in cases that do not have sufficient information to guarantee the outcome. In doing so, plea deals once again facilitate the efficient processing of cases and avoid questionable, and even delayed, trial outcomes in cases where the evidence and circumstances can be challenged and debated extensively among both the actors and jurors.

Lack of familiarity among the members of the courtroom workgroup in a case also breeds uncertainties and, therefore, inefficiencies (Eisenstein and Jacob 1977). It is suggested that judges, prosecutors, and defense attorneys who are regulars or "repeat players" in the system are at an advantage, because they are likely to be more familiar with one another and acquainted with the courthouse norms (Bibas 2004; Eisenstein et al., 1988; Galanter, 1974). This familiarity and experience can improve negotiations and tactics that increase the speed at which cases are processed, and in some circumstances, avoid trial uncertainties (Metcalfe 2016). Ultimately, familiar workgroups operate under a consensual understanding that each person benefits from working together. The system can then continue to operate rationally and in accordance with its bureaucratic goals (Burstein 1979; Clynch and Neubauer 1981; Skolnick 1967).

Essentially, because these three factors increase uncertainties, an informal accommodation arises among actors within the courtroom workgroup in pursuit of the mutual interest to reduce some of these uncertainties and ensure cases are efficiently processed through the system (Burstein 1979; Pollitz Worden 1995). Plea bargaining, as a core technology, maintains the equilibrium of the court system and allows the court system to operate in a more predictable environment (Clynch and Neubauer 1981; Cole 1976). Ultimately, plea bargaining creates an incentive for the organization by decreasing caseloads, eliminating the cost of time and effort involved in trials, preventing an increase in taxes and more frequent jury duty that comes with an escalating numbers of trials, increasing flexibility and discretion, and sidestepping problems related to evidence and witnesses (Alschuler 1968; Galanter 1974; Hessick, III, and Saujani 2002; Padgett 1985; Pollitz Worden 1995). Judges, prosecutors, and defense attorneys also have incentives to plea bargain. For prosecutors, resolving cases through a plea ensures convictions, reduces workload, and maintains a "tough on crime" image with the public (Bibas 2004; Hessick, III, and Saujani 2002; Skolnick 1967). Plea bargaining reduces large caseloads for public defenders, as well, and offers a financial benefit for privately retained counsel. Judges can avoid being overturned on appeal, which maintains their reputation and reduces their extensive caseloads (Alschuler 1976; Hessick, III, and Saujani 2002). With these various incentive structures in place, the result is a system of bargaining that the Supreme Court has recognized as a necessary and indispensable part of the court system (Hessick, III and Saujani 2002).

While trial courts must be responsive to internal bureaucratic pressures, as discussed, they are also susceptible to the influences of their outside environment, also called their task environment

(Thompson, 1967). Court communities function within the context of local political arrangements and statewide legal structures (Ulmer, 1997). Therefore, there exists a means of exchange between a courthouse and its outside environment (Cole, 1970; Seron, 1990). As Ulmer (2012) states, "courtroom workgroup actors' interpretations and acts are embedded in (and maintain or change) local court communities, which are in turn embedded in local socio-cultural contexts" (p. 8). Organizations try to maintain control over the influence of the task environment by minimizing the power of the task environment over them. It is typical for the court organization to create boundaries and interact little with individuals or groups outside of the courtroom workgroup that can potentially disrupt the routine processing of cases (Burstein 1979; Thompson 1967). The external environment can impede the cooperative system of plea bargaining and create more trials, slowing down the court system and ultimately preventing the system from achieving its goal of efficiency.

This outside environment consists of clients, suppliers, regulatory groups, and competitors that exert influence on the court's operations (Flemming et al. 1992; Thompson, 1967). Clients are the people or groups that the court organization interacts with and is dependent upon for resources (Cole 1970). The clients within the court system include criminals, victims, and members of the society at large. Clients and victims are secondary figures within the court system, such that they are outsiders to the court organization. In this role, they generate doubts, contingencies, and pressures that challenge the informal arrangements within the court organization (Blumberg 1967). For example, victims may not want defendants to be offered a plea deal, because they see it as a leniency for a heinous crime committed against them.

Suppliers are those external groups that have some form of power over the courts and can disrupt case processing. Suppliers of court organizations include the police and the legislature. Within designated jurisdictions, police have certain political powers. Prosecutors are often dependent on the police for their input of cases and evidence into the court system and their knowledge about cases, all of which can influence the decision-making process (Cole 1970; Burstein 1979). The legislature has both political and monetary power over the courts, since they make and enact laws related to court procedure and sentencing, and they are responsible for creating and funding lower courts. They also dictate a certain political environment that can influence the courtroom workgroup (Burstein 1979). For example, a release of more punitive sentencing laws may change the approach of the courthouse and can alter the plea deals offered and sentencing procedures. As outsiders to the court system, though, it is not uncommon for these suppliers to sometimes be at odds with the members of the courtroom workgroup. This is especially true of police and prosecutors, for instance, who often disagree on how cases should proceed, placing an extra burden on the prosecutor's office.

Regulators, in the form of the appellate courts, oversee the operations of trial courts and can provide a check on their behavior. The appellate courts create precedent within the realm of case procedure and thereby influence case processing at the trial level. The media can also be seen as a regulator of court behavior through their reporting on particular cases. In certain circumstances, the media can draw unwanted attention to the courts and disrupt the routine processing of cases. In addition, criminal courts have to account for other elements, such as jail size, support for particular sentencing policies, and elections (Eisenstein et al., 1988; Mears, 1998). Fortunately, the court organization does not have to worry about competitors, like other organizations, since the court is a monopoly in its business. Ultimately, though, courthouses are expected to vary from one location to the next, since there are different external pressures within various contexts that change the way they operate. Figure 2.3.2 depicts the court organization within its task environment.

Figure 2.3.2. The Court Organization and It's Task Environment

Although the internal goals of the organization, as well these external pressures, influence the mode of disposition—whether it involves pleading guilty or going to trial—theory and evidence suggests that the influence of the internal bureaucratic goals outweighs that of the external environment. It appears that the American court system, as the embodiment of the rule of law, has shifted focus due to changing demands. More of the court's budget is now allocated for court administration, creating a change of focus from adjudication to administration (Seron 1990). This means the efficient process- ing of cases takes precedence over the maintenance of the cultural values of due process, justice, and fairness within the court organization (Dixon 1995). Evidence shows a trend toward increased used of pre-trial techniques that add greater efficiency and speed to the court system (Seron 1990; Johnson et al. 2014). In federal district courts and other courts, this is a result of the reliance on teamwork among the courtroom actors, as opposed to the dependence on judges as sole decision makers in the court system (Haynes et al. 2010; Seron 1990; Ulmer 1995). The result has been an increase in various forms of dispute resolution, rather than adjudication.

KEY PROPOSITIONS

As stated, the model detailed above attempts to explain case processing within criminal trial courts, as well as the predominant use of guilty pleas to resolve cases. Taken together, the model makes the following propositions in relation to case processing:

1. Courts are organizations that operate under conditions of uncertainty and work towards a sense of stability in case processing. The main goal of the court organization is to efficiently process cases, which is facilitated by the reduction of uncertainties in case processing.

2. Courts are susceptible to influences from both the internal bureaucracy and external environment. Any study of court behavior must take into consideration the pressures exhibited from sources both inside and outside the court organization.

3. Courts are comprised of individuals who work together for the achievement of an agreed-upon objective. Therefore, judges, prosecutors, and defense attorneys, or the courtroom workgroup, cooperate in order to efficiently process cases, fulfilling the goal of the court organization.

4. The demands of the bureaucracy generally lend themselves to informal modes of disposition, such as plea bargaining, while the court's culture and external environment can impose, in certain circumstances, a more adversarial system of trials. For this reason, the court tries to maintain a boundary with its external environment in an attempt to protect informal case processing norms.

5. The goals of the organization trump the ideological goals of the actors within the courtroom workgroup. Although the actors may have their own individual goals, they ultimately work towards the common organizational goal.

6. Plea bargaining is a technique used by the court to foster the reduction of uncertainties and efficient processing of cases, so it is not surprising that the vast majority of cases are resolved through a plea of guilt.

REFERENCES

Albonetti, Celesta A. 1986. Criminality, Prosecutorial Screening, and Uncertainty: Toward a Theory of Discretionary Decision Making in Felony Case Processings. *Criminology* 24: 623–644.

Albonetti, Celesta A. 1987. Prosecutorial Discretion: The Effects of Uncertainty. *Law & Society Review* 21: 291–314.

Albonetti, Celesta A. 1991. An Integration of Theories to Explain Judicial Discretion. *Social Problems* 38: 247–266.

Albonetti, Celesta A. 1999. The Avoidance of Punishment: A Legal-Bureaucratic Model of Suspended Sentences in Federal White-Collar Cases Prior to Federal Sentencing Guidelines. *Social Forces* 78: 303–329.

Alschuler, Albert W. 1968. The Prosecutor's Role in Plea Bargaining. *The University of Chicago Law Review* 36: 50–112.

Alschuler, Albert W. 1976. The Trial Judge's Role in Plea Bargaining, Part I. *Columbia Law Review,* 76: 1059–1154.

Bibas, Stephanos. 2004. Plea bargaining outside the shadow of trial. *Harvard Law Review,* 117: 2463–2547.

Blumberg, Abraham. 1967. The Practice of Law as Confidence Game: Organizational Cooption of a Profession. *Law and Society Review* 1: 15–40.

Burstein, Carolyn. 1979. Criminal Case Processing from an Organizational Perspective: Current Research Trends. *The Justice System Journal* 5: 258–273.

Casper, Jonathan D. 1970. Did you have a lawyer when you went to court? No, I had a public defender. In G. Cole (Ed.), *Criminal Justice: Law and Politics, Second Edition.* North Scituate: Duxbury Press.

Clynch, Edward and David W. Neubauer. 1981. Trial Courts as Organizations: A Critique and Synthesis. *Law and Policy Quarterly* 3: 69–94.

Cole, George. 1970. The Decision to Prosecute. *Law and Society Review* 4: 331–343.

Cole, George. 1976. *Criminal Justice: Law and Politics, Second Edition.* North Scituate: Duxbury Press.

Dixon, Jo. 1995. The Organizational Context of Criminal Sentencing. *The American Journal of Sociology* 100: 1157–1198.

Eisenstein, James, Roy B. Flemming, and Peter F. Nardulli. 1988. *The Contours of Justice: Communities and their Courts.* Boston: Little, Brown and Company.

Eisenstein, James and Hebert Jacob. 1977. *Felony Justice: An Organizational Analysis of Criminal Courts.* Boston: Little, Brown and Company, Inc.

Flemming, Roy B., Peter F. Nardulli, and James Eisenstein. 1992. *The Craft of Justice: Politics and Work in Criminal Court Communities.* Philadelphia: University of Pennsylvania Press.

Frank, Jerome. 1950. *Courts on trial; myth and reality in American justice.* Princeton: Princeton University Press.

Galanter, Marc. 1974. Why the "Haves" Come Out Ahead: Speculations on the Limits of Legal Change. *Law & Society Review* 9: 95–160.

Haynes, Stacy Hoskins, Barry Ruback, and Gretchen Ruth Cusick. 2010. Courtroom Workgroups and Sentencing: The Effects of Similarity, Proximity, and Stability. *Crime & Delinquency* 56: 126–161.

Hessick III, F. Andrew and Reshma M. Saujani. 2002. Plea Bargaining and Convicting the Innocent: the Role of the Prosecutor, the Defense Counsel, and the Judge. BYU *Journal of Public Law* 16: 189–242.

Jacob, H. 1970. Politics and Criminal Prosecution in New Orleans. In G. Cole (Ed.), *Criminal Justice: Law and Politics, Second Edition*. North Scituate: Duxbury Press.

Johnson, Brian D., Cassia Spohn, Ryan D. King, and Besiki Kutateladze. 2014. Understanding Guilty Pleas: The National Science Foundation's Research Coordination Network. *The Criminologist*, 39: 1–6.

Mears, Daniel P. 1998. The Sociology of Sentencing: Reconceptualizing Decisionmaking Processes and Outcomes. *Law & Society Review* 32: 667–724.

Packer, Herbert L. 1968. *The Limits of the Criminal Sanction*. Stanford: Stanford University Press.

Padgett, John. 1985. The Emergent Organization of Plea Bargaining. *The American Journal of Sociology* 90: 753–800.

Parsons, Talcott. 1961. *Theories of society; foundations of modern sociological theory*. New York: Free Press.

Parsons, Talcott. 1969. *Politics and social structure*. New York: Free Press.

Perrow, Charles. 1961. The Analysis of Goals in Complex Organizations. *American Sociological Review* 26: 854–866.

Pollitz Worden, Alissa. 1995. The Judge's Role in Plea Bargaining: An Analysis of Judges' Agreement with Prosecutors' Sentencing Recommendations. *Justice Quarterly* 12: 257–278.

Seron, Carroll. 1990. The Impact of Court Organization on Litigation. *Law & Society Review* 24: 451–465.

Selznick, Philip. 1948. Foundations of the Theory of Organization. *American Sociological Review* 13: 25–35.

Skolnick, Jerome. 1967. Social Control in the Adversary System. *The Journal of Conflict Resolution* 11: 52–70.

Thompson, James D. 1967. *Organizations in Action*. New York: McGraw-Hill.

Ulmer, Jeffrey T. 1997. Social Worlds of Sentencing: Court Communities Under Sentencing Guidelines. Albany: State University of New York Press.

Ulmer, Jeffery T. 1995. The Organization and Consequences of Social Pasts in Criminal Courts. *The Sociological Quarterly*, 36: 587–605.

Ulmer, Jeffrey T. 2012. Recent developments and new directions in sentencing research. *Justice Quarterly*, 29: 1–40.

It's Not the Old Ball Game

Three Strikes and the Courtroom Workgroup

John C. Harris and Paul Jesilow

On March 7, 1994 the governor of California signed into law urgency legislation known publicly as "Three Strikes" (AB971).[1] The same law was passed as a voter initiative (Proposition 184) during June of that year. The legislation provides that persons with one "serious" prior offense who are convicted of a felony are to receive twice the prison term that otherwise would apply to their offenses.[2] For such offenders, a third felony conviction is to receive either three times the punishment that would apply to first offenders or a term of 25 years to life in prison, whichever is greater.[3] These punishments are applicable even if the current felony conviction is not for a serious offense.[4] California's Legislative Analyst's Office reported soon after enactment that 70 percent of "second strikers" and "third strikers" were charged with nonviolent offenses (California Legislative Analyst's Office 1995). More recent (unpublished) data indicate that in most counties, 75% of third strike filings are for nonserious crimes.

In this article we explore the impact of Three Strikes on the courtroom workgroup and the workgroup's response. As predicted by some observers, the workgroup already has begun to mediate and even to nullify some provisions of Three Strikes (Feeley and Kamin

---

[1]   As urgency legislation, the law went into effect immediately.

[2]   Serious felonies are set forth in California Penal Code Section 1192.7(c); these include burglary, lewd acts on a child under 14, and grand theft involving a firearm. Violent felonies are described in California Penal Code Section 667.5(c) and include many of the same offenses as in Section 1192.7(c). Penal Code Section 667.5(c) includes robbery, murder, voluntary manslaughter, mayhem, forcible sodomy, rape, and most violations that involve the use of a firearm or other deadly weapon or result in the infliction of great bodily injury. Offenses of this type are included when committed by a juvenile over age 16, even if they are handled entirely in juvenile court (*People v. Davis* 1997). The statute and the proposition mandate that the district attorney must charge all known qualifying felony prior allegations, although the prosecutor subsequently may dismiss such allegations for lack of proof or in the interests of justice.

[3]   In addition to increased terms, Three Strikes requires that a person subject to enhanced punishment serve not less than 80 percent of the term of imprisonment before any release can be considered. Absent such a provision, most prisoners can receive up to a 50 percent reduction in their prison terms for "good time" and "work" credits.

[4]   Many illegal acts that are misdemeanors are classified as felonies when committed by individuals with prior convictions.

1996). The law is not self-enforcing, and no effective mechanism exists to ensure that prosecutors charge all known prior "strikes" (Feeley and Kamin 1996). The research on which this paper is based suggests that Three Strikes has fundamentally changed the relationships and power among members of the courtroom workgroup, significantly disrupting the efficiency of their work and making the prediction of case outcomes difficult, if not impossible.

The Law

Three Strikes was part of a public and political movement designed to send a message to those who would prey on the innocent. The initiative was presented to the public as a way to prevent politicians from interfering with that directive and to keep dangerous offenders away from society by drastically increasing sentences for repeat offenders ("Argument for Proposition 184" 1994).

Three Strikes limits prosecutors' and judges' discretion in disposing of offenders' cases. Prosecutors are mandated to allege all qualifying prior offenses; and they may dismiss them only if proof of a prior is insufficient or if the dismissal is "in the interest of justice," with reasons stated on the court record. In 1996 the California Supreme Court held that judges had the statutory power to dismiss allegations of prior offenses in "the interest of justice," but cautioned that judges should take care to implement the intent of Three Strikes (*People v. Superior Court* [*Romero*] 1996).[5]

Three Strikes was more than minor modification in the handling of criminal cases. This law has been characterized as the most consistently used sentencing enhancement scheme for repeat offenders that has been enacted by any state (Butterfield 1996; Canon 1996). Three Strikes—its effectiveness at controlling crime and the fairness of its application, particularly in cases where the current charge is not a serious or violent offense—has created substantial and continuing debate ("A Wrong Turn" 1998). Attempts were made in 1997 and 1998 to amend the law to apply only when the current felony was serious, but they were unsuccessful (Vanzi 1998).

Previous Reforms and the Workgroup

Some observers have suggested that Three Strikes ultimately will meet the same fate as other attempts to limit the discretion of the courtroom workgroup: adaptation, flexibility, and mitigation, which will allow the courts, in the end, to operate unchanged (Feeley and Kamin 1996). Historical evidence supports the proposition that members of the courtroom workgroup will act to mediate or nullify legislative enactments that affect the operation of the courts. For example, the "Victims' Bill of Rights," approved by California voters in 1982, was (among other things) supposed to end plea bargaining in felony cases. Despite this mandate, an early study showed that plea rates did not decline (McCoy 1990). Plea bargaining was prohibited only after the information was filed in Superior Court. To comply with the letter of the law, the courtroom workgroup members merely bargained earlier in the process: before or during the preliminary hearing, or when the information was filed.

---

5   This ruling raised concern that judges would gut Three Strikes, but such worries apparently have been misplaced. A review of prison commitments for second- and third-strike defendants both before and after the *Romero* decision shows no major change in the numbers of commitments (California Legislative Analyst's Office 1997).

California is not unique in its experience with courtroom workgroups' nullification of legislation. The New York "Rockefeller Laws," which provided for severe penalties for drug offenses, including life imprisonment, were routinely ignored by some prosecutors or were mediated by plea bargaining (Feeley and Kamin 1996). Because of their activities in these matters, the courtroom actors are blamed for undermining the legal intent of legislators and the electorate.

The Courtroom Workgroup

The courtroom workgroup consists of a judge, a prosecutor, and a defense attorney (Eisenstein and Jacob 1977). In this organizational construct, the workgroup is viewed as an interdependent collection of actors, each with an interest in having the group function effectively (Blumberg 1967; Eisenstein and Jacob 1977). Individual members must participate in the workgroup to deal with the large number of cases they are called on to resolve, many more cases than could be managed without the existence of the workgroup (Blumberg 1967).

The primary activity that brings the courtroom workgroup together, and by which the workgroup's members achieve their individual goals, is the process of plea bargaining. The work of the courts could never be accomplished if all cases went to trial. In addition to the need to manage caseloads, each member of the court has other interests that encourage participation in the workgroup and promote plea bargaining (Blumberg 1967; Eisenstein and Jacob 1977; Heumann 1975; Meyer and Jesilow 1997; Nardulli 1978).

Although great discretionary authority is vested in each member of the courtroom workgroup, the traditional view is that power is distributed among the participants, such that no one member can dominate court operations (Nardulli 1978). For example, the prosecutor's unilateral discretion to charge is balanced by the defense's power to demand trial and by the judge's authority to sentence. This balance of might creates an interdependence among the courtroom workgroup members and supports their continuing relationship to accomplish their common goal: expeditious case processing (Nardulli 1978). Three Strikes has upset this balance of power and has undermined the workgroup's ability to efficiently process defendants through the courts.

METHODOLOGY

In this paper we report the results of interviews and surveys with members of courtroom workgroups in six California counties. Semistructured interviews were conducted with the most senior officials available in each of the six counties, usually including the elected district attorney, the chief public defender, the presiding judge of the superior court, and other high-ranking court administrators. A total of 96 individuals were interviewed: at least four superior court judges, four prosecutors, four public defenders, and support personnel in each county.

[…]

The judges averaged 11.9 years on the bench. The great majority (83.6%) had dealt with felony matters for at least two years before Three Strikes came into effect; almost all (96.4%) had handled felony trials since enactment of the law. More than 70 percent (71.4%) of the responding judges had participated in felony plea negotiations since the enactment of Three Strikes. Because municipal court judges most often conduct preliminary hearings, fewer than 11 percent of the responding judges (all of whom are superior court officials) had participated in these hearings.

The public defenders who responded to the survey were an experienced group: They averaged 14.26 years on the job, and none had been public defenders less than five years. Almost all (94.2%) had handled felonies for at least two years before Three Strikes. Since enactment of the law, 82.7 percent had represented felons at preliminary examinations, 87.8 percent had participated in felony plea negotiations, and 97 percent had participated in felony trials.

Prosecutors averaged 13.4 years in their positions. Almost all (94.4%) had handled felonies for at least two years before the enactment of Three Strikes; 70.6 percent had conducted preliminary examinations since Three Strikes came into effect; 82.5 percent had participated in felony plea negotiations; and 83.9 percent had conducted felony trials since the law was enacted.

RESULTS

The results we reported here are based on the interviews and the surveys. The surveys provide numerical support for issues originally raised in the interviews. Both methods indicate that Three Strikes has significantly disrupted the efficiency of the courtroom workgroup and has made the prediction of case outcomes difficult. The equilibrium among members of the workgroup has been greatly affected. Prosecutors' power to strike prior allegations, and thereby to reduce mandatory 25-years-to-life sentences (e.g., to as low as 32 months in the case of simple drug possession), has made the exercise of that power the central concern of other workgroup members.

A stated purpose of Three Strikes is to limit the discretion of courtroom workgroup members. The law mandates county district attorneys to seek stiff terms for certain repeat offenders by charging all known prior strikes. In most counties, the survey responses from the courtroom workgroup members indicated that they believe prosecutors are complying by alleging all known qualifying prior offenses. Table 2.4.1 presents the workgroup members' estimates of the percentage of cases in which the prosecutor, "in the interest of justice," did not allege known "strike" priors.[6] In only one county, in which the district attorney has taken the position of *not* charging all eligible third strike cases, did the workgroup believe that not all known priors are charged.

Table 2.4.1. Estimated Percentages of Cases Which the District Attorney Did Not File Known Priors: Workgroup Responses Aggregated by County

County	Mean	SD	Median
Alameda	39.29%	20.65	50.00%
Fresno	.80%	2.26	0%
Los Angeles	5.57%	8.99	2.00%
Orange	3.54%	1.45	0%
Santa Clara	9.11%	14.27	1.00%
San Diego	2.84%	8.32	0%

6   We wrote two items to ascertain the courtroom workgroup's perception of the district attorney's policies with regard to alleging prior offenses. "Since the 3 strikes law came into effect ... prosecutors always charge all known prior adult felony strikes" and "Based on your knowledge and experience, among all cases in which the current charge has been (or *could have been*) a third strike, PROSECUTORS have *omitted charging* a prior in the interest of justice in about _____% of these cases."

For most of the elected county district attorneys, alleging all prior strikes is probably a matter of philosophy and politics. They became prosecutors, at least in part, because they believed that certain types of criminals should be behind bars. As elected officials, they are also quite aware that they must go before the voters again if they are to remain in office. The fact that Three Strikes was passed by a sizable majority of the California electorate is an important mandate to them. During the interviews, one county district attorney explained,

> It's my philosophy that when you have a law, you enforce it. If you don't like the law, you go change it in the legislature. But you don't use any of the "Mickey Mouse" or "straw man" type of facades to get around the law. So our view is that if you have two strikes that are legitimate, serious, or violent prior felonies, and you get another felony, we are hammering you, because that is what 84 percent of the public wants in this state.

During the interviews, some members of the courtroom workgroups suggested that counting prior juvenile convictions as strikes might lead to increased litigation in juvenile courts because youths might fear more severe sentences for future misdeeds. In addition, they questioned the fairness of the action. As juveniles, the individuals might have been less likely to admit guilt if they had known that at some time in the future, their admissions would be used to enhance the penalties imposed on them. One deputy district attorney, however, asserted that he did not "have any philosophical problems with it. … Every time I see [juvenile strikes], I allege them." The workgroup members' responses on their surveys confirmed that, for the most part, the prosecutors were using juvenile convictions to allege strikes. Table 2.4.1 includes the workgroup members' estimates of the percentage of cases in which prosecutors allege all juvenile strikes.

PLEA BARGAINING

A major intent of Three Strikes is to thwart the workgroup's most common mechanism for handling its workload, namely the plea bargain. Under Three Strikes, prosecutors are allowed to expunge allegations if they are unprovable, or to do so in the "interest of justice." The legislation, however, specifically prohibits prosecutors from deleting priors merely to induce a plea. The answers we received suggest that the legislation has affected the plea-bargaining process, although not uniformly across counties.

The plea-bargaining system is the outgrowth of years of experience and negotiation. Workgroup members handle cases efficiently because they know how other members will respond to specific circumstances. The mandate of Three Strikes effectively undermined that system by making it difficult for participants to predict the outcome of cases. Workgroup members are concerned about their ability to predict when district attorneys might show some mercy and strike priors "in the interest of justice." During the interviews, a judge noted that in his county, "[i]nitially, the DA had announced criteria to strike priors, but to the best of my knowledge and observation, those criteria were often lost and not consistently or meaningfully followed." He added that the situation was deteriorating as the DA's office began to feel "the pressure of those cases." He concluded that the problem was one of workload ("they have difficulty handling a number of cases"); as evidence of his position he pointed to requests for continuances. The judge inferred that prosecutors might forgive strikes in order to induce pleas and manage their increasing workloads.

Table 2.4.2 presents the courtroom workgroup members' perceptions of the ease of predicting when prosecutors might strike priors. Even in those counties where the decision had been assigned to a single individual or group in the prosecutor's office, substantial numbers of all respondents (including prosecutors) believed they were unable to predict which cases were likely candidates for leniency.

Table 2.4.2. Percentages of Respondents Who Agree with the Statement That It Is Easy to Predict When Prosecutors Will Dismiss Strike Allegations: All Workgroup Members Aggregated by County

County	% Agree	% Disagree
Alameda	50.00	50.00
Fresno	28.57	71.43
Los Angeles	23.64	76.36
Orange	25.00	75.00
Santa Clara	36.36	63.64
San Diego	24.49	75.51

According to the survey responses, predicting the striking of priors is even more difficult when the current case is not a "serious" felony and when the individual has no convictions for violent acts. In practice, such cases commonly involve drug possession or theft, and the defendant previously had committed two serious (but not violent) felonies. Treatment of these defendants can differ substantially across counties. In jurisdictions where the district attorney's policy is to charge all priors, the court actors believe that priors are rarely ignored. Workgroup members in the other counties, however, stated that priors were more likely to be struck (see Table 2.4.3). The inconsistency across counties in the application of the law and the wide variation of opinions among the workgroups indicate that the prediction of case outcomes is difficult for defendants and courtroom actors. Members of the workgroup believed they could predict when priors would be stricken only in the county where the district attorney limits third-strike allegations to cases in which the current charge is a serious or violent offense. In this county, Three Strikes is often ignored, and the workgroup continues to operate as it did in the past.

Table 2.4.3. Estimated Priors Stricken by Prosecutors in the Least Serious Third Strike Cases: Workgroup Members Responses Aggregated by County

County	Mean	SD	Median
Alameda	28.93%	33.82	15%
Fresno	.60%	2.26	0%
Los Angeles	30.27%	24.05	25%
Orange	2.54%	3.78	0%
Santa Clara	34.63%	27.62	40%
San Diego	17.76%	23.26	5%

Overall, judges (40 of 53) and public defenders (131 of 144) felt that prosecutors dismissed prior strike allegations in too few cases. In contrast, a majority of prosecutors in every responding county disagreed with the idea that they struck priors in too few cases.

During the interviews, comments from numerous respondents indicated that prosecutors were placing increased importance on obtaining strike convictions and that they were unlikely to plea-bargain on these matters. A deputy DA reported:

> I'll make it clear. I'm going to walk away from this case with that strike. I'm going to do it one way or another. If I give you a little bit over here, that's fine. But I'm going to get a strike on you right now. I'll tell you that.

In response to the surveys, public defenders (96 of 133) reported that prosecutors were less likely to plea-bargain when strike felonies were alleged than before the passage of Three Strikes. Convictions in such cases make defendants eligible for much more severe punishments if convicted of a later felony. In instances where defendants had no prior strikes, judges in half of the counties agreed with the public defenders' view, but we found no consensus among the judges in the remaining counties. Similarly, prosecutors in none of the counties could agree on whether their own group's plea-bargaining practices had changed in "first strike" cases. Most workgroup members (239 of 290), however, agreed that prosecutors had changed their plea-bargaining position since passage of the law with respect to repeat offenders. Now they were less likely to plea-bargain in instances where the defendant already had a prior strike conviction.[7]

Judges in California have some authority to reduce penalties. The most significant change in the Three Strikes law, the *Romero* decision, made clear that judges had the power to dismiss allegations of prior felonies in second- and third-strike cases "in the interest of justice" (*People v. Superior Court* 1996). The interviews revealed conflict between the district attorneys and judges over this matter. One elected DA, for example, commented that he did not "think the courts should have discretion with regard to Three Strikes." Yet now that the *Romero* decision had made clear that judges could dismiss prior strikes, he expected judges to shoulder some responsibility. He explained:

> I've had judges talk to me personally about what a *de minimis* case was before them as a third strike, and why didn't I do something about it. And I said, "The last time I checked, you could do something about it. You want me to do it instead of you. You do it … I'll put on the record that I oppose it." So what? They're elected officials too. Although the public doesn't know much about it, they ought to. They are accountable to the public if they display an attitude the public disagrees with.

A judge from another county confirmed the words of the elected DA: "I can say," he told us, "that the general attitude of the DA's deputies, consistently, [is] 'ok, judges, you wanted *Romero*, you got it. You exercise it.'"

Judges' decisions to delete priors in strike cases are apparently an attempt to counter the prosecutors' power and restore equilibrium to sentencing. Workgroup members perceived judges as more likely than prosecutors to ignore a prior strike only in the survey responses from counties where prosecutors are likely to charge and pursue all strike priors.[8] In counties where prosecutors are less zealous

---

7 Regardless of the nature of the current felony, the defendant may receive double the punishment. In cases where the current offense is a serious or violent felony, however, convictions make future felonies eligible for treatment as a third strike.

8 The item stated: "Since the *Romero* decision in June, 1996 … judges have been more likely than prosecutors to strike priors in the interest of justice." Among workgroup members in Fresno (20 of 23), Orange (40 of 42), and San Diego (40 of 45) Counties, we found agreement that judges

about filing strikes, judges are less perceived as prone to delete priors. For example, in a county where the district attorney favors filing and pursuing almost all third-strike cases, the workgroup members reported the highest percentage of cases in which judges dismissed strike allegations (mean 28.6%, median 25%). Workgroups' estimates of judges deleting prior strikes were lowest in the county where the district attorney files third-strike cases only in rare instances (mean 4.18%, median 3%).

Before the passage of Three Strikes, plea agreements were accomplished easily among workgroup members: Each knew the "going rate" for offenses. The prosecutor, public defender, and judge needed to discuss particulars only in unusual circumstances. Each could expect that the others would act as they had acted previously. Our interviews and surveys revealed that Three Strikes has given rise to one aspect of sentencing that mimics the old process: The judges are using *Romero* to coax guilty pleas from defendants and to avoid trials; in doing so, they have established a "going rate."

According to the *Romero* ruling, a judge's decision to strike a prior is supposed to be a sentencing determination, made after a guilty plea is entered. Numerous interviewees, however, reported that judges were indicating their intentions to defendants before the defendants entered pleas. A deputy DA, for example, reported that "almost everybody—strike or no strike—when they're pleading, they're pleading with some kind of indication from the court ... I can't stress that strongly enough." Most common, he reported, were court indications of sentencing second-strike defendants to double the mitigated term. "And frankly," he added, "many times that's our offer."

A judge from a different county expressed a similar sentiment. He reported,

> The new charge for a vast majority of cases is a drug charge, and they settle for a stipulated middle term. Thirty-two months to four years is the most likely sentence. I've been watching them come down since *Romero*, and I am amazed at how many are coming down 32 months. That seems pretty much the standard deal.

Workgroup members' responses to the survey also confirmed that judges sometimes suggest to defendants their intent to forgive a prior: More than 80 percent of all respondents reported that judges indicated their intention to strike a prior before the plea. Moreover, almost all respondents in all counties believed that judges were offering the lowest possible term allowed by law in second-strike cases: Almost 80 percent agreed or strongly agreed that judges often indicate their willingness to impose the minimum sentence on such offenders.

TRIALS

The greatest effect of Three Strikes for workgroup members has been an increase in trials. Previously, defendants were usually willing to trade a plea of guilty for a lesser punishment, the mechanism used by the courtroom workgroup to handle their overwhelming caseload. Three Strikes prohibits such deals, however. Defendants, who face extended prison terms, are unlikely to agree to plead guilty.

---

were striking priors more frequently than prosecutors. Among respondents in Alameda (19 of 24), Los Angeles (68 of 99), and Santa Clara (33 of 57) Counties, we gained the impression that judges were not more likely than prosecutors to strike priors. Santa Clara County public defenders were the only exception: The 18 respondents were divided evenly on this item.

"They've nothing to lose" seemed to be the general sentiment expressed by the workgroup members during the interviews.

There is evidence that the number of trials has increased in situations in which offenders are charged with a third strike, but in which their current crime is not serious. Overall the felony trial rate is higher than before Three Strikes but trials of nonstrike cases have decreased dramatically (unpublished data), perhaps as courtroom actors continue to look for ways to decrease their workload.

WORKGROUP MEMBERS

One effect of Three Strikes has been a substantial increase in the workload and in stress for all system participants. Interviewees and survey respondents in every county complained of these increases. Table 2.4.4 presents all workgroup members' estimates of the change for each workgroup position. Public defenders in particular are at or near a crisis: All the workgroup members believe that defenders have experienced the greatest increases in workload and in stress. Two-thirds of all respondents believed that defenders' workloads had increased substantially; three-fourths felt that defenders' stress had increased similarly. As an illustration, one defender wrote on his questionnaire, "I have tried 4 third-strike cases and the stress is insane and will drive me out of the business. Of those 4 [cases] I have 2 acquittals and 1 hung jury. I know that I cannot keep it up and it is killing me."

Table 2.4.4. Change in Workload and Stress Reported by All Workgroup Members for Each Workgroup Position: Percentages

	Decreased	Remained Same	Increased Slightly	Increased Moderately	Increased Substantially
Workload Changes					
Judges	.4	13.9	28.7	34	27
Prosecutors	.8	5.8	15	40	38.5
Defenders	.7	2.6	6.3	24.7	65.7
	Decreased	Remained Same	Increased Slightly	Increased Moderately	Increased Substantially
Stress Changes					
Judges	.8	28.6	27.8	25.8	17.1
Prosecutors	.8	21.7	25.3	28.5	23.7
Defenders	.0	4.9	5.3	12	77.8

The crisis among public defenders is partly attributable to increased workloads, but that is not the primary problem. Defenders, more than other workgroup members, must deal with prosecutors' and judges' inconsistent and unpredictable practices in striking prior allegations; many of their responses reflected this frustration. Certainly much of this stress is due to defenders' uncertainty as to what facts may cause a prosecutor or judge to ignore a prior allegation in any particular case. The uncertainty adds to their workload as they exhaust every possible approach in a strike case. A deputy DA, commenting on the defense attorneys, commented that public defenders "really can't enter into any meaningful negotiations until they know it's a valid strike. And particularly a 1980 juvenile strike from Los Angeles, that's going to be hard to track down." Such tasks increase the attorneys' workload.

Jury nullification is an example of public defenders' actions in cases: Jurors will not convict if they believe the punishment does not fit the crime. Recognizing this, public defenders attempt to inform the jury that the current offense is a third strike. They do so particularly if the current charge is not a serious felony; a drug charge is the most common situation. The public defenders hope that jurors will balk at sending defendants to prison for more than 25 years for minor misdeeds. One elected DA reported,

> My impression is that we probably are not convicting as many strike cases as we are others. The horror stories that I hear have to do with jurors. ... I'll give you an example. We tried a guy not long ago. Tried him twice actually. He was a graduate student at [one of the state universities]. He's got straight As. He has nine prior individual armed robberies. Good-looking black kid. ... He's strung out on crack. So we tried him. The cops were going to stop him, and one cop said he saw him throw some rock cocaine out. He went back to the place where he saw him throw it, and he found it. Another cop in the car didn't see anything, and that was the hang-up. You can't keep all this stuff out from in front of the jury, particularly with lawyers who are willing to be unethical. There are some of those. Probably surprises you guys, but we tried the case. It hung eight to four. We tried it again and it hung at six-up. I said to hell with it, and rather than strike the priors for a plea, I dumped it because we don't strike priors unless there are enormous problems with our case.

As a result of the DA's unwillingness to negotiate, the defendant was released, but only after his attorney defended him twice in court. Before Three Strikes, such cases usually would have resulted in plea agreements and would have been settled quickly.

Some defenders gave overtly hostile responses to what they viewed as political positioning by prosecutors at the expense of justice. "Prosecutors operate in a culture of fear for their careers," said one public defender. "If they err, their careers may end." Such comments may represent "sour grapes" on the part of defense attorneys who cannot persuade prosecutors to drop charges. Again, they may represent the reality of the situation for many deputy DAs, who work for an elected official who is obligated to the voters. The passage of the Three Strikes initiative was itself an intrusion by the public into the court system. Prosecutors have always been affected somewhat by public opinion; Three Strikes probably has increased this pressure.

Another common theme among public defenders was the increased difficulty in dealing with their clients (and the clients' families), who may face 25 years to life in prison for relatively minor offenses. One defender reported that clients had threatened him with violence in third-strike situations. The difficulty arises from the fact that defendants have a certain knowledge of the courtroom workings and expect certain outcomes. They are informed by their own and others' experiences, and they are shocked and angered by public defenders' claims that prosecutors will not offer them a deal. Under these circumstances, defense lawyers often act as grief counselors, trying to help their clients and the clients' families deal with the expected long prison term. One lamented, "Three guys got 25 to life on petty theft, and I got all depressed about it when I had to tell them. The pressure of facing 25 to life is a lot."

Prosecutors do not have an easy time with Three Strikes. They regard themselves as responsible for carrying out the political will of the public in the face of resistance by defenders and the bench. Still, many prosecutors are uncomfortable with the law as drafted and as implemented by their own offices. A number of prosecutors, in responses to open-ended items on the survey, pointed out that inequities existed. Some volunteered that offenders with serious felonies, such as murderers without strike priors, were receiving lighter sentences than strike defendants. Other prosecutors were concerned that life sentences were being imposed for minor offenses. Some prosecutors complained about being required to try cases with significant evidentiary problems because the defendants had strike priors. Many prosecutors apparently are as confused as other members of the workgroup as to when strike allegations will or should be dismissed. They complain about increases in workloads without additions in staff, and wonder how to do their jobs within the straitjacket that is Three Strikes.

Judges' complaints centered on workload issues: the staggering increase in some types of trials as a result of defendants' unwillingness to plead guilty and receive long prison terms. Even judicial suggestions that punishments for pleas of guilty will be decreased slightly may little affect the number of trials, particularly because defendants know that juries may acquit if they learn that the case involves Three Strikes. Still, judges were thought to have suffered the smallest increase in workload and stress as a result of Three Strikes.

[...]

REFERENCES

"Argument for Proposition 184." 1994. California voter pamphlet.

Blumberg, A.S. 1967. *Criminal Justice*. Chicago: Quadrangle Books.

Butterfield, F. 1996. "Three Strikes Rarely Invoked in Courtrooms," 1996. *New York Times*, September 10, pp. Al, A15.

California Legislative Analyst's Office. 1995. "The 'Three Strikes and You're Out Law': A Preliminary Assessment." Retrieved August 31, 1998 (http:// www.law.ca.gov/sc010605).

———. 1997. The "Three Strikes and You're Out" Law: An Update. Retrieved October 14, 1997 (http://www.law.ca.gov/hol01497_3_strikes_update.html).

Canon, A. 1996. "Only California Using '3 Strikes' Law Widely." *Sacramento Bee*, September 10, p. A8.

Eisenstein, J. and H. Jacob. 1977. *Felony Justice: An Organizational Analysis of Criminal Courts*. Boston: Little, Brown.

Heumann, M. 1975. "A Note on Plea Bargaining and Case Pressure." 1975. *Law and Society Review* (Spring): 515–28.

Feeley, M.M. and S. Kamin. 1996. "The Effect of 'Three Strikes and You're Out" on the Courts: Looking Back to the Future." Pp. 135–54 in *Three Strikes and You're Out: Vengeance as Public Policy*, edited by D. Shichor and D.K. Sechrest. Thousand Oaks, CA: Sage.

McCoy, C. 1990, *Politics and Plea Bargaining: Victims' Rights in California*. Philadelphia: University of Pennsylvania Press.

Meyer, J. and P. Jesilow. 1997. *Doing Justice in the People's Court: Sentencing by Municipal Court Judges*. Albany: SUNY Press.

Nardulli, P.F. 1978. *The Courtroom Elite: An Organizational Perspective on Criminal Justice*. Cambridge, MA: Ballinger.

Vanzi, M. 1998. "Senate Committee OKs Bill to Ease Three-Strikes Law", *Los Angeles Times*, April 15, p. A3.

Wolfe, L. 1995. "After Year, '3 Strikes' Called Foul Cure". *San Diego Union-Tribune*, February 26, p. A3. "A Wrong Turn on 'Three Strikes." 1998. *Los Angeles Times*, May 16, p. B7.

CASES CITED

People v. Davis (1997) 15 Cal. 4th 1096

People v. Superior Court (Romero) (1996) 13 Cal.4th 497

DISCUSSION QUESTIONS

1. Why do the media portray courtroom proceedings as exciting and filled with trials when in reality it is the opposite?

2. Why might debating skills be more important than coordination skills in an adversarial proceeding?

3. What are the consequences of defense attorneys serving as double agents?

4. How is the criminal trial court system similar to a business?

5. Describe the problems with an adversarial system of justice.

6. How might the courtroom function if every case were to go to trial?

7. Do plea deals undermine due process? Why or why not?

8. Explain why it is the interest of the courts to remain a closed community.

9. What burdens do three strikes laws place on the courtroom workgroup? How have these laws affected both judges and prosecutors, in particular?

10. With the three strike laws causing more stress on courtroom workgroups, longer prison sentences for minor crimes, and inefficient sentencing, why was it applied?

SECTION 3

COURTROOM WORKGROUPS

Introduction

From an organizational perspective, the courtroom workgroup is a key element in facilitating court operations. Typically, courtroom workgroups refer to the groups of judges, prosecutors, and defense attorneys that handle criminal cases, but they can also include others, such as probation officers and court clerks. These workgroups have the task of processing cases through the court system. Each member of the workgroup has a specialized role and responsibility, but as discussed in Section 2, they tend to work together, mostly in response to some of the organizational demands. It is necessary to understand how this organized group operates and the impact of its organized nature on case processing.

Common Goals and Incentives

It has been proposed that two of the main bureaucratic goals within the court organization are efficiency and uncertainty reduction. James Eisenstein and Herbert Jacob, in "Trial Courtrooms as Organized Workgroups," refer to these as the instrumental goals of the courtroom workgroup, as opposed to the expressive goals of justice and due process. They acknowledge that part of what makes the courtroom workgroup an organized group is the fact that each member is held together by these instrumental goals. As a group, they all have an interest in disposing cases with a minimal number of uncertainties in the outcome, resulting in a tendency to rely on plea bargaining.

This mutual interest calls attention to an important factor—the varying personal incentives that each of the actors has in fulfilling the obligations of the court organization and regularly relying on the plea process. While Skolnick and Metcalfe briefly highlighted some of these incentives, Stephanos Bibas further explains why prosecutors and defense attorneys, in particular, would have an interest in negotiations and plea deals in "Plea Bargaining Outside the Shadow of Trial." Many of the incentives he details for prosecutors can apply to judges as well, who also have to worry about their reputations and getting overturned on appeal.

Bibas recognizes that the incentives faced by prosecutors and defense attorneys can result in un-likely cases being resolved by a plea. For instance, in a logical sense, plea bargaining would seem more likely in cases with extensive evidence and witnesses, where it is clear the person would get convicted at trial. Taking into account the bureaucratic concerns and attorney incentives, the opposite generally happens, such that weak cases are often resolved through the plea process, thereby ensuring speed and finality to the resolution of the case. In this sense, the mode of disposition is heavily influenced by the interests of the courtroom workgroup, meaning that its discretion plays a large role in the process.

The actors also have an interest in doing justice, but in the context of their incentives, this goal can take on different meanings. For example, Eisenstein and Jacob recognize that justice for a defense attorney may come in the form of a reduced sentence for a client. For a prosecutor, justice may be seen in the accrual of high conviction rates. Therefore, in a circumstance where the goals of justice may seem to conflict with the instrumental goals, the "ambiguity" of justice means that the actors can give different meaning to it, so that it fits within their interests and the concerns of the organization.

Workgroup Familiarity

In Section 2, it was noted that familiarity can facilitate cooperation and influence case processing, by making bargaining and negotiation easier. The readings in the current section expand upon this idea of familiarity. Particularly, Eisenstein and Jacob explain that familiarity depends on the (a) stability of the workgroup and (b) size of the pool from which workgroup members are drawn. These two factors call attention to the number of interactions between the same judge, prosecutor, and defense attorney. Presumably, the more often the same judge, prosecutor, and defense attorney work together, the more familiar with one another they become. Having a smaller pool of attorneys will make interactions between the same three actors more likely.

Bibas focuses on a different aspect of familiarity. He recognizes that attorneys who are engaged in more cases and have been practicing for more years develop greater familiarity with the laws. He uses the example of charge and sentence reductions defendants can receive for cooperating with the government, also called substantial assistance departures. Defense attorneys more familiar with the way these departures work can better navigate the process and potentially get a better outcome for their clients. Attorneys with more familiarity also understand the typical outcomes for certain cases and can rely on this information when making negotiations.

In addition to these perspectives, familiarity can be based in the quality of relationships. Although the same three people may have a high degree of familiarity, in that they interact often to handle cases, they may all dislike each other, which is an additional aspect of familiarity. Similarity among the actors may be important as well, such that both demographic and ideological similarities between people often create a positive working relationship. A workgroup can be familiar but have extreme ideological differences, for instance, which can foster tensions and hinder cooperation.

The Prosecutor's Influence

Within the courtroom workgroup, the prosecutor often assumes a dominant role. As Eisenstein and Jacob discuss, the judge is considered the "formal leader" of the courtroom. Although this is true, they recognize that organized groups "display influence relationships which modify the authority relationships." Stated differently, prosecutors or defense attorneys can assume greater influence over judges at any point in time. Because of their role in making the decision to prosecute, deciding the charges against the defendant, and initiating plea negotiations, prosecutors usually take on greater authority within the workgroup. In many circumstances, they possess the most discretion.

Some of this authority may come from the fact that prosecutors' interests, even at the ideological level, are more aligned with the court organization's interests than the other actors. Prosecutors want to portray an image of being tough on crime, which is demonstrated through high conviction rates. In this way, they are particularly supportive of processes, like plea bargaining, that increase efficiency and reduce uncertainties in the outcome (especially when they guarantee a conviction). Alternatively, defense attorneys are ideologically bound to promote due process for their clients and make sure they get their day in court. These ideological goals are contradictory to the organizational needs and also go against defense attorneys' best interests in terms of reducing caseload and increasing financial returns, as Bibas discusses.

Another source of prosecutors' authority stems from sentencing guidelines. Sentencing guidelines at the state and federal level were put in place to limit the discretion of judges at the sentencing phase. It is argued that most of this discretion has been displaced to prosecutors. In many circumstances, prosecutors can use guidelines to their advantage to obtain plea deals, thereby getting the convictions they need. This strategizing puts them in a place of influence where they can absolutely affect the mode of disposition, as well as case outcomes.

Public vs. Private Defense Attorneys

Many defendants that come to the courts are represented by public defenders. The modern public defender system was established after *Gideon v. Wainwright* in order to ensure that indigent defendants received counsel under the Sixth Amendment, which states that "in all criminal prosecutions, the accused shall enjoy the right ... to have the Assistance of Counsel for his defense." *Argersinger v. Hamlin* later clarified that indigents had a right to an attorney for any offense that could result in incarceration.

A common assumption within the court system is that private defense attorneys obtain better outcomes for their clients than public defenders. In "Do You Get What You Pay For? Type of Counsel and Its Effect on Criminal Court Outcomes," Richard Harley, Holly Ventura Miller, and Cassia Spohn explain the reasons for this argument. Public defenders have been criticized for being quick to resort to plea bargains and less effective in representation, especially due to their extremely high caseload. In light of some of the earlier discussions regarding familiarity, though, public defenders could be seen as having an advantage, because they are regulars to the courtroom and often know how the judges and prosecutors operate. Presumably, they would then be able to negotiate better deals for their clients. To an extent, private defense attorneys are outsiders to the system, since they are not always around and do not consistently interact with the judges and prosecutor's office. They may then fair worse in negotiations.

Overall, Harley and colleagues find that case outcomes are largely consistent across public defenders and private attorneys. There are certain circumstances, however, in which public defenders fair better, as well as circumstances in which private defense attorneys get a better outcome for the defendant. The belief commonly held by indigent defendants that their outcomes would have been different had they been represented by a private defense attorney is not necessarily true. There continues to be some support for the idea that public defenders, as an integral part of the court organization, can be at an advantage in case processing.

Trial Courtrooms as Organized Workgroups

James Eisenstein and Herbert Jacob

Persons entering American courthouses expecting to witness trials usually experience swift disappointment. Naive visitors will be bewildered by the throngs in criminal courtrooms where they expected dignified decorum; they will be even more puzzled by the large number of empty courtrooms, after being told by almost everyone associated with law that courts are overwhelmed with work. In the full courtrooms, the observer will hear one case after another called and disposed of within a few seconds or minutes. Over a hundred cases may be handled in this fashion during the course of a day, with scarcely a single proceeding resembling a trial. If the observer settles onto one of the uncomfortable benches of an empty courtroom to wait and see what happens during a morning, he will see attorneys come in and out, transacting business with the court clerk and sometimes disappearing into an unmarked door, which the observer learns takes one to the judge's chambers. He may see the judge emerge for a brief ceremony when several attorneys are in the courtroom. But unless the visitor enjoys exceptionally keen hearing, he will often be unable to hear what the attorneys and judges are saying. The ceremonies end as abruptly as they began, and once more judge and attorneys disappear behind closed doors or into the hallway. A kindly but curious clerk will eventually go to our visitor and ask him what he wants and then lead him to the door with the explanation that there will be no trials today.

Is the busy courtroom an assembly line? Is the empty courtroom testimony to governmental waste and inefficiency? What has happened to the classic adversarial proceedings so dramatically portrayed on stage and screen, where defense counsel and prosecutor vigorously oppose each other in a trial that takes many days? Where is the judge who is supposed to be sitting on his bench? Where is the jury? How does what we see in ordinary courtrooms fit into the exciting description of trials that can be found in almost any daily newspaper?

The answers to these questions rest in an entirely different way of looking at judicial proceedings. Courts are not an occasional assemblage of strangers who resolve a particular conflict and then dissolve, never to work together again. Courts are permanent organizations.[1] Moreover, adversarial proceedings are only one of the techniques available to disputants; trials may become so costly that few people use them. Viewing courtrooms as organized workgroups will enable us to unravel many of the mysteries of the judicial process.

The Courtroom Workgroup

Courtroom workgroups have characteristics commonly found among other organized workgroups.

1. They exhibit authority relationships.
2. They display influence relationship, which modify the authority relationships.
3. They are held together by common goals.
4. They have specialized roles.
5. They use a variety of work techniques.
6. They engage in a variety of tasks.
7. They have different degrees of stability and familiarity.

These traits establish a complex network of ongoing relationships that determines who in the courtroom does what, how, and to whom.

Courtroom Authority Patterns. The judge is the formal leader of most courtrooms.[2] In a sense, the courtroom belongs to him; he enjoys considerable formal powers to force others to conform to his desires. Most decisions the courtroom produces, including those made by others that affect the disposal of cases, usually require formal judicial approval. The judge must ratify the defendant's decision to enter a guilty plea, the prosecutor's decision to dismiss some or all charges, and an agreement on sentence. Finally, by participating in a number of decisions affecting case outcomes, judges gain influence over other courtroom organization members. Judges make preliminary decisions on bail, on motions and hearings. They rule on specific objections during courtroom proceedings and thus

---

1   Our understanding of organizations is based primarily on the work of Herbert A. Simon, *Administrative Behavior,* 2d ed. (New York: Macmillan, 1957); Peter M. Blau and W. Richard Scott, *Formal Organizations: A Comparative Approach* (San Francisco: Chandler, 1962); Amitai Etzioni, *A Comparative Analysis of Complex Organizations* (New York: Free Press, 1961); Charles Perrow, *Organizational Analysis: A Sociological View* (London: Tavistock, 1970); and James D. Thompson, *Organizations in Action* (New York: McGraw-Hill, 1967). As will be evident to the reader familiar with organizational studies, we have been eclectic in our construction of the framework presented in the following pages.

To our knowledge, no organizational analyst has studied courts. However, several students of courts have used fragments of organizational analysis for their presentation. The most influential of these are Abraham S. Blumberg's *Criminal Justice* (Chicago: Quadrangle Books, 1967) and Herbert L. Packer's *The Limits of the Criminal Sanction* (Stanford, Calif.: Stanford University Press, 1968). Neither Blumberg nor Packer, however, lays bare the elements of an operative organizational model for courts. A more recent, but also only partial, attempt to explicate an organizational model for courts is Malcolm Feeley, "Two Models of the Criminal Justice System: An Organizational Perspective," *Law and Society Review* 7 (1973): 407—426; Feeley focuses on court systems rather than courtrooms, and again presents only a very partial model. The organizational context of the work of criminal courts is also emphasized by Lief Carter, although he focuses on the prosecutor's office rather than the courtroom in his analysis; see Lief H. Carter, *The Limits of Order* (Lexington, Mass.: Lexington Books, 1974). Exchange relationships in an organizational context are emphasized by George F. Cole, *Politics and the Administration of Justice* (Beverly Hills, Calif.: Sage Publications, 1973), esp. pp. 200–203.

2   The judge's formal role is the focus of much legal literature. It is epitomized by Bernard Botein, *The Trial Judge* (New York: Simon and Schuster, 1952).

influence whether a compromise is reached—and if so, its content—as well as the verdict when no bargain is consummated.

Judges are universally considered the linchpins of courtroom workgroups. They are the formal leaders of the court and have the formal responsibility for making decisions that affect the flow of cases. They set dates for motions, hearings, trials, and other proceedings. The courtroom's work load is affected by their willingness to grant or deny extensions of deadlines, the time they take to render decisions on motions and in hearings, the procedures they use to empanel juries, the degree to which they cut short attorneys' examination of witnesses, and the amount of time they are willing to work. Judges also govern courtroom conduct. They are responsible for the actual behavior of attorneys, witnesses, spectators, and defendants; for example, they regulate voice level and physical movement, and decide when conversations will be allowed.

Attorneys represent interested parties to a conflict, but the judge is the neutral arbiter; even in criminal trials, he is not supposed to favor the state, even though he is a public official like the prosecutor. He represents the ideals of justice; he sits above the others, wears a robe, and requires all others to show visible respect for him by addressing him as "your honor" and by rising when he enters and leaves the courtroom. No one may openly criticize him in the courtroom; he may charge those who do with contempt of court (not contempt of the judge) and fine or imprison them on the spot. Moreover, this formal authority is often reinforced by the age and experience of the judge. He is often older and more experienced in the law than the attorneys who practice before him.

The judge, however, has less authority than many superiors in workgroups. He does not hire or fire others who work in the courtroom. Almost all of them are assigned by independent authorities—we call them sponsoring organizations—such as the state's attorney, the public defender, the clerk of courts, the sheriff (who assigns the bailiffs in many courtrooms), and the marketplace, which brings private attorneys representing individual clients to the courtroom. Each, of these sponsoring agencies imposes its own requirements on the participants it sends to the courtroom workgroup. Consequently, the judge's authority is quite limited.

Judges also have few budgetary controls over the courtroom. Unlike most workgroups, courtroom workgroups typically do not have their own budget. Each participant brings his own resources to the workgroup and uses them himself or shares them with others. Neither judges nor anyone else in the courtroom workgroup can decide to install a new public address system or to hire several additional clerks; judges cannot reward hardworking prosecutors or bailiffs with a salary raise, nor can they directly withhold salary increments from malingerers. Lacking personnel and budgetary powers, judges have less authority than many workgroup supervisors.

Even on legal matters the judge's authority is not absolute. He renders decisions, of course, and they have the force of law. But they are subject to reversal by other judges. Attorneys sometimes seek to influence their content by citing statutes and appellate decisions. In addition, a judge generally can rule only when someone else raises the issue and requests a decision. Thus, his legal decisions are molded by the activities of others.

Courtroom Influence Patterns. The influence of other participants in the workgroup limits the formal authority of the judge. Their influence stems from formal authority that the law also provides them, and from superior information or control over access to the courtroom.

The law gives the state's attorney the right to determine whom to prosecute and what charges to press. In addition, the prosecutor routinely has more information about a case than anyone else in the courtroom. He possesses the police report, records of previous arrests and convictions, witness reports, laboratory tests, and the physical evidence if there is any. The prosecutor, more than anyone else, knows what the strength of a case is and when it is ready for disposition. Thus in many court-rooms, the prosecutor controls the scheduling of cases and the dispositional pattern. The judge—although possessing greater formal authority—responds to the prosecutor's actions. No experienced prosecutor will routinely overlook the judge's sentiments about how the courtroom is to be run, but many run it instead of the judge. Even where the judge maintains more control, he must take into account the prosecutor's opinion of what should be done.

Defense counsel also possess considerable influence in the work of the courtroom. They are charged with representing their client in a number of crucial proceedings. The defense attorney has a duty to insist that evidence seized illegally be thrown out of court and may ask for a hearing to accomplish that end. He can demand a hearing to determine the legality of an arrest or confession. A conscientious and skilled defense counsel may make the work of a prosecutor much more difficult and may require detailed rulings on the law from the judge.

The defendant is notably absent from most interactions of courtroom workgroups, assuming the role of a very interested spectator with a front row seat.[3] But he possesses several rights—the right to a jury trial being the most important—which cannot be waived without his formal direct participation in a ceremony. Before a defendant can waive his right to a jury trial or enter a plea of guilty, he must be questioned directly by the judge and answer in his own voice, not his attorney's. But defense attorneys may convince defendants to waive these rights and may school them in the proper responses to the judge's questions. If defense counsel is unwilling or unable to influence and control clients most of the time, the smooth operation of the workgroup is jeopardized.

Under some circumstances, clerks also possess some influence in the courtroom workgroup. In busy courtrooms where dockets are not arranged by a central computer, the clerk often determines which case will be heard next. The order in which cases are heard is important for busy lawyers who want to avoid fruitless hours of waiting for their case to be called for a two-minute ritual. Where the sequence of cases has an effect on the outcome (because one case is affected by the outcome of the case just before), the clerk's decision may also lead to more or less severe results for the defendant.

Finally, police have significant influence on the operation of criminal courts. In many cities they determine who will be sent to court by the arrests they make; at the least, they share that determination with the prosecutor. They also are the most frequent witnesses in criminal court. Their appearance or absence, their demeanor, the care with which they preserve evidence—all have a considerable effect on the work of the courtroom. Prosecutors, especially, depend on the police, but defense counsel and judges also have a considerable stake in how the police act in the courtroom.

The precise pattern of influence in courtroom workgroups varies with the degree to which each of the participants possesses these resources and how he uses them. When everything else is equal, an aggressive defense attorney will exert more influence than a reticent one. A diligent prosecutor exerts more influence than one who forgets details of the cases he is handling. An assertive judge retains more of his authority than one who sees his role solely as responding to the initiatives of others in the courtroom. Some courtrooms appear to be governed almost entirely by their judges, although that appearance almost always is an exaggeration. Other courtrooms are ruled by the prosecutor; a few are dominated by defense counsel. Many are governed by a collective decision-making process encompassing judge, prosecutor, defense attorneys, clerks, and police.

---

3   Note the analysis of criminal proceedings from the defendant's perspective by Jonathan Casper, *American Criminal Justice* (Englewood Cliffs, N.J.: Prentice-Hall, 1972).

Shared Goals of Courtroom Workgroups. Courtroom workgroups have a job to do. Like most people pressed for time, their members do not often pause to philosophize about their ultimate purpose or goals. It is difficult enough just to keep going. Although they may not realize it, all courtroom workgroups share values and goals.[4] These shared perspectives undermine the apparent conflicts generated by the formal roles of workgroup members—the prosecutors' push toward convictions, the defense attorneys' quest for acquittals, and judges' inclination toward neutrality.

Four goals present in courtroom workgroups are summarized in Table 3.1.1 They are produced by the interaction of two dimensions: the function performed (expressive or instrumental) and the origins of the goals (external or internal to the group).[5] Expressive goals serve symbolic functions and infuse meaning into activity. Instrumental goals serve material functions and help get things done. Externally oriented goals are imposed by the workgroup's environment. Internal goals are produced by the need of the members to share perspectives that sustain the organization itself.

Table 3.1.1. Goals of Courtroom Workgroups

Function of Goal	Origins of Goal	
	External	Internal
Expressive	Doing Justice	Maintaining Group Cohesion
Instrumental	Disposing of Case Load	Reducing Uncertainty

External goals reflect pressures on the workgroup from outside the immediate bounds of the courtroom and from the sponsoring organizations that send the major participants to the courtroom. The police, the media, governmental agencies, including the legislature and appellate courts, and ultimately the general public, all expect results from the courtroom workgroup. These "outside" groups impose both instrumental and expressive goals on courtroom organization. The most important instrumental goal is that cases should be handled expeditiously. Many people believe that expeditious disposition will deter crime. In addition, quick convictions or acquittals tie up fewer resources of the police. They also fulfill requirements imposed by appellate courts for a speedy trial and might reduce appellate business. They produce a steady flow of news to the media and assure the public that the courts are doing their job. Disposing of cases without attracting undue attention or criticism from outsiders is also interpreted by many as doing justice.

All members of the courtroom workgroup are interested in disposing cases, although the reason for this interest varies. Judges and prosecutors want high disposition rates in order to transmit an aura of efficiency and accomplishment. Prosecutors also prefer speedy dispositions because as cases age, memories dim and witnesses scatter, weakening the evidence and lowering the chances of conviction.

Retained attorneys face a more complicated set of incentives. Most attorneys who specialize in criminal cases depend on a high turnover of clients who can afford only modest fees. Without high volume and the investment of a modest amount of time in each case, many a private defense counsel

---

4   We are conceptualizing goals as incentive mechanisms and the goal structure as multifaceted. They help orient the calculus of decision-makers and serve to bind organization members together. An insightful discussion of the jutiblems associated with operationalizing goals and placing them in a theoretic scheme is Petro Georgiou, "The Coal Paradigm and Notes toward a Counter Paradigm," *Administrative Science Quarterly* 18 (1973): 291–310. Despite Georgiou's arguments, we find the concept of goals and incentive structures essential to die organizational paradigm.

5   This discussion reflects what Mohr calls transitive and reflexive goals. Lawrence B. Mohr, "The Concept of Organizational Goal," *American Political Science Review* 67 (1973): 470–481, esp. 475–476.

would go broke. Yet private counsel must maintain a reputation for vigorous defense in order to attract new clients. Public defender organizations charged with representing all indigent defendants prefer quick disposition because their manpower barely suffices to handle their case load. But they also seek to establish a reputation for effective representation of defendants.

The expressive goal imposed by the external environment is to do justice. All the principal participants are attorneys, and are bound to that goal by their professional training. For that matter, nearly everyone in American society values doing justice. The specific content of the term, however, is ambiguous. For some, justice is done when criminals are caught and severely punished regardless of procedures. For others, adherence to the principles of due process and equal treatment produces justice. The ambiguity and disagreement contained in the notion of justice in society are mirrored in the varying perspectives of workgroup members. For the defense, doing justice may mean either obtaining an acquittal or a mild sentence for its clients, or forcing the prosecution to prove its case beyond a reasonable doubt. The prosecution often sees doing justice in terms of its conviction rates, because it is convinced that most defendants are in fact guilty. Judges generally see this goal as requiring impartial behavior, although their definition of impartiality often favors either the defense or the prosecution. Thus surface agreement within the courtroom organization on the goal of "doing justice" often engenders behavioral conflict.

Internally oriented goals facilitate the functioning of the courtroom workgroup. The expressive form of these goals is maintaining group cohesion.[6] Pervasive conflict is not only unpleasant; it also makes work more difficult. Cohesion produces a sense of belonging and identification that satisfies human needs. It is maintained in several ways. Courtroom workgroups shun outsiders because of their potential threat to group cohesion. The workgroup possesses a variety of adaptive techniques to minimize the effect of abrasive participants. For instance, the occasional defense attorney who violates routine cooperative norms may be punished by having to wait until the end of the day to argue his motion; he may be given less time than he wishes for a lunch break in the middle of a trial; he may be kept beyond usual court horns for bench conferences. Likewise, unusually adversarial defense or prosecuting attorneys are likely to smooth over their formal conflicts with informal cordiality. Tigers at the bench, they become tame kittens in chambers and in the hallways, exchanging pleasantries and exuding sociability.

The instrumental expression of internal goals is reducing or controlling uncertainty.[7] The strong incentives to reduce uncertainty force courtroom members to work together, despite their different orientations toward doing justice. More than anything else, trials produce uncertainty. They require substantial investments of time and effort without any guarantee of the result. The difficulty of estimating how long they will last makes everyone's schedule very uncertain. Even bench trials require some preparation of witnesses and throw the other participants at the mercy of these witnesses, whose behavior on the witness stand is unpredictable. What witnesses say and how they say it may make the difference between conviction and acquittal. Jury trials are even worse, because attorneys must deal with the jurors as well as the witnesses. In ordinary cases very little is known about the jurors,

---

6   For partial evidence in support of the following see "Lawyers with Convictions," in Abraham S. Blumberg, *The Scales of Justice* (Chicago: Aldine, 1970), pp. 51–67; George F. Cole, *The American System of Criminal Justice* (North Scituate, Mass.: Duxbury Press, 1975), pp. 238–241 and 271–272; Carter, *The Limits of Order*, pp. 75–105; Jerome Skolnick, "Social Control in the Adversary System," *Journal of Conflict Resolution* 11 (1967): 51 ff; Lynn M. Mather, "The Outsiders in the Courtroom: An Alternative Role for the Defense," in Herbert Jacob (ed.). *The Potential for Reform of Criminal Justice* (Beverly Hills, Calif.: Sage Publications, 1974), pp. 268–273.
     Note, however, that cohesion is not the only goal of actors and that it sometimes conflicts with others.

7   Cf. Carter, *The Limits of Order*, pp. 19–21.

and jury decisions are proverbially unpredictable. Even after presenting a "dead-bang" case to a jury, prosecutors suffer nervous hours while the jury deliberates. The judge is also committed to avoiding uncertainty. Most judges like to have some control over their dockets; they like to see where actions are heading and what further activity is required of them.

The desire to reduce uncertainty leads to the development of several norms designed to make behavior predictable. One is "stick by your word and never mislead deliberately." Attorneys who violate this norm find they are punished. Another is "no surprises." It is often illegal to call surprise witnesses or to introduce evidence that the opposing counsel is unaware of; it is almost always regarded as a dirty trick.

The instrumental goals we have identified are generally mutually supportive. Caseload disposition and reduction of uncertainty go hand in hand; the former is often articulated (partly because it is directed at the external environment), whereas the latter is more often an unspoken commitment by courtroom members. Expressive goals, however, are not as frequently mutually supportive. The quest for justice often threatens courtroom cohesion, and the desire to maintain a cohesive workgroup may seem to jeopardize the quest for justice. The general political culture more explicitly legitimates the externally oriented goals. There is much public discussion of the need for justice and for the clearing of dockets in criminal courts. Organizational maintenance goals are almost furtive by contrast. They are rarely articulated in public by members of the courtroom organization; they can best be deduced from private statements and courtroom behavior. Although they are not illegitimate, they have not yet been publicly legitimated.

Courtroom workgroups vary in their adherence to these goals. For instance, some workgroups value cohesion less than others because they find conflict less threatening to their survival. But in general we believe that the variation is not great. Nevertheless, it is important to identify these goals, because common adherence to them keeps the groups together.

Workgroup Specialization. Although courtroom participants have common goals, they play radically different roles. The participants rigidly adhere to the specified role differentiation. The judge maintains an air of impartiality; he responds to requests for rulings on the law and makes decisions when called on by others. He may intervene in the scheduling of cases or in questioning witnesses, but he may not take sides. The prosecutor, on the other hand, represents only the state and never the defense. Defense counsel only defend and never prosecute. There is no alternation of roles in the criminal courtroom.

However, the three leading members of the courtroom workgroup—the judge, prosecutor, and defense attorney—are all lawyers and possess the professional qualifications to do each others work. Although role orientations are distinct and specialized, the work these three principals do is very similar. All of them manipulate information in order to reach decisions on the cases before them. They ask questions of witnesses—in private interviews or on the witness stand. They search out relevant aspects of code and case law and seek to apply them to their cases. All three are familiar with the techniques employed in adversarial proceedings; they are equally familiar with negotiations.

Little disagreement exists in the courtroom about this division of tasks and roles, It creates a situation in which everyone quickly fits into his accustomed place and in which the principals readily understand each other's work. Even novices readily fit into the work routine of a courtroom.

The other members of the courtroom workgroup engage in quite different tasks. The clerk keeps records. Although judges and lawyers may keep their own, the clerk's record is the official one. He records decisions, the dates when they occurred, and the motions and appearances that are filed with him. Together with the stenographic record of the proceedings, the clerk's file is the official record of the case and is used by everyone in the courtroom to determine what has happened in the past and what still needs to be done to complete disposition of the case. In addition, the court reporter—often a private contractor—makes a stenographic record of public proceedings. Those records, however, are not transcribed unless the defense or the state asks and pays for the transcription. Finally, bailiffs work in the courtroom to maintain decorum and guard prisoners who appear as defendants or witnesses.

Each of these members of the courtroom workgroup knows his task, role, and physical location in the courtroom. He knows it before he enters the courtroom. Little formal training or socialization occurs in the workgroup. If a participant needs additional skills, he learns them informally.

The Work Techniques of Courtroom Organizations. Organizations are more than stable groups of people who share goals and divide tasks in a purposive manner. Organizations also employ a technology, which in turn helps shape them.[8] The technology consists of procedures to manipulate resources into desired outputs. For courtrooms, resources consist principally of information and the authority to make decisions that bind others. The outputs are dispositions. The courtroom organization s task is to transform information and authority into dispositions by applying its work techniques.

Courtroom workgroups require an externally validated, comprehensive, readily available, and generally accepted set of techniques, because the participants are sometimes unfamiliar with one another. This unfamiliarity means that they have not developed common patterns of interaction. When strangers meet and interact, they fall back on commonly accepted formulas to guide their behavior. The procedures embodied in statute and case law relating to the conduct of trials and the hearing of motions provide such formulas. These techniques are not only justified because they employ norms and values relating to equal justice and due process; the very nature of courtroom workgroups also requires that some work techniques be codified and generally accepted.

Courtrooms use three sets of techniques: (1) unilateral decisions, (2) adversarial proceedings, and (3) negotiations. Each of them requires highly specialized knowledge and involves courtroom members in intense interactions.

Any attorney member of the courtroom workgroup may make unilateral decisions that eventually turn into dispositions. The defense counsel may file a motion; the prosecutor may file a dismissal; the judge or clerk may call up one case rather than another in his docket. In each instance, the participant uses his information and authority to impose a condition on other members of the courtroom team. The extensive interdependence of workgroup members, however, restricts their ability to impose unilateral decisions on the group. Consequently, unilateral decisions play a rather minor role in the courtroom's work.

Adversarial proceedings play a much more prominent role. They may be invoked by any of the three attorney members. Some of them are preparatory proceedings, such as preliminary examinations or hearings on motions; others are full-scale trials before a judge or jury. Adversarial proceedings are highly stylized interactions for revealing and sharing information that can become the basis for a disposition. During adversarial proceedings, information must be elicited in the approved manner, through oral arguments on legal points or questioning of witnesses. Neither prosecution nor defense ordinarily knows the full story a witness may tell, but the side presenting the witness generally knows more about what he might reveal than the opposing party. The judge knows almost nothing. Each side attempts to elicit the information most favorable to its cause while blocking the presentation of damaging information. This activity requires a high degree of skill in questioning and a thorough knowledge of the technical rules of evidence which guides courtroom hearings. Participants whose

---

8   See especially Thompson, *Organizations in Action.*

skills are inadequate not only jeopardize their case, but also hinder the output rate of the courtroom. It is common to see a judge take over questioning from inept prosecutors or defense counsel, or to cut them off when he thinks that sufficient evidence has been presented to reach a disposition. Similarly, counsel often advise judges about the legal basis for a decision.

Hearings require considerable coordination by the prosecutor or defense counsel rather than the judge. Witnesses must be assembled and prepared; each side must have an overview of its argument so that witnesses can be called in the most convincing sequence. Witnesses who might make an unfavorable impression or who appear fragile are often held in reserve and used only if absolutely necessary. If the hearings involve legal as well as evidentiary matters, the attorneys must read up on the law and have appropriate appellate citations at their fingertips. All of this preparation involves coordinating many people outside the ordinary ambit of the courtroom workgroup. Consequently, co-ordinative skills are almost as valuable as debating skills in adversarial proceedings.

Negotiation is the most commonly used technique in criminal courtrooms.[9] Plea bargaining—although most widely publicized—is only one use of negotiation. Continuances and the date of hearings are often bargained; the exchange of information is also commonly negotiated. Negotiation involves persuasion and the search for common ground. The common ground is generally based on agreement about the courtroom's goals; most members of the courtroom implicitly agree on the need to dispose cases and to reduce uncertainty. They also recognize the value of accommodating those on whom they are partially dependent. Each party to the negotiation attempts to convince the other that his solution is acceptable; in the course of negotiations, both parties are likely to move from their original positions toward a mutually acceptable outcome.

Information and the ability to make unilateral decisions that affect others significantly are the principal resources in negotiations. Courtroom participants utilize two types of information. One type is information about legal matters: the character of admissable evidence, the authorized sentence for a particular offense, the meaning of "lesser included offense," and similar matters. Most attorneys who specialize in criminal cases routinely possess this legal information. They also need to know the factual details of the case. Normally the prosecution possesses more information about the incident, on the basis of police reports and sometimes as a result of preliminary interviews with witnesses. Often there are disputes about what "really" happened, with the defense attorney attempting to put a less serious interpretation on the events than the prosecutor. At the same time, the character of the defendant is also in question. The defense attorney often claims to know more about that; he will tell of his client's family background, his employment record, his standing in the community, in addition to any disadvantages he has had to overcome. The prosecutor usually possesses only the defendant's police record. Negotiations proceed through a careful manipulation of this information. Even when both prosecutor and defense make "full disclosure," they often interpret the information at their disposal rather than simply laying it out on the table.

Information about the way in which other courtrooms handle similar incidents is also important in negotiations. What happens in other courts of the city or state is communicated principally through these negotiations. If other courtrooms readily grant continuances, that constitutes a useful argument that a continuance ought to be granted in the case under discussion. If, in an adjoining courtroom, aggravated assault seems to carry a normal sentence of two to four years, defense counsel will try hard

---

9   We have drawn from descriptions of courtroom negotiations by Blumberg, *Criminal Justice*, Casper, *American Criminal Justice;* Carter, *The Limits of Order;* Mather, "The Outsiders in the Courtroom"; and Albert W. Alschuler, 'The Prosecutor's Role in Plea Bargaining," *University of Chicago Law Review* 36 (1968): 50–112.

to achieve at least as low a sentence. Because prosecutors usually work in a single courtroom, whereas private defense counsel circulate throughout several courtrooms in the city, some defense attorneys possess more of this kind of information.

Negotiations also invoke claims on workgroup cohesion. None that we witnessed did so overtly, but many were impregnated with hints that the continuing need to work together required reasonableness in negotiation. Participants joked, about it; at the end of a negotiation, they often stood around and chatted about other matters as if to imply that they were still friendly partners of the same workgroup. Only when negotiations broke down did either prosecutor or defense counsel occasionally stalk out without the usual social amenities.

Clearly the techniques of presentation, the manipulation of information, and the invocation of common workgroup values are quite different in negotiations than in adversarial hearings. Not only are the negotiations much less formal, but they also depend less on the rules of evidence and other legalistic formulas that pervade so much of the adversarial performance. In negotiations much more depends on the long-run relationships between bargaining members of the workgroup. Trust, empathy, mutual understanding are important in negotiations, but matter little in adversarial proceedings. In bargaining, information is narrated; formal testimony from witnesses is the principal mode in adversarial proceedings.

Implicit threats to make unilateral decisions underlie the uses of information in all negotiations. The ability to take such actions gives weight to the efforts to control the exchange of information. Judges can render decisions that affect the outcome of specific cases and the work life of attorneys in general. The prosecutor can proceed to trial on the original charges if the defendant does not plead guilty to them. And the defense attorney can insist on a full jury trial regardless of what anyone else does, unless a complete dismissal is forthcoming. Without the existence of these threats, negotiations based on the exchange of information would carry little weight. Indeed, much of the manipulation of information is directed toward demonstrating what would happen if the case went to trial.

Courtroom Tasks. Courtrooms everywhere must complete similar tasks. These tasks flow from their fundamental responsibility in one way or another to dispose of every defendant charged. That responsibility requires maintaining physical control over defendants who may be prone to flee or to express their anger in violent outbursts. Much record-keeping is also required. A case file must be kept, containing information about all major actions taken. Then cases must be scheduled and the participants for each case assembled at the same time. All major proceedings must be recorded by a court reporter in case verbatim transcripts are required at a later stage. Finally, the law requires a variety of actions at different stages of criminal cases. Defendants must be arraigned and informed of the charges against them. Bond or release conditions must be set. In order to proceed against the defendant, a court must determine whether there is "probable cause," or a grand jury must return an indictment against him. "Discovery"—the exchange of information between prosecution and defense—must take place.

These tasks may be handled in many different ways. In some places, a single courtroom workgroup performs all of them, processing a criminal case from beginning to end. More commonly, courtroom workgroups specialize in subsets of these tasks. For instance, arraignments, bond setting, and preliminary hearings are often handled by one set of workgroups, whereas final dispositions are the domain of another workgroup. In some places, specialized workgroups process all motions; in others, all negotiations take place in a single setting. Specialized workgroups obviously operate differently than generalized ones. The more specialized the tasks of the workgroup, the more it can routinize procedures and the more familiar its members will be with the tasks they perform. On the other hand, specialized workgroups often do not see the final outcome of the case, and their decisions may hinder rather than help the work of other courtroom workgroups that later process the same case.

Workgroup Familiarity. Courtroom workgroupings almost always contain some persons who are quite familiar with one another and some who are more like strangers. The familiarity among major participants is an important characteristic of workgroups, because it has a significant effect on the manner in which they work. The more workgroup members are familiar with one another, the better they can negotiate; the more familiar, the less they need to rely on formalities and the more they can utilize informal arrangements. The more familiar courtroom members are with each other, the more likely it is that they will agree about courtroom values and goals and the less they will conflict with one another.

Workgroup familiarity depends on two factors. The first is the stability of the workgroups themselves.[10] The second is the size of the pool from which workgroup members are drawn; the smaller the number of judges, prosecutors, defense attorneys, clerks, and others working in the courthouse, the more familiar courtroom members will be with each other.

Generally the most stable assignment is that of the judge. Except during vacation or illness, a single judge ordinarily sits for a year or more in a single courtroom. However, in courtrooms hearing misdemeanors, assignments may last for as little as a month; in other courtrooms, where the judges are elected or appointed to the criminal court itself, the assignment may extend over many years. The stabilizing effect of long assignments of judges is well illustrated by what happens when one is temporarily replaced by another judge. Work routines become substantially altered. Everyone suffers from more uncertainty about what to do and how to do it, because an important stranger is in their midst. Where possible, the remaining members postpone significant proceedings until the judge returns. If action cannot be delayed, proceedings switch into an adversarial mode, because the unknown qualities of the substitute judge can best be neutralized in a jury trial.

The assignment of prosecutors and defense attorneys is much more variable. These differences have profound consequences.

The less change there is in workgroup personnel, the more interaction will occur. Frequent interactions produce familiarity with each other's intentions and probable behavior. In stable courtroom workgroups, the principal actors know each other's preferences; they have been able to develop standing accommodations with each other. They work together enough to share organizational maintenance goals; they learn to understand the pressures that each must bear from his sponsoring organization. Thus, prosecutors and defense attorneys learn what information the judge wants in routine cases; they know the sentence he will likely mete out. They know how to present a case in order to provoke the harshest response or the mildest reaction from the judge. They know what plea offers were made in the past, and can evaluate the present case in the light of that common past. The uncertainty in negotiating with each other is considerably reduced by their familiarity with one another. In addition, frequent interactions provide innumerable informal opportunities for negotiation. Prosecutor and defense counsel may talk about a case not only when it is on the docket but during the many other occasions at which they encounter each other. They can test possible compromises informally, without putting the case on the judge's desk for formal decision. By contrast, in fluid workgroups, information about each of the participants is much more sparse; members of the courtroom

---

10   Stability or cohesiveness is taken for granted by many organizational analysts. For instance, the much-cited article by D. S. Pugh, D. J. Hickson, C. R. Hinings, and C. Turner, "Dimensions of Organizational Structure," *Administrative Science Quarterly* (June 1968): 65–106 does not count stability as one of the dimensions of organizational structure.

workgroup deal with each other more as strangers than as friends; formal roles govern them more completely. In fluid workgroups, members work in a much less certain context They are less likely to know the judge's preferences or each other's. They do not have a great storehouse of common experiences by which to evaluate the present case. They have not had an opportunity to develop a set of shared accommodations or an understanding of each participant's work pressures.

Finally, low interaction means that no one heavily depends on the actions of any other individual to accomplish his work. Where the same individuals interact continually, however, strong patterns of mutual dependence and accompanying abilities to influence one another emerge. In addition, if interaction is high, circulation of defense counsel and prosecutors from one courtroom to another will be low. A lower circulation, in turn, facilitates the development of distinctive styles of behavior within the rather isolated courtrooms located in the same building.

Even in unstable workgroups members may be quite familiar with each other, if the pool of active participants in the courthouse is fairly small. Where there are only a handful of judges, a half-dozen prosecutors, and a dozen defense attorneys, familiarity develops as if the workgroups were the same every day. But the familiarity found in smaller cities and in rural areas can be approximated in large cities if a small group of specialized attorneys monopolizes the work.

Plea Bargaining Outside the Shadow of a Trial

Stephanos Bibas

Attorneys and Agency Costs

1. Prosecutors' Pressures and Incentives.—The ideal of the adversary system presumes that prosecutors will decide whom to prosecute based on the evidence, the equities, and the justifications for punishment. In other words, prosecutors should decide to prosecute based on the likelihood of conviction and the need to deter, incapacitate, rehabilitate, reform, and inflict retribution. Of course, prosecutors are supposed to pursue justice, not just convictions. In some cases, doing so means pursuing lower sentences if the equities warrant them, or it may mean not prosecuting at all. While justice should temper the pursuit of punishment, self-interest should not.[1] To be sure, prosecutors may be merciful to sympathetic defendants. In addition, they may not insist on a higher sentence for one defendant when they have recently given a lower sentence to a similarly situated defendant.[2] They may also drive hard bargains on particular crimes to send messages, teach lessons, and deter especially harmful or prevalent crimes. Apart from these considerations, plea bargains should depend only on the severity of the crime, the strength of the evidence, and the defendant's record and need for punishment. This ideal asks prosecutors to be perfectly selfless, perfectly faithful agents of the public interest.

---

1   *See* Transcript of Edited and Narrated Arguments, Gideon v. Wainwright, 372 U.S. 335 (1963) (No. 155) (argument of Abe Fortas for the petitioner) ("[O]ur adversary system ... means that counsel for the state will do his best within the limits of fairness and honor and decency to present the case for the state. ..."), *in* May It Please the Court 185, 187 (Peter Irons & Stephanie Guitton eds., 1993).

2   *See* Milton Heumann, Plea Bargaining: The Experiences of Prosecutors, Judges, and Defense Attorneys 120–21 (1978) (discussing how prosecutors develop "habits of disposition" that lead to like sentences in like cases (quoting a prosecutor)).

The reality is much more complex. The strength of the prosecution's case is the most important factor,[3] but other considerations come into play. Trials are much more time consuming than plea bargains, so prosecutors have incentives to negotiate deals instead of trying cases.[4] Prosecutors have personal incentives to reduce their workloads so that they can leave work early enough to dine with their families. Additionally, prosecutors are paid salaries, not by case or by outcome, so they have no direct financial stake in the outcome.[5] The only countervailing financial incentive is that prosecutors might jeopardize their jobs by losing a string of trials and so drawing supervisors' or voters' wrath. Self-interest, in short, may discourage prosecutors from investing enough work in plea-bargained cases, in which more work might lead to heavier sentences. Some of this plea bargaining serves the public interest by freeing up prosecutors to pursue many more cases.[6] Even if the public might prefer the extra work needed for trial, however, prosecutors have personal incentives to strike plea bargains.[7]

In addition to lightening their workloads, prosecutors want to ensure convictions. They may further their careers by racking up good win-loss records, in which every plea bargain counts as a win but trials risk being losses.[8] The statistic of conviction, in other words, matters much more than the sentence.[9] Favorable win-loss statistics boost prosecutors' egos, their esteem, their praise by colleagues, and their prospects for promotion and career advancement.[10] Thus, prosecutors may prefer the certainty of plea bargains even if the resulting sentence is much lighter than it would have been after trial.[11] The psychology of risk aversion and loss aversion reinforces the structural incentives to ensure good statistics and avoid risking losses.[12] The public also has an interest in certainty of punishment, which plea bargaining will sometimes further. At other times, the public might prefer to gamble on a trial to secure heavier punishment, while the prosecutor's fear of personal embarrassment favors a plea bargain.

Prosecutors are particularly concerned about their reputations because they are a politically ambitious bunch. Most district attorneys are elected, and many have parlayed their prosecutorial successes into political careers: witness Mayors Rudolph Giuliani and Richard Daley, Senators John Kerry and

---

3   *See* Alschuler, *The Prosecutor's Role, supra* note 11, at 58–60; *see also* Dean J. Champion, *Private Counsels and Public Defenders: A Look at Weak Cases, Prior Records, and Leniency in Plea Bargaining,* 17 J. Crim. Just. 253, 257 (1989) (reporting a 1989 study that found that prosecutors have "an overwhelming propensity" to cut lighter deals in weak cases); William F. McDonald et al., *The Prosecutor's Plea Bargaining Decisions, in* The Prosecutor 151, 158 (William F. McDonald ed., 1979) (reporting that most prosecutors admit to giving the most generous deals in the weakest cases).

4   *See* Alschuler, *The Prosecutor's Role, supra* note 11, at 54–55; Joan E. Jacoby, *The Charging Policies of Prosecutors, in* The Prosecutor, *supra* note 15, at 75, 89; Schulhofer, *Criminal Justice Discretion, supra* note 11, at 51.

5   The many part-time prosecutors, however, have financial incentives to speed their dockets so that they can get back to their paying clients. *See* George Fisher, Plea Bargaining's Triumph: A History of Plea Bargaining in America 42–44 (2003); James Eisenstein, *Research on Rural Criminal Justice: A Summary, in* Criminal Justice In Rural America 105, 113–14, 125 (Shanler D. Cronk et al. eds., 1982).

6   *See* Easterbrook, *Criminal Procedure, supra* note 2, at 309.

7   *See* Jeffrey Standen, *Plea Bargaining in the Shadow of the Guidelines,* 81 Cal. L. Rev. 1471, 1495–96 (1993). As a former prosecutor, I can attest that most of the prosecutors and defense counsel with whom I worked were honorable and would not consciously shortchange their cases. Nevertheless, the human desires to relax and have a life beyond the law doubtless have an impact on even the most conscientious employee.

8   *See* Alschuler, *The Prosecutor's Role, supra* note 11, at 106, 109–10; Schulhofer, *Criminal Justice Discretion, supra* note 11, at 51; *cf* James Eisenstein, Counsel For The United States: U.S. Attorneys in the Political and Legal Systems 174 (1978) (noting that prosecutors know their reputations will affect their later prospects in private practice, so they act with a concern for preserving these reputations).

9   *See* Fisher, *supra* note 17, at 48–49 (noting that plea bargains inflate conviction statistics).

10   *See* Catherine Ferguson-Gilbert, Comment, *It Is Not Whether You Win or Lose, It Is How You Play the Game: Is the Win-Loss Scorekeeping Mentality Doing Justice for Prosecutors?,* 38 Cal. W. L. Rev. 283, 291–96 (2001); *see also* Alschuler, *The Prosecutor's Role, supra* note 11, at 106–07 ("Conviction statistics seem to most prosecutors a tangible measure of their success. Statistics on sentencing do not."); *id.* at 106 n.138 ("[P]rosecutors seem to believe the scalps on their belts enter their souls." (quoting a former prosecutor)).

11   *See* Heumann, *supra* note 14, at 110–13.

12   *See infra* section II.D (exploring the psychology of risk aversion and loss aversion).

Robert Dole, Chief Justice Earl Warren, and Attorney General Edwin Meese.[13] Losses at trial hurt prosecutors' public images, so prosecutors have incentives to take to trial only extremely strong cases and to bargain away weak ones.[14] They may push strong or high-profile cases to trial to gain reputation and marketable experience.[15]

This dynamic is the opposite of what one might expect: strong cases should plead guilty because trial is hopeless, while weak cases have genuine disputes that merit resolution at trial. In other words, the shadows of trials in strong cases are so clear and crisp that the shadow-of-trial model predicts settlement. In weak cases, however, the parties have imperfect information about the cases' weaknesses. Trial shadows in these cases may be fuzzy enough that the parties can disagree in predicting trial outcomes, and as a result bargaining may break down. The shadow-of-trial model, in short, predicts that most trials should involve weak cases. Self-interest, in contrast, pushes prosecutors toward trying the strongest cases.[16] Prosecutors can discourage defendants in strong cases from pleading guilty by refusing to make any concessions, while they can make irresistible offers in weak cases.[17]

Thus, instead of allowing juries to air and wrestle with the hard, troubling cases, prosecutors may hide them from view. If, for example, prosecutors bargain away most cases involving dubious confessions, they avert public scrutiny of police interrogation tactics. If they buy off credible claims

---

13 *See* Biographical Directory of the American Congress 1774–1996, at 951, 1329, 1376, 1861 (Joel Treese ed., 1997) (reporting that Robert Dole, John Kerry, Patrick Leahy, and Arlen Specter, among others, all served as prosecutors before election to the U.S. Senate); Michael Barone, *Back in Law Enforcement*, Wash. Post, Jan. 24, 1984, at A13 (reporting that Earl Warren served as Alameda County District Attorney and that, before being nominated to serve as Attorney General, Edwin Meese III served as an Alameda County prosecutor); Kevin Johnson, *Chicago Mayor Closes Gap*, Usa Today, Feb. 21, 1989, at 2A (reporting that Richard Daley served as Cook County state's attorney while running for mayor); Sam Roberts, *La Guardia's Legacy Is Formidable, but It May Be Surpassed*, N.Y. Times, Dec. 31, 2001, at F7 (reporting that concerns regarding crime helped former prosecutor Rudolph Giuliani win the mayoral election in New York, despite his having no experience in elected office).

14 *See* Raymond Moley, *The Vanishing Jury*, 2 S. CAL. L. REV. 97, 103 (1928); Schulhofer, *Criminal Justice Discretion, supra* note 11, at 50. Perhaps in a few rare situations, even losing a high-profile celebrity trial might gain a prosecutor fame or at least notoriety: witness Marcia Clark, the prosecutor in the O.J. Simpson trial. As a rule, however, losses are painful. Prosecutors might enhance their reputations by winning tough trials, but loss aversion means that most prosecutors hate losing more than they like winning. Thus, they will play it safe by trying to rack up their wins and statistics in rock-solid cases. *See infra* section II.D (discussing risk aversion and loss aversion). This phenomenon is particularly strong if outsiders cannot easily distinguish wins in hard-fought cases from wins in slam-dunk cases; each counts equally as a conviction statistic.

15 *See* Daniel Richman, *Prosecutors and Their Agents, Agents and Their Prosecutors*, 103 Colum. L. Rev. 749, 787–88 & n.176 (2003) (citing Richard T. Boylan & Cheryl X. Long, Size, Monitoring, and Plea Rate: An Examination of United States Attorneys 14–17 (Econometric Soc'y, World Congress 2000 Contributed Paper No. 00089, 2000), *available at* http://fmwww.bc.edu/RePEc/es2000/0089.pdf; and Edward L. Glaeser et al., *What Do Prosecutors Maximize? An Analysis of the Federalization of Drug Crimes*, 2 Am. L. & Econ. Rev. 259, 260–61 (2000)); *see also* Glaeser et al., *supra*, at 272, 282–83.

16 One famous study of the jury seems to contradict my assertion. Kalven and Zeisel thought that guilty pleas would siphon off the strongest cases, leaving only weaker, more controversial cases for jury trial. *See* Kalven & Zeisel, *supra* note 2, at 30–31. Their primary evidence was a statistical table of major crimes. The most serious crimes at the top of the table, such as murder, manslaughter, and rape, tended to have the fewest guilty pleas and the highest rates of acquittal at trial. The less serious felonies, such as burglary, auto theft, and forgery, had the most guilty pleas and the fewest acquittals. *Id.* at 20 tbl.2. Kalven and Zeisel concluded that defendants were choosing not to plead when they had significant chances of acquittal at trial. *See id.* at 21–22. But one could just as easily read the causal relationship the other way around. For less serious crimes, prosecutors siphon off the weakest cases with generous plea bargains, leaving only the strong cases for trial. This phenomenon explains the low acquittal rate. For the most serious crimes, especially murder, public scrutiny and press coverage pressure prosecutors not to offer generous plea bargains. Because prosecutors must offer less generous plea bargains, fewer defendants plead guilty. And because prosecutors must try the weaker cases instead of buying them off, more defendants win acquittals.

A further difficulty is that Kalven and Zeisel's statistics show only the charges on which defendants pleaded guilty or were tried. Charge bargaining, however, means that pleas are often misleading. For example, murder defendants often plead to manslaughter rather than murder. This relabeling of crimes partly explains why Kalven and Zeisel report a murder plea rate of 34% and a manslaughter plea rate of 52%. Without data on arrests and charges filed, one cannot compute plea rates by looking simply at the charges to which defendants pleaded guilty.

17 Prosecutors may also try some strong cases in order to strengthen their bargaining hand in future negotiations. When negotiating, they can credibly bluff or threaten to go to trial if they have actually gone to trial with great success recently. See Samuel R. Gross & Kent D. Severed, *Don't Try: Civil Jury Verdicts in a System Geared to Settlement*, 44 Ucla L. Rev. 1, 56 (1996). Prosecutors have a large pool of strong cases from which to choose. Out of this pool, they may choose some for trial based on the defendant's stubbornness in bargaining, on dislike of or disdain for the defendant or his lawyer, or on other factors.

of innocence cheaply, they cover up faulty investigations that mistakenly target innocent suspects. By pressing the easiest cases, prosecutors turn jury trials into rubber stamps or mere formalities.

[...]

2. Defense Attorneys' Pressures and Incentives.—Like prosecutors, defense attorneys are not ideal, perfectly selfless, perfectly faithful agents. They too are human and subject to similar failings and temptations. Some defense attorneys are more talented or more industrious than others, and some desire the fame and fortune that come from a high-profile trial. And like prosecutors, defense lawyers prefer to avoid losing cases at trial, which would harm their reputations.

In some ways, defense representation is even more variable and vulnerable to skewing than is the prosecution. One of the main culprits is funding. Many defense lawyers are public defenders, who are paid fixed salaries to represent large numbers of indigent clients. Others are private appointed lawyers, whom courts appoint and pay fixed fees or low hourly rates subject to caps.[18] Still others are privately retained counsel, who may receive flat fees, retainers plus hourly rates, or simply hourly rates. Some clients of private lawyers have modest means and cannot afford to pay more than a certain amount. This financial constraint may operate as a cap on representation unless the client then qualifies for and seeks court-appointed counsel. For other clients, money is no object.

One obvious problem with this patchwork quilt is that it leads to inconsistent incentives. Though not all lawyers are slaves to their pocketbooks, financial incentives influence many to varying degrees.[19] A lawyer who receives a fixed salary or a flat fee per case has no financial incentive to try cases. On the contrary, flat fees create financial incentives to plead cases out quickly in order to handle larger volumes.[20] A lawyer who receives a low hourly rate or an hourly rate subject to a low cap also has little financial incentive to try cases. The desire for a lighter workload and free time may incline that lawyer toward plea bargaining.[21] Involuntarily appointed private lawyers are especially unlikely to push cases to trial, particularly because courts often compensate poorly.[22] To put it bluntly, appointed or flat-fee defense lawyers can make more money with less time and effort by pushing clients to plead.

---

18 *See generally* Steven K. Smith & Carol J. Defrances, Bureau Of Justice Statistics, U.S. Dep't of Justice, Indigent Defense 1–2 (1996), *available at* http://www.ojp.usdoj.gov/bjs/pub/pdf/id.pdf; William J. Stuntz, *The Uneasy Relationship Between Criminal Procedure and Criminal Justice*, 107 YALE L.J. 1, 10–11 (1997) (collecting statutes that authorize payment of $30 to $40 per hour on average to appointed private counsel, subject to a $500 to $1000 cap on average in noncapital cases, which means zero compensation for hours over twenty-five or so, unless the court, on finding that the case is extraordinary, waives the cap).

19 *See* Alschuler, *The Defense Attorney's Role, supra* note 11, at 1182.

20 *See* Jones v. Barnes, 463 U.S. 745, 761 (1983) (Brennan, J., dissenting) (discussing how flat fees encourage fast dispositions); Recorder's Court Bar Ass'n v. Wayne Circuit Court, 503 N.W.2d 885, 888 (Mich. 1993) (stating that under a fixed-fee system, "[t]he incentive, if a lawyer is not paid to spend more time with and for the client, is to put in as little time as possible for the pay allowed" and that "[u]nder [this] system, a lawyer can earn $100 an hour for a guilty plea, whereas if he or she goes to trial the earnings may be $15 an hour or less" (quoting the special master's findings of fact) (internal quotation marks omitted)); Richard Klein & Robert Spangenberg, Am. Bar Ass'n, The Indigent Defense Crisis 6 (1993); Ken Armstrong et al., *Attorney Profited, but His Clients Lost*, Seattle Times, Apr. 5, 2004, at Ai (reporting that a part-time appointed defense lawyer earned large salaries for disposing of cases after little work, leaving time to earn more money in part-time private practice), 2004 WL 58931017; Ken Armstrong et al., *For Some, Free Counsel Comes at a High Cost*, Seattle Times, Apr. 4, 2004, at Ai (reporting that county's flat-fee system led appointed defense counsel to dispose of staggering caseloads through perfunctory representation, producing the highest guilty-plea rate in Washington State), 2004 WL 58930916.

21 *See* Robert Hermann et al., Counsel for the Poor 158 (1977); Richard Klein, *The Emperor* Gideon *Has No Clothes: The Empty Promise of the Constitutional Right to Effective Assistance of Counsel*, 13 Hastings Const. L.Q. 625, 672–73 (1986); David Luban, *Are Criminal Defenders Different?*, 91 Mich. L. Rev. 1729, 1757 (1993); Schulhofer, *Disaster, supra* note 11, at 1988–90.

22 *See* Eisenstein, *supra* note 20, at 173; Alschuler, *The Defense Attorney's Role, supra* note at 1259; Stuntz, *supra* note 45, at 10–11, 33; *see also* State Bar of Tex. Legal Sevices to the Poor in Criminal Matters Comm., Prosecutor Survey Results, The Status of Indigent Criminal Defense in Texas questions 18, 19, 31 [hereinafter Prosecutor Survey Results] (reporting that Texas defense lawyers who handle both retained and appointed cases devote less time to their indigent clients, are less prepared to defend them, and put on less vigorous defenses; also reporting that a large minority of Texas prosecutors believe that appointed defense counsel are undercompensated), *available at* www.uta.edu/pols/moore/indigent/prosecutor_results.htm (last visited May 4, 2004).

Encouraging pleas out of financial self-interest is part of what Abraham Blumberg famously called "[t] he [p]ractice of [l]aw as [confidence [g]ame."[23]

If a lawyer is bent on plea bargaining and does so all the time, he cannot credibly threaten to go to trial.[24] Prosecutors will offer fewer concessions to these lawyers' clients because they do not have to offer more.[25] In other words, financial conflicts of interest slant many defense attorneys toward pleas, which may mean less favorable negotiating results.[26]

Even if a particular appointed lawyer resists these financial pressures, clients still believe the adage that you get what you pay for.[27] Defendants trust appointed counsel less and so are less likely to heed their advice.[28] Thus, the psychology of trust exacerbates the structural problem of funding indigent defense. This mistrust may somewhat offset bad advice to plead, but it may also poison perfectly sound legal advice.

In contrast, privately retained lawyers who receive generous hourly rates have incentives to bill more hours and to fight matters out and go to trial if necessary. They spend more time preparing their cases and mount more vigorous defenses.[29] As a result, the client's plea-bargaining posture improves, particularly when the attorney has a strong reputation for trial prowess. Unlike appointed lawyers, retained lawyers have an economic incentive to fight hard enough to obtain good results so as to attract future paying clients.[30] Because these lawyers face less pressure to bargain, prosecutors may have to offer them more generous concessions in order to induce guilty pleas.[31] One would expect the same of defense lawyers who volunteer for court appointments to gain experience. If anything, these

---

23 Abraham S. Blumberg, *The Practice of Law as Confidence Game: Organizational Cooptation of a Profession*, 1 Law & Soc'y Rev. 15, 15 (1967); *see id.* at 24–31 (describing defense lawyers as players in a confidence game, influencing clients' choices to serve their own interests in collecting fees without doing much work; and describing defense lawyers' cooperation with prosecutors and court personnel in moving cases along).

24 Thus, defense lawyers who care about their bargaining credibility might maintain it by trying the occasional case. But many defense lawyers do not care to put in the extra work to maintain their credibility, particularly because that extra work is costly, time-consuming, and could result in humiliating defeat. If they are public defenders or handle primarily court appointments, their credibility will not improve their business because their clients have almost no choice of counsel. Even if defense counsel depend on attracting private clients, few clients are well informed enough when choosing a lawyer to monitor attorneys' reputations for toughness in bargaining.

25 *See* Alschuler, *The Defense Attorney's Role, supra* note 11, at 1185–86; Luban, *supra* note 48, at 1744–45 (noting that "harassed and overworked" public defenders tend to engage in "perfunctory advocacy" even though "[t]he credible threat of an aggressive defense … may provide a bargaining chip"); McDonald et al., *supra* note 15, at 159–60 (noting the belief that attorneys who never go to trial have less plea-bargaining leverage and thus wind up with worse deals).

26 *See* Alschuler, *The Defense Attorney's Role, supra* note 11, at 1199–1204; *see also* Recorder's Court Bar Ass'n v. Wayne Circuit Court, 503 N.W.2d 885, 888 n.7 (Mich. 1993) (quoting the special master's finding of fact that fixed-fee compensation for defense counsel "discourages plea bargaining in that the prosecutor is aware that the defense attorney has no financial incentive to go to trial and will assent to a guilty plea to a higher charge" (internal quotation marks omitted)); *id.* at 888 (quoting the special master's finding that the reimbursement system "creates a conflict between the attorney's need to be paid fully for his services and obtaining the full panoply of rights for the client" and that "[o]nly the very conscientious will do the latter against his or her own interests" (internal quotation marks omitted)). The majority of the defense attorneys interviewed by another researcher on the subject admitted that "the energy which they devoted to a case sometimes varied with the amount of the fee they were able to collect." Alschuler, *The Defense Attorney's Role, supra* note 11, at 1203 (citing R. Petty, Fee-Setting and Fee-Collection Practices Among Criminal Defense Attorneys in the State of Texas 15 (fall 1973) (unpublished manuscript, on file with the University of Texas Law School Library)).

27 *See* Alschuler, *The Defense Attorney's Role, supra* note 11, at 1242.

28 *See* Daniel W. Stiller, *Guideline Sentencing: Deepening the Distrust Between Federal Defendant and Federal Defender*, 11 Fed. Sentencing Rep. 304, 304 (1999) (exploring psychosocial factors that cause defendants to distrust their appointed counsel and so hinder defense representation); *see also* Tamara Rice Lave, *Equal Before the Law*, Newsweek, July 13, 1998, at 14, (describing her career as a public defender and reporting that "[m]y clients often think that because I'm court-appointed, I must be incompetent!;] [i]n jailhouse parlance, I am just a 'dump truck,' a person who wants nothing more than to plead them guilty").

29 Prosecutor Survey Results, *supra* note 49, questions 27, 30, 31 (noting that 56.5% of Texas prosecutors reported that retained counsel spend more time preparing than appointed counsel do, and showing that 60.7% of the prosecutors saw defense lawyers mount more prepared, more vigorous defenses for their retained clients than these same lawyers do for their court-appointed clients).

30 *See* Daniel C. Richman, *Cooperating Clients*, 56 OHIO ST. L.J. 69, 116 (1995).

31 *See* Alschuler, *The Defense Attorney's Role, supra* note 11, at 1187. If the hourly rate is high and the lawyer does not have enough other business, the lawyer may dissuade the client from taking a plea bargain that might be in the client's interests. This possibility, however, strikes me as fairly remote.

inexperienced lawyers will be too unyielding in plea bargaining because they want trial experience. The result may be the rejection of a fair plea offer and a harsher sentence after trial.[32]

Another problem is that many public defenders are overburdened. They handle hundreds of cases per year, far more than privately retained attorneys do.[33] This volume ordinarily means that pleas become the norm, making trial a less realistic threat in plea bargaining. In addition, overburdened defense attorneys cannot spend enough time to dig up all possible defenses. The result is fewer plea-bargaining chips and less favorable plea bargains. Financial incentives may also lead some private attorneys to take on more cases than they can handle, with similar results.[34]

Public defenders work closely with prosecutors and judges, developing close relationships that can influence plea bargaining. Judges and clerks put pressure on defense counsel (especially public defenders) to be pliable in bargaining. Repeat defense counsel often must yield to this pressure in order to avoid judicial reprisals against clients and perhaps to continue to receive court appointments.[35] Some clients benefit from this relationship of trust, particularly those whom the public defender believes are innocent. Conversely, public defenders must choose their battles wisely, which may require an implicit tradeoff of some clients against others.[36] There are even occasional anecdotes in which a defense lawyer agrees to trade a concession in case *A* for a harsher sentence in case *B*.[37] The inequity is particularly troubling when a private defense lawyer cashes in favors that he is owed in order to benefit paying clients but not court-appointed clients.[38]

Defense lawyers vary also in bargaining skills and knowledge. Public defenders and some private attorneys are repeat players who come to know prosecutors and judges. As a result, they develop a

---

32 *See id.* at 1260–61. Of course, this analysis assumes that the lawyer has at least some influence over the client's decision to accept or reject a plea, which seems more than plausible. It also assumes that the lawyer does not care greatly about being cooperative enough to please the court in the hope of receiving future court appointments.

33 *See* State v. Peart, 621 So. 2d 780, 784, 788–90 (La. 1993) (finding the New Orleans public defender system presumptively ineffective because counsel handled seventy active felony cases at a time, which amounted to 418 defendants over a seven-month period); Robert Burke et al., Nat'l Legal Aid & Defender Ass'n, Indigent Defense Caseloads and Common Sense: An Update 3–5 (1992); Ken Armstrong & Justin Mayo, *Frustrated Attorney: "You Just Can't Help People"*, Seattle Times, Apr. 6, 2004, at Ai (describing staggering caseloads of public defenders in parts of Washington State), 2004 WL 58931091. Occasionally public defenders stage plea-bargaining strikes, in which they hold out for trial in all cases in an effort to extract more favorable pleas from prosecutors. Sometimes the tactic works; sometimes it does not. *See* Alschuler, *The Defense Attorney's Role, supra* note 11, at 1249–53.

34 *See* Alschuler, *The Defense Attorney's Role, supra* note 11, at 1201.

35 *See id.* at 1237–39, 1240, 1261–62 & n.225; Darryl K. Brown, *Rationing Criminal Defense Entitlements: An Argument from Institutional Design*, 104 Colum. L. Rev. 801, 812 & n.46 (2004) (explaining that courts lean toward appointing defense lawyers who dispose of cases quickly instead of making extra work for judges by filing motions, investigating, or seeking expert witnesses); *see also* Prosecutor Survey Results, *supra* note 49, question 3 (noting that an attorney's reputation for moving cases is the single biggest factor in winning court appointments, and so implying that defense attorneys who wish to keep receiving court appointments must dispose of them efficiently); *cf* Margareth Etienne, *Remorse, Responsibility, and Regulating Advocacy: Making Defendants Pay for the Sins of Their Lawyers*, 78 N.Y.U. L. Rev. 2103, 2171–73 (2003) [hereinafter Etienne, *Remorse, Responsibility, and Regulating Advocacy*] (arguing that judges have incentives to penalize defendants and their counsel for zealous advocacy, leading defense counsel to tread lightly); Margareth Etienne, *The Declining Utility of the Diminished Right to Counsel in Federal Criminal Courts: An Empirical Study on the Role of Defense Attorney Advocacy Under the Sentencing Guidelines*, 92 CAL. L. REV. 425, 429–30 (2004) [hereinafter Etienne, *The Declining Utility of the Right to Counsel*] (same). Judges who prefer plea bargains can punish defendants who go to trial by increasing their post-trial sentences. In that sense, plea bargaining casts its own shadow on trials. Alschuler relates a case in which a judge imposed a 270-year sentence after trial and then told the public defender: "Don't you ever bring a case like this one into my court. You bargain it out first." Alschuler, *The Defense Attorney's Role, supra* note 11, at 1240 n. 172 (internal quotation marks omitted).

36 *See* Heumann, *supra* note 14, at 61–66, 69, 72, 74, 123–26; Alschuler, *The Defense Attorney's Role, supra* note 11, at 1210–11, 1222, 1224; *see also* Rodney Thaxton, *Professionalism and Life in the Trenches: The Case of the Public Defender*, 8 St. Thomas L. Rev. 185, 187 (1995) (comparing public defenders to battlefield triage medics, who must focus their efforts on the most serious cases).

37 *See* David A. Jones, Crime Without Punishment 120–21 (1979) (noting that defense counsel will sometimes concede that one defendant who is uncooperative or has committed a very serious crime deserves a heavier sentence in exchange for a lighter sentence for other defendants, and also noting that whites are more likely to benefit from this practice while minorities are more likely to suffer).

38 *See* Alschuler, *The Defense Attorney's Role, supra* note 11, at 1223.

feel for cases and can gauge the going rate for particular types of crimes and defendants.[39] Public defenders have a particular institutional advantage because they can pool information about judges and prosecutors with others in their offices.[40] Similarly, retained counsel who are former prosecutors have not only experience, skill, and knowledge, but also close relationships with prosecutors and judges.[41] In contrast, inexperienced lawyers have yet to develop an intuitive sense of what a case is worth. Thus, civil lawyers who take court appointments, new defense counsel, and new prosecutors start out at a disadvantage in plea bargaining.[42] Somewhere in between seasoned public defenders and neophytes are both defense attorneys who receive frequent court appointments and retained criminal-defense specialists.

Repeat players understand not only bargaining, but also trials, better than neophytes do. Trials resolve such a small percentage of criminal cases that their shadows are faint and hard to discern.[43] Public defenders in large cities have some sense of shadows because they and their colleagues try hundreds of cases before the same judges each year. Former prosecutors and public defenders have a sense as well, though their knowledge may be dated. But most other lawyers have only a smattering of unrepresentative data points and unreliable courthouse gossip from which to extrapolate.

The most experienced, most talented defense lawyers are very marketable. After they have cut their teeth as prosecutors or public defenders, many of the best lawyers earn much more in the private sector by serving well-to-do clients.[44] At the other end of the spectrum, many criminal defense lawyers provide poor representation. Ineptitude, sometimes combined with inexperience, huge caseloads, or sloth, harms many a defendant's case.[45] Needless to say, inept lawyers are disproportionately likely to represent poor defendants because those with money will be able to hire better counsel.[46]

The constraints on appointed attorneys' funding, time, and working relationships described above appear to influence outcomes. For example, public defenders are more likely to press their clients to plead guilty, or at least defendants perceive this to be true.[47] Retained counsel file more motions than do appointed counsel.[48] They also meet with their clients sooner and more often, getting a head

---

39   *See* Jonathan D. Casper, American Criminal Justice: The Defendant's Perspective 108 (1972); Heumann, *supra* note 14, at 89–91.

40   *See* Alschuler, *The Defense Attorney's Role, supra* note 11, at 1229–30.

41   *See* Rebecca Hollander-Blumoff, Note, *Getting to "Guilty": Plea Bargaining as Negotiation*, 2 Harv. Negot. L. Rev. 115, 146 n.143 (1997) (noting that ex-prosecutors often become private defense lawyers and enjoy strong relationships with current prosecutors).

42   *See* Heumann, *supra* note 14, at 76, 79, 96–97, 102; Alschuler, *The Defense Attorney's Role, supra* note 11, at 1268–70.

43   I am grateful to Al Alschuler for pointing out this problem.

44   Nevertheless, many zealous, public-spirited, and able lawyers work as public defenders even though they could earn more elsewhere. *See* LISA J. McIntyre, The Public Defender: The Practice of Law in the Shadows of Repute 83–86 (1987) (reporting that many lawyers become public defenders at least in part to do public service and reporting, based on anecdotal evidence, that many senior public defenders could take more lucrative private jobs if they wanted to); Con Garretson, *Public Defenders Lauded, Despite Offices*, Marin Indep. J. (Cal.), May 17, 2003 (discussing a grand jury report that found that many zealous public defenders "have a passion" for the job despite low pay), Lexis, News Library, Allnws File; Lave, *supra* note 55 (reporting that Lave, a Stanford Law School graduate, chose to become a public defender rather than work at a law firm).

45   *See generally* Stephen B. Bright, *Counsel for the Poor: The Death Sentence Not for the Worst Crime but for the Worst Lawyer,* 103 Yale L.J. 1835 (1994) (collecting horrifying anecdotes of poor representation).

46   But, as Alschuler notes, clients have difficulty determining a lawyer's quality. They may get word-of-mouth recommendations from inmates, bail bondsmen, or jailers (who may refer clients in exchange for commissions but have difficulty telling which lawyers are good). *See* Alschuler, *The Defense Attorney's Role, supra* note 11, at 1188–91.

47   *See* Hermann et al., *supra* note 48, at 47, 51, 94; Alschuler, *The Defense Attorney's Role, supra* note 11, at 1246–47; *see also* Roger A. Hanson et al., *Effective Adversaries for the Poor, in* The Japanese Adversary System in Context 89, 102 fig.6.5 (Malcolm M. Feeley & Setsuo Miyazawa eds., 2002) (finding, in an empirical study of eleven American communities, that public defenders resolve 95% of their cases by guilty plea, compared with 94% for assigned and contract attorneys and 91% for privately retained attorneys). Indeed, many early advocates of public defender systems touted them as a way to increase guilty-plea rates. *See* Fisher, *supra* note 17, at 194–200.

48   Pauline Houlden & Steven Balkin, *Quality and Cost Comparisons of Private Bar Indigent Defense Systems: Contract vs. Ordered Assigned Counsel,* 76 J. Crim. L. & Criminology 176, 190 (1985); *see also* Kenneth B. Nunn, *The Trial as Text: Allegory, Myth and Symbol in the Adversarial Criminal Process—A Critique of the Role of the Public Defender and a Proposal for Reform,* 32 Am. Crim. L. Rev. 743, 805 (1995).

start on learning the key facts and witnesses.[49] Clients with retained counsel plead guilty later,[50] so their lawyers have more time to investigate their cases and find weaknesses that could serve as plea-bargaining chips. Retained counsel may be more likely to take cases to trial, to win acquittals, to obtain dismissals, to avoid prison sentences, and to win charge reductions.[51]

Another factor that warps plea outcomes is the complexity of modern sentencing law, which puts a premium on lawyers' familiarity with lengthy and intricate rules. Most of the shadow-of-trial literature predates mandatory sentences and sentencing guidelines; scholars have not yet explored how these developments exacerbate discord between plea and trial outcomes. For example, federal sentencing is now governed by a thick manual of sentencing guidelines and appendices that are updated every year.[52] Thousands of cases interpret these guidelines, yielding still more complexity. Complexity favors intelligent, savvy repeat players who build up expertise and who pool information. They are in the best position to master opportunities and ambiguities that are "like little prizes hidden in the guidelines."[53] They may learn, for example, that particular prosecutors and courts are sympathetic to downward departures for single mothers with toddlers but not to departures based on health or aberrant behavior.[54] Or they may propose package deals that involve discounts for global pleas, in which

---

49   *See* Caroline Wolf Harlow, Bureau of Justice Statistics, U.S. Dep't of Justice, Defense Counsel in Criminal Cases 8 tbl.17 (2000) (reporting that 60% of state inmates and 75% of federal inmates with retained counsel met with their attorneys within the first week after arrest, compared with 37% of state inmates and 54% of federal inmates with court-appointed counsel), *available at* www.ojp.usdoj.gov/bjs/pub/pdf/dccc.pdf.

50   *See* Roger A. Hanson et al., Nat'l Ctr. for State Courts, Indigent Defenders Get the Job Done and Done Well 43–44 (1992); Pauline Houlden & Steven Balkin, *Costs and Quality of Indigent Defense: Ad Hoc vs. Coordinated Assignment of the Private Bar Within a Mixed System,* 10 Just. Sys. J. 159, 165 (1985); *cf* Blumberg, *supra* note 50, at 37 tbl.3, 38 (suggesting that time pressure causes appointed counsel to suggest pleas during initial interviews with their clients at much higher rates than do legal-aid or privately retained counsel).

51   *See* Stuntz, *supra* note 45, at 35 & nn. 123–24 (collecting sources and noting that the effects are most notable in studies done after 1980). There is, however, much disagreement about whether and how the type of counsel affects outcomes. *Cf.* Harlow, *supra* note 76, at 1, 3, 5 tbl.9, 6 tbls. 10–11, 8 tbl.17 (reporting that clients of privately retained lawyers were significantly more likely to plead not guilty, significantly less likely to plead guilty without plea bargains, significantly less likely to be incarcerated, and significantly less likely to be released on bail, but that overall acquittal and dismissal rates were roughly the same).

    Easterbrook's response is that the funding and agency-cost problems are no different at trial. *See supra* pp. 2465, 2474; *see also* Easterbrook, *Plea Bargaining, supra* note 2, at 1975–76; *cf.* Church, *supra* note 2, at 516. Agency-cost problems, however, may not be as significant at trial. To preserve their reputations, prosecutors and defense lawyers must adequately prepare opening statements, witnesses, questioning, closing arguments, and jury instructions. Failure to do these tasks at trial invites questioning, disciplinary action, and possibly reversal for ineffectiveness. In contrast, an attorney who failed to do any work at all before a plea would never be noticed. Of course, there are less visible ways to cut corners at or before trial, for example by doing insufficient work on pretrial investigation or motions. *Cf.* p. 2476 (discussing oversight of prosecutors). In addition, not all lawyers care enough about their reputations to work hard, as evidenced by anecdotes of sloppy lawyering at trial. Nonetheless, on average, reputational concerns constrain trial performance more than they do low-visibility plea bargaining. *See* Alschuler, *supra* note 37, at 151; Schulhofer, *Criminal Justice Discretion, supra* note 11, at 58–59. Schulhofer also argues that the fixed costs of going to trial are large, so there is less room to cut corners at trial. Even a bad witness examination takes a fair amount of time, so the gains from shirking are less. *See id.* There is some truth to this point, but there is still a big difference between how much time a diligent lawyer and a lazy lawyer will invest in the same factual investigation, legal research, witness preparation, or opening statement. *Cf. supra* pp. 2474–76 (discussing how similar considerations constrain prosecutors).

    A countervailing factor is that because trials are more complex than pleas, differences in lawyers' skills might matter more at trial than in plea bargaining. Those who are fearsome trial lawyers will extract better bargains in the shadow of that trial skill. Because bargaining is tempered by stable going rates for ordinary crimes, it might even out the playing field to some extent. I am indebted to George Fisher for pointing out this effect.

52   U.S. Sentencing Guidelines Manual (2003).

53   Ilene H. Nagel & Stephen J. Schulhofer, *A Tale of Three Cities: An Empirical Study of Charging and Bargaining Practices Under the Federal Sentencing Guidelines,* 66 S. Cal. L. Rev. 501, 530 (1992); *see also id.* at 529–30 (paraphrasing one public defender as saying "there are numerous opportunities for a creative defense lawyer to find paths to a plea concession," and reporting the observation of probation officers that prosecutors are "outgunned" because of the public defenders' "commitment to the idea that knowledge [of the guidelines] is power" (internal quotation marks ommitted)).

54   *See generally* Michael S. Gelacak et al., *Departures Under the Federal Sentencing Guidelines: An Empirical and Jurisprudential Analysis,* 81 Minn. L. Rev. 299 (1996) (discussing judicial trends in discretionary departures from the Guidelines); Dana L. Shoenberg, *Departures for Family Ties and Responsibilities After Koon,* 9 Fed. Sentencing Rep. 292, 292–93 (1997) (noting that conservative courts such as the Fourth Circuit greatly restrict departures for family circumstances, while more liberal courts such as the Second Circuit readily allow these departures).

all codefendants plead guilty in exchange for an extra sentence reduction.[55] Guidelines neophytes, in contrast, may be ignorant of these opportunities unless they pool information with more experienced colleagues.[56] Knowledge of possible downward departures and adjustments can make a difference of years to a defendant's sentence.

Familiarity with mandatory minima and maxima, and with techniques for evading them, can likewise greatly affect sentences. For example, many federal drug crimes carry mandatory minimum penalties of five or ten years' imprisonment.[57] Knowledgeable defense lawyers who act quickly may strike early charge-bargains before a grand jury indicts. They can, for instance, suggest a plea to using a telephone in the course of drug trafficking in lieu of a substantive drug-trafficking charge. The reward for a quick plea bargain may be a four-year maximum sentence instead of a five- or ten-year minimum.[58] If the defense lawyer suggests this deal only after indictment, the prosecutor may have more difficulty persuading his or her supervisor to drop an already filed charge.[59]

The Federal Sentencing Guidelines have put a huge premium on another plea-bargaining technique: cooperating with the government. This venerable tactic has become much more important in recent years as one of the few ways around sentencing guidelines and mandatory minima. The Federal Guidelines impose stiff sentences and abolish parole. Mandatory minima often require offenders to spend five or ten years in prison before release, particularly for drug and gun convictions.[60] In exchange for substantially assisting the investigation or prosecution of others, defendants may earn sentences

---

55   *See* United States v. Carrozza, 4 F.3d 70, 86 (1st Cir. 1993) (indicating that the trial court departed downward as reward for a package-deal plea that obviated a lengthy trial); United States v. Mosquera, Nos. CR 92-1228 (JBW), CR 93-0036 (JBW), 1994 WL 593977, at *13–15 (E.D.N.Y. Mar. 17, 1994) (report of coordinating counsel appointed by the court in *United States v. Mosquera,* 816 F. Supp. 168, *aff'd mem.,* 48 F.3d 1214 (2d Cir. 1994)).

    Sometimes public defenders use their large caseloads to negotiate package deals of a different sort. By disposing of a large number of cases at once, they can extract larger discounts than a private lawyer with a single case could. *See* Jones, *supra* note 64, at 121–22; *cf. supra* note 60 (discussing strikes by defense counsel to gain bargaining leverage).

56   *See* Douglas A. Berman, *From Lawlessness to Too Much Law? Exploring the Risk of Disparity from Differences in Defense Counsel Under Guidelines Sentencing,* 87 Iowa L. Rev. 435, 444–57 (2002); Alan J. Chaset, *A Teacher at the Top: Another Reason To Have a Representative of the Criminal Defense Bar on the Sentencing Commission,* 11 Fed. Sentencing Rep. 309, 309 (1999) (reporting that many defense lawyers in an advanced sentencing seminar were unaware of sentencing guidelines complexities that could help their clients); *id.* at 309–310 (concluding that "our current guideline system may involve too much law for the average practitioner to keep current with" and that "[e]ven experienced defense counsel must devote considerable time and energy in order to stay fully conversant"); Lisa M. Farabee, *Disparate Departures Under the Federal Sentencing Guidelines: A Tale of Two Districts,* 30 Conn. L. Rev. 569, 616 (1998) (asserting that defense counsel inexperience with the complexity of the Federal Guidelines impairs sentencing advocacy); Owen S. Walker, *Litigation-Enmeshed Sentencing: How the Guidelines Have Changed the Practice of Federal Criminal Law,* 25 U.C. Davis L. Rev. 639, 640, 649 (1992) (reporting that the Guidelines' creation of myriad new rules has given defense counsel many more ways to make mistakes). The same complexity may, of course, bewilder inexperienced prosecutors and limit their bargaining tools.

57   *See, e.g.,* 21 U.S.C. § 841(a)(1), (b)(1)(A)–(B) (2000).

58   *Compare id.* (mandating five- and ten-year minima for substantive drug trafficking), *with id.* § 843(b), (d) (providing a four-year maximum for using a telephone in drug trafficking). *See generally* Frank O. Bowman, III & Michael Heise, *Quiet Rebellion? Explaining Nearly a Decade of Declining Federal Drug Sentences,* 86 IOWA L. Rev. 1043, 1121–22 (2001) (explaining that pleas to "such [phone charges] are almost always Guidelines-evading plea bargains"); Rodney J. Uphoff, *The Criminal Defense Lawyer as Effective Negotiator: A Systemic Approach,* 2 CLINICAL L. REV. 73, 112 (1995) (advising defense counsel to intervene with prosecutors before formal charges are filed to persuade prosecutors to select lesser charges or even none at all).

59   *See* Fisher, *supra* note 17, at 229 (noting that pre-charge bargaining "avoids awkward explanations to superiors and the public about why prosecutors are abandoning charges they once thought worth bringing").

60   *See, e.g.,* 21 U.S.C. § 841(a)(1), (b)(1)(A) (prescribing a ten-year mandatory minimum sentence for various drug offenses, with higher minima for recidivists); 18 U.S.C. § 924(c) (2000) (prescribing a five-year mandatory minimum penalty for using or carrying a firearm during and in relation to a crime of violence or drug trafficking, with a twenty-five year penalty for recidivists); *see also* U.S. Sentencing Comm'n, 2001 Sourcebook of Federal Sentencing Statistics 81 fig. j (2002) [hereinafter Sentencing Sourcebook] (reporting that the mean federal sentences are 115 months in crack cocaine cases, 77 months in powder cocaine cases, and 88.5 months in methamphetamine cases), *available at* www.ussc.gov/ANNRPT/2001/SBTOC01.htm.

far lower than the Guidelines and even mandatory minima would otherwise provide.[61] Cooperation often requires swift action. For example, police may arrest a drug courier and ask the courier to wear a tape recorder the next day while completing a planned drug delivery.[62] Or a prosecutor may indict twenty members of a violent gang and offer cooperation agreements to the first two who will testify against the others. In other words, the first one in the door gets the deal.

A defendant's lawyer can make a big difference in the cooperation process. Experienced criminal defense attorneys understand the potential benefits of fast cooperation and may tell their clients this fact. As repeat players, they may also have developed bonds of trust with prosecutors that can facilitate negotiations over cooperation. A prosecutor who needs only one cooperator in a five-defendant case may incline toward offering the cooperation deal to the client of the experienced attorney. Some experienced attorneys, however, may resist having their clients cooperate. Their motivations range from ideological opposition to snitching, to receiving their fees from a crime boss, to fear that a reputation as a snitches' lawyer will drive away clients.[63] Inexperienced attorneys may not understand the benefits of quick cooperation, or they may be less skilled in persuading prosecutors to offer agreements to their clients. Indigent defendants may distrust public defenders' recommendations to cooperate because they already fear that their free lawyers are pushing pleas to get rid of cases.[64] Also, overburdened public defenders may not meet with their clients in time to arrange for them to cooperate. When quick cooperation is at a premium, these clients may lose out to codefendants who can afford to retain speedier private counsel.[65] These variations create inequities among codefendants, punishing similarly situated defendants differently based on their lawyers' skills, temperaments, and workloads.

Finally, a defense lawyer's adversarial stance may reduce the defendant's plea discount. The Federal Sentencing Guidelines significantly discount the sentences of defendants who accept responsibility in a timely manner, typically by pleading guilty. Defendants whose lawyers take extensive discovery or file many motions may suffer retaliation by judges and prosecutors and thus lose some or all of this discount.[66]

---

61   *See* 18 U.S.C.A. § 3553(e) (West Supp. 2003); U.S. Sentencing Guidelines Manual § 5K1.1 (2003); *see also* Sentencing Sourcebook, *supra* note 87, at 18 tbl.8 (reporting that 17.1% of federal defendants received substantial-assistance departures).

62   *See* Stephanos Bibas, *The Right To Remain Silent Helps Only the Guilty*, 88 Iowa L. Rev. 421, 425–26 (2003).

63   *See* Kim Taylor-Thompson, *Individual Actor v. Institutional Player: Alternating Visions of the Public Defender*, 84 GEO. L.J. 2419, 2457–60 (1996) (noting that community defender offices may sometimes adopt blanket rules against representing clients who wish to "snitch"); *see also* Richman, *supra* note 57, at 117–26 (describing reasons why defense attorneys may deter cooperation).

64   *See* Stiller, *supra* note 55, at 305.

65   *See* Harlow, *supra* note 76, at 8 tbl.17 (citing statistics that show that privately retained counsel meet with their clients more swiftly than do appointed counsel).

66   *See* Etienne, *Remorse, Responsibility, and Regulating Advocacy*, *supra* note 62, at 2104; Etienne, *The Declining Utility of the Right to Counsel*, *supra* note 62, at 474–80; Stiller, *supra* note 55, at 305–06.

Do You Get What You Pay For?

Type of Counsel and Its Effect on Criminal Court Outcomes

Richard D. Hartley, Holly Ventura Miller, and Cassia Spohn

Introduction

The Sixth Amendment to the U.S. Constitution states that "In all criminal prosecutions, the accused shall enjoy the right to have the assistance of counsel for his defense." For many years this was interpreted to mean that if a defendant had an attorney, this attorney could accompany him to court. This was not helpful, however, to the many defendants too poor to hire an attorney and who were therefore prosecuted, convicted and sentenced without legal representation. The Supreme Court eventually recognized that defendants could not be guaranteed due process without the assistance of counsel. Supreme Court decisions in *Powell v. Alabama* (287 US 45 (1932)); *Johnson v. Zerbst* (304 US 458 (1938)); *Gideon v. Wainwright* (372 US 335 (1963)), and *Argersinger v. Hamlin* (407 US 25 (1972)) required federal and state jurisdictions to provide counsel for those who were indigent. Subsequent rulings have also extended the right to counsel to other "critical stages." Today, indigent defendants must be provided with counsel during most proceedings in the criminal justice process.

This expanded interpretation of the Sixth Amendment spurred the development of a variety of systems for representing indigent defendants. At the federal level and in many large urban jurisdictions, indigent defendants are represented by government-funded public defenders. Other jurisdictions rely on local bar associations to act as liaisons to the courts, appointing attorneys to represent indigent defendants on a case-by-case basis, or contracting with law firms to take care of indigent caseloads. Some jurisdictions also use a combination of these systems (Wolf-Harlow, 2000).

The expansion of the right to counsel specifically led to a dramatic increase in the number of public defender offices in the United States. The number of public defender offices grew from seven in 1951 (McIntyre, 1987), to 136 following the *Gideon* decision, to 573 following the *Argersinger* decision. By 2000, roughly 4.2 million indigent defendants were represented by publicly funded counsel (public defender offices represented 82 percent of these defendants) at a cost of 1.2 billion dollars (Defrances & Litras, 2000)). Nationally, about 66 percent of federal felony defendants and 82 percent of state felony defendants were represented by public defenders (Wolf-Harlow, 2000). As these statistics illustrate, public defenders are responsible for the lion's share of indigent defense in the nation.

Public Defense Counsel

The above case law has ensured that most defendants are provided with counsel at critical stages in the criminal justice system. Questions, however, have been raised regarding the quality of legal representation that is afforded by public defenders. As Sterling (1983:166) noted, "the general suspicion is that equal justice is not available to rich and poor alike." Critics charge that defendants represented by public defenders do not get the same quality of legal services as defendants who can afford to retain private attorneys and, as a result, are more likely to be convicted and receive harsher punishments. The charge, in other words, is that Gideon's promise is unfulfilled. That "states have largely, and often outrageously, failed to meet the Court's constitutional command" (Harvard Law Review, 2000:2062). Bright (1994) has similarly argued that although the right to counsel is fundamental to safeguard the rights of those accused of crimes, it has received the least protection.

The purpose of the current study, therefore, is to determine whether defendants represented by a public defender receive significantly different case processing outcomes than defendants who hire a private attorney. This study specifically examines the effect of public defense on a series of four decision-making stages: one release decision (whether the defendant had bail set by the judge or was released on their own recognizance), one plea bargaining decision (whether the primary charge filed by prosecutor was reduced), and two sentencing decisions (whether the defendant was incarcerated and the length of the sentence). No study to date has focused explicitly on the effect of public defense on multiple decision points in the criminal justice process. The current study is an attempt to add to the existing research examining this important question.

Public Defenders Versus Private Attorneys

Some of the criticism of public defense counsel focuses on their non-adversarial relationship with other members of the courtroom workgroup. Public defenders, like prosecutors and judges, want to ensure the smooth and efficient processing of cases; as a result, their relationships with other members of the courthouse community may be characterized more by cooperation than conflict (Bowen, 2009; Eisenstein, Fleming, & Nardulli, 1987; Fleming, Nardulli, & Eisenstein, 1992). This suggests that public defenders play an ambiguous role in the American criminal justice system. Although they are advocates for protecting defendants' rights and saviors for those who are indigent, they are also viewed as "double agents" (Blumberg, 1967; Uphoff, 1992; Worden, 1991) who work not only for their clients but also, and ultimately, for the state. Critics charge that this co-optation by the state means that public defenders are "too quick to bargain away the precious rights of their under-privileged clients" (Albert-Goldberg & Hartman, 1983:67) and too willing to believe that their clients are guilty (Alpert, 1979; Sudnow, 1965).

Private attorneys, on the other hand, are not bound by this court community; largely because they are not as much a regular part of it as the public defender. In other words, private attorneys may not have other cases in the same courtroom with the same prosecutor and same judge. As such, they are not concerned with maintaining relationships with prosecutors and judges or with system efficiency via smooth and efficient case processing in the way that public defenders are.

Others argue that the workgroup's emphasis on cooperation means public defenders will be able to negotiate more favorable outcomes for their clients than privately retained attorneys (Champion, 1989; Stover & Eckhart, 1975). For example, Skolnick (1967) suggested that defendants represented by public defenders will get better plea bargains because prosecutors are more willing to share information with public defenders than with privately retained attorneys. Other researchers agree with this assessment citing studies that reveal criminal defendants represented by public defenders do not fare worse than those represented by private attorneys (Casper, 1972; Levin, 1977; McIntyre, 1987; Oaks & Lehman, 1970; Silverstein, 1965; Wheeler & Wheeler, 1980). These researchers suggest that critics "have tended to underestimate the quality of defense provided by the public defender" (Skolnick, 1967, p. 67). Wice (1985) concludes that the public defender is able to establish a working relationship with prosecutors and judges "in which the exchange of favors, so necessary to greasing the squeaky wheel of justice, can directly benefit the indigent defendant" (p. 65). As part of the courtroom workgroup, in other words, public defenders are in better positions than private attorneys to negotiate favorable plea bargains and to mitigate punishment.

Overall, the evidence regarding the quality of legal representation provided by privately retained attorneys and public defenders is mixed. Wolf-Harlow (2000) reports that conviction rates are similar for both types of attorneys; in state courts, the guilty plea rate was 72.8 percent for defendants represented by privately retained attorneys and 71 percent for those represented by public defenders. Moreover, the percentage of defendants convicted at trial was nearly identical for privately retained attorneys (4.3 percent) and public defenders (4.4 percent). In federal courts, the guilty plea rate was 84.6 percent for defendants represented by privately retained attorneys and 87.1 percent for those represented by public defenders. The percentage of defendants convicted at trial was 6.4 percent and 5.2 percent for privately retained attorneys and public defenders, respectively. Approximately 90 percent of defendants in federal court and 75 percent of defendants in state courts in the 75 largest counties were found guilty, either at trial or through a guilty plea, regardless of the type of attorney.

Sentencing outcomes by attorney type are also varied (Wolf-Harlow, 2000). In federal courts, 88 percent of defendants with public defenders, but only 77 percent of those with privately retained attorneys, were incarcerated. The difference was even larger in state courts: 71 percent versus 54 percent. The pattern for the length of sentence, however, was just the opposite. In federal courts, the average sentence was 62 months for defendants represented by privately retained attorneys, compared to 58 months for those represented by public defenders. The figures for state courts were similar at 38 months for private attorneys and 31 months for public defenders. These statistics suggest mixed outcomes; similar conviction rates for both attorney types, higher incarceration rates for those represented by public defenders, but longer average sentence lengths for those represented by privately retained counsel.

Despite the mixed results above, there is some additional criticism of the public defender system relating to large caseloads and limited resources. Weitzer (1996:313), for example, contends that many public defenders are "grossly underpaid, poorly trained, or simply lack the resources and time to prepare for a case—a pattern documented in cases ranging from the most minor to the most consequential capital crimes" (see also Bright, 1994). Recent reports (American Bar Association, 2004; 2009; Spangenburg Group, 2009) have also highlighted the high caseloads and lack of resources that plague public defender offices around the country and the effect it has on providing adequate defense. Casper's (1972) qualitative research with inmates in a Connecticut jail suggests that even indigent defendants have similarly negative views of public defenders. When Casper asked a prisoner whether or not he had a lawyer when he went to court, the defendant replied no, he didn't—he had a public defender. These criticisms have spurred some empirical research which has attempted to examine the effectiveness of the public defender.

Empirical Research on Attorney Type and Case Outcomes

Empirical research examining the relationship between attorney type and case outcomes is limited but generally reveals that defendants represented by public defenders are not at a disadvantage. For example, Hanson and Ostrom's (1998) study of nine state trial courts revealed that public defenders fare as well as privately retained attorneys in obtaining positive outcomes for their clients. Their analysis of conviction rates revealed no advantage for either type of attorney. Wheeler and Wheeler (1980) and Taylor, Stanley, DeFlorio, and Seekamp (1973) similarly found no effect for attorney type in their study of defendants in Houston and San Diego. Nardulli (1986) found that attorney type had no effect regarding securing plea bargains. Spohn and Holleran (2000) studied three large urban jurisdictions and found no effects for type of attorney on the odds of incarceration. Similarly, research in a northern Florida county by Williams (2002) found no effect of type of attorney for odds of probation, incarceration or sentence length. Finally, Wilson (1984), and Walker, Spohn, and Delone (2004) found attorney type was less predictive of case outcomes than offense seriousness, the defendant's prior record, pretrial status, and type of disposition.

There have been only a few studies that have indicated that privately retained attorneys are able to secure more favorable outcomes (see Beck & Shumsky, 1997; Gitelman, 1971; Nagel, 1973). In a recent study, Hoffman and his colleagues (2005) examined the effectiveness of public defenders vis-à-vis private counsel using felony data from Denver, CO. Results suggested that offenders represented by public defenders received significantly longer prison sentences than those who employed private counsel. There are also studies that report that the effect of attorney type is influential only in certain contexts (see Cohen, Semple, & Crew, 1983; Holmes et al., 1996; Kelly, 1976; Levine, 1975; Spohn, Gruhl & Welch, 1981–82; & Sterling, 1983). This research, however, also produces mixed results; at some stages in the criminal justice process those who retain private attorneys get more favorable outcomes, while at other stages, those with public defenders benefit.

Although the results of the research conducted to date are somewhat inconsistent, the studies generally reveal that type of counsel is not a strong predictor of case processing decisions. However, the inconsistency of the findings, coupled with the fact that most of the extant research has not empirically tested the effect of attorney type across a number of outcomes, suggests that questions regarding the effectiveness of public defenders vis-à-vis private attorneys have not been fully addressed. Previous research has revealed that certain offenders may experience a cumulative disadvantage (Mufioz, Lopez & Stewart, 1998; Spohn, 2009; Zatz, 1987) where "differences at early stages of decision-making (e.g., bail) can accumulate and be compounded further in the system" (Zatz, 1987, p. 307). Examining the effects of attorney type across different case processing stages will also allow an examination of this phenomenon for indigent defendants.

Methodology

DATA

The data for this study are from Cook County (Chicago), Illinois, and are a random sample of 2850 offenders convicted of felonies in Cook County Circuit Court.[1] Cook County represents a large Midwestern jurisdiction which is similar to other large, urban jurisdictions in the country. At the time the data was collected, the jurisdiction had crime rates above the national average; today this is still the case. Illinois also has a determinate sentencing structure, meaning that the sentences imposed by judges are for a fixed term. The classification for felonies in Cook County in decreasing seriousness is as follows: First degree murder, Class X, Class 1, Class 2, Class 3, and Class 4 felonies. Some classes of offenses are not eligible for probation; they must be sentenced to incarceration. These offenders include those who are convicted of first-degree murder or attempted first-degree murder,[2] or a Class X felony.[3]

The courtroom workgroup in Cook County is organized at the local municipal level and is relatively large; for the year that the data was collected, there were 49 judges assigned to the criminal division of the Cook County Circuit Court, 360 assistant state's attorneys, and 113 public defenders. Both prosecutors and public defenders are assigned to courtrooms and handle all of the cases allocated to that courtroom. There are three assistant state's attorneys, and either two or three public defenders assigned to each courtroom. Prosecutors remain in a courtroom for at least six months while public defenders remain from 12 to 18 months. Public defenders, therefore, would presumably work closely with the same judges for at least a year to 18 months and with the same prosecutors for at least 6 months.

DEPENDENT VARIABLES

This study analyzes the effect of attorney type at four critical court processing stages: the bail decision, a plea bargaining decision, and two sentencing decisions. The dependent variable for the bail decision is a measure of whether the defendant was released on recognizance (ROR) or had bail set by the

---

1   The data utilized for this study are from 1993 and were collected by the third author as part of a larger research project.

2   Murder was therefore removed from the analyses of the ROR decision and the incarceration decision. Murder cases, however, were included in the analyses of the primary charge reduction decision (almost 30 percent of murderers had their charge reduced) and the sentence length decision.

3   Despite the requirement by Illinois law that class X offenders cannot be given probation, class X offenses were left in the analyses because roughly 8 percent of those convicted of a class X offense were not incarcerated; further, 10 percent of defendants indicted on a class X offense were released ROR, and 21.5 percent had their primary charge reduced.

judge. Initially, the analysis intended to assess the impact of attorney type on the defendant's pretrial status (whether the defendant was in custody pretrial or released), however, because being released may be a function of ability to pay bail, we decided to use a measure of whether or not bail was set in the case. Furthermore, although the release decision may be a function of the seriousness of the offense, the defendant's attorney may also be an important influence in advocating for the release of the defendant. Ideally, the release decision is based upon the judge's assessment of dangerousness and risk for reoffending or absconding. We argue that it is important therefore to control for theoretically relevant influences of this decision (seriousness of offense and priors) to assess if attorney type is influential net of these effects. If attorney type is a significant predictor of this decision, it would suggest that judges may use legally irrelevant factors in assessments of dangerousness and risk.

The dependent variable for the plea bargaining decision is a measure of whether the defendant had their primary charge reduced. In other words, this is an analysis of whether the original filed charge was greater than the conviction charge. Finally, the dependent variables for the two sentencing decisions include a dichotomous measure of whether the defendant was incarcerated, and for those incarcerated the length of the sentence imposed.

INDEPENDENT VARIABLES

Type of counsel (public defender or private attorney) is the primary independent variable in this study. Other independent variables include both offender and case characteristics that previous research has found to be influential of case processing outcomes. For instance, previous research has revealed that judicial decisions are influenced by offender characteristics including gender (Daly, 1987; Spohn & Beichner, 2000; Steffensmeier, Kramer, & Streifel, 1993), race or ethnicity (Spohn & Holleran, 2001; Steffensmeier & Demuth, 2000; Steffensmeier et al., 1998), and age (Spohn & Holleran, 2000; Steffensmeier et al., 1998; Steffensmeier & Motivans, 2000). These extra-legal factors are therefore also controlled for by including the offender's race, ethnicity, gender (1 = male), age, and employment status (1 = unemployed). Race/ethnicity is measured using three dummy variables: black, Hispanic and white. In all of the models, whites are the reference category. Age is a continuous variable.

Legally relevant variables include prior criminal record, whether a weapon was used during the offense, and whether the defendant was under some type of criminal justice control at the time of the offense. In order to control for an offender's prior criminal record, a variable for number of prior felony convictions (which ranges from zero to six) was included. The variables measuring offense seriousness vary according to the dependent variable. For the bail and charge reduction models, the number of filed charges and the statutory classification of the most serious filed charge are included in the model. For the in/out and sentence length decisions, the number of conviction charges and the statutory classification of the most serious conviction charge are included; for the latter three outcomes, pretrial status will also be included in the model.

The type of offense is also controlled for using variables measuring whether the offender committed a violent, property, or drug offense; violent offenses serve as the reference category. The four case processing outcomes are analyzed using both logistic regression and ordinary least squares (OLS) regression. Logistic regression is employed to analyze whether the defendant was released ROR, whether the primary charge was reduced, and the incarceration decision. Finally, OLS regression is used to analyze sentence length.

Results

Dependent and independent variables, their codes, and frequencies are displayed in Table 3.3.1 Regarding the dependent variables, a majority of the defendants (71.3%) had bail set in their case, most defendants (92.1%) did not have their primary charge reduced, nearly two-thirds (60.6%) of the defendants in Cook County were sent to prison, and the average sentence length was roughly 56 months, or almost five years in prison. Regarding the independent variables, the data in Table 3.3.1 show that of the 2850 defendants, 2610 (91.5%) were represented by public defenders and 240 (8.5%) retained a private attorney. Eighty-one percent of defendants were black, 10.4 percent were Hispanic and the other 8.6 percent were white. Most of the defendants were male (90.5%), unemployed (72.2%), with a mean age of 27.2 years. The largest percentage of cases were class two offenses, drug offenses made up over half of the cases (54.5%) and the typical offender was not under criminal justice control at the time of the offense (80.1%) and did not use a weapon in the commission of their offense (83.9%). The mean number of prior felony convictions was 1.09, and the mean number of filed, and conviction, charges was 1.74 and 1.14 respectively.

Tables 3.3.2 and 3.3.3 present the results of the logistic and OLS regression analyses testing the effect of attorney type on the four case processing outcomes.[4] Table 3.3.2 presents the results of the logistic regression analysis for the bail (ROR) decision[5] and the primary charge reduction (plea bargaining) decision.[6] The results in Table 3.3.2 indicate that attorney type was not a significant predictor of either the decision to release the defendant on their own recognizance or the decision to reduce the defendant's primary charge. In other words, whether a defendant was represented by a public defender or a privately retained attorney did not affect a defendant's likelihood of being released or having their primary charge reduced. Some of the classes of the filed charge, however, are significant in the release and charge reduction decisions. Those charged with offenses other than Class X offenses were all more likely to be released ROR. Results from the offense type variables reveal that property and drug offenders are over 3 and 6 times more likely to be released ROR than violent offenders.

Regarding the primary charge reduction model, all defendants charged with offenses other than class X were significantly less likely to have their primary charge reduced. From these results, it appears that the less serious the case, the more likely the defendant is to be released but the less likely they are to have their primary charge reduced. Regarding offense type, however, drug offenders are more likely than violent offenders to have their primary charge reduced.

Regarding other legal variables, although the number of filed charges or use of a weapon did not affect the release decision, defendants with prior felony convictions and defendants under criminal justice control at the time of offense had reduced odds of ROR. For the primary charge reduction model none of these variables reached significance. The pretrial status of the defendant was influential of the primary charge reduction decision; those who were released were roughly one and a half times more likely to have their primary charge reduced than those who were detained. The disposition of the

---

4   Collinearity diagnostics indicate that variance inflation factor scores are all within acceptable ranges (<4).

5   Only one defendant charged with murder was released; murder cases were therefore excluded from this analysis. Process related variables were also not included in this model due to obvious time order assumptions.

6   There were only three out of 675 defendants charged with class 4 offenses that had the primary charge reduced, therefore, these cases were excluded from the analysis.

Table 3.3.1. Dependent and independent variables: Codes and frequencies

Variable	Code	N	%	Missing
Dependent Variables				
Pretrial Status (ROR)	1 = released	818	28.7	
	0 = detained or	2032	71.3	
	had bail set			
Primary Charge Reduced	1 = yes	225	7.9	
	0 = no	2625	92.1	
Sentenced to Prison	1 = yes	1726	60.6	
	0 = no	1124	39.4	
Mean Sentence Length			56.1	
Independent Variables				
Private Attorney	1 = yes	240	8.5	0
	0 = no	2610	91.5	
Offender's Race/Ethnicity	White	245	8.6	
	Black	2308	81	0
	Hispanic	297	10.4	
Offender's Gender	1 = Male	2581	90.5	0
	0 = Female	269	9.5	
Offender's Mean Age			27.2	0
Employment Status	1 = unemployed	1783	72.2	381
	0 = employed	686	27.8	
Class of Most Serious Filed Charge				
Class X		344	12.1	0
Class 1		509	17.9	
Class 2		948	33.3	
Class 3		374	13.1	
Class 4		675	23.7	
Class of Most Serious Conviction Charge				
Class X		280	9.8	0
Class 1		465	16.3	
Class 2		938	33.1	
Class 3		413	14.5	
Class 4		754	26.5	
Offense Type				
Violent		447	18.1	0
Property		677	27.4	0
Drug		1345	54.5	0
Mean Number of Prior			1.09	0
Felony Convictions				
Under Some Type of CJ Control	1 = yes	567	19.9	0
at the time of the offense	0 = no	2283	80.1	
Guilty Plea	1 = yes	2578	90.5	0
	0 = no	272	9.5	
Mean Number of Filed Charges			1.74	0
Mean Number of Conviction Charges			1.14	0
Weapon Used In Offense	1 = yes	447	16.1	78
	0 = no	2325	83.9	

Table 3.3.2. Logistic regression models of whether or not the defendant was released ROR[a] and whether or not the defendant had the primary charge reduced[b]

	Released ROR			Primary Charge Reduced		
	b	S.E.	EXP (β)	b	S.E.	EXP (β)
Type of Counsel	.10	.18	1.11	.37	.24	1.45
Legal Variables						
Class of Most Serious						
Filed Charge[c]						
Class1	.59*	.26	1.81	−.66*	.24	.52
Class2	.98*	.25	2.65	−1.78*	.26	.17
Class3	1.32*	.29	3.74	−2.11*	.36	.12
Class4	1.32*	.26	3.74			
Offense Type[d]						
Property	1.16*	.28	3.20	.39	.34	1.48
Drug	1.80*	.28	6.04	.77*	.31	2.16
# of Filed Charges	−.02	.03	1.02	.04	.02	1.04
# of Prior felony Convictions	−.66*	.06	.52	−.13	.08	.87
Under CJ Control	−.45*	.15	.64	−.14	.24	.87
Use of a Weapon	−.46	.25	.66	−.17	.29	1.18
Process variables						
Pretrial Status			.48*	.19	1.62	
Guilty Plea			.32	.25	1.38	
Offender Characteristics						
Male	−.66*	.16	.52	.02	.27	1.02
Age	−.01	.01	.99	.01	.01	1.01
Race/Ethnicity[e]						
Black	−.03	.19	.97	−.37	.29	.69
Hispanic	.22	.23	1.24	.33	.32	1.38
Unemployed	−.45*	.11	.64	−.14	.18	.87
Constant		−1.57		−1.97		
Nagelkerke R²		.29		.17		
N		2370		1869		

a. Dependent variable: Released on own recognizance minus murder cases.

b. Dependent variable: Primary charge reduced minus class 4 offenses.

c. Class X offenses serve as the reference category.

d. Violent offenses serve as the reference category.

e. White offenders serve as the reference category.

* Statistically Significant at .05 level.

STAT HELP!

Because the authors use logistic regression, the findings can be interpreted as the odds of (a) being released on recognizance and (b) getting the primary charged reduced. It is easiest to look at the column labeled "EXP(β)." For example, the EXP(β) value for "Type of Counsel" under "Released ROR" shows that the odds of being released on recognizance for those with a private attorney are 1.11 times higher than those without a private attorney. The lack of an asterisk (*), though, indicates that type of attorney does not have a *statistically significant* effect, meaning the odds of being released on recognizance are not statistically different for defendants with and without private attorneys. Stated differently, type of attorney is not influencing whether defendants get released on recognizance. A value less than 1 in this column would suggest lower, as opposed to higher, odds.

Table 3.3.3. Logistic regression model of incarceration decision[a] and OLS regression model of sentence length decision[b]

	Incarceration			Sentence Length		
	b	S.E.	EXP (β)	b	S.E.	β
Type of Counsel	.19	.24	1.21	-.75	4.69	.01
Legal Variables						
Class of Most Serious						
Charge[c]						
Class1	-.73*	.33	.48	-46.72*	4.58	-.34
Class2	-1.40*	.32	.26	-57.83*	4.25	-.51
Class3	-1.57*	.33	.21	-87.38*	4.37	-.58
Class4	-1.80*	.33	.17	-76.85*	4.86	-.55
Offense Type[d]						
Property	-.38	.25	.68	-13.37*	4.39	-.11
Drug	-.23	.25	.80	-26.35*	4.37	-.24
# of Conviction Charges	.43*	.17	1.54	8.44*	2.02	.09
# of Prior felony Convictions	1.22*	.08	3.37	.80	.89	.02
Under CJ Control	.47*	.17	1.60	3.34	2.60	.03
Use of a Weapon	.38	.25	1.46	8.64*	4.33	.07
Process variables						
Pretrial Status	-2.23*	.13	.11	-4.14	3.32	-.03
Guilty Plea	.42	.21	1.52	-11.33*	4.03	-.06
Primary Charge Reduced	.08	.22	1.08	-.86	4.45	-.01
Offender Characteristics						
Male	.86*	.22	2.36	-.77	5.53	-.01
Age	-.01	.01	.99	.32*	.15	.05
Race/Ethnicity[e]						
Black	.54*	.23	1.71	3.32	5.13	-.02
Hispanic	.74*	.28	2.10	4.82	6.10	.03
Unemployed	.12	.14	1.12	7.55*	2.70	.06
Constant			-.47		105.47	
Nagelkerke R²/Adjusted R²			.61		.37	
N			2391		1726	

a. Dependent variable: Sentenced to prison minus murder cases.
b. Dependent variable: Sentence length in months for those incarcerated.
c. Class X offenses serve as the reference category.
d. Violent offenses serve as the reference category.
e. White offenders serve as the reference category.
* Statistically Significant at .05 level.

STAT HELP!

Similar to the previous table, it is easiest to look at the "EXP(β)" column under "Incarceration." For example, the odds of being incarcerated for those with a private attorney are 1.21 times higher than those without a private attorney. For the "Sentence Length" results, it is easiest to look at the "b" values. A negative value indicates a decreased sentence length and a positive value indicates an increased sentence length. For instance, having private counsel decreases the sentence length. Because there are no asterisks (*), though, we can infer that incarceration decisions and sentence lengths for defendants with and without private attorneys are not statistically different. Stated differently, type of attorney is not influencing whether defendants get incarcerated and their length of incarceration.

case (plea or trial), however, had no effect on the decision to reduce the primary charge. Examination of the offender characteristics reveals that males and those unemployed are less likely to be released ROR than female and employed defendants but the defendant's race, ethnicity, or age were not influential of the release decision. None of the offender characteristics is a significant predictor of having the primary charge reduced.

Table 3.3.3 presents the logistic regression model for the in/out decision[7] and the OLS model for the sentence length decision.[8] The results of these models indicate that type of counsel is not a significant predictor of the likelihood of incarceration or the length of sentence handed out by the judge. In other words, the type of attorney a defendant is represented by does not significantly influence these judicial sentencing decisions. All of the class of conviction charge variables, however, are significant and negative. Defendants convicted of offense classes other than Class X are all less likely to be incarcerated and for those sent to prison, received shorter average sentences. The offense type variables did not reach significance for the incarceration model but property and drug offenders receive sentences that are, on average, 13 and 26 months less respectively than the sentences given to violent offenders.

Regarding the incarceration decision, all of the other legally relevant variables except for use of a weapon were significant; defendants with more conviction charges, defendants with prior felony convictions, and defendants who were under some type of criminal justice control at the time of the offense were all more likely to be sentenced to prison. An increase in the number conviction charges and number of prior felony convictions increases the likelihood of being incarcerated by 1.5 and 3.4 times respectively. For the sentence length decision, only the variables for the number of conviction charges and use of a weapon are significant; each additional conviction charge and use of a weapon increase the average sentence length by about 8 months. The defendant's pretrial status significantly affects the incarceration decision but not the sentence length decision; those who were released have lower odds of being incarcerated than those who are detained. Further, those who plead guilty are rewarded by roughly a year less in prison time than those who are convicted at trial.

The gender and race/ethnicity of the defendant are significant predictors of the incarceration decision but do not affect the sentence length decision. Males are 2.4 times more likely than females to be incarcerated and blacks and Hispanics are 1.7 and 2.1 times more likely than whites to be incarcerated. Finally, the age and employment status of the defendant significantly affect the sentence that the judge gives; older defendants are given lengthier sentences and those unemployed receive average sentences that are seven and a half months longer than defendants who are employed.

---

7   Only 1 defendant convicted of murder and 1 defendant convicted of rape were not incarcerated; murder and rape cases were therefore excluded from this analysis.

8   Researchers have noted that sampling selection bias can be problematic in OLS regression analyses since observations are not selected independent of the outcome of interest, specifically that only defendants sent to prison will have a sentence length outcome. Previous studies have utilized the Heckman (1974) two-step procedure as a remedy (see for instance Engen & Gainey, 2000; Steffensmeier et al., 1998; Steffensmeier & Demuth, 2000; Wu & Spohn, 2010). Bushway, Johnson, and Slocum, (2007), however, contend that this is not always an appropriate remedy for selection bias. They state that "the Heckman two-step estimator is specifically a probit model followed by a linear regression, and there is no simple analog of the Heckman method for discrete choice models" (p. 161–162). Bushway et al. (2007) also suggest a better method for controlling selection bias may be to use indicted samples rather than convicted samples. We argue that since our analysis was interested in estimating the effect of attorney type across four distinct stages, which according to formal legal theory should not be related to the outcomes examined, and we used indicted samples at some stages and convicted samples at others, we chose not to include the Heckman procedure in the OLS model and instead utilized what Bushway et al. (2007) refer to as a TPM or two part model. Further, the variables that were found to be significant and the amount of explained variance observed across the two models were different which may suggest small selectivity bias in our sample and therefore no need for the Heckman correction.

These results reveal that net of legally relevant factors, race, ethnicity, and gender are influential of judicial decisions regardless of the type of attorney representing the defendant.

In summary the results of the regression models suggest that that the type of attorney representing the defendant does not have a statistically significant effect on any of the outcomes studied here. To the contrary, this study provides evidence that contradicts the idea that 'you get what you pay for', at least in Cook County. In the four analytic models, the legally relevant variables were the most consistently significant predictors of these case processing outcomes. In some of the models, however, certain offender characteristics also influenced the outcome. Existing research has indicated the importance of testing for interaction effects when analyzing criminal justice outcomes (Miethe & Moore, 1986; Zatz, 1987; Spohn & Holleran, 2000; Steffensmeier & Demuth, 2001; Steffensmeier et al., 1998). To explore the extent to which attorney type might interact with other key variables (both legal and extra-legal), the data were partitioned by class of offense, offense type, employment status, pretrial status, race/ethnicity, sex, and whether the defendant plead guilty or went to trial. The logistic and OLS regression models were then re-estimated using the partitioned data.[9]

Partitioning the data allows for a determination of whether there are differences across these variables in the effect of the type of attorney representing the defendant. Table 3.3.4. presents the results of the logistic and OLS regression analyses testing interaction effects for type of counsel and class of offense, offense type, employment status, pretrial status, race/ethnicity, sex and disposition.[10] Table 3.3.4. reveals that the type of counsel did not have a significant effect for any of the decision-making stages regardless of the class of offense or offense type committed. The results of the data partitioned by employment status, however, reveal that for both employed and unemployed defendants, private attorneys are significantly more likely to get the defendant's primary charge reduced than public defenders, 2.1 and 1.9 times more likely respectively.

Similar results are found regarding the primary charge decision and the defendant's pretrial status. No matter whether the defendant was detained or released, being represented by a private attorney increases the likelihood of getting the primary charge reduced. Interestingly, however, those who are released on bail and represented by a private attorney are twice as likely to be incarcerated as those released on bail but represented by the public defender. In the initial model in Table 3.3.3., the type of attorney did not significantly affect whether the defendant was sent to prison. The results from Table 3.3.4. reveal, however, that the type of attorney likewise has no effect on the incarceration decision for defendants who were detained. For those released on bail, however, having a private attorney doubled the odds of being incarcerated. This finding provides some evidence that the effect of attorney type is contextual; public defenders are more successful than privately retained attorneys at securing non-incarcerative outcomes but only for defendants released on bail. This finding may also provide some support for the notion that public defenders are in a better position to negotiate favorable outcomes for their clients, specifically for clients who are not detained.

The idea of a courtroom workgroup model of negotiated justice is further supported by the results of the analyses partitioned by disposition type. Attorney type has no significant effect on the

---

9   There was some concern that partitioning the data would result in too few cases where the defendant was represented by a private attorney for comparative purposes. Cross tabulations reveal that there were a sufficient number of private attorney cases for each of the variables of interest to run the analyses except where the defendant was female. The number of cases of defendants represented by private attorneys in each category are as follows: Class X, 40; Class 1, 47; Class 2, 58; Class 3, 44; Class 4, 51; Violent, 67; Property, 46; Drug, 127; Employed, 85; Unemployed, 123; In Custody, 99; Released, 141; Plea, 185; Trial, 55; White, 53; Black, 128; Hispanic, 59; Male, 209.

10 For the partitioned models, all other independent variables were included in the models, but only the coefficients for the attorney type variable are presented; full results of these models are available from the first author.

Table 3.3.4. Regression matrix of the effect of attorney type for ROR, primary charge reduction, incarceration decision and sentence length models: Data partitioned by class of offense, employment status, pretrial status, disposition, race/ethnicity, and sex[a]

Dependent Variable	Released ROR			Primary Charge Reduced			Incarceration Decision			Sentence Length		
	b	S.E.	Exp(B)	b	S.E.	Exp(B)	b	S.E.	Exp(B)	b	S.E.	β
Class X		Not Significant			Not Significant			Not Significant			Not Significant	
Class 1		Not Significant			Not Significant			Not Significant			Not Significant	
Class 2		Not Significant			Not Significant			Not Significant			Not Significant	
Class 3		Not Significant			Not Significant			Not Significant			Not Significant	
Class 4		Not Significant			Not Significant			Not Significant			Not Significant	
Violent		Not Significant			Not Significant			Not Significant			Not Significant	
Property		Not Significant			Not Significant			Not Significant			Not Significant	
Drug		Not Significant			Not Significant			Not Significant			Not Significant	
Employed		Not Significant		.75	.36	2.12		Not Significant			Not Significant	
Unemployed		Not Significant		.68	.29	1.96		Not Significant			Not Significant	
Out on Bail		NA		.63	.29	1.88	.71	.28	2.05		Not Significant	
Detained		NA		.75	.36	2.12		Not Significant			Not Significant	
Plea		Not Significant		.77	.25	2.17		Not Significant			Not Significant	
Trial	1.0	.48	2.74		Not Significant		1.25	.56	3.48	46.87	22.70	.19
White		Not Significant			Not Significant			Not Significant			Not Significant	
Black		Not Significant		.67	.31	1.96		Not Significant			Not Significant	
Hispanic		Not Significant			Not Significant			Not Significant			Not Significant	
Male		Not Significant		.80	.23	2.22		Not Significant			Not Significant	

a. Models were run with all the variables included in the original models; full results are available from the first author; all coefficients are significant at the 0.05 level.

STAT HELP!

In this table, the authors predicted the effect of having a private attorney on each of the outcomes separately for all of the variables listed in the left column. For instance, under the "Primary Charge Reduced" column, the results show that among those who pled guilty, the odds of having the primary charge reduced were 2.17 times higher for defendants with a private attorney. Alternatively, at trial, having a private attorney did not have a significant effect on the primary charge being reduced.

incarceration or sentence length decisions for defendants who plead guilty; defendants who exercise their right to a jury trial, however, are more likely to be sent to prison and receive longer sentences if they were represented by a private attorney. In other words, for defendants who go to trial, public defenders are able to secure more favorable outcomes. Defendants with private attorneys who are convicted at trial have almost 3 and a half times greater odds of incarceration and receive average sentences that are 46 months longer than those represented by public defenders. These findings reveal that the so called jury trial penalty might only be applicable for defendants who retain a private attorney.

The tests for interactions between attorney type and demographic variables reveal that type of counsel has a significant effect in some of the models. Regarding race/ethnicity, White defendants are the only defendants who benefit from having a private attorney at the release decision; whites with private attorneys are 2.7 times more likely than whites with public defenders to be released on bail. Attorney type does not affect the bail decision for Black or Hispanic defendants. Black defendants who retain a private attorney, however, are the only defendants to benefit regarding the primary charge decision. Black defendants who retain a private attorney are almost two times more likely to have the primary charge reduced than Black defendants who are represented by a public defender. Attorney type had no significant effects at any of the decision-making stages for Hispanic defendants.

Regarding sex, attorney type was only significant for males at the primary charge reduction decision. Males with privately retained attorneys were almost twice as likely as males with public defenders to have their primary charge reduced. There were not enough female defendants with private attorneys to test the effect of attorney type for females alone. The findings from the analyses of the data partitioned by sex, however, reveal that, at least for males, private attorneys are in a better position to bargain with prosecutors than public defenders. These findings, therefore, are contradictory to the courtroom workgroup model of case processing.

Discussion

The right to counsel is considered fundamental in the United States' legal system. It was included in the Sixth Amendment to the Constitution and the Supreme Court has issued a series of rulings emphasizing the importance of representation by an attorney at critical stages in the criminal justice process. The *Gideon* court stated "It is intolerable in a nation which proclaims equal justice under the law as one of its ideals that anyone should be handicapped in defending himself simply because he happens to be poor" (372 US 335 (1963)). It is important therefore to examine whether this fundamental right has produced fair and neutral outcomes. If defendants represented by public defenders do not get the same "quality of justice" as those represented by privately retained attorneys, questions are raised about the fundamental fairness of the legal system. Ideally, the quality of justice one receives should not be determined by his or her social class. Further, since the vast majority of defendants are represented by public defenders (DeFrances & Litras, 2000), more evaluations of fairness and effectiveness are needed.

The current study sought to investigate the effect of type of counsel on four case processing outcomes using data from Cook County (Chicago), Illinois. This study was also an attempt to add to the existing research by focusing on type of counsel at multiple decision points in the criminal justice process. The overall results of this study generally support the idea that there is no difference between private attorneys and public defenders regarding case outcomes. The type of attorney representing the defendant was not influential on any of the four decision-making points examined here. The results of this study also support previous research which finds that legally relevant factors are the most important predictors of case outcomes. Although some of the process-related factors and offender characteristics were influential of some of the decision-making points, the effects of these variables were not consistently significant compared to the effects of the seriousness of the offense and prior criminal record.

This study suggests that there is little difference in the 'quality' of legal defense provided to defendants by private attorneys and public defenders. Public defenders are as effective as private attorneys in Cook County (Chicago), Illinois. Some results, however, are also in line with previous research indicating a contextual effect for attorney type. The mixed findings from the tests for interaction suggest that a courtroom workgroup justice model, where public defenders will be able to secure more favorable outcomes, is supported in some circumstances and not in others.

Alternatively, perhaps some privately retained attorneys in Cook County also have good working relationships with prosecutors and judges and are as much a part of the courtroom workgroup as the public defenders. As such, for certain offenders and at certain stages (whites at the ROR decision and blacks and males at the primary charge reduction decision) having a privately retained attorney is beneficial. Results, however, also reveal that the courtroom work-group is a benefit to public defenders in certain situations (i.e., if the defendant is out on bail at the incarceration stage or if the defendant goes to trial at both the incarceration and sentence length decision-making stages. Regardless of the seriousness or type of offense, however, the type of attorney representing the defendant did not significantly affect any of the outcomes. This provides evidence that the legally relevant variables are the primary determinants of these case processing decisions.

Although these interaction results are somewhat idiosyncratic, they support the notion that type of counsel has a contextual effect; attorney type interacts with other important variables to produce disparate outcomes for certain offenders at certain stages. These interactive effects also reveal mixed evidence for the idea of a case processing system characterized by negotiated justice where the public defender is in a better position to secure more favorable outcomes for their clients. In some contexts defendants benefited from being represented by the public defender; in other contexts, defendants represented by private attorneys fared better. These more nuanced situational findings regarding the effect of attorney type on outcomes supports testing for interaction effects as well as the added benefit researchers can gain from disaggregating data sets by variables of interest.

Conclusion

This study examined both direct and interactive effects of type of counsel on four different case processing outcomes. Results reveal no significant direct effects, however, some significant effects that were masked in the aggregated models surfaced in the partitioned analyses. There are some limitations, however, which must be taken into account when interpreting these results. This study had no individual information on the public defenders or private attorneys studied here. Therefore, there were no controls for the experience of the attorneys, or the amount of time the attorneys spent on advocacy or investigation for their clients. Due to these limitations, quality of defense in this study does not refer to the time and effort an attorney spent on a client's case but rather the type of outcome the attorney was able to produce for the defendant. Gitelman (1971) contends that the best way to measure effectiveness of attorneys is to look at what happens to the defendants that the attorneys represent; he argues that it is more important to look at outcomes in the criminal justice process rather than focus on subjective measures of quality of defense. This was the approach taken here.

Another limitation is that the data analyzed are from one jurisdiction and are somewhat dated. Examining the effect of type of counsel using more recent data and across a number of jurisdictions would allow for a better investigation of the effectiveness of public defenders. Cook County, however, is not unlike other large, urban jurisdictions throughout the country and thus the results found here may be similar in other large jurisdictions across the country today. The results of this study generally find that indigent defendants are not denied the right to effective counsel in Cook County. In fact, the partitioned analysis reveals that retaining a private attorney may be detrimental to defendants under some circumstances and at certain decision-making points. Given the large number of defendants in the United States annually that rely on public defenders to represent them at the various stages in the criminal justice system, these are welcome and assuring findings. In other words, publicly funded counsel is a benefit to the many indigent defendants being processed in the system and funding to support public defenders' offices needs to continue. Furthermore, if funding was expanded to reduce caseload pressure, public defenders may be even better situated to ensure fair and just outcomes for their clients.

Future research on type of counsel therefore should continue in this vein. Although most research to date finds that the two main determinants of decisions regarding criminal justice outcomes are the legally relevant factors surrounding the seriousness of the offense and the defendant's prior criminal record, under certain circumstances, for certain types of offenders, and in combination with other key variables, extra-legal factors still influence outcomes. This research found that there are certain constellations of factors for which type of counsel will affect case processing decisions.

REFERENCES

Alpert, G. (1979). Inadequate defense counsel: An empirical analysis of prisoner's perceptions. *American Journal of Criminal Law*, 7, 1–21.

Albert-Goldberg, N., & Hartman, M. (1983). The public defender in America. In *The Defense Counsel*. William F. McDonald (ed.). Beverly Hills, CA: Sage.

American Bar Association. (2004). Gideon's broken promise: America's continuing quest for equal justice. ABA Division for Legal Services Standing Committee on Legal Aid & Indigent Defense. Chicago, IL.

American Bar Association. (2009). Eight guidelines of public defense related to excessive workloads. ABA Division for Legal Services Standing Committee on Legal Aid & Indigent Defense. Chicago, IL.

Beck, J. C., & Shumsky, R. (1997). A comparison of retained and appointed counsel in cases of capital murder. *Law and Human Behavior, 21,* 525–538.

Blumberg, A. S. (1967). The practice of law as a confidence game: Organization and cooptation of a profession. *Law and Society Review, 1,* 15–39.

Bowen, D. M. (2009). Calling your bluff: How prosecutors and defense attorneys adapt plea bargaining strategies to increase formalization. *Justice Quarterly, 26,* 2–29.

Bright, S. B. (1994). Counsel for the poor: The death penalty not for the worst crime but for the worst lawyer. *Yale Law Journal, 103,* 1885–1899.

Bushway, S., Johnson, B., & Slocum, L. A. (2007). Is the magic still there? The use of the Heckman two-step correction for selection bias in criminology. *Quantitative Criminology, 23*(2), 151–178.

Casper, J. (1972). American criminal justice: The defendant's perspective. Englewood Cliffs: Prentice Hall.

Champion, D. J. (1989). Private counsels and public defenders: A look at weak cases, prior records, and leniency in plea bargaining. *Journal of Criminal Justice, 17,* 253–263.

Cohen, L. J., Semple, P. B., & Crew, R. E. (1983). Assigned counsel versus public defender systems in Virginia: A comparison of relative benefits. In William F McDonald (ed.). *The Defense Counsel.* Beverly Hills, CA: Sage.

Daly, K. (1987). Structure and practice of familial-based justice in a criminal court. *Law & Society Review, 21,* 267–290.

DeFrances, C., & Litras, M. (2000). Indigent defense services in large counties, 1999. United States Department of Justice, Bureau of Justice Statistics. Washington, DC.

Eisenstein, J., Fleming, R. B., & Nardulli, P. (1987). The contours of justice: Communities and their courts. Boston, MA: Little, Brown and Company.

Engen, R. L., & Gainey, R. R. (2000). Modeling the effects of legally relevant and extralegal factors under sentencing guidelines: The rules have changed. *Criminology, 38,* 1207–1229.

Fleming, R. B., Nardulli, P., & Eisenstein, J. (1992). *The craft of justice: Politics and work in criminal court communities.* Philadelphia, PA: Pennsylvania University Press.

Gitelman, M. (1971). The relative performance of appointed and retained counsel in Arkansas felony cases: An empirical study. *Arkansas Law Review, 24,* 442–452.

Hanson, R. A., & Ostrom, B. J. (1998). Indigent defenders get the job done and done well. In *The Criminal Justice System: Politics and Policies* (7th Ed.). George F. Cole & Marc G. Gertz (ed.). Belmont, CA: Wadsworth.

Harvard Law Review (2000). Gideon's promise unfulfilled: The need for litigated reform of indigent defense. *Harvard Law Review, 113,* 2062–2079.

Heckman, J. J. (1974). Shadow prices, market wages, and labor supply. *Econometrics, 42,* 679–694.

Hoffman, M. B., Rubin, P. H., & Shepherd, J. M. (2005). An empirical study of public defender effectiveness: Self-selection by the "marginally indigent". *Ohio State Journal of Criminal Law, 3,* 223–255.

Holmes, M. D., Hosch, H. M., Daudistel, H. C., Perez, D. A., & Graves, J. B. (1996). Ethnicity, legal resources, and felony dispositions in two southwestern jurisdictions. *Justice Quarterly, 13,* 11–30.

Kelly, H. E. (1976). A comparison of defense strategy and race as influences in differential sentencing. *Criminology, 14,* 241–249.

Levine, J. (1975). The impact of 'Gideon': The performance of public and private criminal defense lawyers. *Polity, 8,* 215–240.

Levin, M. A. (1977). Urban politics and the criminal courts. Chicago, IL: University of Chicago Press.

McIntyre, L. J. (1987). The public defender: The practice of law in the shadows of repute. Chicago, IL: University of Chicago Press.

Miethe, T. D., & Moore, C. A. (1986). Racial differences in criminal processing: The consequences of model selection on conclusion about differential treatment. *The Sociological Quarterly, 27,* 217–237.

Mufioz, E. A., Lopez, D. A., & Stewart, E. (1998). Misdemeanor sentencing decisions: The cumulative disadvantage effect of "Gringo Justice". *Hispanic Journal of Behavioral Sciences, 20,* 298–319.

Nagel, S. S. (1973). Effects of alternative types of counsel on criminal procedural treatment. *Indiana Law Journal, 48,* 404–426.

Nardulli, P. F. (1986). Insider Justice: Defense attorneys and the handling of felony cases. *Journal of Criminal Law and Criminology, 77,* 379–417.

Oaks, D. H., & Lehman, W. (1970). Lawyers for the poor. In *The Scales of Justice,* edited by A. S. Blumberg. Hawthorne, NY: Aldine.

Silverstein, L. (1965). Defense of the poor in criminal cases in American state courts. Chicago, IL: American Bar Foundation.

Skolnick, J. (1967). Social Control in the adversary system. *The Journal of Conflict Resolution, 11,* 52–70.

Spangenburg Group (2009). Assessment of the Washoe and Clark County, Nevada Public Defender Offices Final Report. Center for Justice, Law and Society at George Mason University.

Spohn, C. (2009). Race, sex, and pretrial detention in Federal Court: Indirect effects and cumulative disadvantage. *University of Kansas Law Review, 57,* 879–902.

Spohn, C., & Beichner, D. (2000). Is preferential treatment of female offenders a thing of the past? A multi-site study of gender, race, and imprisonment. *Criminal Justice Policy Review, 11,* 149–184.

Spohn, C., Gruhl, J., & Welch, S. (1981–82). The effect of race on sentencing: A reexamination of an unsettled question. *Law and Society Review, 16,* 71–88.

Spohn, C., & Holleran, D. (2000). The imprisonment penalty paid by young, unemployed black and Hispanic male offenders. *Criminology, 38,* 281–306.

Spohn, C., & Holleran, D. (2001). Prosecuting sexual assault: A comparison of charging decisions in sexual assault cases involving strangers, acquaintances, and intimate partners. *Justice Quarterly, 18*, 651–685.

Steffensmeier, D., & Demuth, S. (2000). Ethnicity and sentencing outcomes in U.S. federal courts: Who is punished more harshly? *American Sociological Review, 65*, 705–729.

Steffensmeier, D., & Demuth, S. (2001). Ethnicity and judges sentencing decisions: Hispanic-black-white comparisons. *Criminology, 39*, 145–177.

Steffensmeier, D., Kramer, J., & Streifel, C. (1993). Gender and imprisonment decisions. *Criminology, 31*, 411–446.

Steffensmeier, D., & Motivans, M. (2000). Older men and older women in the arms of the criminal law: Offending patterns and sentencing outcomes. *Journals of Gerontology Series B: Psychological Sciences & Social Sciences, 55B*, 141–151.

Steffensmeier, D., Ulmer, J. T., & Kramer, J. (1998). The interaction of race, gender, and age in criminal sentencing: The punishment cost of being young, black, and male. *Criminology, 36*, 763–797.

Sterling, J. S. (1983). Retained counsel versus the public defender: The impact of the type of counsel on charge bargaining. In *The Defense Counsel*, edited by W. F. McDonald. Beverly Hills, CA: Sage.

Stover, R. V., & Eckhart, D. R. (1975). A systematic comparison of public defenders and private attorneys. *American Journal of Criminal Law, 3*, 265–300.

Sudnow, D. (1965). Normal crimes: Sociological features of the penal code in a public defender office. *Social Problems, 12*, 255–277.

Taylor, J. G., Stanley, T. P., DeFlorio, B. J., & Seekamp, L. N. (1973). An analysis of defense counsel in the processing of felony defendants in San Diego, California. *Denver Law Journal, 49*, 233–275.

Uphoff, R. J. (1992). The criminal defense lawyer: Zealous advocate, double agent, or beleaguered dealer? *Criminal Law Bulletin, 28*, 419–456.

Walker, S., Spohn, C., & Delone, M. (2004). The color of justice: Race, Ethnicity and crime in America (3rd ed.). Toronto, Ontario: Wadsworth.

Weitzer, R. (1996). Racial discrimination in the criminal justice system: Findings and problems in the literature. *Journal of Criminal Justice, 24*, 309–322.

Wheeler, G. R., & Wheeler, C. L. (1980). Reflection on legal representation of the economically disadvantaged: Beyond assembly line justice. *Crime and Delinquency, 26*, 319–332.

Wice, P. (1985). *Chaos in the courthouse: The inner workings of the urban municipal courts.* New York, NY: Prager.

Wilson, D. (1984). The effects of counsel on the severity of criminal sentences: A statistical assessment. *The Justice System Journal, 9*, 87–101.

Williams, M. (2002). A comparison of sentencing outcomes for defendants with public defenders versus retained counsel in a Florida circuit court. *Justice Systems Journal, 23*, 249–257.

Wolf-Harlow, C. (2000). Defense counsel in criminal cases. United States Department of Justice. Bureau of Justice Statistics. Washington, DC: Author.

Worden, A. P. (1991). Privatizing due process: Issues in the comparison of assigned counsel, public defender, and contracted indigent defense systems. *Justice System Journal, 15*, 390–418.

Wu, J., & Spohn, C. (2010). Interdistrict disparity in sentencing in three U.S. District Courts. *Crime & Delinquency, 56*, 290–322.

Zatz, M. S. (1987). The changing forms of racial/ethnic bias in sentencing. *Journal of Research in Crime and Delinquency, 24*, 69–92.

CASES CITED

Argersinger v Hamlin 407 US 25 (1972).

Gideon v Wainwright 372 US 335 (1963).

Johnson v Zerbst 304 US 458 (1938).

Powell v Alabama 287 US 45 (1932).

DISCUSSION QUESTIONS

1. Why is the common goal of courtroom workgroups more important than their ideological goals? Explain your reasoning.

2. How do court actor incentives influence case processing?

3. Describe why "justice" has different meanings to courtroom actors based on their intrinsic goals.

4. In what ways can greater familiarity among the courtroom workgroup affect case processing?

5. How do the interests of prosecutors affect the courtroom workgroup?

6. How might prosecutorial discretion harm a first-time defendant?

7. In what circumstances might defense attorneys have more influence than prosecutors and judges?

8. Explain why clients of private attorneys might receive longer incarceration sentences compared to the clients of public defenders after a trial.

9. Although studies have shown that having a public versus private defender does not influence judicial sentencing decisions, why do public defenders continue to have a negative stigma?

10. What would happen in the criminal justice system if it were demonstrated that public defenders could not provide equal legal representation compared to private attorneys?

EARLY PHASES OF CASE PROCESSING

Introduction

While a lot of attention among court scholars has been devoted to sentencing, which occurs at the back end of case processing, there is a recognition that more focus needs to be placed on the earlier phases of case processing that occur before sentencing. The decisions made at these earlier phases have implications for sentences defendants receive later and typically rely more on discretionary decision-making among the courtroom workgroup, especially when there are sentencing guidelines in place to control the later processes. The readings in this section review three earlier phases: the decision to prosecute, pretrial detention, and plea bargaining.

Driving Forces in the Decision to Prosecute

One of the first decisions that must be made within the court system is whether a case cleared by the police and turned over to the prosecutor's office should be pursued in court. There are many competing forces that factor into the prosecutor's decision to move a case forward and the charges the prosecutor brings against defendants. George Cole, in "The Decision to Prosecute," outlines several different sources of influence on prosecutors that can alter decisions as the case proceeds, including the police, court system, defense attorneys, and community. Of course, there are organizational and bureaucratic concerns guiding their decisions, as has been discussed. These organizational demands may sway prosecutors from pursuing cases during periods when the caseload is extremely high, for instance, so as to "regulate the flow of cases to the court." Organizational interests also facilitate cooperative relationships with defense attorneys.

Aside from these bureaucratic concerns, though, there are other factors that may influence the prosecutor. The decision to further pursue a case may depend, for instance, on prosecutors' perceptions that the court will convict the person, especially since prosecutors have an interest in high conviction rates. This perception may depend on the judges in the courthouse and how they handle certain cases. To ensure convictions, Cole recognizes that prosecutors rely on some predictability from the judges, and if that is not true for certain cases, prosecutors may avoid pressing those cases further. They also depend on the police to provide quality evidence that will help them get a conviction and may return cases back to the police with not enough evidence.

Cole also highlights additional factors external to the court organization that can affect prosecutorial decision-making. For instance, the prosecutor's office may get an indication from the corrections system that there is limited space in the jails and prisons, which could result in a slowdown of the flow of cases from the prosecutor's office. Prosecutors may also experience pressure from the legislature or the public to pursue certain cases, even when there is limited evidence. The prosecutor's office can then delay the case as much as possible until evidence comes to bare or the public loses interest in the case, and then they can settle it with a plea deal.

The Drawbacks of Pretrial Detention

Pretrial detention is one of the most controversial aspects of early case processing. During the initial appearance or arraignment, the accused is told of the charges, he or she is advised of his/her constitutional rights, and preliminary bail is set. Bail procedures typically vary by jurisdiction. In some instances, particularly when the offense is more serious or the accused is a flight risk, bail is not set, and the person remains detained. The accused can also remain detained, even when bail is set, if s/he cannot afford to pay the bail amount. The underlying notion of the criminal justice system is that defendants are assumed innocent until proven guilty. Detention is sometimes viewed as an early form of punishment that assumes guilt, as opposed to innocence. If detention is a result on the inability to pay bail, detention may disproportionately punish offenders with a lower socioeconomic status.

In "Bail and Sentencing: Does Pretrial Detention Lead to Harsher Punishment," Meghan Sacks and Alissa Ackerman explain how detention can "adversely affect the entire course of a criminal case," such that detention status can influence later sentencing decisions. Defendants who remain detained cannot adequately prepare for their defense in the same way that released defendants can. Unfortunately, they can also be stigmatized by the system when they are brought to court, since they may be perceived as more dangerous, because of their detention status. Many public defender offices, for instance, have a wardrobe room with business attire for detained defendants to change into before going to trial so that their detention status does not influence the jury. The ability to change clothes does not typically happen in earlier hearings, though, and defendants in jail attire can easily be perceived differently by judges than defendants in civilian clothes. Also, unlike the defendants unable to make bail, defendants in the community are able to demonstrate that they can remain within the community without committing a crime, a factor judges may take into consideration. For these reasons, detained defendants may be subject to harsher sentencing outcomes.

Going back to the organizational approach, detention can be seen as a method for inducing a guilty plea. Defendants who are detained want to get out of jail as quickly as possible, which sometimes results in accepting a plea offer that they otherwise would not have accepted had they been out in the community. From a crime control perspective, detention is then favored for its ability to get cases resolved quickly through plea negotiations. The argument is that the efficient flow of cases would be disrupted, creating a substantial backlog, if defendants were not detained.

Weighing the Pros and Cons of Plea Bargaining

Thus far, the key mechanisms that can explain the predominant use of plea bargaining within the criminal court system have been discussed. While plea bargaining does contribute to efficient case processing, there are consequences for the defendant. Douglas Smith presents the arguments in opposition to and favor of plea bargaining in "The Plea Bargaining Controversy." He recognizes that plea bargaining can undermine the effectiveness of punishment, benefit those with more experience in the criminal justice system, and be coercive. There is also evidence to suggest that defendants who plead guilty get lighter sentences than those who go to trial, such that there exists a trial penalty. Defendants who pursue a trial and chose to exercise their due process rights are essentially punished, while those who plead guilty are rewarded.

The extent to which this less severe sentence is a reward remains questionable, though. For instance, innocent people may plead guilty, or defendants might not recognize that pleading guilty results in a conviction on their record, even if they plead no contest. A conviction can influence the ability to stay in public housing, get food stamps, and even vote. Also, many defendants who plead guilty are placed on probation, which is seen as a lighter sentence. The conditions of probation can make completion almost impossible for many offenders, thereby resulting in a revocation of probation and a return into the criminal justice system.

Alternatively, plea bargaining can be seen as beneficial to defendants. In his study, Smith does not find much evidence to suggest that the plea process is coercive. He recognizes that plea bargaining seems to be a rational process that may be able to benefit what he calls "less serious marginal offenders with less evidence against them." Plea bargaining may provide an opportunity to "tailor punishment," especially when penalties dictated by the guidelines seem too harsh. Through the negotiation process, individual characteristics of defendants and the circumstances of the case can be taken into consideration in determining the appropriate punishment, making justice more individualized. A mutual agreement can be reached that benefits both the courtroom workgroup and defendants and does not necessarily have to come at the expense of justice.

Cumulative Disadvantage

A major concern during the earlier phases of case processing is whether the decisions made at these time points are somehow influenced by stereotypes or prejudices against defendants with particular demographic characteristics or backgrounds. Sacks and Ackerman recognize that there is a "funnel of justice," where cases are dropped out at each phase of case processing. In the decision to prosecute, some cases are pursued, and some are dismissed. Among the cases pursued, some defendants are detained, and some are released. Within this pool of defendants, some plead guilty, and others go to trial. Biases can exist if, at any point, these decisions are made in a way that marginalizes a particular group of people.

This concept has been referred to as cumulative disadvantage. For example, minorities may be more likely to be detained, since minorities generally have a lower socioeconomic status. Sacks and Ackerman show that detention is related to longer incarceration sentences. Minorities would then be more prone to getting harsher sentences. The disadvantage minorities were placed at during the detention decision led to a disadvantage at sentencing. This process demonstrates the importance of the decisions made at these earlier phases. It also calls attention to phases that come before those accused are brought to court. If minorities are disproportionately arrested, for instance, this will affect the pool coming into the court system, putting minorities at a disadvantage from the onset.

The Decision to Prosecute

George F. Cole

This paper is based on an exploratory study of the Office of Prosecuting Attorney, King County (Seattle), Washington. The lack of social scientific knowledge about the prosecutor dictated the choice of this approach. An open-ended interview was administered to one-third of the former deputy prosecutors who had worked in the office during the ten year period 1955–1965. In addition, interviews were conducted with court employees, members of the bench, law enforcement officials, and others having reputations for participation in legal decision-making. Over fifty respondents were contacted during this phase. A final portion of the research placed the author in the role of observer in the prosecutor's office. This experience allowed for direct observation of all phases of the decision to prosecute so that the informal processes of the office could be noted. Discussions with the prosecutor's staff, judges, defendant's attorneys, and the police were held so that the interview data could be placed within an organizational context.

The primary goal of this investigation was to examine the role of the prosecuting attorney as an officer of the legal process within the context of the local political system. The analysis is therefore based on two assumptions. First, that the legal process is best understood as a subsystem of the larger political system. Because of this choice, emphasis is placed upon the interaction and goals of the individuals involved in decision-making. Second, and closely related to the first point, it is assumed that broadly conceived political considerations explained to a large extent "who gets or does not get—in what amount—and how, the good (justice) that is hopefully produced by the legal system" (Klonski and Mendelsohn, 1965: 323). By focusing upon the political and social linkages between these systems, it is expected that decision-making in the prosecutor's office will be viewed as a principal ingredient in the authoritative allocation of values.

The Prosecutor's Office In An Exchange System

While observing the interrelated activities of the organizations in the legal process, one might ask, "Why do these agencies cooperate?" If the police refuse to transfer information to the prosecutor concerning the commission of a crime, what are the rewards or sanctions which might be brought against them? Is it possible that organizations maintain a form of "bureaucratic accounting" which, in a sense, keeps track of the resources allocated to an agency and the support returned? How are cues transmitted from one agency to another to influence decision-making? These are some of the questions which must be asked when decisions are viewed as an output of an exchange system.

The major findings of this study are placed within the context of an exchange system (Evan, 1965: 218).[1] This serves the heuristic purpose of focusing attention upon the linkages found between actors in the decisionmaking process. In place of the traditional assumptions that the agency is supported solely by statutory authority, this view recognizes that an organization has many clients with which it interacts and upon whom it is dependent for certain resources. As interdependent subunits of a system, then, the organization and its clients are engaged in a set of exchanges across their boundaries. These will involve a transfer of resources between the organizations which will affect the mutual achievement of goals.

The legal system may be viewed as a set of interorganizational exchange relationships analogous to what Long (1962: 142) has called a community game. The participants in the legal system (game) share a common territorial field and collaborate for different and particular ends. They interact on a continuing basis as their responsibilities demand contact with other participants in the process. Thus, the need for the cooperation of other participants can have a bearing on the decision to prosecute. A decision not to prosecute a narcotics offender may be a move to pressure the United States' Attorney's Office to cooperate on another case. It is obvious that bargaining occurs not only between the major actors in a case—the prosecutor and the defense attorney—but also between the clientele groups that are influential in structuring the actions of the prosecuting attorney.

Exchanges do not simply "sail" from one system to another, but take place in an institutionalized setting which may be compared to a market. In the market, decisions are made between individuals who occupy boundary-spanning roles, and who set the conditions under which the exchange will occur. In the legal system, this may merely mean that a representative of the parole board agrees to forward a recommendation to the prosecutor, or it could mean that there is extended bargaining between a deputy prosecutor and a defense attorney. In the study of the King County Prosecutor's Office, it was found that most decisions resulted from some type of exchange relationship. The deputies interacted almost constantly with the police and criminal lawyers, while the prosecutor was more closely linked to exchange relations with the courts, community leaders, and the county commissioners.

---

1   See also Levine and White (1961: 583) and Blau (1955).

The Prosecutor's Clientele

In an exchange system, power is largely dependent upon the ability of an organization to create clientele relationships which will support and enhance the needs of the agency. For, although interdependence is characteristic of the legal system, competition with other public agencies for support also exists. Since organizations operate in an economy of scarcity, the organization must exist in a favorable power position in relation to its clientele. Reciprocal and unique claims are made by the organization and its clients. Thus, rather than being oriented toward only one public, an organization is beholden to several publics, some visible and others seen clearly only from the pinnacle of leadership. As Gore (1964: 23) notes, when these claims are "firmly anchored inside the organization and the lines drawn taut, the tensions between conflicting claims form a net serving as the institutional base for the organization."

An indication of the stresses within the judicial system may be obtained by analyzing its outputs. It has been suggested that the administration of justice is a selective process in which only those cases which do not create strains in the organization will ultimately reach the courtroom (Chambliss, 1969: 84). As noted in Figure 4.1.1, the system operates so that only a small number of cases arrive for trial, the rest being disposed of through reduced charges, *nolle pros.*, and guilty pleas.[2] Not indicated are those cases removed by the police and prosecutor prior to the filing of charges. As the focal organization in an exchange system, the office of prosecuting attorney makes decisions which reflect the influence of its clientele. Because of the scarcity of resources, marketlike relationships, and the

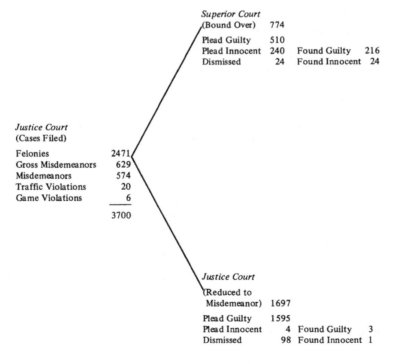

Figure 4.1.1. Disposition of Felony Cases-King County, 1964

---

2   The lack of reliable criminal statistics is well known. These data were gathered from a number of sources, including King County (1964).

organizational needs of the system, prosecutorial decision-making emphasizes the accommodations which are made to the needs of participants in the process.

POLICE

Although the prosecuting attorney has discretionary power to determine the disposition of cases, this power is limited by the fact that usually he is dependent upon the police for inputs to the system of cases and evidence. The prosecutor does not have the investigative resources necessary to exercise the kind of affirmative control over the types of cases that are brought to him. In this relationship, the prosecutor is not without countervailing power. His main check on the police is his ability to return cases to them for further investigation and to refuse to approve arrest warrants. By maintaining cordial relations with the press, a prosecutor is often able to focus attention on the police when the public becomes aroused by incidents of crime. As the King County prosecutor emphasized, "That [investigation] is the job for the sheriff and police. It's their job to bring me the charges." As noted by many respondents, the police, in turn, are dependent upon the prosecutor to accept the output of their system; rejection of too many cases can have serious repercussions affecting the morale, discipline, and workload of the force.

A request for prosecution may be rejected for a number of reasons relating to questions of evidence. Not only must the prosecutor believe that the evidence will secure a conviction, but he must also be aware of community norms relating to the type of acts that should be prosecuted. King County deputy prosecutors noted that charges were never filed when a case involved attempted suicide or fornication. In other actions, the heinous nature of the crime, together with the expected public reaction, may force both the police and prosecutor to press for conviction when evidence is less than satisfactory. As one deputy noted, "In that case [murder and molestation of a six-year-old girl] there was nothing that we could do. As you know the press was on our back and every parent was concerned. Politically, the prosecutor had to seek an information."

Factors other than those relating to evidence may require that the prosecutor refuse to accept a case from the police. First, the prosecuting attorney serves as a regulator of case loads not only for his own office, but for the rest of the legal system. Constitutional and statutory time limits prevent him and the courts from building a backlog of untried cases. In King County, when the system reached the "overload point," there was a tendency to be more selective in choosing the cases to be accepted. A second reason for rejecting prosecution requests may stem from the fact that the prosecutor is thinking of his public exposure in the courtroom. He does not want to take forward cases which will place him in an embarrassing position. Finally, the prosecutor may return cases to check the quality of police work. As a former chief criminal deputy said, "You have to keep them on their toes, otherwise they get lazy. If they aren't doing their job, send the case back and then leak the situation to the newspapers." Rather than spend the resources necessary to find additional evidence, the police may dispose of a case by sending it back to the prosecutor on a lesser charge, implement the "copping out" machinery leading to a guilty plea, drop the case, or in some instances send it to the city prosecutor for action in municipal court.

[…]

COURTS

The ways used by the court to dispose of cases is a vital influence in the system. The court's actions effect pressures upon the prison, the conviction rate of the prosecutor, and the work of probation agencies. The judge's decisions act as clues to other parts of the system, indicating the type of action likely to be taken in future cases. As noted by a King County judge, "When the number of prisoners gets to the 'riot point,' the warden puts pressure on us to slow down the flow. This often means that men are let out on parole and the number of people given probation and suspended sentences increases." Under such conditions, it would be expected that the prosecutor would respond to the judge's actions by reducing the inputs to the court either by not preferring charges or by increasing the pressure for guilty pleas through bargaining. The adjustments of other parts of the system could be expected to follow. For instance, the police might sense the lack of interest of the prosecutor in accepting charges, hence they will send only airtight cases to him for indictment.

The influence of the court on the decision to prosecute is very real. The sentencing history of each judge gives the prosecutor, as well as other law enforcement officials, an indication of the treatment a case may receive in the courtroom. The prosecutor's expectation as to whether the court will convict may limit his discretion over the decisions on whether to prosecute. "There is great concern as to whose court a case will be assigned. After Judge _____ threw out three cases in a row in which entrapment was involved, the police did not want us to take any cases to him." Since the prosecutor depends upon the plea-bargaining machinery to maintain the flow of cases from his office, the sentencing actions of judges must be predictable. If the defendant and his lawyer are to be influenced to accept a lesser charge or the promise of a lighter sentence in exchange for a plea of guilty, there must be some basis for belief that the judge will fulfill his part of the arrangement. Because judges are unable formally to announce their agreement with the details of the bargain, their past performance acts as a guide.

Within the limits imposed by law and the demands of the system, the prosecutor is able to regulate the flow of cases to the court. He may control the length of time between accusation and trial; hence he may hold cases until he has the evidence which will convict. Alternatively, he may seek repeated adjournment and continuances until the public's interest dies; problems such as witnesses becoming unavailable and similar difficulties make his request for dismissal of prosecution more justifiable. Further, he may determine the type of court to receive the case and the judge who will hear it. Many misdemeanors covered by state law are also violations of a city ordinance. It is a common practice for the prosecutor to send a misdemeanor case to the city prosecutor for processing in the municipal court when it is believed that a conviction may not be secured in justice court. As a deputy said, "If there is no case—send it over to the city court. Things are speedier, less formal, over there."

In the state of Washington, a person arrested on a felony charge must be given a preliminary hearing in a justice court within ten days. For the prosecutor, the preliminary hearing is an opportunity to evaluate the testimony of witnesses, assess the strength of the evidence, and try to predict the outcome of the case if it is sent to trial. On the basis of this evaluation, the prosecutor has several options: he may bind over the case for trial in Superior Court; he may reduce the charges to those of a misdemeanor for trial in Justice Court; or he may conclude that he has no case and drop the charges. The President Judge of the Justice Courts of King County estimated that about seventy percent of the felonies are reduced to misdemeanors after the preliminary hearing.

Besides having some leeway in determining the type of court in which to file a case, the prosecutor also has some flexibility in selecting the judge to receive the case. Until recently the prosecutor could file a case with a specific judge. "The trouble was that Judge _____ was erratic and independent, [so] no one would file with him. The other judges objected that they were handling the entire workload, so a central filing system was devised." Under this procedure cases are assigned to the judges in rotation. However, as the chief criminal deputy noted, "the prosecutor can hold a case until the 'correct' judge came up."

DEFENSE ATTORNEYS

With the increased specialization and institutionalization of the bar, it would seem that those individuals engaged in the practice of criminal law have been relegated, both by their profession and by the community, to a low status. The urban bar appears to be divided into three parts. First, there is an inner circle which handles the work of banks, utilities, and commercial concerns; second, another circle includes plaintiff's lawyers representing interests opposed to those of the inner circle; and finally, an outer group scrapes out an existence by "haunting the courts in hope of picking up crumbs from the judicial table" (Ladinsky, 1963: 128). With the exception of a few highly proficient lawyers who have made a reputation by winning acquittal for their clients in difficult, highly publicized cases, most of the lawyers dealing with the King County Prosecutor's Office belong to this outer ring.

In this study, respondents were asked to identify those attorneys considered to be specialists in criminal law. Of the nearly 1,600 lawyers practicing in King County only eight can be placed in this category. Of this group, six were reported to enjoy the respect of the legal community, while the others were accused by many respondents of being involved in shady deals. A larger group of King County attorneys will accept criminal cases, but these lawyers do not consider themselves specialists. Several respondents noted that many lawyers, because of inexperience or age, were required to hang around the courthouse searching for clients. One Seattle attorney described the quality of legal talent available for criminal cases as "a few good criminal lawyers and a lot of young kids and old men. The good lawyers I can count on my fingers."

In a legal system where bargaining is a primary method of decision-making, it is not surprising that criminal lawyers find it essential to maintain close personal ties with the prosecutor and his staff. Respondents were quite open in revealing their dependence upon this close relationship to successfully pursue their careers. The nature of the criminal lawyer's work is such that his saleable product or service appears to be influence rather than technical proficiency in the law. Respondents hold the belief that clients are attracted partially on the basis of the attorney's reputation as a fixer, or as a shrewd bargainer.

There is a tendency for ex-deputy prosecutors in King County to enter the practice of criminal law. Because of his inside knowledge of the prosecutor's office and friendships made with court officials, the former deputy feels that he has an advantage over other criminal law practitioners. All of the former deputies interviewed said that they took criminal cases. Of the eight criminal law specialists, seven previously served as deputy prosecutors in King County, while the other was once prosecuting attorney in a rural county.

Because of the financial problems of the criminal lawyer's practice, it is necessary that he handle cases on an assembly-line basis, hoping to make a living from a large number of small fees. Referring to a fellow lawyer, one attorney said, "You should see _____. He goes up there to Carroll's office with a whole fist full of cases. He trades on some, bargains on others and never goes to court. It's amazing but it's the way he makes his living." There are incentives, therefore, to bargain with the prosecutor and other decisionmakers. The primary aim of the attorney in such circumstances is to reach an accommodation so that the time-consuming formal proceedings need not be implemented. As a Seattle attorney noted, "I can't make any money if I spend my time in a courtroom. I make mine on the telephone or in the prosecutor's office." One of the disturbing results of this arrangement is that instances were reported in which a bargain was reached between the attorney and deputy prosecutor on a "package deal." In this situation, an attorney's clients are treated as a group; the outcome of the bargaining is often an agreement whereby reduced charges will be achieved for some, in exchange for the unspoken assent by the lawyer that the prosecutor may proceed as he desires with the other cases. One member of the King County Bar has developed this practice to such a fine art that a deputy prosecutor said, "When you saw him coming into the office, you knew that he would be pleading guilty." At one time this situation was so widespread that the "prisoners up in the jail had a rating list which graded the attorneys as either 'good guys' or 'sell outs.'"

The exchange relationship between the defense attorney and the prosecutor is based on their need for cooperation in the discharge of their responsibilities. Most criminal lawyers are interested primarily in the speedy solution of cases because of their precarious financial situation. Since they must protect their professional reputations with their colleagues, judicial personnel, and potential clientele, however, they are not completely free to bargain solely with this objective. As one attorney noted, "You can't afford to let it get out that you are selling out your cases."

The prosecutor is also interested in the speedy processing of cases. This can only be achieved if the formal processes are not implemented. Not only does the pressure of his caseload influence bargaining, but also the legal process with its potential for delay and appeal, creates a degree of uncertainty which is not present in an exchange relationship with an attorney with whom you have dealt for a number of years. As the Presiding Judge of the Seattle District Court said, "Lawyers are helpful to the system. They are able to pull things together, work out a deal, keep the system moving."

COMMUNITY INFLUENTIALS

As part of the political system, the judicial process responds to the community environment. The King County study indicated that there are differential levels of influence within the community and that some people had a greater interest in the politics of prosecution than others. First, the general public is able to have its values translated into policies followed by law enforcement officers. The public's influence is particularly acute in those gray areas of the law where full enforcement is not expected. Statutes may be enacted by legislatures defining the outer limits of criminal conduct, but they do not necessarily mean that laws are to be fully enforced to these limits. There are some laws defining behavior which the community no longer considers criminal. It can be expected that a prosecutor's charging policies will reflect this attitude. He may not prosecute violations of laws regulating some forms of gambling, certain sexual practices, or violations of Sunday Blue Laws.

Because the general public is a potential threat to the prosecutor, staff members take measures to protect him from criticism. Respondents agreed that decision-making occurs with the public in mind—"will a course of action arouse antipathy towards the prosecutor rather than the accused?" Several deputies mentioned what they called the "aggravation level" of a crime. This is a recognition that the commission of certain crimes, within a specific context, will bring about a vocal public reaction. "If a little girl, walking home from the grocery store, is pulled into the bushes and indecent liberties taken, this is more disturbing to the public's conscience than a case where the father of the girl takes indecent liberties with her at home." The office of King County Prosecuting Attorney has a policy requiring that deputies file all cases involving sexual molestation in which the police believe the girl's story is credible. The office also prefers charges in all negligent homicide cases where there is the least possibility of guilt. In such types of cases the public may respond to the emotional context of the case and demand prosecution. To cover the prosecutor from criticism, it is believed that the safest measure is to prosecute.

The bail system is also used to protect the prosecutor from criticism. Thus it is the policy to set bail at a high level with the expectation that the court will reduce the amount. "This looks good for Prosecutor Carroll. Takes the heat off of him, especially in morals cases. If the accused doesn't appear in court the prosecutor can't be blamed. The public gets upset when they know these types are out free." This is an example of exchange where one actor is shifting the responsibility and potential onus onto another. In turn, the court is under pressure from county jail officials to keep the prison population down.

A second community group having contact with the prosecutor is composed of those leaders who have a continuing or potential interest in the politics of prosecution. This group, analogous to the players in one of Long's community games, are linked to the prosecutor because his actions affect their success in playing another game. Hence community boosters want either a crackdown or a hands-off policy towards gambling, political leaders want the prosecutor to remember the interests of the party, and business leaders want policies which will not interfere with their own game.

Community leaders may receive special treatment by the prosecutor if they run afoul of the law. A policy of the King County Office requires that cases involving prominent members of the community be referred immediately to the chief criminal deputy and the prosecutor for their disposition. As one deputy noted, "These cases can be pretty touchy. It's important that the boss knows immediately about this type of case so that he is not caught 'flat footed' when asked about it by the press."

Pressure by an interest group was evidenced during a strike by drug store employees in 1964. The striking unions urged Prosecutor Carroll to invoke a state law which requires the presence of a licensed pharmacist if the drug store is open. Not only did union representatives meet with Carroll, but picket lines were set up outside the courthouse protesting his refusal to act. The prosecutor resisted the union's pressure tactics.

In recent years, the prosecutor's tolerance policy toward minor forms of gambling led to a number of conflicts with Seattle's mayor, the sheriff, and church organizations. After a decision was made to prohibit all forms of public gaming, the prosecutor was criticized by groups representing the tourist industry and such affected groups as the bartenders' union which thought the decision would have an adverse economic effect. As Prosecutor Carroll said, "I am always getting pressures from different interests—business, the Chamber of Commerce, and labor. I have to try and maintain a balance between them." In exchange for these considerations, the prosecutor may gain prestige, political support, and admission into the leadership groups of the community.

Summary

By viewing the King County Office of Prosecuting Attorney as the focal organization in an exchange system, data from this exploratory study suggests the market-like relationships which exist between actors in the system. Since prosecution operates in an environment of scarce resources and since the decisions have potential political ramifications, a variety of officials influence the allocation of justice. The decision to prosecute is not made at one point, but rather the prosecuting attorney has a number of options which he may employ during various stages of the proceedings. But the prosecutor is able to exercise his discretionary powers only within the network of exchange relationships. The police, court congestion, organizational strains, and community pressures are among the factors which influence prosecutorial behavior.

REFERENCES

Blau, P. M. (1955) The Dynamics of Bureaucracy. Chicago: Univ. of Chicago Press.

Chambliss, W. J. (1969) Crime and the Legal Process. New York: McGraw-Hill.

Evan, W. M. (1965) "Towards a theory of inter-organizational relations." Management Sci. 11 (August): 218–230.

Gore, W. J. (1964) Administrative Decision Making. New York: John Wiley.

King County (1964) Annual Report of the Prosecuting Attorney. Seattle: State of Washington.

Klonski, J. R. and R. I. Mendelsohn (1965) "The allocation of justice: a political analysis." J. of Public Law 14 (May): 323–342.

Ladinsky, J. (1963) "The impact of social backgrounds of lawyers on law practice and the law." J. of Legal Education 16, 2: 128–144.

Levine, S. and P. E. White (1961) "Exchange as a conceptual framework for the study of inter-organizational relationships." Administrative Sci. Q. 5 (March): 583–601.

Long, N. (1962) The Polity. Chicago: Rand McNally.

Schur, E. M. (1965) Crimes Without Victims. Englewood Cliffs, N.J.: Prentice-Hall.

Skolnick, J. E. (1966) Justice Without Trial. New York: John Wiley.

Bail and Sentencing

Does Pretrial Detention Lead to Harsher Punishment?

Meghan Sacks and Alissa R. Ackerman

A substantial body of research has examined structural flaws in the American criminal justice system. Some scholars concentrate on bail decisions and outcomes (Demuth & Steffensmeier, 2004; Schlesinger, 2005; Turner & Johnson, 2005), and others address plea bargaining practices (Albonetti, 1990; Frenzel & Ball, 2007; Kellough & Wortley, 2002). However, the majority of research to date has focused on inequities in sentencing practices and the possible racial disparities that occur at this phase of the legal process (Demuth & Steffensmeier, 2004; Spohn & Holleran, 2000; Western, 2006).

For several reasons, some obvious, sentencing is usually the focal point of the criminal case process for scholars. As Demuth (2003) points out, sentencing marks the end point of the criminal case and the point when the "real" punishment is pronounced. In her study of factors affecting guilty pleas, Albonetti (1990) also highlights the importance of the finality of the conviction. Demuth notes that the sentencing phase receives more attention than bail in the literature just as sentencing garners more attention from both the legislature and the media. Finally, as Demuth explains, sentencing data are collected, monitored, and made available to researchers.

Studies on this topic have concluded that a variety of factors, both legal and extralegal, affect sentencing decisions. Most notably, several researchers have found that criminal history and the seriousness of the offense are the strongest predictors of sentencing decisions (Gottfredson & Gottfredson, 1988; Neubauer, 2002), whereas other research has demonstrated the strong role that the extralegal variables race and gender play (Albonetti, 1997; Spohn & Holleran, 2000). However, studies on sentencing seldom examine the role of pretrial outcomes on sentencing decisions.

The current study focuses on the potential effects of bail operations on sentencing. Some researchers (Free, 2004; Phillips, 2008; Williams, 2003) have also examined the potential impact of pretrial decisions on conviction and sentencing. However, this body of research is not extensive and more is needed to measure the full extent of pretrial operations on sentencing, particularly given some of the well-known detrimental effects of incarceration on offenders, their family members, and the community. These concerns are intensified because some research has argued that the court's decision to detain a defendant pretrial may be, in effect, a decision to convict. Decisions at the beginning of the criminal case process, such as bail decisions, can affect the entire course of the case and the ultimate punishment handed down in sentencing. That is why it is essential to start from the beginning of a case. The current study provides evidence of the powerful role that bail practices play at each step of criminal case processing and, in particular, sentencing.

[…]

Pretrial Status and Sentencing

The legal factor of pretrial status may significantly affect sentencing, yet this variable is not always included in, or a main focus of, sentencing studies. It appears from current research that offense severity and criminal history are the strongest predictors at all stages of criminal adjudication, including bail decisions, guilty pleas, and sentencing. It is also true that race and gender play a strong role in judicial decision making at various stages of criminal case processing. However, the role of pretrial status should be at the forefront of studies on sentencing, as pretrial decisions can adversely affect the entire course of a criminal case.

Fifty years ago, Foote (1954) postulated that defendants who are held in pretrial detention are not in a position to contribute wholly to their own criminal defense. Twenty-five years later Feeley (1979) detailed the many adverse effects for defendants held in pretrial detention. Recent research regarding the connection between pretrial incarceration and case outcomes shows even more conclusive evidence. Defendants who are detained prior to trial are usually unable to afford representation, a situation that is exacerbated by the increased costs associated with pretrial detention. To make the situation worse, lawyers usually spend less time with their detained defendants than with those released on bail in the community (Allan, Allan, Giles, Drake, & Froyland, 2005).

Detention prior to trial and a defendant's inability to fully participate in his or her own defense can negatively affect the outcome of a case. According to a study of pretrial detention and case outcomes conducted by Phillips (2008) of the New York City Criminal Justice Agency (CJA), pretrial detention had an adverse impact on a final case disposition. More specifically, Phillips found that detention prior to trial increased the odds of conviction, the probability of incarceration, and the length of imprisonment. Findings from earlier work on the effects of pretrial detention acknowledged this effect as well. Specifically, in one of the most notable studies on pretrial detention conducted almost 50 years ago as part of the Manhattan Bail Project, Ares, Rankin, and Sturz (1963) found that defendants held in pretrial detention were more likely to be convicted and incarcerated. A subsequent study conducted by Rankin (1964), in conjunction with the Manhattan Bail Project, reached a similar conclusion.

More recent research confirms the strong link between pretrial detention, conviction, and incarceration. In a study of the impact of pretrial decisions on incarceration, Williams concluded that defendants held in pretrial detention were more likely to receive a sentence of incarceration and lengthier sentences when a term of incarceration was imposed. Other research, though not focusing mainly on pretrial detention, has shown that defendants held in custody were more likely to be convicted (Cohen & Reaves, 2007) and were more likely to receive a term of incarceration (Chiricos & Bales,

1991; Goldkamp, 1980; Harrington & Spohn, 2007; Holmes & Daudistel, 1984), and they received lengthier sentences than their counterparts who were released on bail (Tartaro & Sedelmaier, 2009; Williams, 2003; Willison, 1984).

The legal consequences of incarceration are well known, but incarceration has a myriad of other negative effects on offenders and their families (Travis, 2005; Western, 2002, 2006). When defendants are denied bail or cannot afford to pay the financial bail required, they are usually held in local jails during the pretrial period. According to the Bureau of Justice Statistics (2011), by midyear of 2010, there were approximately 748,728 inmates being held in local jails. Local jails hold offenders who have been convicted and sentenced to serve a term of incarceration (usually 1 year or less and typically for misdemeanors); however, approximately 61% of the total inmates currently detained in jails are being held prior to trial (Bureau of Justice Statistics, 2011). A substantial body of research shows that incarceration is correlated with a number of detrimental effects, including decreased employment rates, lower wages, physical and psychological conditions, damaged familial bonds, and higher rates of recidivism (Allan et al., 2005; Travis, 2005; Western, 2002, 2006), and as Schlesinger (2005) explains, these effects are also experienced by defendants held in pretrial detention.

In sum, evidence has shown that pretrial decisions can adversely affect the entire course of a case. Defendants who receive negative bail decisions cannot participate fully in their defense and, even further, studies show that those detained prior to trial have greater odds of conviction, a greater likelihood of incarceration, and lengthier sentences when imprisonment is imposed. A solid body of research has examined sentencing decisions, particularly within the framework of racial and ethnic differences, but as Foote (1954) suggested many years ago and as McCoy (2007) has echoed in her own work, it may be that earlier case decisions best predict later outcomes.

The Current Study

The literature on factors that affect sentencing practices is vast, yet the research does not usually focus on pretrial detention and, at times, this variable is not included. However, the pretrial decision is one of the first legal proceedings to occur in the criminal justice process and therefore it holds the potential to steer the course of the criminal case, with incarceration as the potential outcome. Given the finality of the criminal justice sentence and the many devastating consequences of incarceration, it is imperative to study not just the factors that affect the pretrial decision but also the role of pretrial outcomes on later decisions. The current study analyzes the legal and extralegal factors that influence both the judicial decision to incarcerate and the sentence length that follows incarceration decisions. We hypothesize that pretrial detention will significantly predict the likelihood of custodial sentences and longer sentences when incarceration is imposed. This study is intended to add to current research on the administration of justice, particularly since the pretrial and sentencing decisions are arguably the two most important decision points in the criminal case process.

Methodology and Data

The research employs individual-level secondary data collected from the State of New Jersey's Criminal Disposition Commission (CDC). In an effort to examine potential systematic inequalities in criminal justice practices, the CDC conducted research in which it recorded all summons and complaints issued in New Jersey on the randomly selected week from October 18, 2004, to October 24, 2004. The progression of these cases from arrest through sentencing (the entire case process) was traced and recorded, which resulted in the creation of a database containing 2,093 initial cases. Of these 2,093 cases, almost half of the sample ($n = 1,118$) cases were "screened out." In New Jersey, the screening process occurs when the County Prosecutor reviews the charges and makes a decision about whether to file them as indictable offenses in Superior Court. Cases that are charged as indictable offenses in Superior Court are classified as "screened in." In this sample ($N = 975$), cases were screened in. Cases may be screened out for a variety of reasons, including lack of evidence and/or a prosecutor's decision to transfer the case to another division, such as Family Court. This process is common in other jurisdictions and exhibits what is known as "the funnel of justice," which refers to the attrition rate of cases as they move through the criminal case process from arrest to sentencing. As demonstrated nicely in a study published by the Vera Institute of Justice (1977), the number of felony arrests decreases substantially as cases are dismissed, downgraded, and decided.

The 975 cases that survived the process of case attrition were further reduced as this analysis focused on those cases that had bail decisions and subsequently proceeded through the entire case process to conviction and sentencing, resulting in a final sample of ($N = 634$) felony cases for this analysis. This sample size is still plenty robust for statistical analyses. The cases included in this sample were collected from all 21 counties in New Jersey, which are representative of all rural, suburban, and urban jurisdictions located in New Jersey. The data include demographic factors, such as race, age, and gender; an expansive list of legal variables, including criminal history and information relevant to offense severity; and information about several decision points in each case.

VARIABLES

Two dependent variables are utilized in this analysis to examine the hypothesis that adverse pretrial decisions will result in adverse sentencing outcomes. The first, a binary variable, measures whether a defendant received a custodial sentence or noncustodial sentence, which includes a punishment such as probation or community service. Second, we examined the length of sentence for individuals who received a sentence of incarceration.

The database used in this study includes both demographic and legal information that were used to create independent variables for our analyses. The demographic variables utilized in this research include the following: race (white/black/Hispanic), gender (male/female), age (in years), jurisdiction type (urban/nonurban), and defense attorney type (public defender/private counsel). Jurisdictions were categorized as urban/nonurban based on the population per square mile of each county. New Jersey is the most densely populated state in the nation though, so no counties could be designated as "rural" compared to less populous states. Unfortunately, the data do not contain direct indicators about the arrestees' socioeconomic status. As such, we use attorney type as a proxy for the defendant's socioeconomic status. Defendants deemed eligible for a public defender are generally categorized as indigent and those who can retain private counsel presumably have some financial means.

This study utilized several legal independent variables relevant to sentencing outcomes. Offense type is measured as a four-category variable comprised of "person and weapons offenses" (violent offenses), property offenses, drug offenses, and other offenses. "Other" offenses include a variety of nonviolent, public order offenses, including crimes such as disorderly conduct, solicitation of prostitution, and "crimes of dishonesty," such as perjury. As previously discussed, offense severity is usually a significant predictor of sentencing decisions. On the basis of this information, we created dummy variables for the latter three offense types, thus utilizing violent offenses as the reference category.[1]

The number of charges involved in each case, a continuous measure of offense severity, is also included in our analyses. In addition to the seriousness of the offense, the defendant's criminal history has been found to be the most powerful predictor of judicial decisions at all stages of criminal case processing (Gottfredson & Gottfredson, 1990). In keeping with previous research, this study includes the number of prior convictions as a continuous measure of a defendant's criminal history. This research adds to the standard list of demographic and legal variables by testing whether pretrial outcomes affect sentencing decisions. Pretrial status is measured by a binary variable indicating whether a defendant was released into the community or held in jail prior to trial.

A few approaches are used in this study to determine the potential impact of bail practices on sentencing. Logistic regression was selected for the analysis involving custodial sentence, where the dependent variable was dichotomized to reflect cases in which defendants were sentenced to a custodial sentence (yes/no).[2] The dependent variable in this analysis is dichotomous and categorical and the independent variables are both categorical and continuous, making logistic regression a preferred statistical procedure, which has been used in similar studies (Mertler & Vannatta, 2005; Williams, 2003). We intended to use OLS (ordinary least squares) regression to examine the dependent variable "sentence length." However, this variable has a lot of values that register zero, which violates the assumptions of multivariate linear regression. Since the study theorizes that the same factors that may influence whether a sentence involves incarceration may also affect the sentence length, a Tobit analysis was utilized to control for bias as a result of left censoring (Albonetti, 1997; Breen, 1996; Bushway, Johnson, & Slocum, 2007).

Some research on judicial decision making has also included the use of interaction terms. Interactions among predictor variables can be helpful in specific analyses in strengthening predictions about the dependent variable (Tabachnick & Fidell, 1996). For example, Nobiling, Spohn, and DeLone (1998) utilized interaction variables of gender and employment status and race and employment status when investigating factors affecting incarceration and sentence severity. Steffensmeier et al. (1998) examined Race x Age and Age x Gender interaction effects in their study on the effect of being young, black, and male involved in criminal sentencing. Spohn (2000) found that interaction effects between legal predictors and race increased sentence severity and that the interaction between race and pretrial detention enhanced sentence severity. In the current study, interaction terms were created between the number of prior convictions and demographic variables (age, race, and gender)

---

1   We note that the group containing "other" offenses comprises a much smaller percentage of cases (see Table 1) and as such we caution the interpretation of the findings. We considered eliminating these cases but ultimately chose to retain them as most of these cases are public order crimes and represent "victimless" crimes, which are qualitatively different from the other offense types in this analysis. Therefore, we chose to retain our "other" cases, similar to several researchers in this field (Frenzel & Ball, 2007; Johnson, 2003; Steffensemeier & Demuth, 2001).

2   More recent research (Harrington & Spohn, 2007; Holleran & Spohn, 2004) has moved away from the use of a dichotomous dependent variable measuring total incarceration. Unfortunately, our data, which were collected by the New Jersey Criminal Disposition Commission, did not allow us to parse out the various custodial and noncustodial options, that is, jail versus prison. We encourage future researchers on this topic to move in this direction; however, for this study we had to rely on the traditional total incarceration variable to measure type of sentence.

and between offense seriousness and demographic variables to determine whether the combination of these variables would produce a more pronounced effect on sentencing decisions. In addition, interaction terms were created between race and pretrial release.

Results

Table 4.2.1 provides the descriptive data for the variables employed in this study. Most of 87% (n = 553) the defendants in this sample were male, and approximately 66% (n = 419) of defendants were ethnic minority. Defendants in this sample had an average of 2.1 prior convictions and 3.8 of charges pending. The offense types were distributed as follows: 30% (n = 187) of all charges involved violent offenses (this category includes the use or sale of firearms), 41% (n = 262) comprised drug offenses, 22% (n = 141) contained property offenses, and 7% (n = 44) involved other types of offenses. Approximately 28% (n = 175) of the arrestees were released on bail, and 72% (n = 459) were held in pretrial detention. The most common bail amount set by the court was US$10,000. Approximately 64% (n = 308) of the defendants in the sample were able to meet bail requirements, whereas about 36% (n = 175) could not meet the financial requirements and were therefore held in jail prior to trial. Regarding attorney type, about 84% (n = 510) of defendants were assigned a public defender and about 16% (n = 98) retained private counsel. When looking at sentencing outcomes, about 59%

Table 4.2.1. Sample Description

Name	Coding	n	%	M	SD
Age	In years			30	9.9
Gender	1 = female	80	12.6		
	0 = male	553	87.4		
Race	1 = white	213	33.7		
	2 = Hispanic	104	16.5		
	3 = black	315	49.8		
County type	1 = urban	451	71.1		
	2 = nonurban	183	28.9		
Offense type	1 = person & weapons	187	29.5		
	2 = property	141	22.2		
	3 = CDS (controlled dangerous substance)	262	41.3		
	4 = other	44	6.9		
Prior convictions	Number of prior convictions			3.1	4.1
Number of counts	Number of current charges			3.8	3.4
Release	1 = release	459	72.4		
0 = in jail	175		27.6		
Defense attorney type	1 = private counsel	98	16.1		
	0 = assigned counsel	510	83.9		
Custodial disposition	1 = yes	372	58.8		
	2 = no	261	41.2		
Incarceration (days)				1095	1144

Note: N = 634.

(n = 372) received a term of incarceration and 41% (n = 261) received a noncustodial sentence. Finally, the average sentence length served in this sample was 1,095 days of imprisonment.

[...]

Table 4.2.2 presents the results of a logistic regression predicting a sentence of incarceration. The analyses reveal some results that conform to the findings of previous studies on the topic. Specifically, the number of charges and the number of prior convictions both significantly predicted a sentence of imprisonment. As previously discussed, both of these continuous variables were recoded as categorical variables. Defendants in categories with one to four prior convictions and five or more prior convictions both had greater odds of receiving a custodial sentence when compared with defendants with no prior convictions (Wald = 11.62, odds = 2.09, p = 001; Wald = 26.10, odds = 4.26, p < .001). Cases with two to five counts and more than five counts were more likely to receive a sentence of incarceration when compared to those cases with only one charge pending (Wald = 7.75, odds = 1.83, p = .005; Wald = 11.57, odds = 2.45, p = .001).

Other significant predictors of incarceration emerged as well. Offense type predicted the odds of a custodial sentence in that defendants charged with property offenses and drug offenses were less likely to receive a term of incarceration when compared to violent offenders (Wald = 4.36, odds = 0.58, p = .037; Wald = 4.11, odds = −0.64, p = .043). Jurisdiction also emerged as a significant predictor of incarceration, however, not in the expected direction. Surprisingly, the odds of incarceration were 38% lower for defendants in urban jurisdictions as compared to their counterparts in nonurban

Table 4.2.2. Logistic Regression: Dependent Variable = Custodial Sentence or No Custodial Sentence.

	B	SE	Wald	Exp (B)
Gender (female)	0.49	0.27	3.16	1.63
Age	−0.01	0.01	0.43	1.00
Race (white)				
Hispanic	0.29	0.28	1.02	1.33
Black	0.17	0.22	0.56	1.18
Attorney type (private)	0.17	0.26	0.40	1.18
County type (nonurban)	−0.48	0.21	5.30	0.62***
Number of counts (1)				
Number of counts 2 to 5	0.60	0.22	7.75	1.83**
Number of counts 5 and more	0.90	0.26	11.57	2.45***
Number of priors (0)				
Number of priors 1 to 4	0.74	0.22	11.62	2.09***
Number of priors more than 5	1.45	0.28	26.10	4.26***
Offense type (violent)				
Property	−0.55	0.26	4.36	0.58*
Drugs	−0.45	0.22	4.11	0.64*
Other	−0.16	0.39	0.17	0.85
Release (in jail)	−0.21	0.22	0.89	0.81
Model χ^2 = 73.48***				
−2LL = 721.881				
Nagelkerke R^2 = .16				

Note: n = 592. Reference categories are in parentheses.
*p < .05. **p < .01. ***p < .001.

STAT HELP!

Because the authors use logistic regression in this table, the findings can be interpreted as the odds of receiving a custodial sentence. It is easiest to look at the column labeled "EXP(B)." For example, the EXP(B) value for "Gender" shows that the odds of males receiving a custodial sentence are 1.63 times higher than the odds of females receiving a custodial sentence. "Female" is in parentheses because it is the comparison category. The lack of an asterisk (*), though, indicates that gender does not have a *statistically significant* effect, meaning the odds of receiving a custodial sentence are not statistically different for males and females. Stated differently, gender is not influencing whether defendants get a custodial sentence. A value less than 1 in this column would suggest lower, as opposed to higher, odds.

jurisdictions (Wald = 5.30, odds = 0.62, $p < .021$). Finally, the variable central to the hypotheses in this study—bail posted—did not have a significant impact on incarceration. This finding does not support the hypothesis that defendants held in pretrial detention are more likely to receive custodial sentences than those who are able to post bail and return to the community prior to trial.

Table 4.2.3 presents the results from a Tobit regression predicting the length of a defendant's term of incarceration in days. Gender emerged as a significant predictor of sentence length and, conforming

Table 4.2.3. Tobit Analysis: Dependent Variable = Sentence Length (Logged)

	Model 1			Model 2		
	Coefficient	*SE*	*T*	Coefficient	*SE*	*t*
Gender (female)	13.10	3.83	3.41***	10.90	3.72	2.93**
Age	0.01	0.02	0.53	−0.11	0.12	−0.87
Race (white)						
Hispanic	6.63	3.69	1.80	4.73	3.56	1.33
Black	7.24	2.93	2.47*	6.12	2.84	2.16*
Attorney type (private)	5.02	3.49	1.44	0.55	3.42	0.16
County type (nonurban)	−3.71	2.68	−1.39	−4.05	2.58	−1.57
Prior convictions	−0.01	0.01	−1.08	2.11	0.33	6.46***
Number of charges	1.16	0.35	3.32***	1.34	0.34	3.97***
Offense type (violent)						
Property	−8.21	3.39	−2.42*	−9.34	3.28	−2.85**
Drugs	−5.14	2.83	−1.82	−6.55	2.72	−2.40*
Other	−6.60	5.05	−1.31	−12.60	5.01	−2.51*
Release (in jail)	−8.24	2.73	−3.02***	−6.35	2.65	−2.39*
Age x Prior Convictions				−5.16	1.51	−3.41***
Model χ^2	73.06 ***			114.55***		
Log likelihood	−1879.55			−1826.41		
Pseudo R^2	.0191			.0304		

Note: n = 589. Reference categories are in parentheses.

*$p < .05$. **$p < .01$. ***$p < .001$.

STAT HELP!

In this table, it is easiest to look at the "Coefficient" column to interpret the results. Positive values suggest an increased sentence length and negative values suggest a decreased sentence length. For example, in both models, males receive longer sentences than females. The only difference between "Model 1" and "Model 2" is that "Model 2" includes what is called an interaction term (labelled "Age x Prior Convictions") that shows older offenders with prior convictions get shorter sentences (so younger offenders with prior convictions get lengthier sentences). One or more asterisks (*) indicate the effect is *statistically significant*.

to the literature on this topic, men received longer sentences than women ($t = 2.93$, $p < .004$). Also corresponding to prior research is the finding that black defendants received lengthier sentences when compared to white defendants ($t = 2.16$, $p < .05$). Consistent with the previous analysis, the number of charges, as well as the number of prior convictions, plays a strong role in sentence length. Specifically, an increasing number of charges and prior convictions increase a defendant's sentence length. Offense type is significant in that property, drug, and other felony offenses all received shorter sentences than violent offenses. The interaction between age and prior convictions is significant, indicating that the relationship between number of prior convictions and sentence length is more pronounced for younger defendants. The variable of most interest to the current study, a defendant's bail posting status, emerged as a significant predictor of sentence length. Specifically, defendants who were held in pretrial detention received longer sentences than those who were able to post bail, confirming one of the main hypotheses of this research.

Discussion

The final decision point, sentencing, marks the end of the criminal case process. As previously discussed, this is the decision point that receives the most attention, particularly from the legislature and the media (Demuth, 2003), since sentencing may provide an opportunity to "see justice served" and as sentencing brings with it the finality to the criminal case process. Several studies have examined variables that affect conviction and sentencing (Neubauer, 2002; Spohn et al., 1981; Steffensmeier, Ulmer, & Kramer, 1998), but only a few of these have included pretrial detention as a possible influence (Phillips, 2008; Williams, 2003). This study examined the determinants of incarceration and sentence length.

As expected, an increasing number of prior convictions increased the likelihood of a custodial sentence and resulted in a lengthier term of incarceration, a finding that is consistent with previous literature (Gottfredson & Gottfredson, 1988; Neubauer, 2002). The number of charges involved in a case also significantly predicted the odds of incarceration and sentence length, in that an increasing number of charges increased sentence length. This finding, also consistent with previous research (Williams, 2003), is logical considering that as the charges pending increase, so do the accompanying penalties. In addition, the findings that cases involving violent offenses are more likely to receive a custodial sentence and lengthier sentences are consistent with previous conclusions that offense severity affects sentencing decisions.

The impact of demographic variables on sentencing decisions was also consistent with previous research: Men received lengthier custodial sentences than women (Albonetti, 1997). Race did not affect the odds of a custodial sentence, but this variable did affect sentence length, in that black defendants received lengthier custodial sentences than their white counterparts. This finding is consistent with a solid body of research concluding that race plays a strong role in these decisions (Kramer & Steffensmeier, 1993; Spohn & Cederblom, 1991), even though some research refutes these results (Engen & Gainey, 2000). The findings also establish that younger defendants receive longer sentences when they have a more extensive criminal history. The finding that young, black, male defendants with extensive criminal histories are sentenced more harshly comports with previous findings linking demographic characteristics such as race and gender with legal factors such as prior criminal record under the framework of attributions of dangerousness (Spohn & Holleran, 2000; Steffensmeier & Demuth, 2001; Steffensmeier et al., 1998).

One result in particular was surprising. Specifically, in this sample, defendants in nonurban jurisdiction were more likely than those in urban counties to receive a sentence of incarceration. This finding implies that nonurban defendants are not treated more leniently by the courts than urban defendants. This finding, though not anticipated, may be related to the political views held by nonurban judges and may indicate a tendency for nonurban judges to be more punitive. Although it is beyond the scope of the current study, this finding could be analyzed more carefully in future research utilizing data that measure court-related characteristics.

In this study we hypothesized that a defendant's bail posting status would significantly predict the decision to incarcerate and the length of sentence. The ability to post bail did not affect whether a defendant received a sentence of incarceration; however, when the court imposed this type of sentence, bail posting played a strong role in dictating the length of the sentence. Defendants who were detained prior to trial received longer sentences than defendants who were released on bail. Several explanations of this finding are possible. More than 50 years ago Foote (1954) posited that defendants who are held in pretrial detention cannot fully participate in their defense, particularly because they spend very little time with their attorneys.

Williams (2003) suggests that judges treat defendants who are released prior to trial more leniently than those who could not afford bail. He reasoned that judges may view detained defendants as being more dangerous and posing a more serious threat to the community. Judges might perceive pretrial incarceration as a measure taken to protect the community rather than detention before trial as an unfortunate result of a lack of financial resources. Logically, defendants who have been released on bail have the opportunity to demonstrate for the court that they do not pose a danger to the community in which they reside.

Similarly, according to Williams (2003), the perception stems from more than a defendant abiding by the terms of his or her release. Good behavior in the community prior to trial suggests to a judge that a defendant does not pose a danger and will make his or her scheduled court appearances. These defendants can keep their jobs or find new employment. They are able to continue attending school and therefore demonstrate ties to the community. Taken together, these factors may contribute to a judge's perception that defendants who are released on bail prior to trial are worthy of more lenient sentences, such as community supervision or other noncustodial sentences. A defendant who is detained pretrial will obviously not have the same opportunity to demonstrate a network of strong community ties and a pattern of good conduct in the community. Therefore, defendants who are released on bail have a distinct advantage at sentencing.

Declaration of Conflicting Interests

The author(s) declared no potential conflicts of interest with respect to the research, authorship, and/or publication of this article.

Funding

The author(s) received no financial support for the research, authorship, and/or publication of this article.

REFERENCES

Albonetti, C. A. (1990). Race and the probability of pleading guilty. *Journal of Quantitative Criminology, 6*, 315–334.

Albonetti, C. A. (1991). An integration of theories to explain judicial decision making. *Social Problems, 38*, 247–266.

Albonetti, C. A. (1997). Sentencing under the federal sentencing guidelines: Effects of defendant characteristics, guilty pleas, and departures on sentence outcomes for drug offenses, 1991–1992. *Law & Society Review, 31*, 789–822.

Alderden, M. A., & Lavery, T. A. (2007). Predicting homicide clearances in Chicago: Investigating disparities in predictors across different types of homicide. *Homicide Studies, 11*, 115–132.

Allan, A., Allan, M., Giles, M., Drake, D., & Froyland, I. (2005). An observational study of bail decision-making. *Psychiatry, Psychology and Law, 12*, 319–333.

Ares, C., Rankin, A., & Sturz, H. (1963). The Manhattan Bail Project: An interim report on the pre-trial use of pre-trial parole. *New York University Law Review, 38*, 67–95.

Baradaran, S., & McIntyre, F. L. (2012). Predicting violence. *Texas Law Review, 90*, 497–540.

Breen, R. (1996). *Regression models: Censored, sample selected, or truncated data.* Thousand Oaks, CA. SAGE.

Brown, D. L., & Warner, B. D. (1992). Immigrants, urban politics, and policing in 1900. *American Sociological Review, 57*, 293–305.

Bureau of Justice Statistics. (2011). *Jail inmates at midyear 2010.* Washington, DC: U.S. Department of Justice. Retrieved from http://www.bjs.gov/index.cfm?ty=pbdetail&iid=2375

Bushway, S., Johnson, B. D., & Slocum, L. A. (2007). Is the magic still there: The use of the Heckman Two-Step Correction for selecting bias. *Journal of Quantitative Criminology, 23*, 151–178.

Chiricos, T., & Bales, W. (1991). Unemployment and punishment: An empirical assessment. *Criminology, 29*, 701–724.

Cohen, T. H., & Reaves, B. A. (2007). *State court processing statistics, 1990–2004: Pretrial release of felony defendants in state courts.* Washington, DC: U.S. Department of Justice.

Demuth, S. (2003). Racial and ethnic differences in pretrial release decisions and outcomes: A comparison of Hispanic, black and white felony arrestees. *Criminology, 41*, 873–907.

Demuth, S., & Steffensmeier, D. (2004). The impact of gender and race-ethnicity in the pretrial release process. *Social Problems, 51*, 222–242.

Engen, R. L., & Gainey, R. R. (2000). Modeling the effects of legally relevant and extralegal factors under sentencing guidelines: The rules have changed. *Criminology, 38*, 1207–1225.

Feeley, M. M. (1979). *The process is the punishment.* New York, NY: Russell Sage.

Foote, C. (1954). Compelling appearance in court: Administration of bail in Philadelphia. *University of Pennsylvania Law Review, 102*, 1031–1079.

Free, M. D., Jr., (2004). Bail and pretrial release decisions: An assessment of the racial threat perspective. *Journal of Ethnicity in Criminal Justice, 2*, 23–44.

Freiburger, T. (2009). Race and the sentencing of drug offenders: An examination of the focal Concerns perspective. *The Southwest Journal of Criminal Justice, 6*, 163–176.

Frenzel, E. D., & Ball, J. D. (2007). Effects of individual characteristics on plea negotiations under sentencing guidelines. *Journal of Ethnicity in Criminal Justice, 5*, 59–82.

Gibbs, A. (1998). *Probation partnerships: A study of roles, relationships and meanings* (Probation Studies Unit Report No. 7). Oxford, UK: University of Oxford.

Goldkamp, J. S. (1980). The effects of detention on judicial decisions: A closer look. *Justice System Journal, 5*, 234–257.

Gottfredson, M. R., & Gottfredson, D. M. (1988). *Decision-making in criminal justice: Toward the rational exercise of discretion.* New York, NY: Plenum.

Gottfredson, M. R., & Gottfredson, D. M. (1990). *Decision making in criminal justice: Toward the rational exercise of discretion* (2d ed.). New York, NY: Plenum.

Greenwood, P. W., & Abrahamse, A. (1982). *Selective incapacitation.* Santa Monica, CA: RAND.

Harrington, M. P., & Spohn, C. (2007). Defining sentence type: Further evidence against use of the total incarceration variable. *Journal of Research in Crime and Delinquency, 44*, 36–63.

Holleran, D. & Spohn, C. (2004). On the use of the total incarceration variable in sentencing research. *Criminology, 42*, 211–240.

Holmes, M. D., & Daudistel, H. C. (1984). Ethnicity and justice in the Southwest: The sentencing of Anglo, Black and Mexican origin defendants. *Social Science Quarterly, 65*, 265–277.

Jenkins, P. (1994). "The ice age": The social construction of a drug panic. *Justice Quarterly, 11*, 7–31.

Johnson, B. D. (2003). Racial and ethnic disparities in sentencing departures across modes of conviction. *Criminology, 41*, 449–489.

Kellough, G., & Wortley, S. (2002). Remand for plea: Bail decisions and plea bargaining as commensurate conditions. *British Journal of Criminology, 42*, 186–210.

Kern, R. P., & Kolmetz, P. F. (1986). *Development of a pretrial risk assessment instrument: A pilot study.* Richmond: Virginia Department of Criminal Justice Services, Statistical Analysis Center.

Kramer, J., & Steffensmeier, D. (1993). Race and imprisonment decisions. *Sociological Quarterly, 34*, 357–376.

Luskin, M. L., & Luskin, R. C. (1986). Why so fast, why so slow?: Explaining case processing time. *Journal of Criminal Law and Criminology, 77*, 190–214.

McCoy, C. (2007). Caleb was right: Pretrial decisions determine mostly everything. *Berkeley Journal of Criminal Law, 12*, 135–149.

Mertler, C. A., & Vannatta, R. A. (2005). *Advanced and multivariate statistical methods: Practical application and interpretation* (2nd ed.). Glendale, CA: Pyrczak Publishing.

Neubauer, D. W. (2002). *America's courts and the criminal justice system.* Belmont, CA: Wadsworth.

Nobiling, T., Spohn, C., & DeLone, M. (1998). A tale of two counties: Unemployment and sentence severity. *Justice Quarterly, 15*, 459–486.

Phillips, M. T. (2008). *Pretrial detention and case outcomes. Part 2: Felony cases.* New York: New York City Criminal Justice Agency.

Phillips, M. T. (2011). *Effect of release type on failure to appear.* New York: New York City Criminal Justice Agency.

Ostrom, B. J., & Hanson, R. A. (1999). *Efficiency, timeliness, and quality: A new perspective from nine state criminal trial courts.* Washington, DC: National Institute of Justice and the State Justice Institute.

Rankin, A. (1964). The effect of pretrial detention. *New York University Law Review, 39*, 641–655.

Sacks, M., & Ackerman, A. (in press). Pretrial detention and guilty pleas: If they can't afford bail they must be guilty. *Criminal Justice Studies.*

Schlesinger, T. (2005). Racial and ethnic disparity in pretrial criminal processing. *Justice Quarterly, 22*, 170–192.

Spohn, C. (2000). *Offender Race and Case Outcomes, Do Crime Seriousness and Strength of Evidence Matter?: Final Activities Report Submitted to the national Institute of Justice.* Washington, DC: National Criminal Justice Reference Service, U.S. Department of Justice.

Spohn, C., & Beichner, D. (2000). Is preferential treatment of female offenders a thing of the past? A Multisite study of gender, race and imprisonment. *Criminal Justice Policy Review, 11*, 149–184.

Spohn, C., & Cederblom, J. (1991). Race and disparities in sentencing: A test of the liberation hypothesis. *Justice Quarterly, 8*, 601–623.

Spohn, C., Gruhl, J., & Welch, S. (1981). The effect of race on sentencing: A re-examination of an unsettled question. *Law and Society Review, 16*, 71–88.

Spohn, C., & Holleran, D. (2000). The imprisonment penalty paid by young, unemployed black and Hispanic male offenders. *Criminology, 38*, 281–306.

Steen, S., Engen, R. L., & Gainey, R. R. (2005). Images of danger and culpability: Racial stereotyping, case processing, and criminal sentencing. *Criminology, 43*, 435–468.

Steffensmeier, D. (1980). Assessing the impact of the women's movement on sex-based differences in the handling of adult criminal defendants. *Crime and Delinquency, 26*, 344–357.

Steffensmeier, D., & Demuth, S. (2000). Ethnicity and sentencing outcomes in U.S. federal Courts: Who is punished more harshly? *American Sociological Review, 65*, 705–729.

Steffensmeier, D., & Demuth, S. (2001). Ethnicity and judges' sentencing decisions: Hispanic-black-white comparisons. *Criminology, 39*, 145–178.

Steffensmeier, D., & Demuth, S. (2006). Does gender modify the effects of race—ethnicity of criminal sanctions? Sentences for male, female, White, Black and Hispanic defendants. *Journal of Quantitative Criminology, 22*, 241–261.

Steffensmeier, D., Kramer, J., & Streifel, C. (1993). Gender and imprisonment decisions. *Criminology, 31*, 411–446.

Steffensmeier, D., Ulmer, J., & Kramer, J. (1998). The interaction of race, gender, and age in criminal sentencing: The cost of being young, black, and male. *Criminology, 36*, 763–798.

Sullivan, L. (2010, January 22). Inmates who can't make bail face stark options. *National Public Radio.*

Tabachnick, B. G., & Fidell, L. S. (1996). *Using multivariate statistics* (3rd ed.). New York, NY: HarperCollins.

Tartaro, C., & Sedelmaier, C. M. (2009). A tale of two counties: The impact of pretrial release, race, and ethnicity upon sentencing decisions. *Criminal Justice Studies, 22*, 203–221.

Thomas, W. H. (1976). *Bail reform in America.* Berkeley: University of California Press.

Tittle, C. R., & Curran, D. A. (1988). Contingencies for dispositional disparities in juvenile justice. *Social Forces, 67*, 23–58.

Toborg, M. (1981). *Pretrial release: A national evaluation of practices and outcomes.* Washington, DC: U.S. Department of Justice, National Institute of Justice.

Travis, J. (2005). *But they all come back: Facing the challenges of prisoner reentry.* Washington, DC: Urban Institute Press.

Turner, K. B., & Johnson, J. B. (2005). A comparison of bail amounts for Hispanics, Whites, and African Americans: A single county analysis. *American Journal of Criminal Justice, 30*, 35–56.

Ulmer, J., & Johnson, B. D. (2004). Sentencing in context: A multilevel analysis. *Criminology, 42*, 137–175.

Vera Institute of Justice. (1977). *Felony arrests: Their prosecution and disposition in New York City courts.* New York, NY: Longman.

Western, B. (2002). The impact of incarceration on wage mobility and inequality. *American Sociological Review, 67*, 526–546.

Western, B. (2006). *Punishment and inequality in America.* New York, NY: Russell Sage. Williams, M. (2003). The effect of pretrial detention on imprisonment decisions. *Criminal Justice Review, 28*, 299–316.

Willison, D. (1984). The effects of counsel on the severity of criminal sentences: A statistical assessment. *The Justice Journal, 9*, 87–101.

The Plea Bargaining Controversy

Douglas A. Smith

G uilty pleas became a major method of case disposition in the late 19th century and today account for over 85% of all felony convictions,[1] yet pleas are a continuing source of controversy. Some critics argue that a system of negotiated justice undermines the deterrent effectiveness of punishment and can be used by influential defendants to evade legal sanctions. Others maintain that defendants with prior criminal records, and hence more firsthand experience with the justice system, are able to negotiate more favorable sentences.[2] Proponents of these views see plea bargaining as undesirable because it weakens the deterrent and incapacitative effectiveness of the law by allowing some defendants to minimize their punishment.

Additional attacks on plea bargaining focus on the alleged coerciveness of the process.[3] This viewpoint characterizes plea bargaining as a series of threats and promises by legal officials that induce defendants to forfeit many of their legal rights and plead guilty. The coercion argument rests on the belief that defendants convicted at trial are sentenced more harshly than those convicted by plea.[4] Since a defendant seeks to minimize his punishment, pleading guilty is made attractive by an explicit agreement or implication that

---

1 *See generally* Alschuler, *Plea Bargaining and Its History*, 79 Colum. L. Rev. 1, 1–43 (1979); Friedman, *Plea Bargaining in Historical Perspective*, 13 Law & Soc. Rev. 247, 247–59 (1979). Heuman, *A Note on Plea Bargaining and Case Pressure*, 9 Law & Soc. Rev. 515, 515–27 (1975).

2 D. Newman, Conviction: The Determination of Guilt or Innocence Without Trial (1966). J.Q. Wilson, Thinking About Crime (1975).

3 *See, e.g.*, Alschuler, *supra* note 1; Blumberg, *The Practice of Law as a Confidence Game: Organizational Cooperation of a Profession*, 1 Law & Soc. Rev. 15, 15–39 (1967); Dash, *Cracks in the Foundation of Justice*, 46 Ill. L.F. 393 (1951).

4 *See, e.g.*, Brereton & Casper, *Does it Pay to Plead Guilty? Differential Functioning of Criminal Courts*, 16 Law & Soc. Rev. 45, 47–70 (1981–82); Nardulli, *Plea Bargaining: An Organizational Perspective*, 6 J. Crim. Just. 217, 217–31 (1978); Uhlman & Walker, *A Plea is no Bargain: The Impact of Case Disposition on Sentence*, 60 Soc. Sei. Q. 218, 218–34 (1979).

his sentence will be reduced in exchange for a guilty plea.[5] This promise convinces defendants that pleading guilty serves their own interests. This dual sentencing structure has been criticized because it penalizes defendants for exercising constitutionally guaranteed legal rights and subordinates due process concerns to crime control objectives.[6]

Not all views of plea bargaining are unfavorable, however. In support of negotiated pleas, some scholars argue that statutory penalties are often too harsh, and that tailoring punishment through charge and sentence "adjustments" makes the criminal justice system more responsive to the exigencies of individual cases.[7] Plea bargaining is also considered an efficient method of allocating justice system resources.[8] Prosecutors seek to maximize the deterrent or incapacitative value of their available resources, while defendants seek to minimize their individual costs of criminal activity.

Plea bargaining also accommodates the interests of both defendants and the state. Prosecutors benefit from plea bargaining because it enables them to secure high conviction rates while avoiding the expense, uncertainty, and opportunity costs of trials. By obtaining guilty pleas, prosecutors can pursue more cases, potentially resulting in greater aggregate deterrent or incapacitative effects with a finite amount of resources.[9]

Defendants may also benefit from plea bargaining, especially if they are factually guilty. Indeed, it is the presumption of factual guilt in cases that are not quickly dismissed that drives the process of negotiation.[10] For the defendant, the presumption of guilt focuses the negotiation on the type and severity of the sentence.[11] A defendant's decision to plead guilty may be rational if the sentence he receives by pleading guilty is implicitly based on both the probability that he would be convicted at trial and the likely sentence if convicted. For example, if the likely sentence following a trial conviction is ten years and the defendant estimates that his probability of conviction is .7, then a plea to a sentence of seven years represents a rational choice. In this example a sentence reduction of 30% would be a rational compromise between the defendant and the state.[12] To the extent that defendants, like prosecutors, face uncertainty in the justice system, pleading guilty may represent a rational means for resolving an uncertain situation.

This article examines several issues in the plea bargaining controversy. First, do defendants convicted by plea receive more lenient sentences than similarly situated defendants convicted by trial? If a sentence differential does exist, what is its magnitude? Is the differential consistent across subcategories of offenders and offenses, or does it vary systematically with case characteristics and offender attributes, such as strength of evidence or prior criminal history? The magnitude of a sentence differential, if any, should provide some evidence as to whether plea negotiations are largely rational or coercive. If sentence differentials vary across offenders, analysis may indicate whether certain types of offenders

5   A. Rosett & D. Cressey, Justice By Consent: Plea Bargains in the American Courthouse (1976).

6   Halberstam, *Towards Neutral Principles in the Administration of Justice: A Critique of Supreme Court Decisions Sanctioning the Plea Bargaining Process*, 73 J. Crim. L. & Criminology 1, 1–49 (1982).

7   *See, e.g.,* P. Utz, Settling the Facts: Discretion and Negotiation in Criminal Courts (1978); Manard, *Defendant Attributes in Plea Bargaining: Notes on the Modeling of Sentencing Decisions,* 29 Soc. Probs. 347, 347–60 (1983).

8   *See, e.g.,* Easterbrook, *Criminal Procedure as a Market System,* 12 J. Leg. Stud. 289, 289–332 (1983).

9   *Id.*

10   W. Rhodes, Plea Bargaining: Who Gains? Who Loses? (1978).

11   Mather, *Some Determinants of the Method of Case Disposition: Decision-making by Public Defenders in Los Angeles,* 8 Law & Soc. Rev. 187, 187–216 (1974).

12   This example may conservatively estimate the rational reduction from expected sentences. Specifically, some argue that defendants and prosecutors discount the value of future time. For example, the possibility of spending the next year in jail may be seen as more severe than the possibility of spending a year in jail seven years from now. If such positive time preferences were operative, reductions in excess of 30% in the instant example would still be consistent with a rational market model of plea bargaining. For a discussion of this position see Easterbrook, *supra* note 8; P. Cook, *Research in the Criminal Deterrence: Laying the Groundwork for the Second Decade,* in 2 Crime and Justice: An Annual Review of Research 211, 211–68 (1980).

systematically benefit from pleading guilty. Answers to these questions provide a tentative empirical basis on which to evaluate the implications of plea bargaining for the allocation of legal sanctions.

Plea Bargaining: A View From the Data

Several studies have examined determinants of guilty pleas and the issue of sentence differentials between pleaded and tried cases. In addition, descriptive case studies have focused on factors which may influence whether a case is pleaded or proceeds to trial. Mather, for example, conducted extensive interviews with court participants and found the strength of the prosecutor's case and the seriousness of the offense increased the likelihood of a negotiated settlement.[13] Other evidence suggests that prosecutors and defense attorneys use similar criteria to establish the worth of a case. One study analyzed interviews with 138 prosecutors and 105 defense attorneys and found that general agreement emerged among court participants about the importance of offense seriousness, offender history, and case strength in determining an appropriate sentence bargain.[14] This study confirmed that prosecutors and defense attorneys generally agree on the "usual" sentence for a given case and that such agreements enhance the likelihood of negotiated pleas.

Quantitative research on plea bargaining has often studied the relationship between mode of disposition (plea vs. trial) and sentence outcomes. Although evidence from numerous studies indicates that defendants who plead guilty are sentenced less severely than defendants convicted at trial, few control variables are generally included in these studies.[15] One notable exception is Brereton and Casper's examination of sentencing dispositions for robbery and burglary defendants in three California jurisdictions.[16] Their analysis included the original charge, mode of disposition, type of attorney, defendant's demographic characteristics, and prior criminal record.[17] The authors found that by controlling for arrest charge and prior criminal record, the sentencing differential between pleaded and tried cases was reduced, but not eliminated.[18] Additionally, the size of this sentencing differential varied considerably across jurisdictions and categories of offenses.[19]

Additional support for sentence differentials between pled and tried cases appears in Uhlman and Walker's study of dispositions of 29,295 convicted felons.[20] Substantial sentence differentials existed between defendants who pled guilty and those convicted at trial.[21] For example, pled cases were 53% less likely to result in incarceration than cases where the defendant was convicted by a jury.[22] When the researchers controlled for severity of charge and crime type, the relationship between disposition mode and sentence outcomes was smaller, but not eliminated.[23] The authors suggested that charge se-

---

13   *See* Mather, *supra* note 11.

14   H. Miller, W. McDonald & J. Cramer, Plea Bargaining in the United States (1980).

15   *See, e.g.,* P. Nardulli, The Courtroom Elite (1979); Hagen, Hewitt & Alwin, *Ceremonial Justice,* 58 Soc. Forces 506, 506–27 (1979); Nardulli, *supra* note 4; Talarico, *Judicial Decisions and Sanction Patterns in Criminal Justice,* 70 J. Crim. L. & Criminology 117, 117–24 (1979); Uhlman & Walker, *supra* note 4.

16   *See* Brereton & Casper, *supr a* note 4.

17   *Id.* at 53.

18   *Id.* at 55.

19   *Id.* at 61.

20   *See* Uhlman & Walker, *supra* note 4, at 230.

21   *Id.* at 224.

22   *Id.*

23   *Id.* at 226.

verity and type of offense influenced the decision to plead guilty or to proceed to trial, and they noted that defendants convicted at jury trials were charged with more serious crimes than those convicted by plea.[24] Thus, while their findings showed that defendants receive a bargain in exchange for a plea of guilty, they concluded that the benefits may be somewhat exaggerated, since defendants who opt for trial may be acquitted.[25]

Two studies take exception to the finding of more lenient dispositions for defendants who plead guilty. Eisenstein and Jacob studied felony cases from criminals courts in Chicago, Detroit, and Baltimore and examined sentence disparities between pleaded and tried cases.[26] Their study included defendant attributes (age, race, prior record, and pre-trial release status), strength of evidence, type of counsel, and a variable which identified the sentencing judge.[27] Their analysis indicated that when these variables were controlled for, the influence of disposition mode in explaining both decisions to incarcerate and sentence length was diminished substantially.[28] In light of these findings, they suggested that tangible sentencing advantages for defendants who pleaded guilty were more imagined than real.[29]

Using a different analytic method, Rhodes examined plea bargaining in the District of Columbia for felony defendants charged with assault, larceny, burglary, or robbery and found no net sentencing differential between pleaded and tried cases.[30] Rhodes estimated the expected sentence defendants would have received if they were convicted at trial from models estimating the probability of conviction at trial and the expected sentence if convicted.[31] These predictions permitted a comparative analysis of actual versus expected outcomes of plead cases. Rhodes concluded that, with the exception of robbery, the sentences received by defendants who entered guilty pleas were roughly equivalent to the expected sentences from conviction at trial. [32]

Studies employing more control variables have found less difference in sentence between pled and tried cases than studies failing to use such variables. The importance of control variables is confirmed by a recent National Academy of Sciences report on sentencing research.[33] The report emphasized that the statistical evidence on sentencing differentials by mode of conviction may be biased by measurement error and selection bias.[34] Moreover, "these potential biases are particularly troubling because they would result in *overestimate* of the effect of the discount."[35] If, for example, offense seriousness was poorly measured or omitted from the analysis, the consequences would be to attribute to the mode of conviction a sentencing differential that was actually due to offense severity.

Finally, some research examined whether certain case or offender characteristics may be related to sentence discounts in exchange for guilty pleas. Research has consistently shown, for example, that prosecutors are less inclined to offer substantial sentence reductions when they have a strong case against a defendant.[36] Other studies suggest that prosecutors are also less likely to offer significant

---

24 *Id.* at 231.

25 *Id.*

26 J. Eisenstein & H. Jacob, Felony Justice (1977).

27 *Id.* at 175.

28 *Id.* at 263.

29 *Id.* at 286.

30 *See* W. Rhodes, *supra* note 10, at 43.

31 *Id.* at 78.

32 *Id.* at 43.

33 A. Blumstein, J. Cohen, S. Martin & M. Tonry, Research on Sentencing: The Search for Reform (1983).

34 *Id.* at 108.

35 *Id.* at 115 (emphasis in original).

36 *See, e.g.,* D. Neubauer, Criminal Justice in Middle America (1974); Alschuler, *supra* note 1; Mather, *supra* note 11.

discounts if the offense is serious or if the defendant has an extensive criminal record.[37] Some studies suggest, however, that defendants with prior records may fare better, or at least no worse, in negotiating sentence reductions than offenders with less experience with the bargaining process.[38]

Data and Variables

The data used in this analysis were collected as part of a larger evaluation of plea bargaining practices by Miller, McDonald and Cramer in 1978.[39] Information on demographic and social characteristics of defendants, the type of offense, pleas entered, evidentiary and case characteristics and sentencing outcomes were collected for 3,397 felony cases in six sites: New Orleans, Norfolk, Seattle, El Paso, Tucson, and Delaware County, Pennsylvania. From these cases, a sample was selected for analysis on the basis of certain criteria. First, only individuals who plead guilty or went to trial were included in the analysis. Second, the analysis was restricted to males charged with robbery or burglary because these offenses represent a large portion of defendants processed by the justice system that frequently result in incarceration. Data from El Paso were also excluded because of large amounts of missing data on key variables. Finally, only cases handled by judges presiding over ten cases or more were included in the final sample so that models could be estimated controlling for the effects of judges on sentencing outcomes. These selection criterion resulted in a final sample of 1,533 pled and 387 tried cases.

[...]

A continuing source of controversy in plea bargaining concerns whether the process is a coercive or rational method of allocating legal sanctions. The coercion argument rests on the claim that plea bargaining makes possible a dual sentencing structure in which defendants who proceed to trial are sentenced more harshly than those who plead guilty. The data examined in this article indicate that when actual sentences are compared to expected sentences, little evidence emerges to support the coercion argument. While a substantial difference exists between the proportion of defendants incarcerated after pleading guilty (.42) compared to those convicted at trial (.71), this difference is largely attributable to two factors: first, not all defendants who pleaded guilty would have been convicted at trial, and second, characteristics of cases convicted by plea differ in important ways from those resulting in conviction at trial. When these factors are taken into account, plea bargaining appears to reflect a rational rather than coercive process.

Data from this study also address the question of whether plea bargaining erodes the deterrent and incapacitative effect of law. While certain defendants do appear to reduce their expected probability of incarceration by pleading guilty, defendants in serious cases and offenders with prior criminal histories do not benefit. Defendants who gain the most from pleading guilty are the less serious marginal offenders with less evidence against them. Conversely, defendants who are on parole or probation at the time of arrest, those with more prior felony arrests and those with histories of drug abuse—factors considered by many to be associated with serious career offenders—do not escape incarceration by pleading guilty.

---

37 *See, e.g.,* W. Chamblis & R. Seidman, Law, Order and Power (1971); H. Miller, W. McDonald & J. Cramer, *supra* note 14; D. Neubauer, *supra* note 36; Lagoy, Senna & Siegel, *An Empirical Study on Information Usage for Prosecutorial Decision Making in Plea Negotiations,* 13 Am. Crim. L. Rev. 435, 435–71 (1976).

38 *See, e.g.,* D. Newman, *supra* note 2; Forst & Brosi, *A Theoretical and Empirical Analysis of the Prosecutor,* 6 J. Leg. Stud. 177, 177–92 (1977).

39 These data are available from the Inter-University Consortium for Political and Social Research at the University of Michigan under the title Plea Bargaining in the United States: 1978.

Collectively, these findings suggest that plea bargaining is a neutral component in the processing of criminal cases which neither erodes the deterrent effect of law nor results in a two tier sentencing system. Perhaps the primary advantage of a system of negotiated pleas is that it allows prosecutors to pursue more cases than otherwise would be possible. Based on current data, for example, prosecutors appear to gain one conviction (which would have been lost at trial) for every five pleas they accept. The manifest consequence of such a system is that legal sanctions are applied to a larger base of offenders, thus heightening the certainty of punishment. Hence, rather than eroding the deterrent effect of punishment, plea bargaining may contribute to the general deterrent effectiveness of legal sanctions.

Finally, much research remains to be done in the area of plea bargaining. First, this research examined incarceration decisions but did not directly examine other aspects of sanction severity, such as sentence length. While the coercion argument is not supported with these data concerning whether defendants go to prison, the findings may not generalize to the issue of sentence length. Further analysis is required to determine whether defendants convicted at trial receive longer sentences than those convicted by plea. Second, results in this paper suggest that plea bargaining and sentence discounts vary substantially across different jurisdictions, and we need to know more about the factors which may contribute to this inter-jurisdictional variation. Third, these results need to be replicated and the base of crime types extended. A number of other data sets may exist that would allow an anaysis similar to the analysis presented in this article. Since results from this article suggest that many commonly held beliefs regarding plea bargaining are more myth than fact, such replication is essential to advance our understanding of plea bargaining.

[…]

DISCUSSION QUESTIONS

1. Discuss some reasons why a prosecutor would go forward with charges even if there was insufficient evidence.

2. What potential ramifications are there if police withhold case information from the prosecutor?

3. What are some of the community pressures faced by prosecutors?

4. Discuss the harms to defendants who cannot afford to pay their bail fee.

5. What are the benefits of detention? Do the benefits of detention outweigh the costs to defendants?

6. What are reasons in favor and against plea deals?

7. Analyze why the plea bargaining process is more rational than coercive.

8. What is the prosecutor's role in the plea bargaining system?

9. Plea bargaining has led to an increase in the certainty of punishment. Explain why this may have a deterrent effect on crime.

10. Explain how sentencing differentials across offenders can be a result of the early phases of case processing.

SENTENCING

Introduction

Sentencing is the final phase of case processing in which the outcome of the case is decided. Sentencing is formally considered a responsibility of judges, but judges can be open to recommendations from other actors, and in plea negotiations, they often approve sentences already decided as an agreement between prosecutors and defense attorneys. There are many different sentencing options, including, but not limited to, fines, restitution, electronic monitoring, community service, probation, incarceration, and the death penalty. The offense committed and the offender's prior record are the two most important factors in predicting the sentence received. Yet, there are still influences on sentencing, aside from these legal factors, that can change the dynamic of the sentencing process.

Justifications for Punishment

To a large extent, sentencing is a reflection of varying punishment ideologies. In "What Drives Punitive Beliefs?: Demographic Characteristics and Justifications for Sentencing," Brian Payne, Randy Gainey, Ruth Triplett, and Mona Danner identify these ideologies as specific deterrence, general deterrence, retribution, rehabilitation, and incapacitation. Some may also include restoration or restorative justice. Deterrence, retribution, and incapacitation generally advocate for a more punitive, or harsher, approach to punishment, as opposed to rehabilitation and restoration.

The former is represented in punishments such as incarceration and the death penalty, whereas the latter is manifested in punishments like probation and community service.

The fact that there exists punishments focused in different ideologies closely ties to the public opinion research of Payne and colleagues. Particularly, they recognize that the public is both punitive and rehabilitative. Support for either approach depends on the type of offense, demographic characteristics, and beliefs about the goals of punishment. In constructing sentencing guidelines and rules, policymakers can be responsive to these sentiments, as well as judges and prosecutors, who are often concerned about how they are perceived by the public. Also, at an individual level, policymakers, judges, and prosecutors have their own beliefs about punishment that can influence their sentencing practices.

While Payne and colleagues demonstrate support for both punitive and rehabilitative approaches, it should be recognized that many of the sentencing policies put in place since the 1970s represent a more punitive approach to punishment. Indeterminate sentencing, which involves judges giving sentences within the guidelines but parole boards determining the amount of time offenders actually serve, was largely replaced by determinate sentencing, or fixed-term sentences based on the sentence imposed, minus credits for good behavior, and the elimination of parole boards. The legislature also instituted mandatory sentences for certain types of offenses and offenders, as well as Three Strikes Laws. Each of these legislative mandates had an enormous impact on the approach to sentencing, contributing to a substantial growth in the prison population. The country is now in a position where it can no longer support prison growth, particularly in certain states, and legislators are now turning to alternatives to incarceration.

Appropriate punishments and sentences are seen differently for various types of offenders. Payne and colleagues recognize that more punitive punishments are supported in circumstances when the offense is more serious, for instance. There is a general understanding within the community that juveniles should be treated differently. Juveniles are still seen as able to be rehabilitated, and therefore, it is believed punishment should be tailored accordingly. In *Roper v. Simmons,* the Supreme Court decided that juveniles charged with murder could not be executed. Later, in *Graham v. Georgia,* the Court ruled that sentences to life in prison without parole for juveniles were cruel and unusual. The public also seems to sympathize with defendants experiencing mental health issues, where the approach has leaned toward treatment over punishment. This sentiment can be seen in the increase in mental health courts across the country, as well as in the decision of *Atkins v. Roper,* when the Court ruled that execution of the mentally ill was cruel and unusual.

Organizational Context

As has been emphasized in the prior sections, the organizational nature of the courts also impacts sentencing. Jo Dixon, in "The Organizational Context of Criminal Sentencing," presents several perspectives to explain sentencing, including an organizational context approach that focuses on the combined influence of legal, social, and organizational factors. This approach acknowledges that in highly bureaucratized, or more organized, courthouses, informal arrangements and incentives to plea will emerge, such that offenders who plea will be rewarded with lighter sentences. Dixon's results suggest that pleas are given lighter sentences in highly bureaucratized courts, but the same is not true in courts with low levels of bureaucratization or organization, where presumably, an informal system of institutionalized pleas is not present.

Legal factors of the case continue to remain important predictors, which supports the formal legal perspective she discusses. This perspective is grounded in the ideals of legal traditionalism, such that sentencing outcomes are only a result of legal rules. Her finding that the organizational context also matters suggests that there is some element of legal realism within the court. Sentences are not just a reflection of legal criteria, but are also a reflection of organizational norms.

Causal Attributions and Focal Concerns

Aside from legal and organizational factors, many studies find that sentencing can vary depending on extralegal factors, such as race, sex, and age. Several propositions have been made in an attempt to explain these differences. Dixon details the substantive political perspective, which proposes that sentencing is used as a tactic among those in more privileged social statuses to condemn those less privileged for their behavior. In this context, defendant class and race would then have an impact on sentencing such that minorities and those of a lower socioeconomic status would be subject to harsher sentences.

Celesta Albonetti, in "An Integration of Theories to Explain Judicial Discretion," identifies how the need to reduce uncertainties within the system can lead to differences in sentences across groups. Specifically, she talks about judicial uncertainty regarding the likelihood of recidivism. In the absence of knowledge about whether an offender will recidivate, judges may develop attributional stereotypes. Attributions are essentially the perceived causes of crime. Those who adopt more dispositional attributions tend to believe that people are born bad, or that crime is an innate feature of individuals. Alternatively, those who adopt situational attributions believe that crime is a result of social circumstances, like neighborhood factors and parenting. Individuals who attribute crime to dispositional causes tend to be more punitive, while those who attribute crime to situational causes are more rehabilitative. Albonetti suggests that decisions about whether a defendant may recidivate could be based on attributions, and these attributions may vary depending on the race or sex of the offender. For instance, crimes committed by minorities may have a greater tendency to be attributed to dispositional causes, resulting in a more punitive stance towards these offenders. While Albonetti focuses specifically on judicial attributions, the attributions of all members of the courtroom workgroup are important, considering their mutual influence on sentencing.

Focal concerns theory, which is presented in "Does Gender Modify the Effects of Race-ethnicity on Criminal Sanctioning? Sentences for Male and Female White, Black and Hispanic Defendants," expands upon Albonetti's approach. Darrell Steffesmeier and Stephen Demuth detail three focal concerns considered by the court actors: blameworthiness, protection of the community, and practical constraints. In assessing these characteristics of a case, judges and other court actors may develop "perceptual shorthands" whereby offenders of certain demographic characteristics are seen as more blameworthy and dangerous. Particularly, they propose that minorities and males are often perceived in this way, resulting in harsher sentences for these defendants.

A final potential explanation to keep in mind is the idea of cumulative disadvantage. As discussed in Section 4, offenders from certain demographic groups can be put at a disadvantage in some of the earlier phases of case processing, and even at arrest. These disadvantages early on can have implications for their sentences. Ultimately, each of these perspectives acknowledges the fact that actors within the court are not robots, as traditionalists espouse. They possess both unconscious and conscious biases that can impact case outcomes for particular defendants.

What Drives Punitive Beliefs?

Demographic Characteristics and Justifications for Sentencing

Brian K. Payne, Randy R. Gainey, Ruth A. Triplett, and Mona J. E. Danner; Ed. Kent B. Joscelyn

Introduction

Numerous criminological studies have examined individuals' attitudes about different aspects of punishment. Those who have been asked about their punishment preferences included *criminal justice officials* (Bayens, Mankse, & Smykla, 1998; Bazemore, Dicker, & Hamad, 1994; Bowers & Waltman, 1994; Frank, Cullen, & Cullen, 1987; Gordon, 1999; Lanier & Miller, 1995; MacDonald, Erickson, & Allen, 1999), *legislators* (Flanagan, McGarrell, & Lizotte, 1989; Sandys & McGarrell, 1994; Welsh, 1993), *members of the public* (Miller, Rossi, & Simpson, 1991; Sundt, Cullen, Applegate, & Turner, 1998; Turner, Cullen, Sundt, & Applegate, 1997), *inmates* (Van Voorhis, Browning, Simon, & Gordon, 1997), and *college students* (Firment & Geiselman, 1997; Miller et al., 1991; Payne & Gainey, 1999). In general, these studies focused on three different areas: (1) how respondents believed offenders should be punished; (2) why respondents believed offenders should be punished; and (3) the factors that influenced individuals' attitudes about punishment. Most often, these areas were addressed separately.

An underlying theme in just about all of these studies was that better understanding of citizens' attitudes towards the punishment of offenders helped criminologists to better understand society in general. Understanding the attitudes of the public is important for theoretical as well as practical reasons. A crucial theoretical question in "the sociology of law is whether the criminal code of a society reflects societal norms ... or serves some other functions that are only coincidentally related to those norms" (Rossi & Berk, 1997, p. 14). This question has practical implications. For example, if the public is found to be overwhelmingly punitive, then actions are warranted to make sure that sanctions are indeed severe. Alternatively, if it is found that the public is relatively forgiving and emphasizes rehabilitative sanctions over punishment, then a completely different reaction would be warranted. Though this makes sense in principle, some research suggests that the way policymakers decide to punish offenders is only loosely, if at all, tied to the desires of the public (Glick & Pruet, 1985; Mande, 1989; Tonry, 1999).

The current research links together past research on punishment attitudes by addressing three primary questions: (1) How punitive are citizens and to what extent do they support various sanctions?; (2) What factors influence individuals' attitudes toward punishment?; and (3) Do the factors that influence attitudes towards punishment differ across race and gender?

Review of Literature

Throughout the evolution of the discipline, criminologists have considered the many reasons offenders were punished by society. In *Essays on Crime and Punishment*, for instance, Beccaria (1764/1963) argued that individuals should be punished in order to prevent future offenses. Durkheim (1947), on the other hand, asserted that punishment fulfilled the important function of demonstrating society's disapproval of certain behaviors. Around that same time, Dubois (1904) contended that society punished offenders, Blacks in particular, "to reduce freed slaves to serfdom" (Gabbidon, 1996, p. 104).

Building on the way early criminologists broadly defined specific reasons for punishment, criminologists now cite five functions fulfilled by punishment: (1) specific deterrence; (2) general deterrence; (3) retribution; (4) rehabilitation; and (5) incapacitation (Van den Haag, 1981). Several different criminologists considered which of these functions of punishment best exemplified why members of the public think individuals should be punished, and how the public believes offenders should be punished. The areas that were considered included punishment and sentencing attitudes, the source of the attitudes, and the importance of studying punishment and sentencing attitudes. These areas were considered in the remainder of this literature review.

PUNISHMENT AND SENTENCING ATTITUDES

Research on punishment attitudes can be distinguished from research on sentencing attitudes. Research on punishment attitudes includes research that focuses on beliefs about *why* individuals should be punished, while research on sentencing attitudes focuses on *how* individuals should be sentenced. Research on *why* individuals should be punished suggests that the public, though punitive, also adheres to a rehabilitative ideal for some offenders under certain conditions (Applegate, Cullen, & Fisher, 1997; Cullen, Skovron, Scott, & Burton, 1990; Immarigeon, 1986; McCorkle, 1993; Shichor, 1992; Sundt et al., 1998). Support for rehabilitation seemed to have peaked in the mid-to late eighties, and decreased some in the nineties, though support remained high for juveniles and nonviolent offenders (Sundt et al., 1998).

Research on *how* offenders should be punished focused on the type of sanction (e.g., incarceration versus a community-based sanction) and the severity of the sanction (e.g., length of sentence). Though some research showed support for community-based sanctions (see Brown & Elrod, 1995; Payne & Gainey, 1999), other research showed that the public preferred relatively long sentences for convicted offenders (Zimmerman, Van Alstyne, & Dunn, 1988). A quote from McCorkle (1993,

p. 251) reconciles these seemingly disparate findings as far as punishment preferences are concerned: "[The public's] priorities seem clear: Incarcerate first, then rehabilitate if possible." Of course lengthy sentences can be costly. Research by Zimmerman et al. (1988) found that if the public's preferred sanctions (from the 1987 U.S. National Punishment Survey) were given to a cohort of offenders convicted in New York, the cost of punishment would increase by 2.5 billion dollars in New York alone.

SOURCE OF ATTITUDES

Research shows there were at least four sources of punishment and sentencing attitudes: (1) research design; (2) offense and offender characteristics; (3) demographic characteristics; and (4) justifications for punishment. The first source, research design, is methodological and concerns measurement. According to Sprott (1999), whether individuals were seen as punitive hinged on whether broad or case specific questions were asked of respondents. The use of single items measuring support for punitive policies was also criticized. Research by Applegate, Cullen, Turner, and Sundt (1996) found that when citizens were asked general questions like whether they favored the death penalty or three strikes legislation, they appeared quite supportive. Alternatively, when citizens were asked about specific cases and were provided with the specifics of a particular case, they tended to be less supportive of various sentencing policies.

Punishment attitudes are also linked to offense and offender characteristics (Durham, Elrod, & Kinkade, 1996; McCorkle, 1993). As implied earlier, individuals are less punitive towards younger offenders (Ghetti & Redlich, 2001; Sundt et al., 1998). Also, violent offenses are responded to more punitively than property crimes and citizens appear to be particularly sensitive to certain types of drug offenses (McCorkle, 1993). For example, Rossi and Berk (1997) showed that individuals who responded to their survey requested much higher sentences for kidnapping and drug trafficking than other street crimes (e.g., bank or street robbery) or white-collar offenses (e.g., embezzlement, bribery).

Research also found different levels of punitiveness across demographic groups, but the relationships were usually not large and were often inconsistent. Some research showed that age was positively associated with more punitive attitudes, though the relationship might be curvilinear with the youngest and oldest groups holding the least punitive attitudes (Rossi & Berk, 1997). Research also showed that men tended to be more punitive than women (Apple-gate, Cullen, & Fisher, 2002), but the differences were sometimes not large and some evidence suggested that women were more punitive for certain types of crimes (Roberts, 1992; Rossi, Berk, & Campbell, 1997; Sprott, 1999). Finally, political ideology and education levels seem to be associated with punitive attitudes—liberals and the more highly educated appear to be less punitive than conservatives and the less educated (see Bowers, 1998; Rossi & Berk, 1997).

Research also found that the relationship between demographic characteristics and punishment attitudes was far from clear-cut. Langworthy and Whitehead (1986) reported that the relationships between demographic characteristics and punishment attitudes could be explained by differing levels of fear and political liberalism. Further, some researchers suggested that the similar levels of punitiveness among Blacks and Whites were produced by unique concerns. According to Cohn, Barkan, and Halteman (1991, p. 287), Whites' punitive attitudes were tied to racial prejudice while Blacks' attitudes towards punishments were tied to their fear of crime.

Finally, there existed a tangential body of literature that focused on the justifications for punishment—that is, why should offenders be sanctioned. This research tended to view justifications as a dependent variable and was largely devoted to whether the public was punitive for its own sake or whether rehabilitation was still an important goal of the criminal justice system (e.g., Applegate et al., 1977; Cullen et al., 1990; Moon, Sundt, Cullen, & Wright, 2000; Sundt et al., 1998). Researchers rarely attempted to link the reasons people feel that offenders should be punished to how severely they think offenders should be sanctioned. Warr and Stafford (1984), however, examined both the determinants of the public's stated goals of punishment and their support for the death penalty. They found that Seattle residents favored retribution as their favored goal of punishment, followed by incarceration and rehabilitation. They also found that respondents who favored retribution and maintaining moral boundaries were the most likely to support capital punishment. This research suggested that punitive attitudes might be tied to societies' perceived goals of punishment. Alternatively, Roberts and Gebotys (1989) found that beliefs in the importance of general deterrence, incapacitation, and rehabilitation were unrelated to punitive sentences.

These inconsistent results may be explained at least in part by methodological differences. In fact, the body of research that focused on the goals of punishment and the extent to which citizens favored punishment or rehabilitation was based on so many different types of samples, measurements of critical variables, and analysis strategies that it was not surprising that the results were mixed. Borrowing from Cohn et al. (1991), however, these mixed results can be understood from a theoretical framework based on an appreciation of subcultural differences among various groups. That is, it may be that different subgroups in society have unique concerns that drive their punitive values. For example, Cohn et al.'s (1991) research suggests that African Americans, because of their higher victimization rates, are more punitive for utilitarian reasons, while Whites are more punitive because of concern, prejudice, and fear of a threatening minority group. A similar argument might be made for gender differences in punitiveness that appear to be either similar in levels or higher for particular types of crimes. Research consistently shows that women are more fearful of crime than are males. Thus, their attitudes towards sentencing may result from utilitarian concerns for keeping an offender from committing future offenses (specific deterrence) or from concerns for deterring prospective offenders from committing like offenses (general deterrence).

Not clearly considered in this past research was the link between demographic characteristics, punishment preferences, and punishment justifications. Although a great deal of research considered the factors that directly influence punishment preferences and their justifications, much less research considered how these relationships interacted with race and gender.

THE IMPORTANCE OF STUDYING PUNISHMENT AND SENTENCING ATTITUDES

Research on the punishment and sentencing attitudes of the public, the sources of these attitudes, and the linkages between citizen beliefs and demographic characteristics is justified on five related grounds. First, this research will inform public policy inasmuch as policymakers are willing to look to public opinion as a guide in their decision making process. If the public supports punitive responses to crime, then sentencing policies can be guided toward that end. On the other hand, if the public shows support for rehabilitative ideals, then thought can be given to providing more support for programs that were shown to be successful in rehabilitating offenders.

Second, research on the public's attitudes about punishment is useful in that it generates understanding about a particular culture's most basic values and beliefs. As Warr and Stafford (1984, p. 108) note "[A]nthropologists and comparative sociologists have long recognized that social norms of justice (that is norms concerning the means and purposes of handling deviants) are among the most telling characteristics of any culture." Certainly a culture that is primarily retributive is distinct from a culture that is primarily rehabilitative. In the United States, for instance, consider the difference between the rehabilitative orientation of the 1960s as compared to the punitive orientation of the 1980s. These differences in punishment attitudes help to define the differences between the two decades and tell a great deal about the values and belief systems in various historical periods.

Third, the overriding attitudes about punishment will influence the way the justice system tends to respond to criminal behavior. Up until the 1960s, the United States tended to rely more on treatment-oriented programs to handle offenders. After the 1960s, and during the shift to a supposedly more punitive culture, programs focusing on rehabilitation were placed on the back burner and policies and practices ensuring a more severe punishment towards offenders were advocated (Clear & Cole, 2001).

Fourth, and related to the previous two points, the behavior of individuals is likely tied to their attitudes about punishment. This is certainly the case with criminal justice officials as research suggests that those who work in the justice system likely act in accordance with their general attitudes about punishment (Gordon, 1999). It is just as feasible that the behavior of law-abiding individuals outside of the justice system is tied to their punishment philosophies. For instance, it could be that those who believe that individuals should be punished as opposed to rehabilitated would be more likely to advocate and use corporal punishment to discipline their children than those who do not. This is not to offer evidence for or against spanking, but it is to suggest that the consequences of punishment philosophies are far reaching.

A final justification for research on punishment and sentencing attitudes is that by learning what the public thinks about punishment justifications, researchers can learn whether citizens are properly educated about various criminal justice responses to offenders (Brown & Elrod, 1995; Payne & Gainey, 1999). As an illustration, if research shows that certain groups are opposed to certain sanctions for reasons that are just plain wrong, because they are ill-informed, lack information, or do not understand the information, then measures can be taken to educate members of those groups. Although educating the public about criminal justice issues is seen as an arduous task by many criminologists, many criminologists nonetheless cite education as influencing individuals' support for or against various sentencing options (Immarigeon, 1986; Lane, 1997; Roberts, 1992; Rogers, 1991; Selke, 1980; Tonry, 2001; Wanner & Caputo, 1987).

With these purposes in mind, the current research addressed the following questions: (1) Are members of the public primarily punitive and how do they justify their attitudes and beliefs regarding punishment?; (2) What factors influence individuals' attitudes about punishment?; and (3) Do the factors that influence punishment attitudes vary across different groups in society? These questions are important for criminal justice theory and have practical implications for policymakers.

Methods

THE SOCIAL AND POLITICAL CONTEXT

As a backdrop, the study was conducted in the Commonwealth of Virginia, a generally conservative state and one that historically emphasized punitive sentences. For example, Virginia ranks second behind Texas in the number of executions since 1977 (U.S. Department of Justice, 2000). The study was originated at a time when debate was surfacing about the way drug offenders should be punished.

Specifically, in 1999 then-Governor James Gil-more proposed changing the drug kingpin laws so that trafficking penalties would increase to life imprisonment and the conditions of a life term would be less stringent (e.g., possessing a smaller amount could result in a life sentence).[1] Given that legislators were considering this sentencing change, the present researchers were afforded the opportunity to see whether the legislators would pass legislation that reflected the wishes of the public or the desire to control offenders.

In early February 2000, a sample of registered voters in Virginia was surveyed as part of a political poll about their attitudes toward punishments. The sample included 387 respondents in the Hampton Roads area in southeastern Virginia and 453 respondents outside this area. Cases were weighted to reflect registered voters in Virginia.[2] A small, unusable number of Asians (n = 6), Hispanics (n = 7), "others" (n = 11), and those who refused this question (n = 13) were excluded from bivariate and multivariate analyses. With listwise deletion of these and other missing data, the final sample size was 734.

MEASURES

Five vignettes of different offenses were developed to measure the respondents' attitudes toward punishment or sentencing severity: (1) an offender sells 200 pounds of marijuana; (2) an offender sells just over two pounds of a substance containing a *detectable* amount of heroin; (3) an individual who is legally intoxicated crashes a car and a passenger is killed; (4) a manufacturer violates occupational safety and health standards causing the death of an employee; and (5) a legal gun dealer sells a gun to a high school student. The first two situations were developed to gauge residents' responses to the kingpin legislation encouraged by the former Governor. The next two situations reflected serious offenses where victims actually died, and a final case was developed because of the timely concern and public panic over school shootings.[3]

For each scenario, respondents were asked how they believed the offender should be punished. Close-ended response categories included: death penalty, life in prison without parole, ten years in prison, five years in prison, probation with treatment, or don't know/undecided. The ordinal response categories ignored the possibility of a variety of lower range sanctions; they were developed, however, to judge Virginians as either supportive or unsupportive of the Governor's platform. Responses were recoded so that higher values indicated greater punitiveness and the mean of the five items were taken as a global measure of punitive attitudes. As a result of missing data, particularly with the occupational death variable, the scale was computed if at least three of the five variables had valid responses.

---

1   Roberts and Gebotys (1989) for example analyzed relatively small nonrepresentative samples of the public and college students, potentially biased and too small to detect small but important correlations. Warr and Stafford (1984) analyzed data from a more representative sample but from a single city. Consistent with the body of literature, different measures of similar theoretical constructs were used and different analytical techniques were conducted; both could help to explain differences in the findings.

2   The sample was supposed to reflect registered adult voters and not the population of Virginia. In comparison to the Virginia population, the sample overrepresented females and underrepresented African Americans. The sample was also somewhat older than the population of Virginians. A small, unusable, number of Asians (*n* = 6), Hispanics (*n* = 7), "others" (*n* = 11), and those who refused this question (*n* = 13) were excluded from bivariate and multivariate analyses. With listwise deletion of these and other missing data, the final sample size was 734.

3   The study was part of a larger political poll funded by a local newspaper with a large readership. The funding source requested the crime scenarios be based on those that were receiving attention in the press at that time. The inclusion of more crime scenarios was desired, but there was a limit placed on the number of questions that could be asked given the nature of the broader survey.

Reliability analyses were conducted on the five items. Given that the contexts of the vignettes were so different, it was felt that the Cronbach's alpha of .69 showed considerable internal reliability even if it did not quite meet certain criteria (see Carmines & Zeller, 1979).

To assess their reasons or justifications for the particular punishment they chose, respondents were simply asked: "Why do you support this sentence?" The close ended response categories were: (1) it keeps the offender from committing another crime (*specific deterrence*); (2) it will keep other people from committing that crime (*general deterrence*); (3) it punishes the offender (*retribution*); and (4) it treats or rehabilitates the offender (*rehabilitation*). From these five responses, five variables were developed that measured consistency in thinking about each of the justifications (e.g., the number of times the person used any one of these categories across the five vignettes).

A number of demographic questions as well as questions concerning self-reported political and philosophical orientation were also asked. *Gender* was coded female = 1 and male = 0, *race* was coded African American = 1 and White = 0, and *age* was coded in years. Respondents were also asked, on ordinal scales, about their *level of education* (a seven-point scale ranging from 1 = less than high school to 7 = graduate/professional degree), and *political orientation* (a five-point scale ranging from 1 = very conservative to 5 = very liberal). Finally, respondents were asked whether *they or a close family member had ever been the victim of a serious crime* (coded yes = 1, no = 0).

[...]

Results

Table 5.1.1 provides descriptive statistics on primary variables of interest and provides information concerning the first research question of interest, which concerns the punitive nature of Virginia residents. Only a minority of respondents favored life in prison or the death penalty (range 13 to 25 percent), and

Table 5.1.1. Descriptive statistics (*n* = 734)

	Minimum	Maximum	Mean	Std. Deviation
Standard independent variables				
Education level	1.00	6.00	4.09	1.46
Conservative to liberal	1.00	5.00	2.70	1.04
Victim of serious crime	.00	1.00	.17	.38
Sex (coded female)	.00	1.00	.59	.49
Race (coded Black)	.00	1.00	.12	.32
Mean age	18.00	100.00	51.10	16.60
Justifications				
Specific deterrence	.00	5.00	1.20	1.35
General deterrence	.00	5.00	.62	.997
Punish offender	.00	5.00	1.35	1.36
Rehabilitate	.00	5.00	.88	1.07
Dependent variable				
Punitive attitudes	1.00	4.00	2.01	.51

a slightly greater percentage were in favor of treatment with probation (range 16 to 30 percent). For the two drug-related cases, examples of the ex-Govenor's proposed legislation which would increase the penalties to life in prison, fully 75 and 77 percent of the respondents favored less severe sanctions. Concerning justifications, or the reasons people ask for various sanctions, they were most likely to choose "to punish the offender" (mean = 1.35). Specific deterrence was also a popular justification and, in fact, was not significantly lower than to punish ($t = 1.87, p > .06$).[4] The third most common reason across situations was rehabilitation (mean = .89), followed by general deterrence (mean = .62).

MULTIVARIATE ANALYSES

The second research question deals with factors affecting punitive attitudes. The first two columns of coefficients in Table 5.1.2 are the unstandardized regression coefficients of two ordinary least

Table 5.1.2. Standardized regression coefficients predicting punitiveness (n = 734)

	Beta	Beta
Education	– .19**	– .16**
Liberal	– .09 *	– .06
Victim	– .00	.00
Female	.09 *	.07 *
Black	.05	.07 *
Age	.09 *	.10**
Specific deterrence		.19**
General deterrence		.12**
Punishment		.10 *
Rehabilitate		– .36**
r-square	.07	.28

* Significant at p <.05.
** Significant at p <.01.

STAT HELP!

In this table, positive "Beta" values indicate increased punitiveness and negative values indicate decreased punitiveness. For example, those with higher levels of education are less punitive. The second column also accounts for the justifications given by the respondents regarding punishment. For instance, those who believe in punishment for the purpose of specific deterrence are more punitive. One or more asterisks (*) indicate the effect is *statistically significant.*

---

4   When the two deterrence items (general and specific) were collapsed to form a composite measure of deterrence, respondents chose deterrence more often than to punish (paired t-test = 5.54, p < .05).

squares regression models predicting more punitive attitudes. The first model includes demographic and other characteristics previously found to be associated with more punitive attitudes. Four of the variables are statistically significant. The strongest variable in the model is education which, consistent with prior research, is negatively related to punitive attitudes. Liberal ideology is also negatively related to punitive attitudes while older people tend to hold more punitive attitudes than younger people and females tend to be somewhat more punitive than males. The model explains a very modest amount of the variance in punitive attitudes (7 percent), which is also consistent with prior research (see Rossi & Berk, 1997).

The second model introduces the justifications of the respondents. The inclusion of these variables greatly increases the ability of the model to explain punitive attitudes. The model explains much more of the variation, increasing the r-square by twenty-one percentage points for a total of 28 percent. The influence of education and gender are reduced slightly but are still statistically significant variables in the model. Liberal ideology is also reduced and is no longer statistically significant, suggesting that liberals and conservatives differ in terms of punitive philosophy because they perceive different goals for punishing offenders. The effect of age remains about the same and there is a slight suppression effect of race, showing that once justifications are controlled Blacks are somewhat more punitive than are Whites. Clearly the justifications are important in understanding individuals' punitive attitudes. Beliefs about the utility of specific and general deterrence and the importance of retribution (punishment) are all positively related to more punitive attitudes, while the belief in rehabilitation is strongly and negatively related to punitive attitudes.

SITUATION SPECIFIC MODELS

To further explore these relationships, separate models were estimated for each of the situations. While the scaled dependent measure of punitiveness could be considered, more-or-less, continuous (Knoke, Bohrnstedt, & Mee, 2002), the individual items or situations are clearly ordinal. Given the nature of the dependent variables ordinal logistic regression techniques (Peterson & Harrell, 1990)

Table 5.1.3. Ordinal logistic regressions for situation specific punitive attitudes (unstandardized coefficients)

	DUI	Occupation	Marijuana	Heroin	Gun
Education	− 0.15**	− 0.13**	− 0.14**	− 0.19**	− 0.17**
Liberal	− 0.21**	− 0.01	− 0.25**	− 0.14	0.21**
Victim	0.23	0.23	− 0.17	− 0.18	− 0.00
Female	0.62**	0.28	− 0.24	− 0.13	0.76**
Black	0.17	0.11	0.32	0.38	0.78**
Age	− 0.01	0.00	0.02**	0.01 *	0.01**
Specific	0.11	0.00	0.32**	0.32**	0.09
General	0.05	0.03	0.40**	0.27**	0.04
Punish	0.07	0.14	0.20 *	0.20 *	− 0.12
Rehabilitation	− 0.82**	− 0.47	− 0.40**	− 0.48**	− 0.53**
Naglkerke r-square	.25	.12	.22	.20	.19

* Significant at $p < .05$.
** Significant at $p < .01$.

STAT HELP!

This table reports the results specific to each of the five vignettes. Once again, positive values indicate increased punitiveness and negative values indicate decreased punitiveness. Concerning the DUI vignette, for instance, those who are educated are less punitive toward the DUI offender. Educated respondents are also less punitive in the four other scenarios. One or more asterisks (*) indicate the effect is *statistically significant*.

were used to model the influence of the demographic characteristics and punitive justifications on the punitive response to each of the situations. The results, unstandardized coefficients, are presented in Table 5.1.3.

The results of the separate analyses were interesting in several ways. First, although the items scaled reasonably well, the factors associated with attitudes towards punishing offenders in each case varied considerably. The most consistent predictor was education, which was significant and negative in each situation. Liberal attitudes for the most part were also significant and negative; the major exception being attitudes toward punishing a gun dealer who inappropriately sold merchandise to an underage person. This was of course consistent with the liberal-conservative debate regarding guns in this society (Kleck & Kates, 2001; Sheley & Wright, 1995).

Where statistically significant, females tend to be more punitive than males, but the coefficients change direction (but do not reach statistical significance) for drug related offenses. Females seem to be more punitive than males in cases where there are more directly apparent negative consequences to victims or potential victims than in seemingly "victimless" crimes (Meier & Geis, 1997). Similarly, the data suggests that Blacks are particularly punitive in cases involving guns, but there is little evidence of racial differences in other situations. Age has a significant positive effect on punitive attitudes across items dealing with illegal drugs and guns. There is no relationship between age and punitive attitudes towards the occupational crime, but there is a negative effect of punitiveness on the drinking under the influence situation.

Finally, the analyses suggested that punitive justifications were for the most part consistent with the analyses of the scaled dependent variables, but were most consistent with the drug related crimes. The most consistent predictor was rehabilitative justification, which was consistently negatively related to punitive attitudes. Interestingly, a rehabilitative ideal was the only justification factor to significantly affect punitive attitudes towards the DUI and the gun sales situations. Across items, the models seemed to explain an important amount of the variation in the dependent variables (19–25 percent); the one exception being the situation dealing with occupational hazards, where only 12 percent of the variation was explained. It could well be that the respondents were not as well "educated" on this item through the media and had thought less about this particular issue.

[…]

Discussion

The findings of this study were intriguing in that they provided qualified answers to research questions. First, is the public (e.g., the voting public in Virginia) primarily retributive or rehabilitative? The findings suggested that the public could be best characterized as mixed, but it was clear that the public was not primarily retributive and the majority of the sample did not support life imprisonment for drug possession with intent to distribute as defined by Governor Gilmore's proposed legislation. Incidentally, the legislation was passed despite the lack of public support found in the current study. Second, as far as the source of punitive attitudes, gender, age, education level, and political ideology were found to be related to punitiveness in ways consistent with past literature. That is, there were some important demographic differences which varied across situations, but none of these were terribly strong predictors of attitudes toward punishment. Further, punishment justifications were strongly related to sentencing severity, especially for the drug-related situations. Finally, the findings suggested that while the overall models did not differ much across gender or race, the effect of the general deterrence justification was much stronger among females and African Americans and was nonexistent among males and Whites. Taken together, these results have important implications for policy and research.

Based on the finding that the public holds mixed attitudes about punishment, three points relevant to sentencing policy can be made. First, when developing sentencing policies, it is imperative that policymakers not assume that all citizens are punitive for all offenses. Indeed, the variation found here suggests that the public continues to support rehabilitative ideals for some offenses. Second, policymakers should expect, and welcome, a mixed response regarding punishment attitudes, if for no other reason, because varied opinions about the goals of punishment will enhance the likelihood that goals are fulfilled in responding to different types of crimes (Wright, 1981). Third, it appears necessary that criminologists generate more understanding among the public about the role of deterrence and rehabilitation.

[...]

REFERENCES

Applegate, B., Cullen, F. T., & Fisher, B. (1997). Public support for correctional treatment: The continuing appeal of the rehabilitative ideal. *Prison Journal*, 77, 237–258.

Applegate, B., Cullen, F. T., & Fisher, B. (2002). Public views toward crime and correctional policies. *Journal of Criminal Justice*, 30, 89–100.

Applegate, B., Cullen, F. T., Turner, M., & Sundt, J. (1996). Assessing public support for three-strikes-and-you're-out laws: Global versus specific attitudes. *Crime and Delinquency*, 42, 517–534.

Bayens, G., Mankse, M., & Smykla, J. (1998). The attitudes of criminal justice workgroups toward intensive supervised probation. *American Journal of Criminal Justice*, 22, 189–206.

Bazemore, G., Dicker, T., & Hamad, A. (1994). The treatment of ideal and detention reality: Demographic, professional/occupational and organizational influences on detention worker punitiveness. *American Journal of Criminal Justice*, 19, 21–41.

Beccaria, C. (1764/1963). *On crime and punishment*. Indianapolis, IN: Bobbs-Merrill Publishing Co.

Bowers, D., Jr. (1998). Giving people what they want: An exploratory analysis of felony sentencing in 49 states. *International Journal of Comparative and Applied Criminal Justice*, 22, 119–130.

Bowers, D., Jr., & Waltman, J. (1994). Are elected judges more in tune with public opinion? A look at sentences for rape. *International Journal of Comparative and Applied Criminal Justice*, 18, 118–133.

Brown, M. P., & Elrod, P. (1995). Electronic house arrest: An examination of citizen attitudes. *Crime and Delinquency*, 41, 332–346.

Carmines, E. G., & Zeller, R. A. (1979). *Reliability and validity assessment*. Beverly Hills, CA: Sage.

Chow, G. C. (1960). Tests of equality between sets of coefficients in two linear regressions. *Econometrica*, 28, 591–605.

Clear, T., & Cole, G. (2001). *American corrections: An introduction.* Belmont, CA: Sage.

Cohn, S., Barkan, S., & Halteman, W. (1991). Punitive attitudes toward criminals: Racial consensus or racial conflict? *Social Problems, 38,* 287–296.

Cullen, F. T. (1995). Assessing the penal harm movement. *Journal of Research in Crime Delinquency, 32,* 338–358.

Cullen, F. T., Clark, G., & Wozniak, J. (1985). Explaining the get tough movement: Can the public be blamed? *Federal Probation, 49,* 16–24.

Cullen, F. T., Fisher, B., & Applegate, B. (2000). Public opinion about punishment and corrections. *Crime and Justice: A Review of Research, 27,* 1–79.

Cullen, F. T., Skovron, S. E., Scott, J. E., & Burton, V. S., Jr. (1990). Public support for correctional treatment: The tenacity of rehabilitative ideology. *Criminal Justice and Behavior, 17,* 6–18.

DeJong, C. (1997). Survival analysis and specific deterrence: Integrating theoretical and empirical models of recidivism. *Criminology, 35,* 561–575.

Doob, A., & Roberts, J. (1983). *Sentencing: An analysis of the public's view of sentencing.* Ottawa, Ontario: Department of Justice.

Dubois, W. E. B. (1904). *Some notes on Negro crime, particularly in Georgia.* Atlanta, GA: Atlanta University Press.

Durham, A., Elrod, H. P., & Kinkade, P. (1996). Public support for the death penalty: Beyond Gallup. *Justice Quarterly, 13,* 337–342.

Durkheim, E. (1947). *The division of labor in society* (G. Simpson, Trans.). New York: Free Press.

Firment, K., & Geiselman, E. (1997). University students' attitudes and perceptions of the death penalty. *American Journal of Forensic Psychology, 15,* 65–89.

Flanagan, T., McGarrell, E., & Lizotte, A. (1989). Ideology and crime control policy positions in a state legislature. *Journal of Criminal Justice, 17,* 87–101.

Frank, J., Cullen, F., & Cullen, B. (1987). Sources of judicial attitudes toward criminal sanctioning. *American Journal of Criminal Justice, 11,* 151–164.

Gabbidon, S. (1996). An argument for including W.E.B. Dubois in the criminology/criminal justice literature. *Journal of Criminal Justice Education, 7,* 99–109.

Gebotys, R. J., & Roberts, J. V. (1987). Public views of sentencing: The role of offender characteristics. *Canadian Journal of Behavioral Science, 19,* 479–488.

Ghetti, S., & Redlich, A. (2001). Reactions to youth crime: Perceptions of accountability and competency. *Behavioral Sciences and the Law, 19,* 33–52.

Glick, H., & Pruet, G. (1985). Crime, public opinion and trial courts: An analysis of sentencing policy. *Justice Quarterly, 2,* 319–343.

Gordon, J. (1999). Do staff attitudes vary by position? A look at one juvenile correctional center. *American Journal of Criminal Justice, 24,* 81–93.

Gottfredson, M., & Hirschi, T. (1995). National crime control policies. *Society, 32,* 30–36.

Gray, T. (1994). Using cost-benefit analysis to measure rehabilitation and special deterrence. *Journal of Criminal Justice, 22,* 569–575.

Immarigeon, R. (1986). Surveys reveal broad support for alternative sentencing. *Journal of National Prison Project, 9,* 1–4.

Kleck, G., & Kates, D. B. (2001). *Armed: New perspectives on gun control.* Amherst, NY: Prometheus.

Knoke, D., Bohrnstedt, G. W., & Mee, A. P. (2002). *Statistics for social data analysis.* Itasca, IL: F.E. Peacock.

Lab, S. P., & Whitehead, J. T. (1990). From nothing works to the appropriate works. *Criminology, 25,* 405–417.

Lane, J. (1997). Can you make a horse drink? The effects of a corrections course on attitudes toward criminal punishment. *Crime and Delinquency, 43,* 186–202.

Langworthy, R. H., & Whitehead, J. T. (1986). Liberalism and fear as explanations of punitiveness. *Criminology, 24,* 575–591.

Lanier, M., & Miller, C., III (1995). Attitudes and practices of federal probation officers toward pre-plea/trial investigative report policy. *Crime and Delinquency, 41,* 364–377.

Lawrence, R. (1991). The impact of sentencing guidelines on corrections. *Criminal Justice Policy Review, 5,* 207–224.

MacDonald, S., Erickson, P., & Allen, B. (1999). Judicial attitudes in assault cases involving alcohol or other drugs. *Journal of Criminal Justice, 27,* 275–286.

Mande, M. (1989). *The effect of public opinion on correctional policy: A comparison of opinions and practices.* Denver: Colorado Division of Criminal Justice.

McCorkle, R. (1993). Research note: Punish and rehabilitate? Public attitudes toward six common crimes. *Crime and Delinquency, 39,* 240–252.

Meier, R. F., & Geis, G. (1997). *Victimless crime? Prostitution, drugs, homosexuality, and abortion.* Los Angeles: Roxbury.

Miller, J., Rossi, P., & Simpson, J. (1991). Felony punishments: A factorial survey of perceived justice in criminal sentencing. *Journal of Criminal Law and Criminology, 82,* 396–422.

Moon, M. M., Sundt, J. L., Cullen, F. T., & Wright, J. P. (2000). Is child saving dead? *Crime and Delinquency, 46,* 38–61.

Paternoster, R., Brame, R., Mazerolle, P., & Piquero, A. (1998). Using the correct statistical test for the equality of regression coefficients. *Criminology, 36,* 859–866.

Payne, B., & Gainey, R. (1999). Attitudes toward electronic monitoring among monitored offenders and criminal justice students. *Journal of Offender Rehabilitation, 29,* 195–208.

Peterson, B., & Harrell, F. (1990). Partial proportional odds models for ordinal response variables. *Applied Statistics, 39,* 205–217.

Roberts, J. (1992). Public opinion, crime and criminal justice. In M. Tonry (Ed.), *Crime and justice: A review of research* (Vol. 16, pp. 99–180). Chicago: University of Chicago Press.

Roberts, J., & Gebotys, R. (1989). The purposes of sentencing: Public support for competing aims. *Behavioral Sciences and the Law, 7*, 387–402.

Rogers, R. (1991). The effects of educational level on correctional officer job satisfaction. *Journal of Criminal Justice, 19*, 123–138.

Rossi, P., & Berk, R. (1997). *Just punishments: Federal guidelines and public views compared.* Hawthorne, NY: Aldine de Gruyter.

Rossi, P., Berk, R., & Campbell, A. (1997). Just punishments: Guideline sentences and normative consensus. *Journal of Quantitative Criminology, 13*, 267–290.

Sandys, M., & McGarrell, E. (1994). Attitudes toward capital punishment among Indiana legislators: Diminished support in light of alternative sentencing options. *Justice Quarterly, 11*, 651–677.

Selke, W. (1980). The impact of higher education on crime orientations. *Journal of Criminal Justice, 8*, 175–184.

Sheley, J. F., & Wright, J. D. (1995). *In the line of fire: Youth, guns, and violence in urban America.* Hawthorne, NY: Aldine de Gruyter.

Shichor, D. (1992). Following the penological pendulum: The survival of rehabilitation. *Federal Probation, 56*, 19–25.

Sprott, J. (1999). Are members of the public tough on crime?: The dimensions of public punitiveness. *Journal of Criminal Justice, 27*, 467–474.

Sundt, J., Cullen, F., Applegate, B., & Turner, M. G. (1998). The tenacity of the rehabilitative ideal revisited: Have attitudes toward offender treatment changed? *Criminal Justice and Behavior, 25*, 426–442.

Taxman, F., & Piquero, A. (1998). On preventing drunk driving recidivism: An examination of rehabilitation and punishment approaches. *Journal of Criminal Justice, 26*, 129–143.

Tonry, M. (1999). Why are U.S. incarceration rates so high? *Crime and Delinquency, 45*, 419–437.

Tonry, M. (2001). Unthought thoughts: The influence of changing sensibilities on penal policies. *Punishment and Society, 3*, 167–181.

Turner, M. G., Cullen, F. T., Sundt, J. L., & Applegate, B. K. (1997). Public tolerance for community-based sanctions. *Prison Journal, 77*, 6–26.

U.S. Department of Justice. (2000). *Capital punishment, 1999: Bulletin* (NCJ 184795). Washington, DC: Author.

Van den Haag, E. (1981). Punishment as a device for controlling the crime rate. *Rutgers Law Review, 33*, 706–719.

Van Voorhis, P., Browning, S., Simon, M., & Gordon, J. (1997). The meaning of punishment: Inmates' orientation to the prison experience. *Prison Journal, 77*, 135–167.

Wanner, R., & Caputo, T. (1987). Punitiveness, fear of crime, and perceptions of violence. *Canadian Journal Sociology, 12*, 331–344.

Warr, M., & Stafford, M. (1984). Public goals of punishment and support for the death penalty. *Journal of Research in Crime Delinquency, 21*, 95–111.

Weisburg, S. (1985). *Applied linear regression* (2nd ed.). New York: John Wiley and Sons.

Welsh, W. (1993). Ideologies and incarceration: Legislator attitudes toward jail overcrowding. *Prison Journal, 73*, 46–71.

Wright, K. (1981). The desirability of goal conflict within the criminal justice system. *Journal of Criminal Justice, 9*, 209–218.

Zimmerman, S., Van Alstyne, D., & Dunn, C. (1988). The national punishment survey and public policy consequences. *Journal of Research in Crime Delinquency, 25*, 120–149.

The Organizational Context of Criminal Sentencing[1]

Jo Dixon

reading 5.2

Introduction

Drawing from a variety of disciplinary perspectives, a substantive body of knowledge about the social organization of criminal sentencing has evolved. However, the empirical research on criminal sentencing has not produced an agreed-upon theory of criminal sentencing processes or a widely accepted set of determinants of sentencing outcomes.

One of the most controversial theoretical debates centers on whether sentencing processes reflect a formal legal, substantive political, or organizational maintenance rationality: the formal legal theory of sentencing predicts that sentencing is primarily determined by legal variables; the substantive political theory predicts that sentencing is determined by legal and social status variables; and the organizational maintenance theory predicts that sentencing is determined by legal and processing variables. A careful review of the empirical findings on sentencing indicates the degree to which this issue is unresolved. Studies that find minorities receiving harsher penalties than nonminorities interpret this finding as evidence that sentencing processes reflect political oppression or substantive political rationality (Garfinkel 1949; Spohn, Gruhl, and Welch 1982; Thomson and Zingraff 1981). Other studies argue that sentencing processes mirror formal legal rationality and that variations in sentencing can be attributed to legal factors. Thus, racial differentials in sentencing occur because of legal attributes correlated with race, for example, offense

1 This research was supported by a grant from the National Institute of Justice and a New York University Vladeck Presidential Fellowship. I am indebted to David Greenberg, Christine Harrington, Wolf Heydebrand, Robert Jackson, David Knoke, Mary Lee Luskin, Bernice Pescosolido, Brian Powell, Marjorie Zatz, members of the New York University Institute for Law and Society, and several *AJS* reviewers for helpful comments. Direct all correspondence to Jo Dixon, Sociology Department, New York University, 269 Mercer Street, New York, New York 10003.

seriousness, prior record, number of charges, harm inflicted, and weapon use (Clarke and Koch 1977; Chiricos and Waldo 1975). A third set of studies claim support for organizational maintenance rationality in sentencing and argues that variations in sentencing outcomes are due to a combination of legal factors and processing procedures related to sentence reduction, for example, plea disposition (Brereton and Casper 1982; Nardulli 1979; Bernstein, Kelly, and Doyle 1977). Finally, several recent studies observing both direct effects of legal variables and interactions between race and plea maintain that substantive political and organizational maintenance processes operate simultaneously such that legal factors increase sentences to a greater degree for minority populations and pleas are more likely to reduce sentences for nonminority populations (Zatz 1985).

In this article, I integrate the previous sentencing theories into an organizational context perspective on sentencing (Flemming, Nardulli, and Eisenstein 1992; Eisenstein, Flemming, and Nardulli 1988; Hagan, Hewitt, and Alwin 1979; LaFree 1985). This approach suggests that the predominant rationality in the organization of sentencing varies across courts diverging in the organization of judicial and prosecutorial activities. To assess the validity of the organizational context approach, I use ordinary least squares (OLS) and logistic regression techniques to analyze the effects of racial, legal, and processing variables on imprisonment and sentence length in courts varying in the bureaucratization of the technology used to organize the work of prosecutors and judges.

[...]

The first theory of sentencing argues that the organization of sentencing is based on substantive political rationality; the second maintains that the organization of sentencing reflects formal legal rationality; and the third portrays sentencing as a natural system based on organizational maintenance rationality. While not a separate perspective, a fourth approach combines the ideas of the substantive political and the organizational maintenance perspectives and argues that these rationalities converge to dilute formal legal rationality. Taken alone, none of these theories can successfully explain the divergent sentencing systems that form the focus of this paper. However, these general theories have implications for explaining variations in sentencing processes across courts that differ in the degree of bureaucratization in the organization of prosecutorial and judicial activities. After specifying the assumptions of each of the aforementioned approaches and assessing the empirical evidence for each, I use an organizational context perspective to formulate an explanation of the organization of sentencing that incorporates various aspects of the existing theories.

THE SUBSTANTIVE POLITICAL PERSPECTIVE

The first approach views the organization of sentencing from a substantive political perspective. One version of this theory views sentencing as a form of political oppression. Fostered by the classic works of Karl Marx (1859) and Thorsten Sellin (1938) and the more contemporary ideas of Richard Quinney (1970), this version argues that the administration of sentencing is a politically organized system wherein the powerful use the police power of the state to reinforce their privileged position by reducing their legal liability for illegal behavior. This line of reasoning focuses on the influence that social class or social status characteristics have on sentencing outcomes (Quinney 1970). A second version of the substantive political perspective also focuses on the influence that social class or social status factors have on sentencing, but explains these effects in terms of social welfare (Savelsberg 1992; Nonet and Selznick 1978; Levin 1977). According to this version, welfare rationalities have motivated the introduction of a substantive political sentencing structure that can influence the relationship between social status and sentencing. Thus, sentencing in the modern welfare state often deems the conditions associated with offenders of lower economic and social status as mitigating or aggravating circumstances for determining sentencing outcomes.

Regardless of which version of the substantive political theory one accepts, it is assumed that economic and social, as well as legal, factors influence sentencing. The substantive political theory of sentencing would predict that extralegal factors such as class and race, as well as legal factors, play a role in sentencing. Some of the early empirical research on sentencing finds that minorities such as blacks receive harsher sentences than whites, especially blacks who murder whites (Martin 1934; Johnson 1957; Garfinkel 1949). Although these findings are often interpreted as evidence for the substantive political model of sentencing, their use of bivariate statistics renders them weak at best. Only a few contemporary studies find a direct link between social class and/or race once legal attributes are controlled (Spohn et al. 1982; Unnever, Frazier, and Henretta 1980). Most of the results from recent studies that include class or racial and legal variables find support for the formal legal perspective.

THE FORMAL LEGAL PERSPECTIVE

According to the formal legal approach, the organization of bureaucratic and legal decision making is perceived as a technically rational machine. Accepting Weberian descriptions of modern organization as technically rational and applying Weber's argument to the organization of sentencing decisions, followers of the formal legal perspective submit that formal legal rules govern sentencing decisions via the application of these rules to specific cases. Hence, in addition to being predictable, sentencing outcomes are primarily the result of legal rules and criteria applied equally to all classes and races (Lukács 1971).

From the viewpoint of the formal legal theory, one would expect legal factors to be the major determinants of sentencing outcomes. Thus, offenders with different class or status characteristics committing crimes of equal severity would receive similar sentences.

Unlike earlier bivariate research, most contemporary research employs multivariate models that include social class or race, as well as measures of legal variables correlated with class and race. The results from the majority of these studies indicate that class and race become statistically insignificant once legal attributes such as offense severity and prior record are controlled (Chiricos and Waldo 1975; Bernstein et al. 1977; Burke and Turk 1975). Hence, most contemporary research supports formal legal explanations of sentencing processes. Given the scarce evidence for the substantive political model, Hagan (1974) and Kleck (1981) conclude that offender characteristics such as race contribute little to understanding sentencing differentials. Similarly, in a more recent review of the numerous studies of sentencing, Wilbanks (1987) infers that racial and class variations in sentencing are generally reduced to zero when legal variables are controlled and that claims of a racist criminal justice system in the United States are based largely on myth rather than reality.

While most contemporary models of sentencing include the legal variables needed to test the merits of the substantive political and formal legal perspectives, many of them lack the processing variables needed to simultaneously test the merits of the organizational maintenance theory of sentencing.

THE ORGANIZATIONAL MAINTENANCE PERSPECTIVE

Repudiating the Weberian perception of the organization of sentencing as a technically rational machine, as well as the Marxian perception of it as a political machine, the organizational maintenance perspective depicts the organization of sentencing as a natural system that operates on the basis of "Michels's law." According to Michels (1915), the imperatives of organizational maintenance deflect the system from the pursuit of formal rational goals and result in the development of operating goals by organizational elites. When Michels's law is applied to the sentencing process, the organization of sentencing is perceived to be an organizational maintenance process created by courtroom elites. Because a complex network of ongoing informal relationships among court actors is formed, a cooperative effort to efficiently dispose of cases evolves, with effects not envisioned by the substantive political or formal legal models. Courtroom elites come to share common interests in disposing of cases, and the mutual interdependence that develops institutionalizes the presumption of guilt and plea bargaining (Eisenstein and Jacob 1977).

Moreover, an elaborate incentive system for plea inducement emerges. Numerous scholars elaborate on the various incentives that police, prosecutors, defense lawyers, and judges have for cooperating in the inducement of guilty pleas (Newman 1956; Blumberg 1967; Sudnow 1965). Adopting this approach, the central problem for understanding the organization of sentencing becomes defining the operational rather than the political or formal legal goals of sentencing. Because attention is diverted from political or formal rules, attention is given to the role that informal rules and incentives play in organizational maintenance and survival.

The sentencing theory emerging from this approach defines efficient case disposition as the operational goal that maintains a stable and orderly sentencing system. Because all members of the courtroom work group receive benefits from disposing of cases with minimal effort, incentives emerge that positively reward pleas via reduced sentences. Accordingly, "the state, at the relatively small cost of charge reduction or sentence leniency, gains the numerous advantages of the plea of guilty over a long, costly and always uncertain trial" (Newman 1956). An organizational maintenance approach to sentencing would predict that offenders who plead guilty would be rewarded with shorter sentences than those with trial dispositions. From the viewpoint of organizational maintenance theory, one would expect both legal criteria and plea dispositions to have an effect on sentencing independent of the social status of an offender. Because the emphasis is on organizational maintenance, however, social status characteristics such as class and race would have no significant relationship to sentence outcomes.

A COMBINED SUBSTANTIVE POLITICAL/ORGANIZATIONAL MAINTENANCE APPROACH

Claiming that political and organizational maintenance goals are simultaneously operating to displace formal legal rationality, some maintain that politics are institutionalized in organizational practices (Selznick 1966). Hence, bias against minorities in sentencing is an indirect political process that is institutionalized behind the facade of organizational maintenance in courts. According to Chambliss and Seidman (1971), certain categories of offenders, specifically whites, are induced to enter pleas that reduce their sentences, while other categories, specifically non whites, are processed in ways that fail to reduce their sentences. Because substantive political and organizational maintenance rationality erode formal legal rationality, processing variables and racial variables interact to affect sentencing. Although legal variables affect sentencing, there is also an interaction between the effects of class or race and plea. Hence, minorities or lower-class individuals with plea dispositions do not receive the sentence reductions given to whites or upper-class individuals who plead guilty.

Findings from research incorporating processing variables such as plea into models with racial and legal variables indicate that plea directly affects sentencing or that race and processing modes interact to affect sentencing (Hagan 1975; Lizotte 1978; LaFree 1980; Bernstein et al. 1977; Spohn et al. 1982; Brereton and Casper 1982; Uhlman and Walker 1980; Zatz 1985). Hence, the results are interpreted as evidence for either the organizational maintenance or the combined substantive political/organizational maintenance theories. While these models contain the legal, racial, and processing variables necessary to determine which of the aforementioned theories of sentencing is supported, they are not capable of answering questions about court variations in sentencing processes.

THE ORGANIZATIONAL CONTEXT PERSPECTIVE

Taken alone, none of these sentencing theories can fully explain variations in sentencing across courts. Since each perspective begins with the assumption that courts operate with a unitary system of sentencing, some rationality of sentencing is stressed with the exclusion or diminution of others. An alternative and less-utilized approach to the study of sentencing, the contextual approach, provides an analytical tool for capturing variations in sentencing processes across courts. A contextual perspective on sentencing maintains that the sentencing of individuals in a given court is influenced by the political, social, and organizational context of the court. If we accept this premise, it is possible to synthesize the theoretical ideas from the existing models of sentencing and formulate a contextual perspective that ignores neither the formal legal nor the political and organizational maintenance rationalities operating in sentencing processes (Savelsberg 1992).

Reviews of the sentencing literature indicate the need for a contextual analysis of sentencing processes (Hagan and Bumiller 1983; Farrell and Holmes 1991; Savelsberg 1992). Although the few studies of the context of sentencing primarily focus on the influence of social and political environments outside the court on sentencing (Balbus 1977; Levin 1977; Myers and Talarico 1986), several recent studies employ an organizational framework that explores the effects of the formal and informal organizational contexts of courts on sentencing (Hagan 1977; Hagan et al. 1979; LaFree 1985; Nardulli, Eisenstein, and Flemming 1988; Eisenstein et al. 1988; Flemming et al. 1992; Myers and Talarico 1986, 1987). For example, in an analysis of the sentencing of white-collar offenders, Benson and Walker (1988) suggest that differences in court contexts explain the incongruencies between their findings and the earlier findings of Wheeler, Wiseburd, and Bode (1982). A debate continues in the organizational context literature on criminal sentencing over the role that the bureaucratic organization of court work plays in determining which of the various theories of sentencing is supported in nonbureaucratic and in bureaucratic contexts. Most of the empirical work addressing this problem examines the effects of legal variables, social class or status, and plea bargaining on sentencing in rural and urban courts.

[…]

The Data

The sample of 1,532 cases for this study comes from the Minnesota State Court Administrator's case-tracking system and consists of all felony cases ending in conviction initiated in the first six months of 1983.[2] The data come from four sources. (1) Information on the offense severity, prior record, race, sentence type, and sentence length comes from the Minnesota Sentencing Commission's database for convicted cases in Minnesota.[3] (2) Attorney-type and disposition-type information comes from the statewide case-tracking system of the Minnesota State Court Administrator's Office. The assistant director and staff members of the Minnesota State Court Administrator's Office and the director and staff members of the Minnesota Sentencing Guidelines Commission provided invaluable assistance in preparing the data for analysis and spent numerous hours explaining the Minnesota court rules and sentencing guidelines. (3) The information on the organization of the work of the judges comes from responses to telephone interviews with the judicial administrators of the 10 judicial districts in the state of Minnesota. Interviews with the Minnesota assistant state court administrator informed us of the types of variations in the organization of judicial activities in Minnesota. The Minnesota State Court Administrator's Office provided maps of each of the 10 judicial districts and the names of the judicial administrators for each of the 10 districts. They also contacted the judicial administrators and informed them that they would be receiving a phone call from us and that they were to provide us with information on the types of docket and calendaring systems used by judges in each county. We conducted telephone interviews with all of the judicial administrators. They provided us with the information on docket and calendaring systems in each county in Minnesota, as well as other information on judicial assignments. (4) The information on the organization of the prosecutors' offices comes from responses to a questionnaire given to the chief prosecutor in each county. Before designing the questionnaire, we interviewed the director of the Minnesota County Attorney's Association, a previous court administrator for Minneapolis, and several previous chief prosecutors in Minneapolis to gain information about the various ways the prosecutors organize the work in their offices. In addition, several judicial administrators and prosecutors pretested the prosecutor questionnaire on the organization of prosecutorial activities. The director of the Minnesota County Attorney's Association provided us with the name and address of the chief prosecutor in each county. We mailed a revised questionnaire to the chief prosecutor in each county. In order to better understand the organization of each prosecutor's office, we asked them to return any existing written organizational chart of their office with their questionnaire. For offices with no existing organizational chart, we asked the chief prosecutor to sketch a chart indicating departments, divisions, and lines of authority. After receiving the returned questionnaires, we conducted interviews with the chief prosecutors in Minneapolis and Saint Paul.[4] It was our intention to examine organizational variations in the public defenders' offices, but an interview with the director of the Minnesota Association of Public Defenders revealed that their organizational structures were relatively uniform across courts since their control was state rather than county based. Although Hagan et al.'s (1979) work on the influence of probation officers

---

2 Because the percentage of cases censored, i.e., not completed before the end of the data collection period, is extremely small and the residuals from an OLS regression approximate the normal distribution, the censored cases in this sample do not present problems for estimation.

3 There is no problem with missing data on the case information variables since the number of cases with missing data is minuscule.

4 Information on the judicial administration was obtained for all of the counties in Minnesota, while information on the prosecutors' offices was obtained for 84% of the counties. A careful examination of other characteristics of the missing courts gives no evidence of selection bias. These courts are located in various geographic areas and do not come from any particular judicial district.

on sentencing is important in some contexts, it is not applicable in Minnesota since the introduction of sentencing guidelines in Minnesota was accompanied by the elimination of probation officer sentencing recommendations.

It is important to note that Minnesota is a sentencing guidelines state. In fact, Minnesota was the first state to implement both presumptive dispositional and durational guidelines for sentencing. The guidelines went into effect for any felony conviction after May 1, 1980 (for a detailed description of the guidelines, see Miethe and Moore [1985], Martin [1983], Minnesota Sentencing Guidelines Commission [1984], Knapp [1982], and von Hirsch et al. [1987]). The intent of the guidelines was to establish a set of consistent standards for sentencing that would increase uniformity in both the dispositional (in/out) and durational (sentence length) aspects of sentencing decisions. A "modified deserts" standard was adopted whereby presumptive sentencing dispositions and durations are determined by the severity of the conviction offense and, to a lesser extent, the criminal history of the offender. The presumptive sentencing dispositions and durations for each combination of severity/criminal history were determined by the Minnesota Sentencing Guidelines Commission and are presented in the form of a sentencing grid.

Although the Minnesota system is considered one of the most comprehensive determinate sentencing systems, there is sufficient opportunity for sentencing disparities. For example, judges may diverge from presumptive sentences within a 15 % range without departing from the guidelines. In one evaluation, Miethe and Moore (1985) find that the likelihood of receiving an aggravated departure from the guidelines is influenced by the socioeconomic attributes of defendants. While evaluations of the role of offense severity, prior record, plea, and race under the Minnesota guidelines have been performed (Minnesota Sentencing Guidelines Commission 1984; Miethe and Moore 1985; Moore and Miethe 1986; Miethe 1987), these previous studies are unable to gauge court variations in the predictors of sentencing outcomes. It is also true that these studies were conducted shortly after the implementation of sentencing guidelines. If, as some authors have suggested, sentencing practices in Minnesota adhered to guideline standards during early implementation, but have shifted toward pre-guideline patterns in the later years of institutionalization, then it is important to continually monitor sentencing processes (von Hirsch et al. 1987).

[...]

These results demonstrate the strengths and limitations of each of the major perspectives on criminal sentencing by indicating the organizational context in which each theoretical perspectives applies. It is not surprising that the effects of legal variables are significant and strong regardless of the organizational context; this finding suggests that the formal legal perspective on sentencing must be considered in all court contexts. The processing measure of plea significantly affects sentencing in particular organizational contexts in a manner consistent with the precepts of the organizational maintenance theory. When compared with the results of previous research, these findings suggest the need to develop theories and empirical models that consider and directly measure the organizational as well as other contexts in which sentencing takes place.

The formal legal theory receives the type of support under conditions of low judicial and prosecutorial bureaucratization that it often receives in the noncontextual research. Verification of the formal legal theory and negation of the organizational maintenance, substantive political, and combined substantive political/organizational maintenance theories is consistently shown in the low-bureaucratization models of sentencing, where legal variables are the primary determinants of imprisonment and sentence length. The fact that neither plea nor race affects sentencing in counties with low levels of judicial and prosecutorial bureaucratization indicates that an institutionalized system of sentence reduction based on race discrimination or plea bargaining is absent in this organizational context. The findings for the models predicting imprisonment and sentence length under conditions of low bureaucratization correspond to early noncontextual studies finding positive effects of legal variables and no effect of either processing or racial variables on sentencing disposition and duration. However, the limitations of the formal legal theory are shown in the models predicting sentence type and length under conditions of high judicial and prosecutorial bureaucratization. Using a sample from a sentencing guidelines state favors the formal legal theory in all contexts; state policies endorsing uniformity and the exclusion of social and processing considerations in sentencing determinations increases the importance of legal factors and minimizes the probability that race and plea will effect sentencing in any context. Hence, effects of race and plea in any organizational context in a sentencing guidelines state would provide strong evidence for the substantive political perspective and the organizational maintenance perspectives, respectively.

The validity of the organizational maintenance theory is evident in the models predicting imprisonment and length under conditions of high bureaucratization in judicial and prosecutorial administrative structures. The strong negative effect of plea, coupled with the positive effect of legal variables, in these models is consistent with the empirical sentencing literature, arguing that sentencing processes reflect organizational maintenance processes. The evidence from this research shows that sentence reduction for pleading guilty is institutionalized in courts where the work of prosecutors and judges is bureaucratically structured. What is most notable is the consistent patterns for the plea effect across the various dimensions of prosecutorial bureaucracy; plea is consistently insignificant in the low-bureaucratization models and consistently significant in the high-bureaucratization models. While the organizational maintenance theory is substantiated under conditions of high bureaucratization, its lack of predictive ability under conditions of low judicial and prosecutorial bureaucratization reveal its limitations.

Although findings supporting the substantive political or the combined substantive political/ organizational maintenance model of sentencing are lacking in this research, this may be the result of several factors associated with Minnesota. First, the racial composition of the general and the criminal population in Minnesota is largely white. This racial composition probably affects the relationship between race and sentencing; further research should extend the newly emerging research agenda on contextual effects by examining the results from my model in states that have different racial compositions. For example, when my findings are compared to those of Myers and Talarico (1987), I do not find the racial effects that they report. This is not surprising, however, since their data comes from a southern nonguidelines state where there is a predominately minority criminal population with a greater racial mix in the general population. A second characteristic that distinguishes Minnesota is the sentencing guidelines policy; this policy favors the formal legal theory of sentencing and, hence, affects the relationship between race and sentencing. The lack of a significant relationship between race and sentencing in my analysis may not be found in studies of sentencing in states without sentencing guidelines. Moreover, the absence of racial effects for sentencing in Minnesota does not imply that there are no effects of race on other dispositions, since many have argued that there is a hydraulic displacement of racial discretion from sentencing to plea bargaining in sentencing guidelines states. Differences in the effects of race on plea bargaining and sentencing across states with differing sentencing policies only reinforces the premise of this research that sentencing processes vary across settings.

A serious consideration of the organizational context perspective on sentencing reveals that what appear to be competing theories of sentencing are actually complementary theories that are capable of predicting the organization of sentencing in particular contexts. The consistent finding that legal variables related to offense severity and criminal history are important for predicting sentencing under conditions both of low and of high bureaucracy, while plea dispositions take on an added importance in the high-bureaucracy context, reveals the importance of the judicial and prosecutorial context in structuring sentencing. Comparisons of sentencing in courts with low and with high levels of bureaucracy fail to support Tepperman's supposition that bureaucratically organized courts render sentencing processes that are less affected by legally irrelevant factors than nonbureaucratically organized courts. In fact, the results are more consistent with Eisenstein et al. (1988), who argue that the greater division of labor and decentralized decision making in bureaucratic courts creates loosely coupled unstable work groups that use individual discretion such that legally irrelevant factors influence sentencing. While my findings are consistent with the theories of Eisenstein et al. (1988), they are in no way a direct test since I offer no direct measure of either the informal relations or tightness of coupling among court actors in the bureaucratic and nonbureaucratic contexts. It is quite possible that tight coupling among court actors only occurs if the court actors are in contexts in which the organization of work is nonbureaucratic and they are regular participants in a local legal and community culture. The assumption that courts in rural areas are nonbureaucratized and involve tight coupling among court actors engaging in other informal relationships in the community merits further investigation since rural courts often share personnel in a manner that does not ensure that the judge hearing a case in a particular court belongs to a stable local legal culture or even the local community culture.

What are the consequences of the variation in sentencing processes across courts with different organizational structures in a sentencing guidelines state as evidenced in this study? Criminal justice professionals have attempted to establish an objective categorical system of sentencing to guard against the introduction of legally irrelevant criteria in sentencing decisions concerning imprisonment and sentence length. My results should not be seen as an indictment of attempts to improve sentencing consistency. On the contrary, the explicit criteria set forth in the Minnesota sentencing guidelines may have attenuated the effects of race on sentencing outcomes. The intent of this study is to demonstrate that, even with carefully drawn standards, sentencing will vary across courts that vary in their formal and informal organization. Professions seek legitimacy by demonstrating the objective nature of their decision making. This trend toward seeking consistency and fairness in sentencing is admirable, but a false sense of confidence in objective measures is created if we ignore the local context of sentencing. I hope that I have shown that it is premature to close the issue of the effects of legal, social, and processing factors on sentencing decisions until the contextual effects of the organizational, as well as social, environments of courts have been examined.

REFERENCES

Austin, Thomas. 1981. "The Influence of Court Location on Type of Criminal Sentence: The Rural-Urban Factor." *Journal of Criminal Justice* 9:305–16.

Balbus, Isaac D. 1977. *The Dialectics of Legal Repression*. New Brunswick, N.J.: Transaction.

Benson, Michael, and Esteban Walker. 1988. "Sentencing the White-Collar Offender." *American Sociological Review* 53:294–302.

Bernstein, Ilene Nagel, William Kelly, and Patricia Doyle. 1977. "Societal Reaction to Deviants: The Case of Criminal Defendants." *American Sociological Review* 42:743–55.

Blau, Peter. 1974. *On the Nature of Organizations*. New York: Wiley.

Blumberg, Abraham. 1967. "The Practice of Law as a Confidence Game." *Law and Society Review* 1:15–39.

Brereton, David, and Jonathan D. Casper. 1982. "Does It Pay to Plead Guilty? Differential Sentencing and the Function of Criminal Courts." *Law and Society Review* 16:45–70.

Burke, Peter, and Austin Turk. 1975. "Factors Affecting Postarrest Dispositions: A Model for Analysis." *Social Problems* 22:313–32.

Chambliss, William, and Robert Seidman. 1971. *Law, Order and Power.* Reading, Mass.: Addison-Wesley.

Champion, Dean, ed. 1989. *The U.S. Sentencing Guidelines.* New York: Praeger.

Chiricos, Theodore G., and Gordon P. Waldo. 1975. "Socioeconomic Status and Criminal Sentencing: An Empirical Assessment of a Conflict Perspective." *American Sociological Review* 40:753–72.

Clarke, Stevens H., and Gary G. Koch. 1977. "Alaska Felony Sentencing Patterns: A Multivariate Statistical Analysis." Anchorage: Alaska Judicial Council.

Eisenstein, James, Roy Flemming, and Peter Nardulli. 1988. *The Contours of Justice: Communities and Their Courts.* Boston: Little, Brown.

Eisenstein, James, and Herbert Jacob. 1977. *Felony Justice: An Organizational Analysis of Criminal Courts.* Boston: Little, Brown.

Farrell, Ronald, and Malcolm Holmes. 1991. "The Social and Cognitive Structure of Legal Decision-Making." *Sociological Quarterly* 32:529–42.

Flemming, Roy, Peter Nardulli, and James Eisenstein. 1992. *The Craft of Justice: Politics and Work in Criminal Court Communities.* Philadelphia: University of Pennsylvania Press.

Garfinkel, Harold. 1949. "Research Note on Inter- and Intra-Racial Homicides." *Social Forces* 27:369–81.

Greenberg, David, and Drew Humphries. 1980. "The Co-optation of Sentencing Guidelines." *Crime and Delinquency* 26:206–25.

Greenwood, Peter, Joan Petersilia, and Franklin Zimring. 1980. *Age, Crime and Sanctions: The Transition from Juvenile to Adult Court.* Report R-2642-NIJ. Santa Monica, Calif.: RAND.

Haas, Eugene, Richard Hall, and Norman Johnson. 1966. "Toward an Empirically Derived Taxonomy of Organizations." In *Studies on Behavior in Organizations,* edited by Raymond V. Bowers. Athens: University of Georgia Press.

Hagan, John. 1974. "Extra-Legal Attributes and Criminal Sentencing: An Assessment of a Sociological Viewpoint." *Law and Society Review* 8:357–83.

———. 1975. "Parameters of Criminal Prosecution: An Application of Path Analysis to a Problem of Criminal Justice." *Journal of Criminal Law, Criminology and Police Science* 65:536–44.

———. 1977. "Criminal Justice in Rural and Urban Communities: A Study of the Bureaucratization of Justice." *Social Forces* 55:597–612.

Hagan, John, and Kristin Bumiller. 1983. "Making Sense of Sentencing: A Review and Critique of Sentencing Research." Pp. 1–54 in *Research in Sentencing: The Search for Reform,* edited by A. Blumstein, J. Cohen, S. E. Martin, and M. H. Tonry. Washington, D.C.: National Academy of Science.

Hagan, John, John Hewitt, and Duane Alwin. 1979. "Ceremonial Justice: Crime and Punishment in a Loosely Coupled System." *Social Forces* 58:506–27.

Hagan, John, Ilene Nagel, and Celesta Albonetti. 1980. "The Differential Sentencing of White-Collar Offenders in Ten Federal District Courts." *American Sociological Review* 45:802–20.

Hage, Gerald, and Michael Aiken. 1969. "Routine Technology, Social Structure and Organizational Goals." *Administrative Science Quarterly* 14:366–77.

Hall, Richard, J. Eugene Haas, and Norman Johnson. 1967. "Organizational Size, Complexity and Formalization." *American Sociological Review* 32:903–12.

Heckman, James. 1979. "Sample Selection Bias as a Specification Error." *Econometrica* 47:153–61.

Heumann, Milton. 1975. "A Note on Plea Bargaining and Caseload Pressure." *Law and Society Review* 9:515–28.

———. 1978. *Plea Bargaining: The Experiences of Prosecutors, Judges and Defense Attorneys.* Chicago: University of Chicago Press.

Heumann, Milton, and Colin Loftin. 1979. "Mandatory Sentencing and the Abolition of Plea Bargaining: The Michigan Felon Firearms Statute." *Law and Society Review* 13:393–430.

Holmes, Malcolm, Howard Daudistel, and William Taggart. 1992. "Plea Bargaining Policy and State District Court Caseloads: An Interrupted Time Series Analysis." *Law and Society Review* 26:139–59.

Johnson, Elmer. 1957. "Selective Forces in Capital Punishment." *Social Forces* 36: 165–69.

Kleck, Gary. 1981. "Racial Discrimination in Criminal Sentencing: A Critical Evaluation of the Evidence with Additional Evidence on the Death Penalty." *American Sociological Review* 46:783–805.

Knapp, Kay. 1982. "Impact of the Minnesota Sentencing Guidelines on Sentencing Structures." *Hamline Law Review* 5:237–70.

LaFree, Gary. 1980. "The Effect of Sexual Stratification by Race on Official Reactions to Rape." *American Sociological Review* 45:842–54.

———. 1985. "Adversarial and Nonadversarial Justice: A Comparison of Guilty Pleas and Trials." *Criminology* 23:289–312.

———. 1989. *Rape and Criminal Justice: The Social Construction of Sexual Assault.* Belmont, Calif.: Wadsworth.

Levin, Martin. 1977. *Urban Politics and the Criminal Courts.* Chicago: University of Chicago Press.

Lizotte, Alan J. 1978. "Extra-Legal Factors in Chicago's Criminal Courts: Testing the Conflict Model of Criminal Justice." *Social Problems* 25:564–80.

Lukács, Georg. 1971. *History and Class Consciousness.* Cambridge, Mass.: MIT Press.

Luskin, Mary Lee, and Robert Luskin. 1986. "Why So Fast? Why So Slow? Explaining Case Processing Time." *Journal of Criminal Law and Criminology* 77: 190–214.

Martin, Roscoe. 1934. *The Defendant and Criminal Justice.* Bulletin no. 34–37. University of Texas, Bureau of Research in the Social Sciences.

Martin, Susan. 1983. "The Politics of Sentencing Reform: Sentencing Guidelines in Pennsylvania and Minnesota." Pp. 265–304 in *Research in Sentencing: The Search For Reform,* edited by A. Blumstein, J. Cohen, S. Marti, and M. H. Tonry. Washington, D.C.: National Academy of Science.

Marx, Karl. 1859. *A Contribution to the Critique of Political Economy.* New York: Vintage.

Meeker, James, and Henry Pontell. 1985. "Court Caseloads, Plea Bargains and Criminal Sanctions: The Effects of Section 17 P.C. in California." *Criminology* 23: 119–43.

Michels, Robert. 1915. *Political Parties.* Glencoe, Ill.: Free Press.

Miethe, Terrance. 1987. "Charging and Plea Bargaining Practices under Determinant Sentencing: An Investigation of the Hydraulic Displacement of Discretion. "*Journal of Criminal Law and Criminology.* 78:101–22.

Miethe, Terrance, and Charles Moore. 1985. "Socioeconomic Disparities under Determinant Sentencing Systems: A Comparison of the Preguideline and Postguideline Practices in Minnesota." *Criminology* 23:337–63.

Minnesota Sentencing Guidelines Commission. 1984. *The Impact of the Minnesota Sentencing Guidelines Commission: Three Year Evaluation.* Saint Paul: Minnesota Sentencing Guidelines Commission.

Moore, Charles, and Terrance Miethe. 1986. "Regulated and Unregulated Sentencing Decisions: An Analysis of First-Year Practices under Minnesota's Felony Sentencing Guidelines." *Law and Society Review* 20:253–77.

Myers, Martha, and Gary LaFree. 1982. "Sexual Assault and Its Prosecution: A Comparison with Other Crimes." *Journal of Criminal Law and Criminology* 73: 1282–1305.

Myers, Martha, and Susan Talarico. 1986. "Urban Justice, Rural Injustice: Urbanization and Its Effect on Sentencing." *Criminology* 24:367–91.

———. 1987. *The Social Contexts of Criminal Sentencing.* New York: Springer.

Nardulli, Peter. 1979. *The Courtroom Elite.* New York: Ballinger.

Nardulli, Peter, James Eisenstein, and Roy Flemming. 1988. *The Tenor of Justice.* Urbana: University of Illinois Press.

Newman, Donald J. 1956. "Pleading Guilty for Considerations." *Journal of Criminal Law, Criminology and Police Science* 46:780–90.

Nonet, Philippe, and Philip Selznick. 1978. *Law and Society in Transition: Toward Responsive Law.* New York: Octagon.

Pope, Carl. 1976. "The Influence of Social and Legal Factors on Sentencing Dispositions: A Preliminary Analysis of Offender Based Transaction Statistics." *Journal of Criminal Justice* 4:203–21.

Pugh, Derek, David Hickson, C. R. Hinings, and C. Turner. 1968. "Dimensions of Organizational Structure." *Administrative Science Quarterly* 13:65–105.

Quinney, Richard. 1970. *The Social Reality of Crime.* Boston: Little, Brown.

Savelsberg, Joachim. 1992. "Law That Does Not Fit Society: Sentencing Guidelines and Substantivized Law." *American Journal of Sociology* 97:1346–81.

Sellin, Thorsten. 1938. *Culture, Conflict and Crime.* New York: Social Science Research Council.

Selznick, Philip. 1966. *TVA and the Grass Roots.* New York: Harper & Row.

Spohn, Cassia, John Gruhl, and Susan Welch. 1982. "The Effect of Race on Sentencing: A Re-Examination of an Unsettled Question." *Law and Society Review* 16: 71–88.

Sudnow, David. 1965. "Normal Crimes: Sociological Features of the Penal Code in a Public Defender Office." *Social Problems* 12:255–76.

Tepperman, L. 1973. "The Effects of Court Size on Organization and Procedure." *Canadian Review of Sociology and Anthropology* 10:346–65.

Thomson, Randall J., and Mathew T. Zingraff. 1981. "Detecting Sentence Disparity: Some Problems and Evidence." *American Journal of Sociology* 86:869–80.

Uhlman, Thomas, and Darlene Walker. 1980. "He Takes Some of My Time; I Take Some of His: An Analysis of Judicial Sentencing Patterns in Jury Cases." *Law and Society Review* 14:323–41.

Unnever, James D., Charles Frazier, and John C. Henretta. 1980. "Race Differences in Criminal Sentencing." *Sociological Quarterly* 21:197–207.

von Hirsch, Andrew, Kay Knapp, and Michael Tonry. 1987. *The Sentencing Commission and Its Guidelines.* Boston: Northeastern University Press.

Warriner, Charles, Richard Hall, and Bill McKelvey. 1981. "The Comparative Description of Organizations: A Research Note and Invitation." *Organizational Studies* 2:100–120.

Weber, Max. 1954. *Law in Economy and Society.* Edited by Max Rheinstein and translated by Edward Shils and Max Rheinstein. Cambridge, Mass.: Harvard University Press.

Wheeler, Stanton, David Wiseburd, and Nancy Bode. 1982. "Sentencing the White- Collar Offender: Rhetoric and Reality." *American Sociological Review* 47:641–59.

Wilbanks, William. 1987. *The Myth of a Racist Criminal Justice System.* Monterey, Calif.: Brooks/Cole.

Wooldredge, John. 1989. "An Aggregate-Level Examination of the Caseload Pressure Hypothesis." *Journal of Quantitative Criminology* 5:259–83.

Zatz, Marjorie S. 1985. "Pleas, Priors and Prison: Racial/Ethnic Differences in Sentencing." *Social Science Research* 14:169–93.

Zatz, Marjorie, and John Hagan. 1985. "Crime, Time and Punishment: An Exploration of Selection Bias in Sentencing Research. "*Journal of Quantitative Criminology* 1:103–26.

An Integration of Theories to Explain Judicial Discretion

reading 5.3

Celesta A. Albonetti

A review of sentencing research indicates progress toward greater statistical rigor and model specification but with little development of a theoretical framework for understanding the inconsistent findings of the effect of the extra-legal variables (i.e., race, ethnicity, gender, and class position) and the consistent findings of the effect of defendant's prior record of conviction on sentence severity. While labelling and conflict theories have since the 1960s provided the perspectives from which the legal/extra-legal debate emerged, little theoretical formulation has followed in the past two decades of sentencing research. The lack of theoretical development may result from a singular interest in uncovering discrimination in the exercise of discretion and a neglect of explanations of the consistent findings of the influence of prior record, bail outcome, and guilty plea. Excepting the work of Farrell and Swigert (1978a), with interest centering on the net effect of extra-legal variables on sentence severity, factors such as prior record of conviction, typically treated as a legally relevant variable, are relegated to a secondary, or peripheral place in discussions of judicial decision making. In an attempt to stimulate further theory development, the research herein presents an integration of two theoretical perspectives on discretionary decision making and uses this integration as the basis for generating empirical specifications and hypotheses for main and interaction effects in an analysis of the variables affecting sentence severity.

Theoretical Perspective

The theoretical perspectives for this research are the structural organizational approach represented in the work of March and Simon (1958; Simon 1957), and Thompson (1967) and the social psychological orientation evidenced in the work of attribution theorists such as Carroll and Payne (1976; Carroll 1978), Fontaine and Emily (1978), Hawkins (1980, 1981), Livermore (1978), and Shaver (1975). The salience of these two theoretical perspectives to judicial sentencing decisions lies in each perspective's sensitivity to discretionary use of information in decision making.

Structural organizational theorists assert that rational choice models of decision making provide a useful point of departure for understanding the exercise of discretion. To be fully rational a decision must be made with knowledge of all possible alternatives, though in reality decision makers rarely, if ever, possess complete information (Simon 1957). The underlying supposition is that complete knowledge eliminates uncertainty in decision making and decision outcomes. In the situation of having incomplete knowledge, the actor attempts to reduce uncertainty by relying upon a rationality that is the product of habit and social structure.

According to Simon (1957: 102–103), these limits to decision making rationality are overcome through organizational arrangements such as established operating procedures, a division of labor, a hierarchy of authority, formal channels of communication, professional training, and, finally, indoctrination. These structures absorb uncertainty resulting in a "bounded rationality" (March and Simon 1958:109). The result is decision making made on the "basis of past experience, stereotypes, prejudices, and highly particularized views of present stimuli" (Clegg and Dunkerley 1980:265). Decision makers seek to achieve a measure of rationality by developing "patterned responses" that serve to avoid, or at least, reduce uncertainty in obtaining a desired outcome. According to these theorists, problem solving is based on a limited search for "satisficing" rather than optimizing solutions.

Pursuing further a theory of uncertainty avoidance in decision making, Thompson (1967) identifies two dimensions around which decision makers organize efforts to reduce uncertainty. He suggests that uncertainty surrounding (1) beliefs about cause and effect relationships, and (2) preferences among possible outcomes is crucial to understanding the use of discretion. Of the two dimensions, uncertainty associated with cause and effect relationships is particularly salient to judicial exercise of discretion at sentencing. This dimension of uncertainty relates offender characteristics, case processing outcomes, and punishment to the goal of reducing the likelihood of recidivism.

In large urban courts with a well defined division of labor, as the one under study, sentencing judges do not exert direct influence on early pretrial processing decisions. Thus, they have little, if any, control over the certainty and celerity of processing, but they do control punishment severity. This observation is essential to specifying the sources of uncertainty in decision making relevant to the sentencing decision. From an uncertainty avoidance perspective, case information salient to reducing recidivism will affect judicial discretion. The direction of the effect is dependent on whether the information increases or decreases the likelihood that the offender will avoid future criminal activity. In other words, proponents of this perspective would argue that in the face of uncertainty characterizing the link between sentence severity and likelihood of recidivating, case information thought to predict future criminal behavior is expected to increase the severity of the sanction imposed. Conversely, case information stereotypically thought to decrease the likelihood of recidivating is expected to decrease sanction severity.

March and Simon's (1958) concept of "patterned response" provides a link to the second theoretical perspective useful to an understanding of discretionary decision making, that of causal attribution in punishment. The development of "patterned responses" in decision making situations characterized by high discretion can be further understood by the theoretical framework found in the work of Carroll and Payne (1976), Hawkins (1980), and Shaver (1975). Drawing from Heider (1958), these theorists suggest that judgments of causality are premised on both personal and environmental forces that are thought to contribute to behavior. Shaver (1975) maintained that individuals attribute causation in terms of the above two forces.

Shaver (1975) examined the relationship between the perceiver's characteristics and attributions of responsibility. Hawkins, referring to Shaver's work, notes that

> perceivers' attributional choice may affect their perception of remedies or control mechanism needed where perceived behavior is negatively valued. Crime represents a form of negatively valued behavior, and criminal punishment represents a means of control. Therefore, the perception of criminal behavior may involve processes of attribution and perceptions for punishment. For example, a perceiver may believe that a violent criminal offender is an aggressive person or alternatively that environmental factors precipitated the criminal act. Perceptual differences such as this may in turn lead to conclusions regarding the possibility of the offender's rehabilitation potential, the threat posed to society, and the type of criminal sanction imposed (Hawkins 1981: 280).

Fontaine and Emily (1978) investigated the relationship between causal attribution and judicial discretion among municipal court judges. Relying on verbal statements made by the judge at the time of sentencing, Fontaine and Emily concluded that judges do attribute meaning to past and future behavior consistent with stereotypes associated with membership in such social categories. Their findings are consistent with Lippman's (1922) research showing a link between social category and attributions of particular traits and behaviors and Stephan's (1975) work indicating that membership in a certain social category influences verdicts and sentences. Also consistent Carroll (1978) found that "the higher the stability of the attributions regarding the cause of the parole applicant's offense, the higher is the Board member's prediction of the risk of future crime, and the more reluctant he or she is to grant parole" (1978:1510).

Based on the work on uncertainty avoidance and causal attribution in punishment, judges would attempt to manage uncertainty in the sentencing decision by developing "patterned responses" that are themselves the product of an attribution process influenced by causal judgments. Judges would rely on stereotypes that link race, gender, and outcomes from earlier processing stages to the likelihood of future criminal activity. Imposing punishment in the criminal justice system, similar to other highly discretionary decisions, is the result of "satisficing" or simplifying causal assumptions in an effort to achieve rationality.

In summary, uncertainty surrounding the sentencing decision arises from an inability to predict accurately future criminal behavior. Using defendant characteristics, circumstances of the crime, and case processing outcomes, judges assess the defendant's disposition toward future criminal activity. Attributions of a stable and enduring disposition are expected to increase sentence severity. Attributions of a temporary or situational involvement in crime are expected to decrease sentence severity. These attributions provide a basis for arriving at rational decision in a domain of responsibility characterized by uncertainty. Caroll and Payne (1976) refer to this simplification of decision making as involving causal attribution about the crime and the offender.

Combining the two perspectives on discretionary decision making provides a useful reconceptualization of sentencing research. This reconceptualization provides an understanding of prior research findings indicating the importance of such case information as defendant's race, gender, prior record of conviction, and earlier decision outcomes to the sentencing decision. Discrimination and disparity in sentencing decisions, the underlying focus of the legal/extra-legal debate, may be the product of judicial attempts to achieve a "bounded rationality" in sentencing by relying on stereotypical images of which defendant is most likely to recidivate.

[...]

The theoretical perspective brought to this research does not excuse discriminatory sentencing practices, but rather it helps us to understand how racial stereotypes can be salient to decision making in the criminal justice system. Such stereotypes increase uncertainty in achieving a successful outcome, resulting in an increase in sanction severity. In other words, when judges attribute stable, enduring causes of crime to black offenders, the defendant's race affects the exercise of discretion. I suggest that it is an attribution link between race, stability of disposition to commit future criminal behavior, and uncertainty that explains the observed race effect on sentence severity. The link between attribution and attempts to avoid uncertainty provides an explanation of the effect of variables heretofore treated as legally relevant to sentencing discretion in jurisdictions using indeterminant sentencing.

REFERENCES

Atkinson, David N., and Dale A. Newman 1970 "Judicial attitudes and defendant attributes: Some consequences for municipal court decision-making." Journal of Public Law 19: 68–87.

Baab, George W., and William R. Furgenson 1967 "Texas sentencing practices: A statistical study." Texas Law Review 45: 471–503.

Balbus, Issac D. 1973 The Dialetics of Legal Repression: Black Rebels Before the American Criminal Courts. New York: Russell Sage Publications.

Berk, Richard A. 1983 "An introduction to sample selection bias in sociological data." American Sociological Review 48: 386–398.

Berk, Richard A., and Subhash C. Ray 1982 "Selection bias in sociological data." Social Science Research 11:352–398.

Bernstein, Ilene Nagel, John Cardascia, and Catherine E. Ross 1979 "Defendants's sex and criminal court decisions." In Discrimination in Organizations, ed. R. Alvarez, K.G. Lutterman and Associates, San Francisco: Jossey-Bass.

Bernstein, Ilene, William Kelly, and Patricia Doyle 1977 "Societal reaction to deviants: The case of criminal defendants." American Sociological Review 42: 743–755.

Brereton, David, and Jonathan Casper 1981–82 "Does it pay to plead guilty? Differential sentencing and the functioning of criminal courts." Law and Society Review 16: 45–70.

Burke, Peter and Austin Turk 1975 "Factors affecting postarrest disposition: A model for analysis." Social Problems 22: 313–332.

Carroll, John S. 1978 "Causal theories of crime and their effect upon expert parole decisions." Law and Human Behavior 2: 377–388.

Carroll, John S., and John W. Payne 1976 "The psychology of the parole decision process: A joint application of attribution theory and information processing psychology." In Cognition and Social Behavior, ed. John S. Carroll and John W. Payne, 109–123, Hillsdale, N.J.: Erlbaum.

Chambliss, William J., and John T. Liell 1966 "The legal process in the community setting: A study of law enforcement." Crime and Delinquency 12: 310–317.

Chambliss, William J., and Robert B. Seidman 1971 Law, Order and Power. Reading, Mass.: Addison-Wesley.

Chiricos, Theodore G., and Waldo, Gordon P. 1975 "Socioeconomic status and criminal sentencing: An empirical assessment of a conflict proposition." American Sociological Review 40: 753–772.

Cohen, Jacob, and Patricia Cohen 1983 Applied Multiple Regression/Correlation Analysis for the Behavioral Sciences. Hillsdale, N.J.: Lawrence Erlbaum Associates.

Clegg, Stewart, and David Dunkerley 1980 Organization, Class and Control. Boston: Routledge and Kegan Paul.

Dawson, Robert 1969 Sentencing: The Decision As to Type, Length and Conditions of Sentence. Boston: Little Brown.

Eisenstein, James, and Herbert Jacob 1977 Felony Justice: An Organizational Analysis of Criminal Courts. Boston: Little Brown.

Farrell, Ronald A., and Victoria Swigert 1978a "Prior offense as a self-fulfilling prophecy." Law and Society Review 12: 437–453. 1978b "Legal disposition of inter-group and intra-group homicides." Sociological Quarterly 19: 565–576.

Fontaine, Gary, and Catherine Emily 1978 "Causal attribution and judicial discretion." Law and Human Behavior 2: 323–337.

Green, Edward 1961 Judicial Attitudes in Sentencing. London: Macmillian. 1964 "Inter- and intra-racial Crime relative to sentencing." Journal of Criminal Law, Criminology, and Police Science 55: 348–358.

Greenwood, Peter C., Sorrel Wildhom, Eugene C. Poggio, and Michael J. Strumwasser 1973 Prosecution of Adult Defendants in Los Angeles County: A Policy Persective. Santa Monica, Calif.: Rand.

Goldberger, Arthur S. 1982 "Linear regression after selection." Journal of Econometrics 15: 357–366.

Gottfredson, Don M., and B. Stecher 1979 Sentencing Policy Models. Newark, N.J.: School of Criminal Justice, Rutgers University, manuscript.

Gottfredson, Michael R., and Don M. Gottfredson 1980 Decision Making in Criminal Justice. New York: Plenum Press.

Hagan, John 1974 "Extra-legal attributes and criminal sentencing: An assessment of a sociological viewpoint." Law and Society Review 8: 357–383. 1975a "The social and legal construction of criminal justice: A study of the pre-sentencing process." Social Problems 22: 620–637. 1975b "Parameters of criminal prosecution: An application of path analysis to a problem of criminal justice." Journal of Criminal Law, Criminology, and Police Science 65: 536–544.

Hagan, John, John Hewitt, and Duane Alwin 1979 "Ceremonial justice: Crime and punishment in a loosely coupled system." Social Forces 58: 506–527.

Hagan, John, Ilene Nagel, and Celesta Albonetti 1980 "The differential sentencing of white collar offenders in ten federal district courts." American Sociological Review 45: 802–820.

Hagan, John, and Patricia Parker 1985 "White-collar crime and punishment: The class structure and legal sanctioning." American Sociological Review 50: 302–316.

Hawkins, Darnell F. 1980 "Perceptions of punishment for crime." Deviant Behavior 1: 193–215. 1981 "Causal attribution and punishment for crime." Deviant Behavior 2: 207–230.

Hayduck, Leslie A., and Thomas Wonnacott 1980 " 'Effect equation' or 'effect coefficient': A note on the visual and verbal presentation of multiple regression interactions." Canadian Journal of Sociology 5: 399–404.

Heckman, James J. 1976 "The common structure of statistical models of truncation, sample selection and limited dependent variables and a simple estimation for such models." Annals of Economic and Social Measurement 5: 475–492. 1979 "Sample selection bias as a specification error." Econometrica 47: 153–161.

Heider, Fritz 1958 The Psychology of Interpersonal Relations. New York: Wiley.

Horton, John 1966 "Order and conflict theories of social problems." American Journal of Sociology 31: 701–713.

Johnson, Elmer H. 1957 "Selective forces in capital punishment." Social Forces 36: 165–169.

Klepper, S., D. Nagin, and L. Tierney 1983 "Discrimination in the criminal justice system: A critical appraisal of the literature," In Research on Sentencing: The Search for Reform, vol. II, ed. A. Blumstein, Jacqueline Cohen, Susan E. Martin, and Michael H. Tonery, 55–128, Washington, D.C.: National Academy Press.

Levin, Martin A. 1977 Urban Politics and the Criminal Courts. Chicago: University of Chicago Press.

Lippman, W. 1922 Public Opinion. New York: Harcourt Brace.

Livermore, Joseph M. 1978 "Contributions of attribution theory to the law." Law and Human Behavior 2: 389–393.

Lizotte, Alan J. 1978 "Extra-legal factors in Chicago's criminal courts: Testing the conflict model of criminal justice." Social Problems 25: 564–580.

March, James G., and Herbert A. Simon 1958 Organizations. New York: Wiley.

Mather, Lynn 1979 Plea Bargaining or Trial? Lexington, Mass.:Lexington Books.

Miethe, Terance D., and Charles A. Moore 1986 "Racial differences in criminal processing: The consequences of model selection on conclusions about differential treatment." The Sociological Quarterly 27: 217–237.

Nardulli, Peter 1979 The Courtroom Elite. New York: Ballinger.

Neubauer, David 1974 "After the arrest: The charging decision in Prairie City." Law and Society Review 8: 495–517.

Newman, Donald J. 1966 Conviction: The Determination of Guilt or Innocence Without Trial. Boston: Little Brown.

Peterson, Ruth, and John Hagan 1984 "Changing conceptions of race: Towards an account of anomalous findings of sentencing research." American Sociological Review 49: 56–70.

Pope, C. E. 1975a Sentencing of California Felony Offenders. Washington, D.C.: National Criminal Justice Information and Statistics Service. U.S. Government Printing Office. 1975b The Judicial Processing of Assault and Burglary Offenders in Selected California Courts. Washington, D.C.: National Criminal Justice Information and Statistics Service. U.S. Government Printing Office.

Quinney, Richard 1970 The Social Reality of Crime. Boston: Little Brown. 1972 "From repression to liberation: Social theory in a radical age." In Theoretical Perspectives on Deviance, ed. Robert Scott and Jack Douglass, 317–341. New York: Basic Books.

Rosett, A., and Donald Cressey 1976 Justice By Consent: Plea Bargains in the American Courthouse. Philadelphia: J.B. Lippincott.

Schur, Edwin 1965 Victimless Crimes. Englewood Cliffs, N.J.: Prentice Hall.

Shaver, Kelly G. 1975 An Introduction to Attribution Process. Cambridge, Mass.: Winthrop.

Simon, Herbert A. 1957 Administrative Behavior: A Study of Decision Making Processes in Administrative Organizations. New York: Macmillian.

Skolnick, Jerome H. 1966 Justice Without Trial: Law Enforcement in Democratic Society. New York: Wiley.

Smith, Douglas A. 1986 "The plea bargaining controversy." The Journal of Criminal Law and Criminology 77: 949–968.

Spohn, Cassia, John Gruhl, and Susan Welch 1981–82 "The effect of race on sentencing: A re-examination of an unsettled question." Law and Society Review 16: 72–88.

Stephan, Charles 1975 "Selectivity characteristics of jurors and litigants: Their influences on juries' verdicts," In The Jury System in America: A Critical Overview, ed. Rita J. Simon, 43–59. Beverley Hills, Calif.: Sage.

Stinchcombe, Arthur L. 1963 "Institutions of privacy in the determination of police administrative practice." American Journal of Sociology 69: 150–160.

Sutherland, Edwin H. 1949 White Collar Crime. New York: Dryden Press.

Sutton, Paul A. 1978 Federal Sentencing Patterns: A Study of Geographical Variations. Albany, N.Y.: Criminal Justice Research Center. 1987 "Comment—The effect of Spohn and Welch on sentencing research: An examination of their assumption that any one measure is adequate." Justice Quarterly 4: 303–307.

Swigert, Victoria L., and Ronald A. Farrell 1977 "Normal homicides and the law." American Sociological Review 42:16–32.

Thompson, James D. 1967 Organizations in Action. New York: McGraw-Hill.

Thomson, Randall J., and Matthew T. Zingraff 1981 "Detecting sentence disparity: Some problems and evidence." American Journal of Sociology 86: 869–880.

Uhlman, T.M., and N. D. Walker 1979 "A plea is no bargain: The impact of case disposition on sentence." Social Science Quarterly 60: 218–234. 1980 "He takes some of my time: I take some of his: An analysis of judical sentencing patterns in jury cases." Law and Society Review 14: 323–341.

Unnever, James D., Charles E. Frazier, and John C. Henretta 1980 "Race differences in criminal sentencing." The Sociological Quarterly 21: 197–206.

Vetri, Domenick R. 1964 "Guilty plea bargaining: Compromises by prosecutors to secure guilty pleas." University of Pennsylvania Law Review 112: 865–887.

Willick, Daniel H., Gretchen Gehlker, and Anita McFarland Watts 1975 "Social class as a factor affecting judicial disposition: Defendants charged with criminal homosexual acts." Criminology 12: 57–69.

Wolfgang, Marvin, and R. Marc Riedel 1973 "Race, judicial discretion and the death penalty." The Annals of the American Academy of Political and Social Sciences 407: 119–133.

Zatz, Marjorie, and John Hagan 1985 "Crime, time, and punishment: An exploration of selection bias in sentencing research." Journal of Quantitative Criminology 1: 103–126.

Zatz, Marjorie 1985 "Pleas, priors, and prison: Racial/ethnic differences in sentencing." Social Research 14: 169–193.

Does Gender Modify the Effects of Race–Ethnicity on Criminal Sanctioning?

Sentences for Male and Female White, Black, and Hispanic Defendants

Darrell Steffensmeier and Stephen Demuth

Introduction

Whether the criminal justice system and other societal institutions are fair, or whether they are biased along racial, ethnic, or gender lines is a pressing policy and theoretical issue that adjoins larger political concerns of American society as well as broad-based substantive interests within law, criminology, and the social sciences. Politically, because the symbolism of equality before the law is at the heart of our legal system, racial–ethnic or gender bias in the enforcement of law threatens the value we place on equity in this system (Hagan 1987). Substantively, because race–ethnicity and gender stratify and differentiate U.S. society, research on the effects of race–ethnicity or gender on criminal justice processing encompasses larger concerns with inequality and social stratification (Feree and Hall 1996). It is hardly surprising, therefore, that the search for racial and/or gender influences on legal and criminal justice outcomes has been a major enterprise in sociology and criminology.

[...]

Prior Research

RACE–ETHNICITY AND GENDER EFFECTS

An abundance of research on criminal sentencing has focused on possible disparities in sentence outcomes between black and white defendants. In their extensive review of these

Darrell Steffensmeier and Stephen Demuth, "Does Gender Modify the Effects of Race-Ethnicity on Criminal Sanctioning?: Sentences for Male and Female White, Black, and Hispanic Defendants," *Journal of Quantitative Criminology*, vol. 22, no. 3, pp. 241-248, 251-257, 259-261. Copyright © 2006 by Plenum Publishing. Reprinted with permission.

studies, Chiricos and Crawford (1995; see also Kramer and Steffensmeier 1993; Zatz 2000) conclude that findings of racial disparity in the in/out decision (i.e., whether to incarcerate) are relatively common in the sentencing literature. They conclude that, on average, the extant research finds that black defendants are more likely to be sentenced to jail or prison than white defendants upon conviction, net of controls. In contrast, a less consistent black disadvantage is found for sentence length decisions. Earlier studies often failed to differentiate between the two decisions, hence, muddying the influence of race on sentencing and leading to inaccurate conclusions of no race effect. The findings of several, recently published studies on sentencing decisions in state courts (Spohn and Holleran 2000; Steffensmeier et al. 1998) and in federal courts (Steffensmeier and Demuth 2000) reach a similar conclusion—i.e., a black disadvantage and a white advantage in incarceration decisions but small or negligible black–white differences in sentence-length decisions.

Far fewer sentencing studies examine Hispanic-white differences (but see, e.g., Holmes and Daudistel 1984; Klein et al. 1990; La Free 1985; Welch et al. 1984; Welch et al. 1985; Zatz 1984), due partly to the small number of Hispanics in many localities as well as the frequent practice of classifying Hispanics for reporting purposes into the "white" racial category (Steffensmeier and Demuth 2001). The paucity of research on the treatment of Hispanics in the criminal justice system is particularly alarming given that recent sophisticated studies provide evidence that Hispanic defendants are sentenced more harshly than white (and sometimes black) defendants (e.g., Engen and Gainey 2000; Spohn and Holleran 2000; Steffensmeier and Demuth 2000, 2001; Ulmer and Johnson 2004) and that Hispanics receive less favorable guidelines departure decisions than whites (and sometimes blacks) (Johnson 2003; Kramer and Ulmer 2002). Indeed, the failure to consider defendants' Hispanic ethnicity (i.e., by combining Hispanics and whites together into a single "white" group) in race-sentencing studies may result in race findings that significantly underestimate black–white sentencing differences (Steffensmeier and Demuth 2001). But, despite an increasing interest in the sentencing of Hispanic defendants, research on Hispanic-white and Hispanic-black differences in sentencing remains considerably underdeveloped relative to research on race and sentencing.

Lastly, compared to race effects, gender effects—that adult female defendants receive more lenient sentences than adult male defendants—are more consistently found in statistical sentencing studies (for reviews, see Bickle and Peterson 1991; Daly and Bordt, 1995; Spohn 2002; Steffensmeier et al. 1993). Gender differences apparently are stronger in imprisonment decisions than in conviction and sentence length decisions (Daly and Bordt 1995; Spohn 2002; Steffensmeier et al. 1993). The increasing attention to gender effects on court sanctioning notwithstanding, the existing studies have been criticized for "weak" controls for legally relevant variables like prior record and offense conduct, relying on a small number of cases, and an absence of contextual analysis to assess the possible interaction effects of gender and race–ethnicity on sentencing practices.

INTERSECTION OF GENDER AND RACE–ETHNICITY

There are few prior quantitative studies that have as their main objective to examine the interactive effects of gender and race on sentence outcomes net of controls for legal variables (e.g., Spohn et al. 1985; Steffensmeier et al. 1998).[1] At issue is whether *all* female defendants receive preferential

---

1   The research literature also provides some anecdotal observations of the intersection of gender and race–ethnicity at sentencing (see Daly 1994).

treatment in the criminal justice system regardless of their race–ethnicity; or whether this benefit is granted to white women but not necessarily to "women of color," as some writers contend (Belknap 1996, p. 70; Farnworth and Teske 1995; Klein and Kress 1976).

In the first empirical study to focus on the interaction between gender and race at sentencing, Spohn et al. (1985) find that black women are sentenced less harshly than black men, but receive sentences that are comparable to those of white men. There were an insufficient number of white females in the analysis to allow for a comparison of white males and white females. In spite of Spohn et al.'s (1985) interaction findings, the question of whether the effects of race–ethnicity and gender interact at sentencing has received little attention from sentencing researchers. This inattention is surprising because studies of interaction effects may help to explain the somewhat inconsistent findings of sentencing studies that emphasize only the main effects of race–ethnicity and/or gender (see for discussion, Steffensmeier et al. 1998).

In a more recent study, Steffensmeier et al. (1998) derive five main conclusions from their examination of the main and interactive effects of race (black–white), gender, and age on sentencing outcomes. First, women defendants receive more lenient treatment in court decisions than similarly situated male defendants—i.e., within-race comparisons show white females are sentenced more leniently than white males and black females are sentenced more leniently than black males. Second, black defendants are sentenced more severely than similarly situated white defendants—i.e., within-sex comparisons show black males are sentenced more severely than white males and black females are sentenced *slightly* more severely than white females (i.e., the race effect is *weaker* for female defendants). Third, young male defendants and especially young black male defendants receive the harshest sentences, whereas older male defendants—whether white or black—receive sentences more comparable to those of similarly aged female defendants. These patterns together yield a small or negligible race x gender interaction effect but significant race x gender x age effects. Fourth, a consistent gender effect of more lenient sentencing of female offenders persists not only across race (i.e., white and black) groups but also across any race x age grouping. The only instances of females receiving harsher sentences than males occurs when young female defendants (under age 30) are compared to older male defendants (aged 50 and over), and these differences are quite small. A fifth conclusion is that the overall race effect is smaller for female defendants than male defendants and is due to the relatively harsher sentencing of young black males.

In addition to the small number of studies that specifically explore the interaction between race and gender at sentencing, there does exist a small but growing number of studies that present either race-specific models (controlling for sex) or sex-specific models (controlling for race) and thus allow for a comparison of coefficients across groups (Albonetti 1997; Crawford 2000; Crawford et al. 1998; Kramer and Ulmer 2002; Spohn and Beichner 2000; Steffensmeier et al. 1993; Zatz 1984). For example, Zatz (1984) examines white–black-Hispanic differences in the effects of legal and extra-legal factors on sentence length. Although gender is not the focus of her analysis, she reports gender coefficients in her regression models that show no within- or between-group gender differences. In a study examining the sentencing of offenders under the Florida habitual offender statute, Crawford (2000) finds that among offenders eligible for habitual sentencing, the odds of habitualization are nearly twice as large for black female offenders as for white female offenders. A similar race effect is also found among male offenders in a previous study by the author and colleagues (Crawford et al. 1998). The authors conclude that "black status" similarly disadvantages both male and female defendants. In contrast, Spohn and Beichner's (2000) analysis of the effects of gender and race on sentence outcomes for offenders convicted of felonies in Chicago, Kansas City, and Miami shows that blacks are sentenced more harshly than whites among male defendants, but not among female defendants. And, similar to the findings of Steffensmeier et al. (1998), Spohn and Beichner (2000) find that women are treated more leniently than men regardless of racial category.

Last, we were able to locate only one study that compared gender differences in sentence outcomes for Hispanic as well as white and black defendants. In an analysis of federal drug sentencing practices, Albonetti (1997) reports that female defendants are sentenced less harshly across all racial–ethnic groups but that the gender gap in sentence outcomes is smaller for Hispanic defendants than for white or black defendants (who do not differ from each other).

Taken together, these studies which essentially involve black–white comparisons indicate that (i) female defendants on the whole are likely to receive more lenient sentences than their same-race male counterparts; (ii) the gender gap in sentencing is fairly robust across both white and black groups; and (iii) some evidence suggests (see Steffensmeier et al. 1998; Spohn and Beichner 2000) a smaller race effect among female than male defendants—i.e., greater similarity in the sentences of white and black females than in the sentences of white and black males.

Theoretical Framework

In light of the mixed findings and the scarcity of research on gender by race–ethnicity effects, the present study examines the extent to which the gender gap in sentence outcomes is similar or different across Hispanic, black, and white defendant groups. Or, stated differently, are the effects of race–ethnicity on sentence outcomes similar or different for male and female defendants? Our analysis is framed by the *focal concerns* theory of judicial decision making, first articulated by Steffensmeier (1980) and then expanded on by others (Spohn and Holleran 2000; Steffensmeier et al. 1998, 1993; Steffensmeier and Demuth 2001; Ulmer 1997; Ulmer and Johnson 2004). The key notion is that judges and other court actors are guided by three focal concerns in reaching sentencing decisions: blameworthiness, protection of the community, and practical constraints and consequences. *Blameworthiness* is associated with defendant culpability and having the punishment fit the crime. *Protection of the community* draws on similar concerns but emphasizes the goals of incapacitation and general deterrence, and on assessments about offenders' future behavior such as dangerousness or recidivism. *Practical constraints and consequences* include concerns about the organizational costs incurred by the criminal justice system, the disruption of ties to children or other family members, and potential impact of offender recidivism on the court's or the judge's standing in the public's eye. Importantly, the defendant's present offense and prior criminal conduct play a prominent role in the determination of sentences based on behavioral expectations concerning the focal concerns. However, it is argued that all of these focal concerns may be influenced by the offender's position in the social structure in ways that contribute to disparate treatment of racial or ethnic minorities.

Legal decision making is complex, repetitive, and frequently constrained by time and resources in ways that may produce considerable ambiguity or uncertainty for arriving at a "satisfactory" decision (Farrell and Holmes 1991; Albonetti 1991). The complexity and uncertainty stem partly from the multiple and sometimes conflicting sentencing goals faced by judges (see focal concerns above) and from the difficulty inherent in predicting the risk and seriousness of recidivism. While sometimes there is little definitive information on the background and character of the defendant, it also appears that judges and other court actors cannot easily digest the information that they do have at their disposal (Kramer and Ulmer 2002). Pre-sentence reports, which tend to be quite detailed, may in fact produce an "overload" of simultaneous information that is difficult to cognitively process or use. As an adaptation to these constraints, a "perceptual shorthand" (see Steffensmeier et al. 1998) for decision making emerges among judges and other court actors that utilizes attributions about case and defendant characteristics to manage the uncertainty and the case flow. Then, once in place and continuously reinforced, such patterned ways of thinking and acting are resistant to change. Indeed, prior studies examining the decisions of "courtroom workgroups" provide evidence that an inability to internalize crime attributions threatens the effectiveness of an overloaded court system (Eisenstein and Jacob 1977; Nardulli et al. 1988). In effect, judges make situational imputations about defendants' character and expected future behavior, and assess the implications of these imputations for the focal concerns describe above.

For our purposes here, although the use and reliance on these focal concerns *in the abstract* may be postulated to be universal or even-handed, it is likely that *in practice* the meaning, relative emphasis and priority, and situational interpretation of them is shaped both by the defendants' position in the social structure such as gender or racial or ethnic status and by political and public concerns regarding crime control and community safety. Regarding *gender*, therefore, more lenient sentencing decisions may be imposed on women because judges and other court actors view females as less dangerous and less of a public safety risk than males, tend to see women's crimes as an outgrowth of their own victimization (e.g., by coercive men or drugs), and because of judges' beliefs that the social costs of detaining women are higher since they are more likely than males to have child care responsibilities and mental or health problems that could not be treated in a jail setting (Steffensmeier et al. 1993). Also, women are perceived to maintain community ties more so than males (e.g., with children, parents) and are more closely bonded to conventional institutions that also serve to reduce the likelihood future involvement with the criminal justice system (see also Daly 1994).

Concerning *race–ethnicity*, more harsh sentences are likely to be imposed on black and Hispanic defendants than white defendants because of court actors' beliefs that blacks and Hispanics are more dangerous, more likely to recidivate, and less likely to be deterred. Research on labeling and stereotyping of black and Hispanic offenders reveals that court officials (and society-at-large) often view them as violent-prone, threatening, disrespectful of authority, and more criminal in their lifestyles (Bridges and Steen 1998; Mann and Zatz 1998; Russell 1998; Spohn and Beichner 2000; Swigert and Farrell 1976). Both Hispanic and black defendants are more likely than white defendants to lack the resources to thwart the imposition of sanctions (Bridges et al. 1987). Additional problems may face some Hispanic defendants (and especially recently immigrated Hispanic defendants): difficulty with the English language, general ignorance about or distrust of the criminal justice system, and an unwillingness to cooperate with authorities out of fear of deportation of family and friends. Defendants with limited English-speaking ability are probably less capable of mounting a strong criminal defense that could reduce criminal sanctions. Furthermore, unfamiliarity with or distrust of the criminal justice system, combined with a fear of retaliation by immigration officials, could make Hispanics less forthcoming to court employees and, as a result, more "deserving" of punishment.

Hypotheses

Prior research and our theoretical framework suggest the following key hypotheses, net of controls for legal, extralegal, and contextual factors:

i.   Female defendants will receive more favorable sentence outcomes than male defendants. That is, female defendants will be less likely to be incarcerated and, if incarcerated, will receive shorter jail or prison terms.

ii. Black and especially Hispanic defendants will receive less favorable sentence outcomes than white defendants, net of controls for legal, extralegal, and contextual factors.

iii. The gender effect on sentence outcomes will persist across the racial–ethnic comparison groups.

iv. The race–ethnicity effect on sentence outcomes will persist among both male and female defendants but the effect will be weaker among female defendants.

Hypotheses 3 and 4 are at odds with the view of some writers that white women, but not necessarily black or Hispanic women, are advantaged and will receive preferential treatment in the criminal justice system because they benefit from chivalrous attitudes and because they tend to be more deferential to legal functionaries than black or Hispanic women (Belknap 1996; Farnworth and Teske 1995; Klein and Kress 1976). As Belknap (1996, p. 70) writes, "women of color may not receive the chivalry accorded white women" [because women of color] "may not appear and behave in ways perceived by men as deserving of protection." Drawing instead on the focal concerns perspective, along with several recent studies showing a persistent gender effect in sentencing outcomes across subgroup comparisons (Daly 1994; Spohn and Beichner 2000; Steffensmeier et al. 1998), we expect *all* female defendants to benefit from beliefs viewing them as less culpable, as less dangerous, as less likely to recidivate (partly because of stronger ties to kin/family including children), and as more essential for providing child care.

[…]

Data and Method

In the present study, we use individual-level data compiled by the State Court Processing Statistics (SCPS) program of the Bureau of Justice Statistics on the processing of a sample of formally charged felony defendants in the State courts of the nation's most populous counties in 1990, 1992, 1994, and 1996. The SCPS data (1) provide information on both in-out and length-of-term sentencing decision; (2) provide important demographic, case, and contextual information such as gender, ethnicity, age, criminal history, arrest and conviction offense, and jurisdiction that might affect decisions at various stages of the process; (3) furnish adequate numbers of cases across all gender and racial/ethnic groups of interest at the sentencing stage; and (4) permit considerable generalizability of findings since the counties sampled represent courts that handle a substantial proportion of felony cases in the United States.

Findings

We are theoretically and empirically interested in the effects of gender and ethnicity on sentencing outcomes. First, we examine descriptive statistics at the sentencing stage, focusing on differences between male and female white, black, and Hispanic defendant groups. Second, we present the results of multiple regression analyzes examining the main effects of gender and race–ethnicity and other extralegal and legal factors on incarceration (in/out) and sentence-length outcomes. Third, we show the results of analyzes that examine the joint effects of gender and race–ethnicity on in/out and sentence length outcomes. In particular, we are interested in whether the racial–ethnic (and gender) gaps found in our analysis of main effects are similar or different across the different gender (and racial– ethnic) defendant groups.

DESCRIPTIVE STATISTICS

Table 5.4.1 provides descriptive statistics for the sentencing outcomes and legal and extralegal characteristics of each gender/racial–ethnic defendant subsample in the study. Among convicted defendants,

Table 5.4.1. Descriptive statistics for male and female defendants by race/ethnicity

	Female				Male			
	Total	White	Black	Hispanic	Total	White	Black	Hispanic
Measure								
Age	30.7	31.2	30.5	30.6	29.1	30.0	29.0	28.2
Robbery (%)	1.9	0.9	2.4	2.7	5.5	3.1	7.1	5.4
Assault (%)	5.0	3.5	6.2	4.5	6.5	6.1	6.3	7.1
Other violence (%)	1.9	2.2	1.7	1.5	3.4	4.5	2.3	4.1
Burglary (%)	4.0	2.9	3.6	7.4	10.8	11.9	10.1	10.9
Theft (%)	16.5	18.2	15.3	16.6	11.4	13.4	10.5	10.9
Other property (%)	14.9	16.2	15.5	10.7	8.8	11.7	8.2	6.5
Drug trafficking (%)	14.4	11.6	14.3	20.3	16.6	10.2	17.5	21.8
Other drug (%)	18.8	22.1	16.6	18.2	14.7	13.2	16.4	13.3
Other felony (%)	6.3	5.2	7.2	5.9	9.4	10.1	8.4	10.2
Misdemeanor (%)	16.3	17.2	17.2	12.1	13.0	15.8	13.0	9.9
Multiple charges (%)	50.4	49.8	49.3	54.8	53.1	55.6	50.5	54.8
Prior FTA (%)	31.8	28.0	32.9	36.3	38.2	33.5	42.8	35.4
Active CJ status (%)	33.8	33.6	32.6	37.4	42.3	37.7	45.0	42.7
Criminal history	1.4	1.2	1.4	1.4	1.9	1.6	2.1	1.8
Guilty plea (%)	94.2	95.1	93.0	95.5	91.1	93.6	88.0	93.8
Bench trial (%)	4.8	3.5	6.2	3.6	6.2	4.5	8.4	4.1
Jury trial (%)	1.0	1.4	0.8	0.9	2.7	1.9	3.6	2.1
Incarcerated (%)	56.1	53.9	53.4	67.3	70.7	63.0	70.6	79.2
Sentence length (in months)	21.5	20.5	24.3	17.1	32.5	29.0	38.5	26.2
N	3729	1292	1776	661	20525	5822	9339	5364

about 56% of women and 71% of men are sentenced to prison or jail; approximately 44% of women and 29% of men receive probation or some other nonincarcerative sentence (e.g., a fine). Notably, there is considerable racial–ethnic variation in the likelihood of receiving an incarceration sentence for both female and male defendants. Among females, white and black defendants have similar levels of incarceration: 54% and 53% respectively. But, Hispanic females are considerably more likely to be incarcerated than black and white females. Almost 67% of Hispanic women receive incarceration sentences. A somewhat different pattern emerges for male defendants. White male defendants are the least likely to be incarcerated (63%) and Hispanic males are the most likely to be incarcerated (79%); black male defendants rest in the middle (71%).

For defendants sentenced to incarcerative terms in prison or jail, female defendants receive average sentences of 22 months and male defendants receive average sentences of 33 months. A similar racial–ethnic pattern emerges for both male and female defendants. Among both females and males, Hispanic defendants receive the shortest sentences (17 and 26 months), black defendants receive the longest sentences (24 and 39 months), and white defendants rest in the middle (21 and 29 months).

The overall higher incarceration rates of male, black, and Hispanic defendants are, in part, a function of offense severity and criminal history. For example, male defendants are overrepresented in violent offenses (15% of offenses for males versus 9% of offenses for females) that are especially likely to result in prison sentences. Also, male defendants tend to have higher average criminal history scores than female defendants (1.9 for males versus 1.4 for females). Similarly, black and Hispanic defendants tend to be convicted of more serious, violent offenses than white defendants. Black and Hispanic defendants also have higher average criminal history scores than white defendants.

MAIN EFFECTS OF GENDER AND RACE–ETHNICITY

In this section, we provide the results of multivariate regression analyzes which examine whether gender and racial/ethnic differences in incarceration and sentence length persist net of statistical controls for legal, extralegal, and contextual factors.

Table 5.4.2 contains the results of logistic and OLS regression models for the incarceration and sentence length decisions, respectively.[2] Importantly, the legal variables are associated most strongly with sentencing outcomes. Beginning with the incarceration model (1 = incarcerated, 0 = not incarcerated), defendants convicted of the most serious crimes (e.g., robbery) are the most likely to receive incarceration sentences. Also, defendants with multiple charges, an active criminal status, a prior FTA (failure to appear for scheduled court hearing), and a more extensive criminal history are more likely to be incarcerated relative to defendants with a single charge, no active criminal status, no prior FTA, and a less extensive criminal history. And, for mode of conviction, defendants convicted at a jury or bench trial are significantly more likely to receive incarceration sentences than defendants who entered a guilty plea. The odds of incarceration for defendants convicted by a jury or judge are 2.01 and 1.19 times the odds of incarceration for defendants convicted through a guilty plea, respectively.

Turning to the gender and race–ethnicity incarceration findings, female defendants are much less likely to be incarcerated than male defendants. The odds of incarceration for male defendants are about 71% higher than the odds of incarceration for female defendants. Black and Hispanic

---

2   Contextual variables for county and sentencing year are omitted from the tables for space reasons. Regression results for these variables are available from the authors upon request.

Table 5.4.2. Logistic and OLS regression models for in/out and sentence length decisions

Measure	In/Out [odds ratio]	Sentence length [log (months)]
(Female) Male	1.706***	0.226***
	(0.045)	(0.033)
(White) Black	1.282***	0.048
	(0.041)	(0.027)
Hispanic	1.315***	0.074*
	(0.049)	(0.030)
Age	0.999	0.001
	(0.002)	(0.001)
Age^2	0.999***	−0.000
	(0.0001)	(0.0001)
Robbery	6.271***	1.190***
	(0.124)	(0.058)
Assault	1.384***	0.446***
	(0.082)	(0.050)
Other violence	1.476***	0.390***
	(0.108)	(0.063)
Burglary	1.475***	0.368***
	(0.074)	(0.043)
(Theft) Other property	0.681***	−0.171***
	(0.068)	(0.047)
Drug trafficking	1.724***	0.315***
	(0.065)	(0.040)
Other drug	0.824**	−0.248***
	(0.064)	(0.040)
Other felony	1.016	−0.206***
	(0.073)	(0.044)
Misdemeanor	0.487***	−1.205***
	(0.065)	(0.047)
Multiple charges	1.323***	0.205***
	(0.036)	(0.023)
Prior FTA	1.244***	−0.024
	(0.043)	(0.025)
Active CJ status	1.447***	0.230***
	(0.041)	(0.025)
Criminal history	1.423***	0.221***
	(0.014)	(0.012)
(Guilty plea) Bench trial	1.192*	0.301***
	(0.075)	(0.050)
Jury trial	2.010***	0.945***
	(0.129)	(0.062)
Hazard	—	0.823***
		(0.167)
−2 Log L/R^2	22754.17	0.328
N	24254	16605

* $P < 0.05$

** $P < 0.01$

*** $P < 0.001$; County and year dummy variables are included in the regression models; Numbers in parentheses are standard errors

STAT HELP!

Under the "In/Out" column, the findings can be interpreted as the odds of receiving an incarceration sentence. For example, the value for "Male" indicates that the odds of males receiving an incarceration sentence are 1.706 times higher than the odds of females receiving an incarceration sentence. In the "Sentence length" column, positive values represent an increase in sentence length and negative values represent a decrease in sentence length. Therefore, sentences for males are longer than females, for instance. In both columns, one or more asterisks (*) indicate the effect is *statistically significant.*

defendants are both more likely to be incarcerated than white defendants. The odds of incarceration for black defendants are 28% greater than the odds of incarceration for white defendants; the odds of incarceration for Hispanic defendants are 32% greater than the odds of incarceration for white defendants. Although the odds of incarceration are slightly higher for Hispanic defendants than black defendants, the black-Hispanic difference is not statistically significant.

For the sentence length decision (sentence length in months is logged), the effects of legal variables closely mirror the effects of legal variables found in the incarceration decision model. Regarding the effects of gender, male defendants sentenced to incarceration terms receive sentence lengths that are longer than female defendants, net of controls. Male sentences are about 20% (exp[0.226]) longer than female sentences. Looking at race-ethnicity, Hispanic defendants receive sentences that are about 8% longer than white defendants. The black–white difference for sentence length is not significantly different.

These findings are consistent with our theoretical expectations and provide support for Hypotheses 1 and 2. We turn next to the main focus of our analysis, whether the effects of gender and/or race–ethnicity are additive and consistent or whether the effect of gender is contextualized by race–ethnicity and vice versa.

INTERACTION EFFECTS OF GENDER AND RACE–ETHNICITY

[…] First, in general, female defendants receive more favorable incarceration and sentence length decisions than males across all racial-ethnic groups. Second, the gender gap or difference in both the in/out and the sentence length decisions is smallest among white defendants (male odds ratio of incarceration = 1.399, male sentence length = 0.130). For the in/out decision, the gender gap is largest among Hispanic defendants (odds ratio = 2.183), followed by black defendants (odds ratio = 1.773). Furthermore, both the Hispanic-white difference ($P < 0.001$) and the black–white difference ($P < 0.05$) in the gender gap are statistically significant. For the sentence length decision, black defendants ($b = 0.287$) have the largest gender gap followed closely by Hispanic defendants ($b = 0.219$). Here, the black–white difference is statistically significant ($P < 0.05$); there is no statistically significant Hispanic-white difference in the gender gap for the sentence length outcome.

[…] For both the in/out and sentence length decisions, there are no statistically significant racial-ethnic differences among female defendants. In contrast, racial-ethnic differences in sentencing decisions do exist for males. Black and Hispanic males are more likely to be incarcerated and receive longer sentence terms than similarly situated white males. The odds of incarceration for black and Hispanic males are about 40% higher than the odds of incarceration for white males. Also, black and Hispanic males receive sentence terms that are approximately 8% longer than the sentence terms for white males. In addition, z-tests of differences between race–ethnicity coefficients across male and female models show that the effects of race–ethnicity on the in/out decision are greater among male defendants than female defendants ($P < 0.01$). For the sentence length decision, only the black effect is statistically different for male and female defendants ($P < 0.01$).

Thus, two main findings emerge from our analysis of interaction effects depending on whether we are looking at the gender difference or at the racial–ethnic difference. First, the gender difference in sentencing is not uniform across racial–ethnic groups—the difference in both incarceration and sentence length outcomes is smaller for white defendants and larger for Hispanic and black defendants. Second, neither are racial–ethnic differences in sentencing the same between male and female offenders—for both the in/out and sentence length decisions, there are no racial–ethnic differences for female defendants, but racial– ethnic differences do exist for male defendants.

[…]

Summary and Discussion

Our main goal in this analysis has been to examine the intersection of defendants' gender and race–ethnicity on sentence outcomes in large urban felony courts, *with particular focus on how gender might affect the extent that black and Hispanic offenders are sentenced more harshly than white offenders.* Drawing from the focal concerns perspective on decisions and practices of court officials, we expected that female defendants would receive more favorable sentence outcomes than male defendants, that white defendants would receive more favorable treatment than black or Hispanic defendants, and that this main effect would persist fairly evenly across gender and racial–ethnic subgroup comparisons (because, like white males, white females would receive more lenient sentences than black or Hispanic females). The findings were generally supportive of these hypotheses but with an important qualification. We discovered a notable interaction effect, namely, that the influence of race–ethnicity in sentencing depends on the defendant's gender—to the extent that racial–ethnic bias exists in sentencing, it does so for male defendants but not for female defendants.

Thus, our key findings are as follows. In addition to the strong effects of prior record and offense seriousness on sentence outcomes, both gender and race–ethnicity have significant direct effects on sentence outcomes. Female defendants receive more lenient sentences than male defendants. Black and Hispanic defendants receive less favorable treatment than white defendants. These main effects, however, depend on whether the defendant sample is partitioned by race–ethnicity or gender. Specifically, we find (i) that race–ethnicity influences sentencing in the case of male defendants but not female defendants, and (ii) that gender strongly influences sentencing across all within-race comparisons but there essentially are no differences in the sentences received by white, black, and Hispanic *female* defendants. Apparently one or more of the following are operative: white male defendants are penalized for being "male" but benefit from being white rather than a "minority" (black or Hispanic); black and Hispanic male defendants are penalized for being both "male" and a "minority"; white female defendants benefit from being "female" but do not benefit from being "white"; black and Hispanic females benefit from being "female" but are not penalized for being "minority."

While these findings support the general hypothesis that *all* women defendants will tend to receive more lenient treatment in court decision making than similarly situated male defendants, the findings are sharply at odds with the traditional view that chivalry or leniency in court sanctioning typically by-passes "women of color" (Klein and Kress 1976; Belknap 1996). Instead, consistent with some prior research (Steffensmeier et al. 1998; Spohn and Beichner 2000), it appears that black and Hispanic female defendants actually benefit more from their "female" status than would be expected *all else equal* (i.e., given their racial–ethnic status).

[…]

Acknowledgments

This research was supported by grants from the American Statistical Association/Bureau of Justice Statistics Statistical Methodological Research Program and the Law and Society Program of the National Science Foundation. Core support was provided by the Population Research Institute at The Pennsylvania State University and the Center for Family and Demographic Research at Bowling Green State University.

REFERENCES

Albonetti CA (1991) An integration of theories to explain judicial discretion. Soc Probl 38:247–266 .

Albonetti CA (1997) Sentencing under the federal sentencing guidelines: effects of defendant characteristics, guilty pleas, and departures on sentence outcomes for drug offenses, 1991–1992. Law Soc Rev 31:789–822.

Belknap J (1996) The invisible woman: Gender, crime, and criminal justice. Wadsworth, Belmont, CA.

Berk RA (1983) An introduction to sample selection bias in sociological data. Am Sociol Rev 48:386–398.

Bickle GS, Peterson RD (1991) The impact of gender-based family roles on criminal sentencing. Soc Probl 38:372–394.

Bridges GS, Crutchfield RD, Simpson EE (1987) Crime, social structure, and criminal punishment: white and nonwhite rates of imprisonment. Soc Probl 34:345–361.

Bridges GS, Steen S (1998) Racial disparities in official assessments of juvenile offenders: attributional stereotypes as mediating mechanisms. Am Sociol Rev 63:554–570.

Bureau of Justice Statistics (1999) Felony defendants in large urban counties, 1996. Department of Justice, Washington, DC.

Chiricos TG, Crawford C (1995) Race and imprisonment: a contextual assessment of the evidence. In: Hawkins DF (ed) Ethnicity, race, and crime: perspectives across time and place. State University of New York Press, Albany, NY, pp 281–309.

Clogg CC, Petkova E, Haritou A (1995). Statistical methods for comparing regression coefficients between models. Am J Sociol 100:1261–1293.

Crawford C (2000) Gender, race, and habitual offender sentencing in Florida. Criminology 38:263–280.

Crawford C, Chiricos T, Kleck G (1998) Race, racial threat, and sentencing of habitual offenders. Criminology 36:481–511.

Daly K (1994) Gender, crime, and punishment. Yale University Press, New Haven, CT.

Daly K, Bordt RL (1995) Sex effects and sentencing: an analysis of the statistical literature. Justice Q 12:143–177.

Demuth S (2002) The effect of citizenship status on sentencing outcomes in drug cases. Fed Sentencing Rep 14:271–275.

Eisenstein J, Jacob H (1977) Felony Justice: an organizational analysis of Felony courts. Little Brown, Boston.

Engen RL, Gainey RR (2000) Modeling the effects of legally relevant and extralegal factors under sentencing guidelines: the rules have changed. Criminology 38:1207–1230.

Farnworth M, Teske R Jr.(1995) Gender differences in felony court processing: three hypotheses of disparity. Women Crim Justice 62:23–44.

Farrell RA, Holmes MD (1991) The social and cognitive structure of legal decision-making. Sociol Q 32:529–542.

Ferree MM, Hall E (1996) Gender, race, and class in mainstream textbooks. Am Sociol Rev 61:929–950.

Hagan J (1987) Review essay: a great truth in the study of crime. Criminology 25:421–428.

Holleran D, Spohn C (2004) On the use of the total incarceration variable in sentencing research. Criminology 42:211–240.

Holmes MD, Daudistel HC (1984) Ethnicity and justice in the southwest: the sentencing of Anglo, black, and Mexican origin defendants. Soc Sci Q 65:263–277.

Johnson BD (2003) Racial and ethnic disparities in sentencing departures across modes of conviction. Criminology 41:449–490.

Johnston J, DiNardo J (1997) Econometric methods. McGraw-Hill, New York.

Klein D, Kress J (1976) Any women's blues: a critical overview of women, crime, and the criminal justice system. Crime Soc Justice 5:34–59.

Klein S, Petersilia J, Turner S (1990) Race and imprisonment decisions in California. Science 247:812–816.

Klepper S, Nagin D, Tierney L (1983) Discrimination in the criminal justice system: a critical appraisal of the literature. In: Blumstein et al. (eds) Research on sentencing: the search for reform. National Academy Press, Washington, DC, pp 55–128.

Kramer J, Steffensmeier D (1993) Race and imprisonment decisions. Sociol Q 34:357–76.

Kramer JH, Ulmer JT (2002) Downward departures for serious violent offenders: local court "corrections" to Pennsylvania's sentencing guidelines. Criminology 40:897–932.

LaFree GD (1985) Official reactions to Hispanic defendants in the southwest. J Res Crime Delinquency 22:213–237.

Mann CR, Zatz MS (eds) (1998) Images of color, images of crime: readings. Roxbury, Los Angeles.

Massey D (1993) Latinos, poverty, and the underclass: a new agenda for research. Hispanic J Behav Sci 15:449–475.

Melendez E, Rodriguez C, Figueroa JB (eds) (1996) Hispanics in the labor force: issues and policy. Plenum, New York.

Nardulli PF, Eisenstein J, Flemming RB (1988) The tenor of justice: criminal courts and the guilty plea process. University of Illinois Press, Urbana, IL.

Paternoster R, Brame R, Mazerolle P, Piquero A (1998) Using the correct statistical test for the equality of regression coefficients. Criminology 36:859–866.

Portes A, Rumbaut R (1996) Immigrant America: a portrait. University of California Press, Berkeley, CA.

Russell KK (1998) The color of crime: racial hoaxes, white fear, black protectionism, police harassment, and other macroaggressions. New York University Press, New York.

Sandefer G, Tienda M (1988) Divided opportunities: minorities, poverty, and social policy. Plenum, New York.

Spohn CC (2002) How do judges decide?: the search for fairness and justice in punishment. Sage, Thousand Oaks, CA.

Spohn C, Beichner D (2000) Is preferential treatment of female offenders a thing of the past? A multi-site study of gender, race, and imprisonment. Crim Justice Policy Rev 11:149–184.

Spohn C, Holleran D (2000) The imprisonment penalty paid by young, unemployed black and Hispanic male offenders. Criminology 38: 281–306.

Spohn C, Welch S, Gruhl J (1985) Women defendants in court: the interaction between sex and race in convicting and sentencing. Soc Sci Q 66:178–185.

Steffensmeier D (1980) Assessing the impact of the women's movement on sex-based differences in the handling of adult criminal defendants. Crime Delinquency 26:344–357.

Steffensmeier D, Demuth S (2000) Ethnicity and sentencing outcomes in U.S. federal courts: Who is punished more harshly? Am Sociol Rev 65:705–729.

Steffensmeier D, Demuth S (2001) Ethnicity and judges' sentencing decisions: hispanic-black-white comparisons. Criminology 39:145–178.

Steffensmeier D, Kramer J, Streifel C (1993) Gender and imprisonment decisions. Criminology 31:411–446.

Steffensmeier D, Kramer J, Ulmer J (1995) Age differences in sentencing. Justice Q 12:583–602.

Steffensmeier D, Ulmer J, Kramer J (1998) The interaction of race, gender, and age in criminal sentencing: the punishment cost of being young, black, and male. Criminology 36:763–798.

Swigert V, Farrell R (1976) Murder, inequality, and the law: differential treatment in the legal process. Heath, Lexington, MA.

Ulmer JT (1997) Social worlds of sentencing: court communities under sentencing guidelines. State University of New York Press, Albany, NY.

Ulmer JT, Johnson B (2004) Sentencing in context: a multilevel analysis. Criminology 42:137–178.

Welch S, Gruhl J, Spohn C (1984) Dismissal, conviction, and incarceration of Hispanic defendants: a comparison with Anglos and blacks. Soc Sci Q 65:257–264.

Welch S, Spohn C, Gruhl J (1985) Convicting and sentencing differences among black, hispanic, and white males in six localities. Justice Q 2:67–77.

Zatz MS (1984) Race, ethnicity, and determinate sentencing. Criminology 22:147–171.

Zatz MS (2000) The convergence of race, ethnicity, gender, and class on court decisionmaking: looking toward the 21st century. In: Horney J (ed) Criminal Justice 2000, vol 3: policies, processes and decisions of the Justice system. Department of Justice, Washington, DC.

DISCUSSION QUESTIONS

1. Explain the primary motivations of punishment and how they can change throughout time.

2. Why has support for rehabilitation remained high for juveniles and nonviolent offenders?

3. Analyze why the United States was in favor of rehabilitation in the 60s and then shifted towards a more punitive ideal. How does this impact sentencing?

4. How can differences in the justifications for punishment among judges impact their sentencing behavior?

5. Analyze which theories of sentencing promote efficient case processing.

6. If a judge is uncertain, should relying on his or her personal experiences be a first option?

7. Explain why offenders with certain demographic backgrounds may get different sentences.

8. How might the defendant's race/ethnicity affect the exercise of discretion among the court actors?

9. Explain some of the reasons as to why women sometimes receive more lenient sentences in comparison to men.

10. Why would there be a large sentencing difference between white and non-white males but not between white and non-white females?

THE CRIMINAL APPEAL PROCESS

Introduction

Whereas the trial courts are not given much attention by the public, appellate courts are constantly in the limelight. For this reason, the decisions of appellate courts are often subject to more scrutiny. Their role is quite different than that of the trial courts, because they have appellate jurisdiction, meaning, in most circumstances, they are not the first to hear a case. Also, as opposed to a single judge presiding over trial cases, appellate cases are heard by a panel of judges or justices. This means that judges take on a more prominent role within the appellate process, and they are given greater discretionary power in making decisions. Fully explaining the appellate court process, though, requires an understanding of judges' powers and limits and how these factor into their decision-making.

Sources of Judicial Power

Alexander Hamilton, in Federalist No. 78, said "the judiciary, from the nature of its functions, will always be the least dangerous to the political rights of the Constitution; because it will be least in a capacity to annoy or injure them." There is a lot of debate surrounding this argument that the court is the "least dangerous" of the three branches of government. The court system, and the appellate courts in particular, possess important powers that give them prominence and authority on issues of the law.

Typically, cases that come to the appellate courts are those in which there was a trial court error, such as a search warrant without probable cause, improper instruction of the jury, or a cruel and unusual sentence, to name a few. While the first appeal is guaranteed as a right, any subsequent appeals are heard by the appellate courts at their discretion after a petition is filed. Judges can decide whether to grant certiorari or hear the case, and the reasons for this decision do not need to be justified. The Supreme Court, for instance, receives about 7,000 to 8,000 petitions a year and grants about 80 of them, which is close to 1 percent. This discretionary appellate jurisdiction gives them legal power.

When the appellate courts decide to hear a case, they are responsible for issuing an opinion with their decision regarding the legal question posed, as well as an order to the lower courts. This decision becomes law. In this way, appellate judges are important policy-makers. Their ability to make policy is fostered by the power of judicial review. This power was established by Justice John Marshall in *Marbury v. Madison.* The Judiciary Act of 1789 gave the Supreme Court original jurisdiction to issue a writ of mandamus. The Supreme Court is given original jurisdiction in certain cases, but these cases are restricted to those listed in Article III of the Constitution. In *Marbury*, the court struck down the law from the legislature as unconstitutional, because it went against Article III.

From this point on, the courts would continue to exercise its authority in correcting acts from state and federal legislatures that deviated from the rights guaranteed in the U.S. Constitution and state constitutions. This authority gave the courts substantial power within the checks and balances structure and has been used many times to inform and correct laws pertaining to criminal justice issues and procedures.

Limits on Judicial Power

Despite these powers, appellate judges have important limits on their authority. Although they have the ability to overturn and correct laws, they cannot do so unless the case is brought to them. In writing opinions, they must completely justify their decisions, relying on precedent to make and support their arguments. In making decisions as a panel, appellate judges must consider competing interpretations of the law, and decisions may not always go in their favor (i.e., they may not be part of the majority on a decision). Of primary importance, though, is the fact that judges cannot enforce their decisions and are dependent upon the executive branch to do so. Lower courts and other branches of the government can easily avoid, limit, and defy decisions of the appellate courts, and they do not have a means for punishing such behavior. The legislature can even propose amendments to reverse decisions or enact laws specifically rejecting a court's interpretation. This lack of enforcement power has repercussions on judges' decision-making and calls attention to the political structure of the judiciary.

In "Decisionmaking in the U.S. Circuit Courts of Appeals," Frank Cross recognizes four different methods of judicial decision-making. In the legal model, decisions are assumed to be the product of impartial application of legal rules, which is essentially a traditionalist understanding of the court system. Judges are thought to be completely objective and neutral in their application of the law. The ideals of the legal model tie into the concept of an independent judiciary, where judges are seen as free from the political whims of the people. At the federal level, this independence is promoted through the appointment of justices, set salaries, and life tenure. To a certain extent, as Cross finds, decisions made by judges are based on legal rules.

Cross also finds, though, that judges can be influenced by ideological preferences and political goals, which represents a more realist view of the courts. He also presents a strategic model, whereby judges make decisions in consideration of external responses. He specifically focuses on the circumstances in which intermediate appellate judges may take into consideration the preferences of the courts of last resort, including state Supreme Courts and the U.S. Supreme Court, when making decisions. However, Kevin McGuire and James Stimson, in "The Least Dangerous Branch Revisited: New Evidence on Supreme Court Responsiveness to Public Preferences," find that appellate court judges are particularly responsive to the general public.

This responsiveness to public opinion is a byproduct of their lack of enforcement power. If judges want to have an influence on public policy through their decisions, they need to consider whether those implementing their decisions would find them acceptable and worthy of implementation. In constructing their decisions, judges may then consider the likelihood that "popular decision-makers will support their policy initiatives." The fact that they are responding to public opinion makes the appellate courts political.

Maintaining Legitimacy

If the appellate courts want decisions enforced that are not in line with public opinion, they must be seen as a legitimate institution that can be trusted and respected. In their discussion of "Public Opinion and the Court," McGuire and Stimson call attention to important research in this area. Legitimacy is grounded in diffuse support, or the goodwill that the court has generated, such that the people will continue to support the court and its decisions, even when they are contrary to popular opinion. There is also specific support, which involves the support given to specific cases based on whether the outcome of the case appeases the public and meets their demands for justice.

When the courts make a decision, certain people are rewarded, and others are deprived. Those who are rewarded, in that the decision supports their position on an issue, have specific support for the decision that was made. When the courts make decisions that are favorable to the majority of the public, they continue to garner specific support that translates into diffuse support, or favorable attitudes towards the courts. McGuire and Stimson state that "the Constitution affords the Supreme Court institutional independence, but it in no way guarantees the prestige upon which its success is so highly dependent." Essentially, the courts rely on this diffuse support to keep their prestige and authority.

If they make too many decisions against public opinion, the courts begin to lose their legitimacy. It is particularly detrimental when those more attentive to the courts continue to be deprived by their decisions. Most of the public does not actively keep up to date on the latest decisions of the courts. The lower courts, executive branch, and legislative branch, are more aware of the appellate courts' decision-making, because their decisions often have consequences for these groups. Therefore, the courts would be most concerned with losing support from these "relevant publics." The media is also a "relevant public," and presents a challenge in that they can call attention to decisions that would have otherwise gone unnoticed by the general public, who are typically apathetic to the courts. In this way, the media can sway the general public against the appellate courts, greatly influencing the courts' legitimacy. Therefore, in decision-making, judges have to consider the potential backlash from these relevant groups and the consequences of this backlash.

Overall, public opinion polls show that there is more support for the judiciary than the other branches of government. However, recent trends suggest that trust in the judiciary has fallen from prior years. There are many factors that can explain this decline, and lack of support for decisions is one. Of the three branches, it could be argued that the judiciary has the most to lose by this lack of trust.

Marbury v. Madison

5 U.S. 137 (1803)

[Marbury was appointed a justice of the peace, a minor judicial officer, in the District of Columbia, by President Adams—a few days before President Jefferson took office after defeating Adams in the election of 1800. Marbury's position was one of 42 positions created by the lame duck Congress (dominated by Adams' Federalist party). Ironically, his appointment was signed by Adams' Secretary of State, John Marshall, who also was appointed and sworn-in as the Chief Justice of the Supreme Court only days before Jefferson took office. Oddly, neither Adams nor Marshall delivered the commission to Marbury before they left office, creating the basic circumstances from which this dispute arose.]

MARSHALL, CHIEF JUSTICE

At the last term on the affidavits then read and filed with the clerk, a rule was granted in this case, requiring the secretary of state to show cause why a mandamus should not issue, directing him to deliver to William Marbury his own commission as a justice of the peace for the county of Washington, in the District of Columbia.

No cause has been shown, and the present motion is for a mandamus. The peculiar delicacy of this case, the novelty of some of its circumstances, and the real difficulty attending the points which occur in it, require a complete exposition of the principles on which the opinion to be given by the court is founded.

. . . .

In the order in which the court has viewed this subject, the following questions have been considered and decided.

1st.   Has the applicant a right to the commission he demands?

2d.   If he has a right, and that right has been violated, do the laws of his country afford him a remedy?

3d.   If they do afford him a remedy, is it a mandamus issuing from this court?

The first object of inquiry is . . . [h]as the applicant a right to the commission he demands?

His right originates in an act of Congress passed in February 1801, concerning the District of Columbia. After dividing the district into two counties, the 11th section of this law enacts, "that there shall be appointed in and for each of the said counties, such number of discreet persons to be justices of the peace as the president of the United States shall, from time to time, think expedient, to continue in office for five years.["] It appears from the affidavits, that in compliance with this law, a commission for William Marbury as a justice of peace for the county of Washington, was signed by John Adams, then president of the United States; after which the seal of the United States was affixed to it; but the commission has never reached the person for whom it was made out.

In order to determine whether he is entitled to this commission, it becomes necessary to inquire whether he has been appointed to the office. For if he has been appointed, the law continues him in office for five years, and he is entitled to the possession of those evidences of office, which, being completed, became his property.

The 2d section of the 2d article of the constitution declares, that "the president shall nominate, and, by and with the advice and consent of the senate, shall appoint ambassadors, other public ministers and consuls, and all other officers of the United States, whose appointments are not otherwise provided for."

The 3d section declares, that "he shall commission all the officers of the United States."

An act of congress directs the secretary of state to keep the seal of the United States, "to make out and record, and affix the said seal to all civil commissions to officers of the United States to be appointed by the president, by and with the consent of the senate, or by the president alone; provided that the said seal shall not be affixed to any commission before the same shall have been signed by the president of the United States."

These are the clauses of the constitution and laws of the United States, which affect this part of the case. . . .

[The Court then examined whether the technical requirements for appointment of Mr. Marbury had been completed in compliance with the requirements of the federal statute and the Constitution.]

Mr. Marbury, then, since his commission was signed by the president and sealed by the secretary of state, was appointed; and as the law creating the office gave the officer a right to hold for five years independent of the executive, the appointment was not revocable, but vested in the officer legal rights which are protected by the laws of his country.

To withhold the commission, therefore, is an act deemed by the court not warranted by law, but violative of a vested legal right.

This brings us to the second inquiry; which is . . . if he has a right, and that right has been violated, do the laws of his country afford him a remedy?

The very essence of civil liberty certainly consists in the right of every individual to claim the protection of the laws, whenever he receives an injury. One of the first duties of government is to afford that protection. In Great Britain the king himself is sued in the respectful form of a petition, and he never fails to comply with the judgment of his court. . . .

. . . .

The government of the United States has been emphatically termed a government of laws, and not of men. It will certainly cease to deserve this high appellation, if the laws furnish no remedy for the violation of a vested legal right.

If this obloquy is to be cast on the jurisprudence of our country, it must arise from the peculiar character of the case. It behooves us then to inquire whether there be in its composition any ingredient which shall exempt from legal investigation, or exclude the injured party from legal redress. In pursuing this inquiry the first question which presents itself is, whether this can be arranged with that class of cases which come under the description of *damnum absque injuria*; a loss without an injury.

The description of cases never has been considered, and it is believed never can be considered as comprehending offices of trust, of honour or of profit. The office of justice of peace in the District of Columbia is such an office; it is therefore worthy of the attention and guardianship of the laws. It has received that attention and guardianship. It has been created by special act of congress, and has been secured, so far as the laws can give security to the person appointed to fill it, for five years. It is not, then, on account of the worthlessness of the thing pursued, that the injured party can be alleged to be without remedy.

Is it in the nature of the transaction? Is the act of delivering or withholding a commission to be considered as a mere political act belonging to the executive department alone, for the performance of which entire confidence is placed by our constitution in the supreme executive; and for any misconduct respecting which, the injured individual has no remedy.

That there may be such cases is not to be questioned; but that every act of duty, to be performed in any of the great departments of government, constitutes such a case, is not to be admitted.

. . . .

If some acts be examinable, and others not, there must be some rule of law to guide the court in the exercise of its jurisdiction. In some instances there may be difficulty in applying the rule to particular cases; but there cannot, it is believed, be much difficulty in laying down the rule.

By the constitution of the United States, the president is invested with certain important political powers, in the exercise of which he is to use his own discretion, and is accountable only to his country in his political character and to his own conscience. To aid him in the performance of these duties, he is authorized to appoint certain officers, who act by his authority, and in conformity with his orders.

In such cases, their acts are his acts; and whatever opinion may be entertained of the manner in which executive discretion may be used, still there exists, and can exist, no power to control that discretion. The subjects are political. They respect the nation, not individual rights, and being entrusted to the executive, the decision of the executive is conclusive. . . .

[The Court then reasoned that once the appointment was complete, the delivery of the appointment was not a political act.]

But when the legislature proceeds to impose on that officer other duties; when he is directed peremptorily to perform certain acts; when the rights of individuals are dependent on the performance of those acts; he is so far the officer of the law; is amenable to the laws for his conduct; and cannot at his discretion sport away the vested rights of others.

The conclusion from this reasoning is, that where the heads of departments are the political or confidential agents of the executive, merely to execute the will of the President, or rather to act in cases in which the executive possesses a constitutional or legal discretion, nothing can be more perfectly clear than that their acts are only politically examinable. But where a specific duty is assigned by law, and individual rights depend upon the performance of that duty, it seems equally clear that the individual who considers himself injured, has a right to resort to the laws of his country for a remedy.

If this be the rule, let us inquire how it applies to the case under the consideration of the court.

. . . .

That, having this legal title to the office, he has a consequent right to the commission; a refusal to deliver which is a plain violation of that right, for which the laws of his country afford him a remedy.

It remains to be inquired whether . . . [h]e is entitled to the remedy for which he applies. This depends on,

1st. The nature of the writ applied for; and,
2d. The power of this court.
3d. The nature of the writ.

. . . .

[The Court then considered whether this was an appropriate case for a writ of mandamus.]

This, then, is a plain case of a mandamus, either to deliver the commission, or a copy of it from the record; and it only remains to be inquired, [w]hether it can issue from this court.

The act to establish the judicial courts of the United States authorizes the supreme court "to issue writs of mandamus in cases warranted by the principles and usages of law, to any courts appointed, or persons holding office, under the authority of the United States."

The secretary of state, being a person holding an office under the authority of the United States, is precisely within the letter of the description, and if this court is not authorized to issue a writ of mandamus to such an officer, it must be because the law is unconstitutional, and therefore absolutely incapable of conferring the authority, and assigning the duties which its words purport to confer and assign.

The constitution vests the whole judicial power of the United States in one supreme court, and such inferior courts as congress shall, from time to time, ordain and establish. This power is expressly extended to all cases arising under the laws of the United States; and consequently, in some form, may be exercised over the present case; because the right claimed is given by a law of the United States.

In the distribution of this power, it is declared that "the Supreme Court shall have original jurisdiction in all cases affecting ambassadors, other public ministers and consuls, and those in which a state shall be a party. In all other cases, the Supreme Court shall have appellate jurisdiction."

It has been insisted at the bar, that as the original grant of jurisdiction, to the Supreme and inferior courts, is general, and the clause, assigning original jurisdiction to the Supreme Court, contains no negative or restrictive words; the power remains to the legislature to assign original jurisdiction to that court in other cases than those specified in the article which has been recited; provided those cases belong to the judicial power of the United States.

If it had been intended to leave it in the discretion of the legislature to apportion the judicial power between the supreme and inferior courts according to the will of that body, it would certainly have been useless to have proceeded further than to have defined the judicial power, and the tribunals in which it should be vested. The subsequent part of the section is mere surplusage, is entirely without meaning, if such is to be the construction. If congress remains at liberty to give this court appellate jurisdiction where the constitution has declared it shall be appellate; the distribution of jurisdiction, made in the constitution, is form without substance.

Affirmative words are often, in their operation, negative of other objects than those affirmed; and in this case, a negative or exclusive sense must be given to them, or they have no operation at all.

It cannot be presumed that any clause in the constitution is intended to be without effect; and, therefore, such construction is inadmissible, unless the words require it.

If the solicitude of the convention, respecting our peace with foreign powers, induced a provision that the Supreme Court should take original jurisdiction in cases which might be supposed to affect them; yet the clause would have proceeded no further than to provide for such cases, if no further restriction on the powers of congress had been intended. That they should have appellate jurisdiction in all other cases, with such exceptions as congress might make, is no restriction; unless the words be deemed exclusive of original jurisdiction.

When an instrument organizing fundamentally a judicial system, divides it into one supreme, and so many inferior courts as the legislature may ordain and establish; then enumerates its powers, and proceeds so far to distribute them, as to define the jurisdiction; of the Supreme Court by declaring the cases in which it shall take original jurisdiction, and that in others it shall take appellate jurisdiction, the plain import of the words seems to be, that in one class of cases its jurisdiction is original, and not appellate; in the other it is appellate, and not original. If any other construction would render the clause inoperative, that is an additional reason for rejecting such other construction, and for adhering to the obvious meaning.

To enable this court then to issue a mandamus, it must be shown to be an exercise of appellate jurisdiction, or to be necessary to enable them to exercise appellate jurisdiction.

It has been stated at the bar that the appellate jurisdiction may be exercised in a variety of forms, and that if it be the will of the legislature that a mandamus should be used for that purpose, that will must be obeyed. This is true, yet the jurisdiction must be appellate, not original.

It is the essential criterion of appellate jurisdiction, that it revises and corrects the proceedings in a cause already instituted, and does not create that cause. Although, therefore, a mandamus may be directed to courts, yet to issue such a writ to an officer for the delivery of a paper, and, therefore, seems not to belong to appellate, but to original jurisdiction. . . .

The authority, therefore, given to the Supreme Court, by the act establishing the judicial courts of the United States, to issue writs of mandamus to public officers, appears not to be warranted by the constitution; and it becomes necessary to inquire whether a jurisdiction so conferred can be exercised.

The question, whether an act, repugnant to the constitution, can become the law of the land, is a question deeply interesting to the United States; but, happily, not of an intricacy proportioned to its interest. It seems only necessary to recognize certain principles, supposed to have been long and well established, to decide it.

That the people have an original right to establish, for their future government, such principles as, in their opinion, shall most conduce to their own happiness is the basis on which the whole American fabric has been erected. The exercise of this original right is a very great exertion; nor can it nor ought it to be frequently repeated. The principles, therefore, so established, are deemed fundamental. And as the authority from which they proceed is supreme, and can seldom act, they are designed to be permanent.

This original and supreme will organizes the government, and assigns to different departments their respective powers. It may either stop here, or establish certain limits not to be transcended by those departments.

The government of the United States is of the latter description. The powers of the legislature are defined and limited; and that those limits may not be mistaken or forgotten, the constitution is written.

To what purpose are powers limited, and to what purpose is that limitation committed to writing, if these limits may, at any time, be passed by those intended to be restrained? ...

Between these alternatives there is no middle ground. The constitution is either a superior paramount law, unchangeable by ordinary means, or it is on a level with ordinary legislative acts, and like other acts, is alterable when the legislature shall please to alter it.

. . . .

Certainly all those who have framed written constitutions contemplate them as forming the fundamental and paramount law of the nation, and consequently the theory of every such government must be, that an act of the legislature repugnant to the constitution, is void.

This theory is essentially attached to a written constitution, and is consequently to be considered by this court as one of the fundamental principles of our society. It is not therefore to be lost sight of in the further consideration of this subject.

. . . .

It is emphatically the province and duty of the judicial department to say what the law is. Those who apply the rule to particular cases, must of necessity expound and interpret that rule. If two laws conflict with each other, the courts must decide on the operation of each.

So if a law be in opposition to the constitution; if both the law and the constitution apply to a particular case, so that the court must either decide that case conformably to the law, disregarding the constitution; or conformably to the constitution, disregarding the law; the court must determine which of these conflicting rules governs the case. This is of the very essence of judicial duty.

If, then, the courts are to regard the constitution, and the constitution is superior to any ordinary act of the legislature, the constitution, and not such ordinary act, must govern the case to which they may both apply.

Decisionmaking in the U.S. Circuit Courts of Appeals

Frank B. Cross

Introduction

Legal scholarship often presumes that judges capture the complete reasoning behind their decisions in their written opinions. However, a long-standing and growing body of research calls this presumption into question. Researchers in other social sciences, such as economics and political science, typically reject conventional legal wisdom and contend that judicial decisions are explained by factors that have little to do with what is conventionally known as law. This Article reviews, evaluates, and tests competing theories of the factors that influence circuit court decisions.

This Article focuses on the decisions of the U.S. Circuit Courts of Appeals, which are probably the decisions of greatest importance for the development of the law in the United States.[1] Although decisions of the U.S. Supreme Court are preeminent, circuit court decisions are far more numerous and of far greater practical significance. Circuit courts are the courts of last resort for the vast majority of litigants and, hence, for the vast majority of contested legal issues. While circuit court decisions are less dramatic than those of the Supreme Court, circuit courts "are major political institutions that function not only as norm enforcers but also as important creators of public policy."[2] These are the courts that define and develop "principles of law and policy directly governing their respective regions and indirectly affecting the rest of the nation."[3]

---

1   I, like others who seek to understand circuit court decisionmaking, am indebted to the pathbreaking work in the field, J. Woodford Howard, Courts of Appeals in the Federal Judicial System (1981). My research builds on this book, with the benefit of considerable intervening research and data now available.

2   Donald R. Songer et al., Continuity and Change on the United States Courts of Appeals 3 (2000).

3   Tracey E. George, *Developing a Positive Theory of Decisionmaking on U.S. Courts of Appeals*, 58 Ohio St. L.J. 1635, 1636 (1998).

Frank B. Cross, "Decisionmaking in the U.S. Circuit Courts of Appeals," *California Law Review*, vol. 91, no. 6, pp. 1459-1464, 1471-1476, 1482-1485, 1490-1494, 1497-1498, 1514-1515. Copyright © 2003 by University of California Berkeley School of Law. Reprinted with permission.

Ascertaining the determinants of circuit court decisionmaking is, therefore, central to any under-standing of the forces that shape the law. Describing what drives judicial decisions, however, has prov-en perplexing.[4] One may rule out certain factors that have no logical bearing on decisionmaking, such as income. For instance, because circuit judges' salaries are largely fixed, judges' interest in personal wealth maximization have little bearing on their decisions. Similarly, because federal judicial tenure is lifelong, judges' concern for job preservation has no effect on their decisionmaking processes. The judiciary, nonetheless, remains free to base its decisions on factors other than income. This Article explores those factors.

[…]

Theories of Judicial Decisionmaking

This Part reviews the four primary theories of the determinants of legal decisions, as explicated by considerable research in law, political science, and economics. The first theory is the legal model. Proponents of this theory claim that the legal reasons judges give in their decisions reflect the actual logic the judges followed in reaching their conclusions. This is the "traditional legal analysis" as it is typically taught in law schools. The second theory is the political model, sometimes called the attitudinal model.[5] Advocates of the political model contend that judicial outcomes are driven by the ideological preferences of the judges hearing the case. The third theory is the strategic model. Proponents of this model largely accept the premises of the political model but suggest that judges are more sophisticated and consider external responses to their decisions that would alter the decisions' ideological effect. The fourth theory is a litigant-driven model. Under this theory, judicial outcomes have little to do with the judges themselves. Instead, they are determined by the strategic assessments of the parties to the action, who may settle or litigate vigorously, depending upon their interests and the circumstances of the case.

THE LEGAL THEORY OF DECISIONMAKING

The most obvious and straightforward theory of judicial decisionmaking is the legal one. According to this theory, judges decide cases through systematic application of the external, objective sources of authority that classically comprise the law. When judges write opinions or orally explain their deci-sions from the bench, they justify their conclusions by reasoned application of those authorities to the facts of the instant case. This model reflects the theory of judicial decisionmaking commonly taught in law school: judicial decisions are the product of impartial, reasoned analysis grounded in accepted sources of authority.

---

4. *See* Richard A. Posner, *What Do Judges and Justices Maximize? (The Same Thing Everybody Else Does)*, 3 Sup. Ct. Econ. Rev. 1, 2 (1993) (stating that the problem of explaining the economic behavior of the judiciary is a "mystery that is also an embarrassment").

5 *See* Frank B. Cross, *Political Science and the New Legal Realism: A Case of Unfortunate Interdisciplinary Ignorance*, 92 Nw. U. L. Rev. 251, 265–79 (1997) (reviewing the attitudinal model of judicial decisionmaking).

THE THEORY

Various legal theories of judicial decisionmaking have come into being over the past century. While some dispute exists over the precise details of the legal model,[6] one feature of that model is clear: when properly performed, judicial decisionmaking should not be in any way contingent on the preferences of the judges making the decision. As Kathleen Sullivan described the position: "Courts are to stick to law, judgment, and reason in making their decisions and should leave politics, will, and value choice to others."[7] Such legal analysis "can and should be free from contaminating political or ideological elements."[8] The law is separate from politics.

Though the classical legal theory of decisionmaking assumes a formal process, this process cannot be reduced to an algorithm.[9] The legal model states that judges take the applicable authorized legal tools—the rules, standards, and principles embodied in authoritative sources, such as statutory text and precedent—and use reasoned decisionmaking to apply those legal tools to the facts of the case in order to reach a judgment.[10] If a statute or precedent case plainly proscribes behavior, the court will so hold. If the scope of a statute is ambiguous, the court will use tools of interpretation, such as the canons of construction, and perhaps a sense of the purpose underlying the statute to determine whether it should apply. In undertaking this decisionmaking, a court may be influenced by the preferences of the lawmaking legislature but is not to take into account its own preferences.

Several schools of jurisprudence faithful to this concept have gained prominence. The legal process school arose in the 1950s to "relegitimate the judiciary" after the rise of the legal realist school.[11] For the legal process school, the law was less about substantive standards and outcomes than about a particular process and rules of adjudication.[12] Principled reason was the key to these processes and rules. In the legal process conception of jurisprudence, decisions were founded on reason, and "judicial activity motivated by personal instinct or by considerations of policy [was] purged from the system."[13]

The contours of legal process theory, like those of any other broad theory, were imprecise. Legal process theory emphasized the importance of procedure over substantive values in law. It focused on principles of rationality. A key element of the theory, as of all legal model theories, is the principle that judges make decisions without regard to their own personal political views.

Legal process theory also inspired the more controversial Wechslerian "neutral principles."[14] For Herbert Wechsler, judicial decisionmaking must rest upon neutral principles, which are "standards

---

6   Commentators generally agree upon the characteristic sources, such as statutes and precedents, but some, such as Ronald Dworkin, would expand those sources to include broader moral and political principles underlying the law. *See generally* Ronald Dworkin, Freedom's Law: The Moral Reading of the American Constitution (1996) (arguing that certain moral principles imbue the Constitution and its legal interpretation).

7   Kathleen M. Sullivan, *The Supreme Court, 1991 Term—Foreword: The Justices of Rules and Standards,* 106 Harv. L. Rev. 22, 64–65 (1992).

8   Anthony T. Kronman, The Lost Lawyer: Failing Ideals of the Legal Profession 250(1993).

9   The legal model may take a variety of forms, ranging from classical Langdellian formalism to a more flexible approach. Central to the legal model, though, is some element of formalism, because the legal model implies that the law itself can provide certain correct answers to legal questions without reference to external sources.

10   *See* Frank B. Cross & Blake J. Nelson, *Strategic Institutional Effects on Supreme Court Decisionmaking,* 95 Nw. U. L. Rev. 1437, 1439–43 (2001) (reviewing legal model of judicial decisionmaking).

11   *See* Kimberle Crenshaw & Gary Peller, *The Contradictions of Mainstream Constitutional Theory,* 45 UCLA L. Rev. 1683, 1712 (1998).

12   *See, e.g.,* Neil Duxbury, Patterns of American Jurisprudence 210 (1995) (noting that "the study of law became the study of a procedure by which judges, rather than simply apply doctrine in a mechanical fashion, use doctrine in the process of reasoning towards a decision").

13   *Id* at 261–62.

14   The jurisprudence of neutral principles is traced to Herbert Wechsler's seminal 1959 lecture at Harvard Law School. *See* Herbert Wechsler, *Toward Neutral Principles of Constitutional Law,* 73 Harv. L. Rev. 1 (1959).

that transcend the case at hand."[15] They are "criteria that can be framed and tested as an exercise of reason and not merely as an act of willfulness or will."[16] Ultimately, in this view, "integrity," decisionmaking by "disinterested and objective standards," and the pursuit of "impartial justice *under law*" characterize judging.[17] While the academy has criticized and even ridiculed Wechslerian neutral principles, they remain a commonly used model of judicial decisionmaking.[18]

Over the years, numerous critics have attacked various aspects of the legal model of decisionmaking; legal process theory "has been killed again and again, but has always refused to stay dead."[19] The attack on the legal model has commonly centered on its theoretical and empirical indeterminacy. While some measure of indeterminacy is inescapable, indeterminacy itself does not doom the formalistic legal theory of judicial decisionmaking.[20] Steven Burton, for example, recognizes that judges act within a discretionary space, due to the indeterminacy of legal materials, but argues that this discretion is bounded and that, within the discretionary space, judges are to act in a "good faith" effort to find the result that is legally best.[21] At minimum, even absent this good faith, the legal theory holds that the law serves as an objective constraint on the discretion of judges.[22] If the legal theory fails to describe all judicial behavior, it may still provide an accurate prediction of most outcomes.

The legal theory also has normative support: one generally considers judging according to the law to be the duty of the judiciary.[23] However, one cannot merely presume that judges consistently do their duty; the legal model may be no more than an idealized notion that poorly reflects the reality of judicial decisionmaking. The accuracy of the legal model is a descriptive question that must find factual, as well as theoretical, support.

[...]

THE POLITICAL THEORY OF DECISIONMAKING

While judges' opinions almost universally explain their decisions by reference to the legal model, many have questioned whether the case results are truly explained by the law. Political scientists and a considerable number of legal scholars argue that decisions are driven instead by the personal ideologies of judges. Judges, like other officers of government, seek to project their views of justice onto society

---

15 *Id.* at 17.

16 *Id.* at 11.

17 Terri Jennings Peretti, In Defense of a Political Court 81 (1999).

18 *See* Jon O. Newman, *Between Legal Realism and Neutral Principles: The Legitimacy of Institutional Values*, 72 Calif. L. Rev. 200, 215–16 (1984) (suggesting that while judicial

19 Ernest J. Weinrib, *Legal Formalism: On the Immanent Rationality of Law*, 97 Yale L.J. 949, 951 (1988). Some measure of formalism has an inexorable appeal to legal academics. *See, e.g.,* Cross & Nelson, *supra* note 14, at 1441 (maintaining that at least some degree of legal formalism is irresistible to law professors).

20 *See* Weinrib, *supra* note 23, at 1008–12 (describing how perfect determinacy of outcomes in individual cases is not necessary to legal formalism).

21 *See generally* Steven J. Burton, Judging in Good Faith (1992).

22 Peretti, *supra* note 21, at 38.

23 *See* Ruth Gavison, *The Implications of Jurisprudential Theories for Judicial Election, Selection, and Accountability*, 61 S. Cal. L. Rev. 1617, 1640–41 (observing that all "agree that it is a prime duty for a judge to obey the law"); Weinrib, *supra* note 23, at 985–86 (describing the role of the judge "as the guardian and expositor of whatever is non-politically legal"); *see also Marbury v. Madison*, 5 U.S. (1 Cranch) 137, 177 (1803) (stating that it is "the province and duty of the judicial department to say what the law is").

through the force of their decisions.[24] While many criticize the concept of political decisionmaking, some praise it.[25] The concern of this Article is simply descriptive.

THE THEORY

Adherents of the political theory of judicial decisionmaking do not claim that judges are political in the same way that legislators or executive officers are political. Judges, at least at the federal circuit level, do not engage in the campaigning and partisanship of the political branches. Nor does the political theory of judicial decisionmaking refer to politics in the broadest sense, such as a devotion to democracy or individual rights. Viewed at a sufficiently high level, all law is a translation of some political concept. Ronald Dworkin, for example, thus recognizes that his concept of law is "deeply and thoroughly political."[26]

Rather, according to the political theory, judges are dedicated to advancing their own personal ideological preferences, which generally fall along a conventional liberal-to-conservative continuum.[27] Because judges' compensation does not depend on their adherence to the law,[28] one might expect judges' "policy goals" to exert considerable influence on their decisions.[29] Judge Posner suggests that judges may wish to "impose their political vision on society" through rulings, just as an artist imposes an aesthetic vision on society.[30] Judges are officers of the government, with the ability to achieve political goals through legal rulings. One might reasonably expect them to take advantage of that ability and deploy their personal political predilections in their decisions.

The political theory gained prominence through the legal realist movement in the first half of the twentieth century.[31] Legal realists argued that the indeterminate materials available to judges at the appellate level could not clearly resolve the disputes these judges confronted.[32] Consequently, the determinants of legal outcomes came from individuating characteristics of individual judges.

This view retains considerable currency.[33] One observer suggests that "circuit judges frequently encounter cases where their policy preferences are likely to come into play and where the costs of heeding them are acceptable."[34] Others suggest that the growth in the use of law clerks has enabled judges to be more ideological and to rely on the clerks to draft opinions that are "just briefs to support a predetermined result."[35] Some behavioralist or attitudinalist advocates of the ideological model of

---

24 *See* Richards & Kritzer, *supra* note 71, at 305 (noting that attitudinalists view the Supreme Court as equivalent to a "small legislative body" in its decisionmaking).

25 *See, e.g.,* Peretti, *supra* note 21, at 133.

26 Ronald Dworkin, A Matter of Principle 146 (1985).

27 For a good review of the development of this theory, see George, *supra* note 3, at 1646–50.

28 *See* Cross, *supra* note 9, at 295–96 (explaining how conventional economic explanations of human behavior do not apply well to judging).

29 Richard A. Posner, Overcoming Law 372 (1995).

30 *Id.* at 121.

31 For a good review of this movement, see Brian Leiter, American Legal Realism (2002) (University of Texas School of Law Public Law & Legal Theory Research Paper No. 042), *available at* http://ssm.com/abstract_id=339562 (last visited July 26, 2003).

32 *See id.* at 3 (discussing how legal realists argued both that the law was rationally indeterminate, such that legal reasons could not dictate a unique decision, and causally indeterminate, so that those reasons could not explain the specific decisions reached by judges).

33 *See, e.g.,* Mark V. Tushnet, *Following the Rules Laid Down: A Critique of Interpretivism and Neutral Principles*, 96 Harv. L. Rev. 781, 821–22 (1983) (contending that one can manipulate legal rules so much that judges are largely free to fulfill their preferences while apparently remaining within those rules).

34 Klein, *supra* note 38, at 15; *see also* Gillman, *supra* note 49, at 471 (discussing the belief that the "constraints under which the [Supreme Court] Justices decide their cases do not inhibit them from expressing their preferences insofar as voting on the cases before them is concerned").

35 John Kester, *The Law Clerks Explosion*, 9 Litigation 20, 20 (1983), *quoted in* Jonathan Matthew Cohen, Inside Appellate Courts 10 (2002).

decisionmaking believe that the legal model is useless. They have been "remarkably dismissive" of the traditional legal model, characterizing it as "meaningless" or "silly."[36]

Social scientists are skeptical of the theory underlying the legal model, because it assumes that judges actually do what they are supposed to do. Meanwhile, economists and political scientists tend to assume that people are more likely to conduct themselves as they prefer than to act as they are supposed to behave, at least without external checks. Even if one accepts the possibility that people can be authentically altruistic at times, it is difficult to claim that people are primarily altruistic in their behavior. For example, some people contribute to charities, but very few people give more money to charities than they spend on themselves. Correspondingly, adherents to political theories do not necessarily claim that judges never follow their legal responsibilities; supporters of the political model simply maintain that such behavior is not the norm.

As a preempirical matter, however, there is no basis for the social scientists' dismissiveness. Without any motivation to follow the legal model, of course, it seems likely that judges would generally render justice as they see fit on the basis of their ideological predispositions.[37] The question, therefore, is whether some countervailing force constrains those innate inclinations. Attitudinalists may believe that judges likely care more for ideological results than for legal results, but this is by no means self-evident.

It is perfectly plausible to suggest that "judges derive utility from legal procedures as well as from policy outcomes."[38] Judges assume a role in which they are expected to follow the law, after having spent much of their life in training under the legal model.[39] This role may become an "intervening variable between institutional and personality factors in the judicial process."[40] James Gibson describes role orientation as "a psychological construct which is the combination of the occupant's perception of the role expectations of significant others and his or her own norms and expectations of proper behavior for a judge."[41] Gibson contends that role orientation mediates ideological attitudes, but does not completely supplant those attitudes in judicial decisionmaking.[42]

Judges may thus gain utility from adhering to the standards of their profession. Circuit court judges share

> most of the elements that students of the subject consider requisite for the professionalization of an occupation: a basic body of theory or specialized tech-niques, authority recognized by clientele groups and sanction by the community,

---

36 *See* Cross, *supra* note 9, at 264.

37 The response of a circuit court judge in an interview illustrates this phenomenon well: "Of course, if within applicable precedent you can choose one or the other, you will take the one that leads to the good outcome...Klein, *supra* note 38, at 22.

38 Linda R. Cohen *&* Matthew L. Spitzer, *Solving the* Chevron *Puzzle*, 57 Law & Contemp. Probs. 65, 71 (1994); *see also* Ethan Bueno de Mesquita & Matthew Stephenson, *Informative Precedent and Intrajudicial Communication*, 96 Am. Pol. Sci. Rev. 755, 755 (2002) (noting that a legal-model judge would "maximize utility by adhering faithfully to these internal rules, regardless of the external result"); Cross & Nelson, *supra* note 14, at 1443 (noting that "[t]here is nothing intrinsically inconceivable about the notion that judges might value accurate legal decisionmaking, independent of [political] results").

39 On the socializing effect of legal training and experience, see, for example, Robert Carp & Russell Wheeler, *Sink or Swim: The Socialization of a Federal District Judge*, 21 J. Pub. L. 359 (1972), and Beverly B. Cook, *The Socialization of New Federal Judges: Impact on District Court Business*, 1971 Wash. U. L.Q. 253. *See also* Sara C. Benesh, The U.S. Court of Appeals and the Law of Confessions 17 (2002) (listing factors, including socialization, that explain lower courts' compliance with Supreme Court decisions); Donald R. Songer et al., *A Reappraisal of Diversification in the Federal Courts: Gender Effects in the Courts of Appeals*, 56 J. Pol. 425,436 (1994) (suggesting that socialization explains the lack of gender effect on outcomes in obscenity cases).

40 Howard, *supra* note 1, at xxiii.

41 James L. Gibson, *Judges' Role Orientations, Attitudes, and Decisions: An Interactive Model*, 72 Am. Pol. Sci. Rev. 911,917 (1978).

42 *Id.* at 922.

a code of ethics regulating relations of professionals with clients and colleagues, self-consciousness and a 'professional culture' sustained by at least the rudiments of formal associations to guard over standards of training, performance, and mutual protection.[43]

As an occupation becomes more professionalized, "conformity to occupational expectations [will increasingly tend to] be achieved through internalized values and peer-group pressure."[44] Judges may simply "feel an obligation to do the job right."[45] This concern may be referred to as "craft values" or "reasoning utility," and it may countermand political concerns.[46] Even narrow economic models of rationality make some allowance for "rule-abiding attitudes" and "altruism."[47]

Other actors in the legal system may reinforce the judicial desire to perform as the judicial oath prescribes. One economist suggests that "peer pressure and public scrutiny" help to "induce judges to abide by their oath."[48] Judges may care about their reputation with the lawyers and litigants who appear before them.[49] Dedication to the values of the judicial craft through conscious adherence to the legal model may enhance the judge's prestige in the legal community.[50] The combination of concern for reputation in the legal profession and a desire to promote stability and continuity in the law may combine to induce judges to follow the legal model.[51] David Klein has observed that "[w]e may sometimes internalize norms to the point where we follow them unthinkingly, but often we adhere to them because we desire the respect and good opinion of others or ourselves."[52] Both pressures combine to promote some level of judicial adherence to the legal model of decisionmaking.[53]

Moreover, it is "highly likely that at least some judges find the search for good answers to legal questions intrinsically rewarding" and that the "challenge of reaching decisions supported by legal

---

43   Howard, *supra* note 1, at 89.

44   *Id.* at 122. Howard notes, though, that "[t]his is not to say that professionalism necessarily supplants personal predilections in Courts of Appeals." *Id.*

45   Thomas O. McGarity, *On Making Judges Do the Right Thing*, 44 Duke L.J. 1104, 1105 (1995); *see also* Lawrence Baum, The Puzzle of Judicial Behavior 61 (1997) (suggesting that "it pleases judges to carry out what they conceive as the judge's role"); Malcolm M. Feeley & Edward L. Rubin, Judicial Policy Making and the Modern State 213–14 (1998) (suggesting that "since judges are supposed to decide cases by following legal doctrine, the inclination to do so is part of their more general desire to act in the proper fashion," which is "a well-recognized motivation").

46   *See, e.g.,* Christopher R. Drahozal, *Judicial Incentives and the Appeals Process*, 51 SMU L. Rev. 469, 474 (contrasting ideological utility and reasoning utility as factors in judicial decisionmaking); Sidney A. Shapiro & Richard E. Levy, *Judicial Incentives and Indeterminacy in Substantive Review of Administrative Decisions*, 44 Duke L.J. 1051, 1058 (1995) (noting reputational significance of adherence to judicial craft values).

47   Ha-Joon Chang, *The Economics and Politics of Regulation*, 21 Cambridge J. Econ. 703, 722 (1997); *see also* Richard S. Kay, *American Constitutionalism, in* Constitutionalism: Philosophical Foundations 16, 46 (Larry Alexander ed., 1998) (contending that judges are driven to follow legal rules in part because of innate human tendencies to do so, as well as because of their background and training and the manner in which cases are presented to them).

48   Dennis C. Mueller, Constitutional Democracy 284 (1996).

49   Robert D. Cooter, *The Objectives of Public and Private Judges,* 41 Pub. Choice 107, 129 (1983); *see also* Ronald A. Cass, *Judging: Norms and Incentives of Retrospective Decision-Making,* 75 B.U. L. Rev. 941, 971 (1995) (suggesting that "[j]udges gain the respect of professionals—lawyers, fellow judges, law professors—for operating within the model").

50   *See, e.g.,* Drahozal, *supra* note 100, at 475 (claiming that judges "gain respect within the legal community based on how well they apply professional norms of legal reasoning in deciding cases"); Thomas J. Miceli & Metin M. Cosgel, *Reputation and Judicial Decision-Making,* 23 J. Econ. Behav. & Org. 31, 49 (1994) (suggesting that judges trade off their "private utility" in the outcome of the case with "reputational utility" in their expectation of how observers would view the opinion); Shapiro & Levy, *supra* note 100 (noting reputational significance of adherence to judicial craft values).

51   *See* Sisk et al., *supra* note 5, at 1497–98 (explaining why judges follow precedent).

52   Klein, *supra* note 38, at 11.

53   The effect of reputation on legal model adherence is contested. For instance, it may be that even the groups forming the judiciary's constituency are not very committed to the sincere legal model. *See, e.g.,* Frederick Schauer, *Incentives, Reputation, and the Inglorious Determinants of Judicial Behavior,* 68 U. Cin. L. Rev. 615, 630 (2000) (suggesting that "judicial craft is far less important to these esteem-granting groups, and sympathy with the outcome is far more important").

reasoning actually attracts judges to their profession."[54] Interviews with trial judges reveal that they "derive their satisfaction from the activities and behaviors which are associated with judging" more than "the achievement of particular substantive results."[55] Judge Posner has analogized the judging process to a "game" with rules.[56] These rules include legal model constraints, which affect judicial outcomes.[57] Viewing judicial decisionmaking as a sort of game does not exclude political considerations, but suggests that judges playing the game may also follow legal rules in good faith.[58]

Finally, adherence to legal rules is itself ideological. Judges may pursue the legal model precisely in order to achieve relative legal stability.[59] Decisionmaking according to law furthers political ends. While these ends may not seem ideological, in that they are not stereotypically liberal or conservative, they nonetheless reflect a notion of the good society. Impartial decisionmaking, according to the rule of law, may be viewed as intrinsic to fairness and may also have pragmatic value. A growing number of empirical studies have shown that rule-of-law decisionmaking furthers economic growth.[60]

For the above reasons, the descriptive power of the political theory is not self-evident. Judges may reasonably prefer to adhere to their legal responsibilities or to the challenge of the judicial game rather than effect their political preferences. On the other hand, it is not self-evident that judges prefer legal decisionmaking to political decisionmaking. Other government officers, in the legislative and executive branches, clearly act for ideological reasons. One might expect the same of judges. Resolution of the issue requires empirical evidence.

[...]

THE STRATEGIC THEORY OF DECISIONMAKING

A strategic theory of judicial decisionmaking recently has gained increasing acceptance among political scientists. Proponents of this theory generally accept the political theory of judicial motivations, though this presumption is not essential to the strategic theory.[61] The strategic theory suggests that judges, regardless of what they are trying to achieve, are mindful of the positions and powers of other institutions and external forces that could affect the judges' attainment of their goals.

THE THEORY

The strategic theory derives from rational choice theory, a commonly accepted methodology used in political science and economics to explain individual decisionmaking. Under this theory, a circuit court judge realizes that she cannot ensure the effectuation of her ideological preferences simply by deciding a case in accord with those preferences, if that holding would subsequently be reversed by

---

54 Klein, *supra* note 38, at 12.

55 Austin Sarat, *Judging in Trial Courts: An Exploratory Study*, 39 J. Pol. 368, 376 (1977).

56 Posner, *supra* note 83, at 109–44.

57 *See id.* at 134 (suggesting that "a legislature can expect a fair degree of compliance by the judges with its rules even though there is no sanction for noncompliance").

58 *See generally* Hutchinson, *supra* note 46 (contending that judicial decisionmaking is gamelike, as judges strive to reach preferred decisions only insofar as the legal materials allow).

59 *See* de Mesquita & Stephenson, *supra* note 92, at 757.

60 *See* Frank B. Cross, *Law and Economic Growth*, 80 Tex. L. Rev. 1737, 1768–69 (2002) (summarizing recent studies).

61 *See* Segal & Spaeth, *supra* note 32, at 52 (noting that theorists of the rational choice strategic model "hold open the possibility that judges have legal considerations as goals" but "typically conceive of justices as primarily interested in policy outcomes"); de Mesquita & Stephenson, *supra* note 92, at 755 n.1 (observing that both the attitudinal model and the strategic model typically assume that judges are policy-oriented).

the Supreme Court. Hence, the strategic judge would account for the preferences of the Supreme Court in rendering opinions and would avoid issuing rulings that may be reversed.

The strategic theory of circuit court decisionmaking implies, generally, that the Supreme Court truly controls the output of lower courts. As the peak of the judicial hierarchy, the Supreme Court has the ability to reverse the rulings of all lower courts. Some argue that the circuit courts will fall into line in response to Supreme Court preferences.[62] McNollgast presents a more sophisticated theory recognizing the limited resources of the Supreme Court and proposing that the Court allows some doctrinal interval around its precise preferences but effectively can prevent decisions that stray too far outside that interval.[63]

There is substantial theoretical reason to doubt the significance of the strategic theory of appellate court decisionmaking under either model, primarily due to the very low rate of Supreme Court review of circuit court opinions. While the circuit courts decide tens of thousands of cases per year, the Supreme Court recently has reviewed fewer than one hundred of those decisions, or less than 3% of the petitions filed, per year.[64] Hence, as Songer has stated, "the decision of the court of appeals was left undisturbed in 99.7[%] of [those courts'] cases."[65] Some argue that "[t]he sheer number of cases heard by appeals courts makes it impossible for the Supreme Court to adequately monitor the lower courts."[66] Peter Strauss has suggested that "the Court's awareness [of] how infrequently it is able to review lower court decisions has led it to be tolerant, even approving, of lower court and party indiscipline in relation to existing law."[67] For circuit courts, "being overturned is not a likely prospect and is becoming less so."[68]

A low rate of review does not intrinsically disprove the strategic theory, however, as "appellate judges no more need to review every decision below than a teacher must admonish every child to maintain order on a playground."[69] One need not exact punishment if the subject parties are intimidated into compliance by the prospect of punishment. Surely there must be some credible threat of review, though, for the theory to operate. In the context of circuit court decisionmaking, the question is whether nine "teachers," who are capable of reprimanding fewer than one hundred "students," can maintain order in a playground filled with tens of thousands.

The strategic control problem is compounded by the limited sanctions available for noncompliance. If a reviewing court could wield a severe sanction for misbehavior, the expected punishment, a function both of its frequency and its severity, might be sufficient. However, the Supreme Court does not wield this sort of power. A reversal will alter the policy consequence of the circuit court decision, but this leaves the lower court no worse off than if it had acquiesced in the first place, so there is no

---

62 *See, e.g.,* Linda R. Cohen, *Politics and the Courts: A Comment on McNollgast,* 68 S. Cal. L. Rev. 1685 (1995); Lewis A. Kornhauser, *Adjudication by a Resource-Constrained Team: Hierarchy and Precedent in a Judicial System,* 68 S. Cal. L. Rev. 1605 (1995).

63 *See* McNollgast, *Politics and the Courts: A Positive Theory of Judicial Doctrine and the Rule of Law,* 68 S. Cal. L. Rev. 1631 (1995).

64 In 1999, for example, the circuit courts terminated more than 54,000 cases, while the Supreme Court granted only 92 petitions for certiorari. *See* Cohen, *supra* note 89, at 43 tbl.2; *see also* Lee Epstein et al., The Supreme Court Compendium: Data, Decisions, and Developments 83 tbl.2-6 (2d ed. 1996).

65 Songer et al., *supra* note 2, at 17.

66 *Id.* at 132–33.

67 Peter L. Strauss, *One Hundred Fifty Cases Per Year: Some Implications of the Supreme Court's Limited Resources for Judicial Review of Agency Action,* 87 Colum. L. Rev. 1093, 1095 (1987). This lament has been updated: "[W]hen the Court was deciding only 150 cases a year, it was tolerating widespread undiscipline by lower federal courts; now that it has cut that number almost in half, it is forsaking responsibility for holding lower courts in line." Paul D. Carrington, *Restoring Vitality to State and Local Politics by Correcting the Excessive Independence of the Supreme Court,* 50 Ala. L. Rev. 397, 401 (1999) (citation omitted).

68 Cohen, *supra* note 89, at 42.

69 Howard, *supra* note 1, at 82.

meaningful sanction for nonacquiescence. For circuit court judges primarily concerned about case outcomes, deference to the Supreme Court is not the rational choice.[70]

Nor do reversals of circuit court judges' rulings by the Supreme Court cause personal harm to judges. It is possible that Supreme Court reversals will carry some stigma that will cause the circuit court judges to be disrespected or "reduce [their] opportunities for professional recognition and advancement."[71] Yet this consequence is not plainly evident. Howard found that "[c]ircuit reputations appear to be independent of Supreme Court support."[72] Indeed, during the Warren Court era, some judges "wore reversals as badges of honor."[73] Insofar as decisions of the Supreme Court are ideological, generally a premise of the strategic model, reversal should carry with it no disrepute.[74] Some have hypothesized that frequent reversals would hurt a judge's chances for promotion to the Supreme Court and thereby influence appellate judicial behavior, though evidence has not confirmed this hypothesis.[75]

One further problem with the strategic model is more practical. Judges' cognitive limitations, reinforced by the time constraints and heavy caseloads of the appellate judiciary, may "make it impossible for judges to act strategically all the time."[76] In addition, circuit court judges inevitably lack the complete information necessary to make accurate strategic decisions. Such decisions require a reliable assessment of the probability of appeal, the probability of settlement, the probability of the Court's granting certiorari, and the precise preferences of the justices in order to calculate the risk of reversal. Without a reliable estimate of those probabilities, it is impossible for a court to make a strategic choice.

Without the ability and information necessary to make a correct strategic choice, an attempt to be strategic could well be counterproductive. In this circumstance, the more rational choice might well be for a circuit court panel to render its preferred opinion without regard for the risk of reversal rather than needlessly compromise its preferences due to an inaccurate fear of reversal. Even if the difficulty of strategic decisionmaking precludes its universal operation, though, the consideration might remain an important one in some subset of cases where the risk of reversal is clear.

[...]

THE LITIGANT-DRIVEN THEORY OF DECISIONMAKING

A final set of theories of judicial decisionmaking—associated more with economics than with political science—claims that litigants, rather than judges, drive judicial outcomes. Under these theories, litigants' decisions affect results regardless of whether judges produce outcomes based on formal legal reasoning, personal ideology, or anticipated Supreme Court preferences. Proponents of litigant-driven theories maintain that the actual decisions produced by courts will be controlled largely by the strategic litigation decisions made by the parties to the action.

---

70   Benesh, *supra* note 93, at 26–30.

71   Evan H. Caminker, *Precedent and Prediction: The Forward-Looking Aspects of Inferior Court Decisionmaking*, 73 Tex. L. Rev. 1, 77 (1994); *see also* Benesh, *supra* note 93, at 17 (suggesting that some stigma may attach to a judge's reversal rate).

72   Howard, *supra* note 1, at 139.

73   *Id* at 140.

74   *See* Cass, *supra* note 103, at 985 (noting that judges may perceive reversal "as criticism on grounds that are more political than professional" and hence "may find little discomfort in being reversed").

75   *See* Richard S. Higgins & Paul H. Rubin, *Judicial Discretion*, 9 J. Legal Stud. 129 (1980).

76   Klein, *supra* note 38, at 14.

THE THEORY

The key to litigant-driven theories of judicial decisionmaking is the fact that decisions do not represent a complete or random sample of legal disputes found in the real world, or even a random sample of those disputes that produce actual lawsuits. Courts are constrained by their "procedural passivity," their ability to act only "upon a request by litigants."[77] Cases proceed to a judicial decision only when the parties have decided to force this sort of outcome to their dispute. It is "[l]itigants, not judges, [who] set court agendas."[78] The vast majority of cases of all types settle before the judge reaches a final decision.[79] Those cases that reach a judicial decision are the cases that the parties have chosen not to settle and thus represent a subset of disputes chosen by the parties, not by the judges. The same theoretical analysis generally applies to decisions pursued on an appeal.

George L. Priest and Benjamin Klein articulated the seminal litigant-driven theory.[80] They noted that settlement is more efficient for parties than litigation. If the parties have accurate expectations of the outcome of a suit based on settled law and information about the judge, they should settle for an amount approximating the expected outcome after trial.[81] When cases do proceed to trial or are appealed, the parties presumably have significantly divergent expectations about the outcome. The plaintiff, for example, may expect a positive verdict, while the defendant may expect to prevail on the merits or to pay only minimal damages. Priest and Klein hypothesized that only close cases in untested areas of the law would produce the divergence that results in litigation.[82] Because the tried cases are not a representative sample of all filed cases but a sample of cases on the margin, Priest and Klein expected that plaintiffs and defendants would each win about 50% of the time.

This simple 50% hypothesis unrealistically assumes that both parties have equivalent, if not perfect, information about the likely outcome if the case were tried. Theorists have noted that the 50% prediction cannot hold if the parties possess asymmetric information about probable outcomes.[83] If one party has better information about the likely outcome upon litigation, its settlement decisions will be wiser. The ill-informed party will settle some cases it should win and refuse to settle other cases that it likely will lose. Thus, in a higher proportion of cases, the party with the better information on probable litigation outcomes will win.[84]

The most significant theoretical problem with the 50% hypothesis occurs when the parties have unequal stakes in the litigation. The basic version of the Priest-Klein hypothesis assumes that both parties are only interested in the outcome of the particular case. In practice, though, one of the parties may have a more substantial interest in the litigation, including an interest not just in the outcome of the case but also in the precedent set by that outcome. A more sophisticated model suggests that if one party has precedential interest, that party will strive to appeal only cases that it is likely to win and will settle marginal cases. The party will pick cases strategically and pursue those with the best facts or

---

77   Carlo Guarnieri & Patrizia Pederzoli, The Power of Judges: A Comparative Study of Courts and Democracy 10–11 (2002).

78   Howard, *supra* note 1, at 17.

79   *See, e.g.,* Janet Cooper Alexander, *Do the Merits Matter? A Study of Settlements in Securities Class Actions,* 43 Stan. L. Rev. 497, 498 (1991) (reporting that only about 5% of filed cases are tried to judgment); Russell Korobkin & Chris Guthrie, *Psychological Barriers to Litigation Settlement: An Experimental Approach,* 93 Mich. L. Rev. 107, 107 n.l (1994) (noting evidence that most cases settle).

80   George L. Priest & Benjamin Klein, *The Selection of Disputes for Litigation,* 13 J. Legal Stud. 1 (1984).

81   *Id.* at 16–17.

82   *Id*

83   *See, e.g.,* Keith N. Hylton, *Asymmetric Information and the Selection of Disputes for Litigation,* 22 J. Legal Stud. 187 (1993).

84   *See, e.g.,* Lucian Arye Bebchuk, *Litigation and Settlement Under Imperfect Information,* 15 Rand J. Econ. 404 (1984); Hylton, *supra* note 234.

with the potential for a particularly sympathetic hearing on appeal.[85] The party with the interest in the precedent set by the case will "settle strategically in cases where the type of judge or set of facts seems likely to lead to unfavorable precedent."[86] This refinement of the litigant-driven theory suggests:

> Sophisticated "haves" presumably only appeal cases they are likely to win, whereas "have nots" often cannot afford to appeal and are presumably more haphazard in their selections of cases when they can. The result theory tells us that the mix of cases heard by appellate courts is dominated by cases that "haves" have selected because they are likely to win. Missing from the mix are potentially important, precedent-setting cases that "have nots" are likely to win. When a "have not" threatens to appeal such a case, the "have," motivated by his or her interest as a repeat player, typically settles, on the plaintiffs terms if necessary, to prevent the appellate court from setting an adverse precedent.[87]

This so-called "strategic settlement" hypothesis predicts outcomes far different from those of the simple 50% hypothesis. Repeat players will not allow the marginal cases to go to trial or judgment, because those cases present a real risk of creating adverse precedent. Instead, repeat players will push cases they are likely to win and settle the marginal cases. Hence, this refined hypothesis predicts that such repeat players will prevail in a disproportionate number of cases.

The intersection of the litigant-driven hypothesis (generally propounded by economists)[88] and the judge-driven hypotheses (typically advanced by political scientists) has not been extensively explored. For instance, even assuming that judges tend to decide cases ideologically or strategically, litigants concerned about economical consequences would be well aware of that tendency when making litigation and settlement decisions. Consequently, any judicial bias would not necessarily affect actual judicial outcomes. As the judiciary became more conservative, aware litigants would have realized that the ideological location of the marginal case had shifted to the right with the judiciary. As this occurred, cases formerly at the ideological center would have been settled, and a set of relatively more conservative cases would have been pursued to an outcome.[89]

Under the 50% hypothesis, a change in the ideological makeup of the judiciary would not change the frequency of conservative and liberal outcomes, though the conservative outcomes would be relatively more conservative.[90] Likewise, a change in a legal standard under the legal model would alter

---

85   *See* Leandra Lederman, *Precedent Lost: Why Encourage Settlement, and Why Permit Non- Party Involvement in Settlements?*, 75 Notre Dame L. Rev. 221, 241 (1999) (discussing "strategy of picking cases with favorable facts and sympathetic plaintiffs"). The theory of strategic precedent manipulation is discussed at greater length in Frank B. Cross, *In Praise of Irrational Plaintiffs*, 86 Cornell L. Rev. 1, 6–8 (2000).

86   Einer R. Elhauge, *Does Interest Group Theory Justify More Intrusive Judicial Review?*, 101 Yale L.J. 31, 78 (1991); *see also* Martin J. Bailey & Paul H. Rubin, *A Positive Theory of Legal Change*, 14 Int'l Rev. L. & Econ. 467 (1994) (contending that parties with the greatest interest in precedent will tend to prevail more often in setting precedents).

87   Richard Lempert, *A Classic at 25: Reflections on Galanter's "Haves" Article and Work It Has Inspired*, 33 Law & Soc'y Rev. 1099, 1109 (1999). "Haves" are repeat players with large financial interest in the status of legal doctrine. *See id.*

88   *See, e.g.*, Robert D. Cooter & Daniel L. Rubinfeld, *Economic Analysis of Legal Disputes and Their Resolution*, 27 J. Econ. Literature 1067, 1091 (1989) (noting how economists have focused on litigants and not on the role of judges in decisionmaking).

89   Before the ideological shift in the judiciary, those more conservative cases would appear to be too conservative to succeed and would be settled. After the shift, those more conservative cases would appear to litigants to be on the margin, with a reasonable prospect for success; therefore, they would be tried.

90   *See, e.g.*, George L. Priest, *Selective Characteristics of Litigation*, 9 J. Legal Stud. 399, 408 (1980) (suggesting that once a judge's attitudes are known, the litigants will adapt to them and only "raise the most troublesome issues for a person with the judge's attitudes to decide"); Priest & Klein, *supra* note 231, at 36 (contending that this problem illustrates "the failure of the attempts of an extensive and ambitious political science literature to measure the effect of judicial attitudes").

the composition of cases tried to judgment but should not affect the 50% distribution of outcomes. In sum, under the 50% hypothesis, the litigant-driven model subsumes all of the judge-driven models.

Under the strategic settlement hypothesis, though, it is plausible that a more conservative judiciary would produce more conservative outcomes than liberal outcomes. Conservative repeat players would push relatively more cases to judgment, knowing that their overall chances of success were greater. As courts become more conservative, an increasing number of conservative outcomes would become possible. Strategic litigants would drive more of them to resolution and the consequent production of favorable precedents.

The litigant-driven hypothesis of decisionmaking makes sound theoretical sense, if its assumptions are valid. However, some of those assumptions are quite debatable. Litigants may not be exclusively interested in settling for money. The settlement market may not be an efficient one, preventing strategic case selection from operating efficiently. Problems of imperfect information about the prospects of any particular case before any particular judge also undermine the theory to a degree. Empirical inquiry is necessary to evaluate the theory's accuracy.

[...]

Empirically Testing the Theories of Judicial Decisionmaking

This Part employs empirical methods to evaluate the four theories of judicial decisionmaking. Each test builds upon the results of the test for the prior theory. The result of the final test is a model that simultaneously considers the factors focused on by all four theories as potential determinants of judicial outcomes in the circuit courts of appeals.

The basic data for this test come from the Appeals Court Database, compiled under a National Science Foundation grant by a group led by Professor Donald Songer,[91] and the Database on the Attributes of United States Appeals Court Judges, compiled by Gary Zuk, Gerard S. Gryski, and Deborah J. Barrow[92] in order to associate judges with the parties of their appointing presidents. These data cover decisions issued between 1928 and 1992.

[...]

The results of this study shed considerable light on the nature of judicial decisionmaking. The traditional legal model clearly explains a significant part of this decisionmaking, even after controlling for ideology and other variables. The legal model obviously leaves room for other considerations, though, since judicial ideology is also consistently a significant determinant of some decisions. The strategic model appears to explain little, if any, circuit court decisionmaking. The litigant-driven model, likewise, fails to offer adequate explanation for judicial decisions.

---

91 The United States Courts of Appeals Database, developed by Professor Donald Songer of the University of South Carolina, is available through the Program for Law and Judicial Politics at Michigan State University. *See* Program for Law and Judicial Politics, Department of Political Science, Michigan State University, Research Databases and Data Archives—U.S. Courts of Appeals, *at* http://www.polisci.msu.edu/pljp/ctadata.html (last visited July 26, 2003). *See generally* Frank B. Cross, *Comparative Judicial Databases*, 83 Judicature 248 (2000) (reviewing this database in contrast to others).

92 Gary Zuk et al., Multi-User Database on the Attributes of United States Appeals Court Judges (Jan. 9, 1997), *available at* http://ssdc.ucsd.edu/ssdc/icp06796.html (last visited July 26, 2003).

The dispute among theories of legal decisionmaking has been too binary (or quaternary, given the four theories discussed here), proceeding as if one theory must prevail and dispel the validity of all other theories. Weinrib's defense of legal formalism cautions that "once we step outside the most rigorous notion of internal coherence, the slide to nihilism is swift and easy."[93] Yet this claim is false. Acknowledging a material role for politics or strategy in judicial decisionmaking does not mean that legal reasoning is necessarily meaningless. The law may moderate the effects of political leanings in some cases or supplant them entirely in others. The presence of ideological or other determinants in some cases leaves a considerable role for the accurate operation of the traditional legal model.

The results of this analysis are also quite general and cannot necessarily be interpolated into particular areas of judicial decisionmaking. This study included all cases, or all criminal cases, in order to expand the sample size of the cases analyzed and to produce general conclusions about judicial decisionmaking. It is distinctly possible that studies of specific areas of the law could produce results varying from those found here. Thus, in cases of great political importance, the ideological effect might be greater than that identified in this research. This suggestion finds support in other research that has examined discrete areas of the law, such as review of administrative agency decisions.[94]

The results of this research illuminate Gibson's characterization of judicial decisionmaking as influenced by judicial preferences, judicial duties, and judicial abilities, complemented by the external effects of the parties to litigation.[95] This study indicates, though, that judicial duty, or the legal model, is the most powerful determinant. It generally explains more than do judicial preferences or the political model. There is no evidence that judicial abilities affect outcomes, when those abilities are operationalized as Supreme Court preferences and risk of reversal, though other constraints on judicial abilities could well explain some decisionmaking. The greatest constraint appears to be that of the law: the "neutral principles"[96] of the traditional legal model fare quite well as a descriptive model for judicial decisionmaking.

---

93 Weinrib, supra note 23, at 1016.

94 *See, e.g.,* Cross & Tiller, *supra* note 153, at 2173 (showing a much greater percentage of ideological decisionmaking in application of the *Chevron* doctrine).

95 *See* Gibson, *supra* note 8.

96 *See supra* note 18 and accompanying text.

The Least Dangerous Branch Revisited

New Evidence on Supreme Court
Responsiveness to Public Preferences

Kevin T. McGuire and James A. Stimson

A mong the more vexing issues for judicial scholars is the role of public opinion in the Supreme Court. For quite some time, political scientists have debated, both theoretically and methodologically, whether and how popular preferences are translated into judicial policy. To some, appointed justices with lifetime tenure are insulated from popular pressure (Segal and Spaeth 2002). To others, the Supreme Court's dependence upon other institutions to give force to its rulings creates a need to remain attentive to the changing course of popular attitudes (Adamany and Grossman 1983). In addition to the competing expectations created by constitutional design, the evidence on this question is equally uncertain. Empirically, there is strong evidence that both corroborates and contradicts the causal link between public preferences and Supreme Court decision making (Mishler and Sheehan 1993, 1994; Norpoth and Segal 1994). Indeed, the most recent analyses conclude that, while individual justices respond to public sentiment (Flemming and Wood 1997), the extent to which the Court's policies represent popular opinion is indeterminate at best (Stimson, MacKuen, and Erikson 1995; cf. Erikson, MacKuen, and Stimson 2002)). How does one resolve these competing perspectives?

We believe that there is good reason for the justices to be attentive to public opinion. Specifically, we posit that, since the justices do not have the institutional capacities to give their rulings full effect, they must calculate the extent to which popular decision makers will support their policy initiatives. Thus, while the Court is certainly not electorally accountable, those responsible for putting its rulings into effect frequently are. For that reason, strategic justices must gauge the prevailing winds that drive reelection-minded politicians and make decisions accordingly (Murphy 1964). That is, justices who want to see their personal preferences expressed in public policy know that the effectiveness of such policy depends upon whether it is accepted by its implementers and those to whom they are responsible. By this logic, a Court that cares about its perceived legitimacy must rationally anticipate whether its preferred outcomes will be respected and faithfully followed by relevant publics. Consequently, a Court that strays too far from the broad boundaries imposed by public mood risks having its decisions rejected. Naturally, in individual cases, the justices can and do buck the trends of public sentiment. In the aggregate, however, popular opinion should still shape the broad contours of judicial policymaking.

[…]

Public Opinion and the Court

By constitutional design, the nexus between public opinion and public policy is more limited for the Supreme Court than it is for the President and members of Congress. Yet this institutional insularity actually belies interesting relationships that exist between the judicial branch and mass publics. Citizens, it turns out, respond to the Court and its policies in systematic ways. Among other things, research has illuminated the sources of political support for the Court, as well as how the justices' decisions have shaped opinions on specific issues (see, e.g., Caldeira and Gibson 1992; Franklin and Kosaki 1989; Hoekstra 2000; Marshall 1989; Mondak 1992). Thus, a good deal is known about how public opinion moves in response to the Court's outputs.

Reversing the causal arrow, scholars have likewise contemplated the impact of public preferences on judicial policy. Few dispute that public opinion is reflected in the choices of the Court. The mechanism by which it takes place, though, has been subject to considerable disagreement. One highly plausible hypothesis is that public opinion determines Supreme Court policy indirectly: elections determine the composition of Congress and the White House, whose members in turn select the justices. Presidents and Senators, who necessarily reflect majority preferences, are motivated to select justices with whom they share an ideological affinity (Segal and Spaeth 2002). As a result, the ideological orientation of the Court generally corresponds to the attitudes of the electorate (Dahl 1957; Funston 1975; see also Gates 1987).

There is considerable intuitive appeal to this explanation, inasmuch as it under-girds the most widely accepted explanation for the observed changes in Supreme Court policy. Under the precepts of the attitudinal model, the preferences of the justices are virtually the sole determinant of their voting behavior (Segal and Spaeth 2002). Barring changes in the Court's docket, any variation in the ideological direction of the Court's outputs is necessarily a function of membership change, a process that is highly likely to produce justices who serve as contemporaneous reflections of the electorate's preferences. That the Supreme Court's outcomes may comport with popular opinion is scarcely a wonder; it is merely a manifestation of selecting ideologically driven justices whose preferences roughly match those of the electorate more generally. Illustrating this view, Justice Scalia has noted that "it's a little unrealistic to talk about the Court as though it's a continuous, unchanging institution rather than to some extent necessarily a reflection of the society in which it functions. Ultimately, the justices of the Court are taken from society … and however impartial they may try to be, they are going to bring with them those societ[al] attitudes" (quoted in O'Brien 2000, 343). Whether this forecloses the possibility of a Supreme Court that responds more immediately to changes in popular opinion is certainly debatable. Taken on its own terms, though, there is little doubt that this indirect influence is a principal determinant of the Court's decisional outcomes.

In addition to this indirect linkage, scholars have also posited a direct causal connection between public preferences and Supreme Court policy. In this tradition, some scholars have painted with a fairly broad brush, noting the general correspondence between public opinion and judicial outcomes. So, for instance, the Court's proclivity for countermajoritarianism seems to be dependent upon popular preferences. In fact, the justices' protection of minority interests tends to occur only when public opinion supports such outcomes (Barnum 1985; see also Dahl 1957). The absence of careful control for alternative explanations, however, leaves substantial room for disagreement about the degree to which mass opinion actually moves the Court in one direction or another (Caldeira 1991, 314).

Other scholars have proceeded with somewhat greater analytic rigor, examining whether the Court's liberalism follows the ebb and flow of public mood, after controlling for its indirect effects. Methodological sophistication, however, has hardly generated consensus. Holding constant the justices' preferences, there is evidence of a significant causal connection between mass opinion and Supreme Court policy, both in the aggregate and within individual issue areas (Link 1995; Mishler and Sheehan 1993). Indeed, part of this pathway may be attributable to public opinion actually shaping the justices' preferences over the long term (Mishler and Sheehan 1996). Telling as these results are, they do necessitate some circumspection, since the estimated effects of public opinion may be quite sensitive to modest changes in the specification of predictive models (Norpoth and Segal 1994; see also Mishler and Sheehan 1996, 176).

At the level of the individual justice, voting appears to be significantly affected by the changing patterns of public preferences over time, if only marginally so (Flemming and Wood 1997; Mishler and Sheehan 1996; cf. Norpoth and Segal 1994). That the votes of a given member of the Court are influenced by mass opinion does not demonstrate—at least not directly—that the Court's cases are decided any differently as a consequence (Flemming and Wood 1997, 472). After all, if public opinion truly matters to the Court, then the justices ought to take it into account and (their own preferences notwithstanding) actually decide cases in ways that reflect the tenor of public mood. It is this link between public preferences and substantive policy outcomes that we are keen to examine in this analysis.

On the face of it, of course, there is little reason to suspect that the justices care about public opinion at all. With agenda control, lifetime tenure, and no political constituencies that must be appeased, the justices are largely free to make decisions that accord with their personal preferences (Segal and Spaeth 2002). State judges, who must often stand for reelection are one thing (Hall 1992), but the electorally unaccountable members of the U.S. Supreme Court are quite another. Its members do not (at least as far as we know) consult the polls prior to rendering their decisions.

At the same time, governmental actors of all kinds care a good deal about maintaining their ability to craft meaningful public policies. The precise mechanisms that constrain political decision making vary across institutions, obviously. Still, in one way or another, public officials in a constitutional system require support— from legislators, from bureaucrats, from judges, and ultimately from the public— in order to achieve and sustain their objectives.

One way in which policy makers ensure that support is by conforming their behavior to fit the preferences of those whose backing they will later require. Through rational anticipation, governmental actors "sense the mood of the moment, assess its trend, and anticipate its consequences for [the] future . . ." (Stimson, MacKuen, and Erikson 1995, 545). For some, the need to monitor the political winds is especially acute; election-minded members of Congress, for example, rapidly adjust their policies in response to the changing tastes of voters. Presidents, as well, find that the success of their policy ambitions rise and fall with the tide of public sentiment; so they, too, must forecast the effects of popular opinion.

The Supreme Court, by contrast, need not worry over the same practical concerns as elected officials. Still, it does not necessarily follow that the justices are indifferent to changes in public preferences. To the contrary, it has long been suspected that the justices are quite mindful of the imperative of maintaining societal acceptances of their powers and policies. "To a large extent," according to Justice Frankfurter, "the Supreme Court, under the guise of constitutional interpretation of words whose contents are derived from the disposition of the Justices, is the reflector of that impalpable but controlling thing, the general drift of public opinion" (1939, 197). The principal reason, as Alexander Hamilton so sagely observed, is that the Court "has no influence over either the sword or the purse; no direction either of the strength or of the wealth of the society, and can take no active resolution whatsoever. It may truly be said to have neither force nor will but merely judgment; and must ultimately depend upon the aid of the executive arm even for the efficacy of its judgments" ([1787–88] 1961, 465). By this reckoning, the Court is "the least dangerous" branch because it depends upon the good will of other institutions in order for its policies to have genuine force. Justices who sought to raise any reasonable degree of political capital would surely need to consider whether their preferred policies would be met with acclaim or disdain. Estimating the nature of public mood, they should temper their ambitions, as circumstances warrant.

This is, we think, a classic case of rational anticipation by policy makers. Yet we are hardly the first to posit such a relationship. At least since Walter Murphy's *Elements of Judicial Strategy*, scholars have pondered how a rational justice might behave when "the Justice anticipates that at this time a certain decision or the announcement of a policy in an opinion would stir a political reaction which would gravely threaten that policy and probably judicial power itself" (1964, 171). Notwithstanding the absence of an electoral motive, a justice who wished to maintain institutional legitimacy for the future would have substantial incentive to trim his sails and follow popular sentiment in the present.

The reasons for such behavior are not terribly mysterious. The justices may well want to see their preferences reflected in policy outcomes, but that ambition would be fairly hollow if those policies, once promulgated, had no practical effect. The Court requires the cooperation of legislative and executive officials, many of whom are themselves careful auditors of mass opinion. For that reason, the members of the Court must reflect on how well their preferred outcomes will be received and supported by implementers. By no means does this imply that the Court cares about public opinion in the same ways that elected officials do, but we do think it entirely reasonable to assume that justices want their policies to be taken seriously by relevant publics.[1]

This is not just our opinion, of course. There is abundant evidence of resistance, avoidance, and downright defiance from various constituencies of the Court (Canon and Johnson 1999). It is only when popular opinion supports the Court's goals that its policies have their full effects (Rosenberg 1991). To be sure, the Constitution affords the Supreme Court institutional independence, but it in no way guarantees the prestige upon which its success is so highly dependent.

Hence, from our theoretical perspective, we see the role of rational anticipation in the Court vis-à-vis Congress and the President to be a difference of degree, rather than kind. The justices may be comparatively insulated from public pressure, but that does not guarantee that they will be oblivious to it. The mechanism that would impel the justices to follow public opinion, we hypothesize, is the Court's expectations about the future consequences of its decisions. Public mood, then, should be

---

1   At the very least, they want to avoid the bureaucratic hassle of having to revisit the same issue repeatedly to "demand" conformance, as they did in the case of school desegregation, for example (Rosenberg 1991).

a barometer by which the justices estimate the extent to which their preferred policies will likely be accepted and put into effect.

[…]

We set out trying to determine whether the Supreme Court responds directly to movements in public opinion and whether the data used in prior analyses undercut accurate estimation of this relationship. We have unusually clear answers to both. The decisions to affirm are unquestionably bad measures of the Supreme Court's position at best, a reversal of the state of affairs at worst. And, once that is taken into account, public opinion is a powerful influence on the decisions of the Supreme Court. Both conclusions are decisively supported by the evidence.

The net result of these findings is two-fold. First, from a methodological perspective, we have illustrated some quite significant complications that flow from inappropriate measurement of the justices' behavior. Scholars of the Supreme Court are increasingly interested in the ramifications of selection bias that stem from the justices' nonrandom agenda setting (see, e.g., Smith 2000). Our analysis highlights one such problem, and a very severe one, at that; there is systematic contamination in the most widely used measure of Supreme Court outputs. We can only speculate, of course, about its implications for others who care about statistical accounts of the Court, but we can well imagine that many empirical models would produce vastly different results and interpretations if they were to employ the more valid indicator of judicial policymaking.

Second and more substantively, we have found that the Court's policy outcomes are indeed affected by public opinion, but to a degree far greater than previously documented. At the same time, we have hardly eliminated the indirect influence of mass opinion wrought by the appointment process. Reliance upon a better measure of the Court's behavior reveals the justices to be highly motivated by their personal preferences, even after the significant effect of direct public preferences are held constant.

That the justices rationally anticipate the future consequences of their actions speaks well of the system of dynamic representation. After all, a Court that requires the support of others to give life to its pronouncements must surely work within the broad boundaries of public acceptability. We certainly do not expect this analysis to be the last word on the role of public opinion in the judicial branch. Given our results, however, we do believe that a system of popular representation is alive and well in the Supreme Court.

REFERENCES

Adamany, David, and Joel Grossman. 1983. "Support for the Supreme Court as a National Policy Maker." *Law and Policy Quarterly* 5 (October): 405–37.

Barnum, David G. 1985. "The Supreme Court and Public Opinion: Judicial Decision Making in the Post-New Deal Period." *Journal of Politics* 47(2): 652–65.

Baum, Lawrence. 1997. *The Puzzle of Judicial Behavior.* Ann Arbor: University of Michigan Press. Caldeira, Gregory A. 1991. "Courts and Public Opinion." In *American Courts: A Critical Assessment*, eds. John B. Gates and Charles A. Johnson. Washington: Congressional Quarterly, Inc.

Caldeira, Gregory A., and James L. Gibson. 1992. "The Etiology of Public Support for the Supreme Court." *American Journal of Political Science* 36(3): 635–64.

Canon, Bradley C., and Charles E. Johnson. 1999. *Judicial Policies: Implementation and Impact.* Washington: Congressional Quarterly Inc.

Dahl, Robert A. 1957. "Decision-Making in a Democracy: The Supreme Court as a National Policy-Maker." *Journal of Public Law* 6(2): 279–95.

Erikson, Robert S., Michael B. MacKuen, and James A. Stimson. 2002. *The Macro Polity.* Cambridge: Cambridge University Press.

Flemming, Roy B., and B. Dan Wood. 1997. "The Public and the Supreme Court: Individual Justice

Responsiveness to American Policy Moods." *American Journal of Political Science* 41(2): 468–98. Frankfurter, Felix. 1939. *Law and Politics: Occasional Papers of Felix Frankfurter*, eds. Archibald

MacLeish and E. F. Prichard, Jr. New York: Harcourt, Brace and Co.

Franklin, Charles H., and Liane Kosaki. 1989. "The Republican Schoolmaster: The Supreme Court,

Public Opinion and Abortion." *American Political Science Review* 83(3): 751–72.

Funston, Richard. 1975. "The Supreme Court and Critical Elections." *American Political Science Review* 69(3): 795–811.

Gates, John. 1987. "Partisan Realignment, Unconstitutional State Policies, and the U.S. Supreme Court, 1837–1964." *American Journal of Political Science* 31(2): 259–80.

George, Tracey E., and Lee Epstein. 1992. "On the Nature of Supreme Court Decision Making." *American Political Science Review* 86(2): 323–37.

Hagle, Timothy M., and Harold J. Spaeth. 1992. "The Emergence of a New Ideology: The Business Decisions of the Burger Court." *Journal of Politics* 54(1): 120–34.

Hall, Melinda Gann. 1992. "Electoral Politics and Strategic Voting in State Supreme Courts." *Journal of Politics* 54(2): 427–46.

Hamilton, Alexander, James Madison, John Jay. [1787–88] 1961. *The Federalist Papers*. New York: New American Library.

Hoekstra, Valerie J. 2000. "The Supreme Court and Local Public Opinion." *American Political Science Review* 94(1): 89–100.

Link, Michael W. 1995. "Tracking Public Mood in the Supreme Court: Cross-Time Analyses of Criminal Procedure and Civil Rights Cases." *Political Research Quarterly* 48(1): 61–78.

Marshall, Thomas. 1989. *Public Opinion and the Supreme Court*. New York: Longman.

McGuire, Kevin T., Charles E. Smith, Jr., and Gregory A. Caldeira. 2004. "A Spatial Model of Supreme Court Voting." Presented at the annual meeting of the Midwest Political Science Association.

Mishler, William, and Reginald S. Sheehan. 1993. "The Supreme Court as a Countermajoritarian Institution? The Impact of Public Opinion on Supreme Court Decisions." *American Political Science Review* 87(1): 87–101.

Mishler, William, and Reginald S. Sheehan. 1994. "Response: Popular Influence on Supreme Court Decisions." *American Political Science Review* 88(3): 716–24.

Mishler, William, and Reginald S. Sheehan. 1996. "Public Opinion, the Attitudinal Model, and Supreme Court Decision Making: A Micro-Analytic Perspective." *Journal of Politics* 58(1): 169–200.

Mondak, Jeffrey. 1992. "Institutional Legitimacy, Policy Legitimacy, and the Supreme Court." *American Politics Quarterly* 20(4): 457–77.

Murphy, Walter F. 1964. *Elements of Judicial Strategy*. Chicago: University of Chicago Press.

Norpoth, Helmut, and Jeffrey A. Segal. 1994. "Comment: Popular Influence on Supreme Court Decisions." *American Political Science Review* 88(3): 711–16.

O'Brien, David M. 2000. *Storm Center: The Supreme Court in American Politics*. 5th ed. New York: W.W. Norton and Company.

Rosenberg, Gerald N. 1991. *The Hollow Hope: Can Courts Bring About Social Change?* Chicago: University of Chicago Press.

Segal, Jeffrey A., and Harold J. Spaeth. 2002. *The Supreme Court and the Attitudinal Model Revisited*. Cambridge: Cambridge University Press.

Smith, Charles E., Jr. 2000. "An Attitudinal Model of Certiorari Voting: Toward a Solution to the Selection Bias Problem." Presented at the annual meeting of the Midwest Political Science Association.

Songer, Donald R., Jeffrey A. Segal, and Charles M. Cameron. 1994. "The Hierarchy of Justice: Testing a Principal-Agent Model of Supreme Court–Circuit Court Interactions." *American Journal of Political Science* 38(3): 673–96.

Stimson, James A. 1999. *Public Opinion in America: Moods, Cycles, and Swings*. 2nd ed. Boulder: Westview Press.

Stimson, James A., Michael B. MacKuen, and Robert S. Erikson. 1995. "Dynamic Representation." *American Political Science Review* 89(3): 543–65.

DISCUSSION QUESTIONS

1. Explain why the judiciary is considered the "least dangerous" branch of government. Is it the "least dangerous" branch?
2. What is judicial review, and why is it considered a power of the courts?
3. Discuss why the Supreme Court has both original jurisdiction and appellate jurisdiction.
4. In what way are political figures similar and different from appellate court justices?
5. Compare the legal model, political model, strategic model, and litigant-driven model of judicial decision-making. Which are based in legal traditionalism, and which are based in legal realism? Why?
6. How might the panel structure of the appellate courts impede judicial decision-making?
7. Explain why lack of enforcement power is one of the greatest weaknesses of the appellate courts.
8. Should appellate court justices consider public sentiment?
9. What potential problems would arise if Supreme Court justices were elected instead of nominated?
10. Why do the courts depend on their prestige and legitimacy?

Introduction

If appellate courts, in crafting decisions to legal disputes, are making and correcting policy, then the impact of their policies should be considered. The appellate courts can have a (a) legal impact on the lower courts, (b) political impact on the other branches of government, and (c) social impact on the community. The extent to which their decisions are effective and influential in each of these areas depends on a number of factors.

Following the Majority

Traditionally, the legislature is seen as the branch responsible for *making* the law, while the judiciary is responsible for *interpreting* the law. Judicial decisions, though, have the force of law, so many would argue that the courts are policy-makers too. This is particularly important in the context of the courts' presumed apolitical role. One of the reasons the judiciary was designed to be independent was to ensure that judges could be the voice of the minority. While the legislative and executive branches were structured to be responsive to the majority will, the judiciary would be responsible for protecting minority rights. If the courts are, in fact, protecting minorities in their decisions, Robert Dahl, in "Decision-Making in a Democracy: The Supreme Court as a National Policy-Maker," says that policy is being made that "denies popular sovereignty and political equality."

Dahl recognizes that the Court has struck down many provisions of federal law as unconstitutional and has modified several others. Each of these laws was initially passed by majorities of those voting in the Senate and the House. They also had the President's formal approval. In this circumstance, the court is overturning laws popularly supported in the interests of the minority. In some contexts, this would seem necessary in order to ensure the minority view is protected, but decisions constantly made in rejection of majority views can actually be harmful to the courts' legitimacy, hindering their impact.

In his analysis of Supreme Court decisions, Dahl actually finds that "the policy views dominant on the Court are never for long out of line with the policy views dominant among the lawmaking majorities of the U.S." The truth is that the courts often make policies that are in line with public opinion, mostly because the likelihood of their decisions being enforced depends on it, as discussed in Section 6. At least at the federal level, judges are nominated by the President and confirmed by the Senate. Presidents often nominate judges with the same ideological beliefs, assuming that their decisions will then reflect these political leanings. The relevance of political ideology in the appointment process can be seen in the discussions surrounding the appointment of new justices to the Supreme Court. The President makes sure to appoint someone who will support and uphold many of the administration's policy platforms. In this context, Dahl argues that it would be unrealistic to think that judges appointed in this manner "would long hold to norms of right or justice substantially at odds with the rest of the political elite."

Ultimately, the appellate courts can be seen as having a greater impact when they reinforce the policies of the majority. In this way, they guarantee that their decisions will be enforced and supported. When the decisions of the courts go against public opinion, they run the risk of being defied and rejected.

Additional Factors Affecting Impact

Aside from following public opinion, other factors can guarantee that the decisions made have an impact. The courts' legitimacy and prestige can ensure that their decisions are respected and followed. If the courts issue a direct order to an official, these orders are likely to be obeyed. Cases that are clearly in the courts' jurisdiction also have more impact. Generally, the courts are supposed to avoid "political questions," meaning they should not decide on issues that fall within the jurisdiction of the legislature. When the courts make decisions regarding "political questions," they sometimes run the risk of being challenged for interjecting into political life. It helps the courts if the constitutional standard is simple and easy to interpret, and the judiciary can have some form of control over its enforcement. Effective decisions are also likely when the public is less invested in the decision and accepts the decision with little disagreement.

Some contend that decisions have more force when they are unanimous, especially in the Supreme Court. In many controversial cases, the justices are fairly split, with one or two justices serving as swing votes. One of the nuances of *Brown v. Board of Education*, which was read in Section 1, was that all nine justices were in agreement. At the time, Justice Earl Warren felt that it was essential for the justices to come together in crafting the decision so that their decision had more immediate force, especially since it was calling for the desegregation of schools. It was thought that a united front could have a greater impact on the community.

To a certain extent, the impact of the courts' decisions also depends on their "magic." Jerome Frank, the author of "Courts on Trial" in Section 1, referred to this concept as the "cult of the robe." In society, judges assume a special status. They are referred to as "your honor" and when they walk in a room, everyone, without a question, stands. This image commands respect and admiration. Many find comfort in the fact that judges are supposed to be independent from politics. Despite whether that is factually true, the public often operates with an understanding that the courts can be impartial decision-makers, and as such, the public and other branches of government should adhere to their decisions. This view of the court gives their decisions greater meaning and influence.

Having a Symbolic Impact

While these scenarios present circumstances in which appellate courts can affect change, it is better to view the courts as *catalysts* to change, focusing more on their symbolic impact as opposed to their operational impact. This perspective can be demonstrated in *Miranda v. Arizona*. In the *Miranda* decision, the Court told police officers the exact wording they must use when arresting a suspect in order to ensure a legal confession. This wording has come to be known as the Miranda Warning and is heard in countless movies and television shows. The Court was hoping to protect suspects from feeling obligated to talk to the police by making sure the police notified suspects of their rights ahead of time. After *Miranda*, many different studies were conducted to try and understand the extent to which *Miranda* influenced law enforcement.

As a result of *Miranda*, many researchers questioned whether confession rates, clearance rates, and conviction rates had gone down. George Thomas, III, and Richard Leo in "The Effects of *Miranda v. Arizona*: "Embedded" in Our National Culture?" provide a synopsis of studies focusing on the effects of *Miranda*. The first generation of studies shortly following *Miranda* show that many police agencies immediately began complying with the warning requirements, while others ignored the decision. Suspects still continued to waive their rights and talk to the police, and most interrogation methods remained unchanged. There is some evidence to suggest that clearance rates fell temporarily, but overall the decision did not seem to have a large short-term impact on law enforcement.

Later studies beginning largely in the 1990s demonstrate that the police continue to use the *Miranda* warnings but have found ways to adapt and work around some of the *Miranda* requirements. Suspects with criminal records appeared to be the least likely to waive their rights. While it is clear from both the earlier and later studies that *Miranda* did not have the exact impact that was intended, it did create a greater level of professionalism in the interrogation process and raised awareness of suspects' constitutional rights. In *Dickerson v. United States*, the Supreme Court upheld the *Miranda* decision, recognizing that the *Miranda* warning has "become part of our national culture." In this way, *Miranda*'s impact was achieved more at a symbolic level than an operational level.

Decision-Making in a Democracy

The Supreme Court as a National Policy-Maker

Robert A. Dahl

To consider the Supreme Court of the United States Strictly as a legal institution is to underestimate its significance in the American political system. For it is also a political institution, an institution, that is to say, for arriving at decisions on controversial questions of national policy. As a political institution, the Court is highly unusual, not least because Americans are not quite willing to accept the fact that it *is* a political institution and not quite capable of denying it; so that frequently we take both positions at once. This is confusing to foreigners, amusing to logicians, and rewarding to ordinary Americans who thus manage to retain the best of both worlds.

A policy decision might be defined as an effective choice among alternatives about which there is, at least initially, some uncertainty. This uncertainty may arise because of inadequate information as to (a) the alternatives that are thought to be "open"; (b) the consequences that will probably ensue from choosing a given alternative; (c) the level of probability that these consequences will actually ensue; and (d) the relative value of the different alternatives, that is, an ordering of the alternatives from most preferable to least preferable, given the expected consequences and the expected probability of the consequences actually occurring. An *effective* choice is a selection of the most preferable alternative accompanied by measures to insure that the alternative selected will be acted upon.

No one, I imagine, will quarrel with the proposition that the Supreme Court, or indeed any court, must make and does make policy decisions in this sense. But such a proposition is not really useful to the question before us. What is critical is the extent to which a court can and does make policy decisions by going outside established "legal" criteria found in precedent, statute, and constitution. Now in this respect the Supreme Court occupies a most peculiar position, for it is an essential characteristic of the institution that from time to time its members decide cases where legal criteria are not in any realistic sense adequate to the task. A distinguished associate justice of the present Court has recently described the business of the Supreme Court in these words:

> It is essentially accurate to say that the Court's preoccupation today is with the application of rather fundamental aspirations and what Judge Learned Hand calls "moods," embodied in provisions like the due process clauses, which were designed not to be precise and positive directions for rules of action. The judicial process in applying them involves a judgment.... that is, on the views of the direct representatives of the people in meeting the needs of society, on the views of Presidents and Governors, and by their construction of the will of legislatures the Court breathes life, feeble or strong, into the inert pages of the Constitution and the statute books.[1]

Very often, then, the cases before the Court involve alternatives about which there is severe disagreement in the society, as in the case of segregation or economic regulation; that is, the setting of the case is "political." Moreover, they are usually cases where competent students of constitutional law, including the learned justices of the Supreme Court themselves, disagree; where the words of the Constitution are general, vague, ambiguous, or not clearly applicable; where precedent may be found on both sides; and where experts differ in predicting the consequences of the various alternatives or the degree of probability that the possible consequences will actually ensue. Typically, in other words, although there may be considerable agreement as to the alternatives thought to be open [(a)], there is very serious disagreement as to questions of fact bearing on consequences and probabilities [(b) and (c)], and as to questions of value, or the way in which different alternatives are to be ordered according to criteria establishing relative preferability [(d)].

If the Court were assumed to be a "political" institution, no particular problems would arise, for it would be taken for granted that the members of the Court would resolve questions of fact and value by introducing assumptions derived from their own predispositions or those of influential clienteles and constituents. But, since much of the legitimacy of the Court's decisions rests upon the fiction that it is not a political institution but exclusively a legal one, to accept the Court as a political institution would solve one set of problems at the price of creating another. Nonetheless, if it is true that the nature of the cases arriving before the Court is sometimes of the kind I have described, then the Court cannot act strictly as a legal institution. It must, that is to say, choose among controversial alternatives of public policy by appealing to at least some criteria of acceptability on questions of fact and value that cannot be found in or deduced from precedent, statute, and Constitution. It is in this sense that the Court is a national policy-maker, and it is this role that gives rise to the problem of the Court's existence in a political system ordinarily held to be democratic.

Now I take it that except for differences in emphasis and presentation, what I have said so far is today widely accepted by almost all American political scientists and by most lawyers. To anyone who believes that the Court is not, in at least some of its activities, a policy-making institution, the discussion that follows may seem irrelevant. But to anyone who holds that at least one role of the Court is as a policy-making institution in cases where strictly legal criteria are inadequate, then a serious and much debated question arises, to wit: Who gets what and why? Or in less elegant language: What groups are benefited or handicapped by the Court and how does the allocation by the Court of these rewards and penalties fit into our presumably democratic political system?

In determining and appraising the role of the Court, two different and conflicting criteria are sometimes employed. These are the majority criterion and the criterion of Right or Justice.

---

1 Frankfurter, The Supreme Court in the Mirror of Justices, 105 U. of Pa. L. Rev. 781, 793 (1957).

Every policy dispute can be tested, at least in principle, by the majority criterion, because (again: in principle) the dispute can be analyzed according to the numbers of people for and against the various alternatives at issue, and therefore according to the proportions of the citizens or eligible members who are for and against the alternatives. Logically speaking, except for a trivial case, every conflict within a given society must be a dispute between a majority of those eligible to participate and a minority or minorities; or else it must be a dispute between or among minorities only.[2] Within certain limits, both possibilities are independent of the number of policy alternatives at issue, and since the argument is not significantly affected by the number of alternatives, it is convenient to assume that each policy dispute represents only two alternatives.[3]

If everyone prefers one of two alternatives, then no significant problem arises. But a case will hardly come before the Supreme Court unless at least one person prefers an alternative that is opposed by another person. Strictly speaking, then, no matter how the Court acts in determining the legality or constitutionality of one alternative or the other, the outcome of the Court's decision must either (1) accord with the preferences of a minority of citizens and run counter to the preferences of a majority; (2) accord with the preferences of a majority and run counter to the preferences of a minority; or (3) accord with the preferences of one minority and run counter to the preferences of another minority, the rest being indifferent.

In a democratic system with a more or less representative legislature, it is unnecessary to maintain a special court to secure the second class of outcomes. A case might be made out that the Court protects the rights of national majorities against local interests in federal questions, but so far as I am aware, the role of the Court as a policy-maker is not usually defended in this fashion; in what follows, therefore, I propose to pass over the ticklish question of federalism and deal only with "national" majorities and minorities. The third kind of outcome, although relevant according to other criteria, is hardly relevant to the majority criterion, and may also be passed over for the moment.

One influential view of the Court, however, is that it stands in some special way as a protection of minorities against tyranny by majorities. In the course of its 167 years, in seventy-eight cases, the Court has struck down eighty-six different provisions of federal law as unconstitutional,[4] and by interpretation it has modified a good many more. It might be argued, then, that in all or in a very large

---

2   Provided that the total membership of the society is an even number, it is technically possible for a dispute to occur that divides the membership into two equal parts, neither of which can be said to be either a majority or minority of the total membership. But even in the instances where the number of members is even (which should occur on the average only half the time), the probability of an exactly even split, in any group of more than a few thousand people, is so small that it may be ignored.

3   Suppose the number of citizens, or members eligible to participate in collective decisions, is n. Let each member indicate his "most preferred alternative." Then it is obvious that the maximum number of most preferred alternatives is n. It is equally obvious that if the number of most preferred alternatives is more than or equal to $n/2$, then no majority is possible. But for all practical purposes those formal limitations can be ignored, for we are dealing with a large society where the number of alternatives at issue before the Supreme Court is invariably quite small. If the number of alternatives is greater than two, it is theoretically possible for preferences to be distributed so that no outcome is consistent with the majority criterion, even where all members can rank all the alternatives and where there is perfect information as to their preferences; but this difficulty does not bear on the subsequent discussion, and it is disregarded. For an examination of this problem, consult Arrow, Social Choice and Individual Values (1951).

4   Actually, the matter is somewhat ambiguous. There appear to have been seventy-eight cases in which the Court has held provisions of federal law unconstitutional. Sixty-four different acts in the technical sense have been construed, and eighty-six different provisions in law have been in some respects invalidated. I rely here on the figures and the table given in Library of Congress, Legislative Reference Service, Provisions of Federal Law Held Unconstitutional By the Supreme Court of the United States 95, 141–47 (1936), to which I have added United States v. Lovett, 328 U.S. 303 (1946), and United States ex rel. Toth v. Quarles, 350 U.S. 11 (1955). There are some minor discrepancies in totals (not attributable to the differences in publication dates) between this volume and Acts of Congress Held Unconstitutional in Whole or in Part by the Supreme Court of the United States, in Library of Congress, Legislative Reference Service, The Constitution of the United States of America, Analysis and Interpretation (Corwin ed., 1953). The difference is a result of classification. The latter document lists seventy-three acts held unconstitutional (to which Toth v. Quarles, supra, should be added) but different sections of the same act are sometimes counted separately.

number of these cases the Court was, in fact, defending the rights of some minority against a "tyrannical" majority. There are, however, some exceedingly serious difficulties with this interpretation of the Court's activities.

One problem, which is essentially ideological in character, is the difficulty of reconciling such an interpretation with the existence of a democratic polity, for it is not at all difficult to show by appeals to authorities as various and imposing as Aristotle, Locke, Rousseau, Jefferson, and Lincoln that the term democracy means, among other things, that the power to rule resides in popular majorities and their representatives. Moreover, from entirely reasonable and traditional definitions of popular sovereignty and political equality, the principle of majority rule can be shown to follow by logical necessity.[5] Thus to affirm that the Court supports minority preferences against majorities is to deny that popular sovereignty and political equality, at least in the traditional sense, exist in the United States; and to affirm that the Court *ought* to act in this way is to deny that popular sovereignty and political equality *ought* to prevail in this country. In a country that glories in its democratic tradition, this is not a happy state of affairs for the Court's defenders; and it is no wonder that a great deal of effort has gone into the enterprise of proving that, even if the Court consistently defends minorities against majorities, nonetheless it is a thoroughly "democratic" institution. But no amount of tampering with democratic theory can conceal the fact that a system in which the policy preferences of minorities prevail over majorities is at odds with the traditional criteria for distinguishing a democracy from other political systems.[6]

Fortunately, however, we do not need to traverse this well-worn ground; for the view of the Court as a protector of the liberties of minorities against the tyranny of majorities is beset with other difficulties that are not so much ideological as matters of fact and logic. If one wishes to be at all rigorous about the question, it is probably impossible to demonstrate that any particular Court decisions have or have not been at odds with the preferences of a "national majority." It is clear that unless one makes *some* assumptions as to the kind of evidence one will require for the existence of a set of minority and majority preferences in the general population, the view under consideration is incapable of being proved at all. In any strict sense, no adequate evidence exists, for scientific opinion polls are of relatively recent origin, and national elections are little more than an indication of the first preferences of a number of citizens—in the United States the number ranges between about forty and sixty per cent of the adult population—for certain candidates for public office. I do not mean to say that there is no relation between preferences among candidates and preferences among alternative public policies, but the connection is a highly tenuous one, and on the basis of an election it is almost never possible to adduce whether a majority does or does not support one of two or more policy alternatives about which members of the political elite are divided. For the greater part of the Court's history, then, there is simply no way of establishing with any high degree of confidence whether a given alternative was or was not supported by a majority or a minority of adults or even of voters.

In the absence of relatively direct information, we are thrown back on indirect tests. The eighty-six provisions of federal law that have been declared unconstitutional were, of course, initially passed by majorities of those voting in the Senate and in the House. They also had the president's formal approval. We could, therefore, speak of a majority of those voting in the House and Senate, together with the president, as a "lawmaking majority." It is not easy to determine whether any such constellation of forces within the political elites actually coincides with the preferences of a majority of American adults or even with the preferences of a majority of that half of the adult population which, on the

---

5   Dahl, A Preface to Democratic Theory, c. 2 (1956).
6   Compare Commager, Majority Rule and Minority Rights (1943).

average, votes in congressional elections. Such evidence as we have from opinion polls suggests that Congress is not markedly out of line with public opinion, or at any rate with such public opinion as there is after one discards the answers of people who fall into the category, often large, labelled "no response" or "don't know." If we may, on these somewhat uncertain grounds, take a "lawmaking majority" as equivalent to a "national majority," then it is possible to test the hypothesis that the Supreme Court is shield and buckler for minorities against national majorities.

Under any reasonable assumptions about the nature of the political process, it would appear to be somewhat naive to assume that the Supreme Court either would or could play the role of Galahad. Over the whole history of the Court, on the average one new justice has been appointed every twenty-two months. Thus a president can expect to appoint about two new justices during one term of office; and if this were not enough to tip the balance on a normally divided Court, he is almost certain to succeed in two terms. Thus, Hoover had three appointments; Roosevelt, nine; Truman, four; and Eisenhower, so far, has had four. Presidents are not famous for appointing justices hostile to their own views on public policy nor could they expect to secure confirmation of a man whose stance on key questions was flagrantly at odds with that of the dominant majority in the Senate. Justices are typically men who, prior to appointment, have engaged in public life and have committed themselves publicly on the great questions of the day. As Mr. Justice Frankfurter has recently reminded us, a surprisingly large proportion of the justices, particularly of the great justices who have left their stamp upon the decisions of the Court, have had little or no prior judicial experience.[7] Nor have the justices—certainly not the great justices—been timid men with a passion for anonymity. Indeed, it is not too much to say that if justices were appointed primarily for their "judicial" qualities without regard to their basic attitudes on fundamental questions of public policy, the Court could not play the influential role in the American political system that it does in reality play.

Table 7.1.1 The Interval Between Appointments to the Supreme Court.

Interval in Years		Per Cent of Total Appointments	Cumulative Per Cent
Less than 1	. . . .	21	21
1	. . . .	34	55
2	. . . .	18	73
3	. . . .	9	82
4	. . . .	S	90
5	. . . .	7	97
6	. . . .	2	99
———	. . . .	———	———
12	. . . .	1	100
Total	. . . .	100	100

Note: The table excludes the six appointments made in 1789. Except for the four most recent appointments, it is based on data in the Encyclopedia of American History 461–62 (Morris ed., 1953). It may be slightly inaccurate because the source shows only the year of appointment, not the month. The twelve-year interval was from 1811 to 1823.

---

7   Frankfurter, op. cit. supra note 1, at 782–84.

The fact is, then, that the policy views dominant on the Court are never for long out of line with the policy views dominant among the lawmaking majorities of the United States. Consequently it would be most unrealistic to suppose that the Court would, for more than a few years at most, stand against any major alternatives sought by a lawmaking majority. The judicial agonies of the New Deal will, of course, quickly come to mind; but Mr. Roosevelt's difficulties with the Court were truly exceptional. Generalizing over the whole history of the Court, the chances are about one out of five that a president will make one appointment to the Court in less than a year, better than one out of two that he will make one within two years, and three out of four that he will make one within three years. Mr. Roosevelt had unusually bad luck: he had to wait four years for his first appointment; the odds against this long an interval are four to one. With average luck, the battle with the Court would never have occurred; even as it was, although the "court-packing" proposal did formally fail, by the end of his second term Mr. Roosevelt had appointed five new justices and by 1941 Mr. Justice Roberts was the only remaining holdover from the Hoover era.

It is to be expected, then, that the Court is least likely to be successful in blocking a determined and persistent lawmaking majority on a major policy and most likely to succeed against a "weak" majority; e.g., a dead one, a transient one, a fragile one, or one weakly united upon a policy of subordinate importance.

An examination of the cases in which the Court has held federal legislation unconstitutional confirms, on the whole, our expectations. Over the whole history of the Court, about half the decisions have been rendered more than four years after the legislation was passed.

Of the twenty-four laws held unconstitutional within two years, eleven were measures enacted in the early years of the New Deal. Indeed, New Deal measures comprise nearly a third of all the legislation that has ever been declared unconstitutional within four years after enactment.

Table 7.1.2 Percentage of Cases Held Unconstitutional Arranged by Time Intervals Between Legislation and Decision.

Number of Years	New Deal Legislation %	Other %	All Legislation %
2 or Less	92	19	30
3 – 4	8	19	18
5 – 8	0	28	24
9 – 12	0	13	11
13 – 16	0	8	6
17 – 20	0	1	1
21 or More	0	12	10
Total	100	100	100

Table 7.1.3 Cases Holding Legislation Unconstitutional Within Four Years After Enactment.

Interval in Years	New Deal No.	%	Other No.	%	Total No.	%
2 or Less	11	29	13	34	24	63
3 to 4	1	3	13	34	14	37
Total	12	32	26	68	38	100

It is illuminating to examine the cases where the Court has acted on legislation within four years after enactment—where the presumption is, that is to say, that the lawmaking majority is not necessarily a dead one. Of the twelve New Deal cases, two were, from a policy point of view, trivial; and two, although perhaps not trivial, were of minor importance to the New Deal program.[8] A fifth[9] involved the NRA, which was to expire within three weeks of the decision. Insofar as the unconstitutional provisions allowed "codes of fair competition" to be established by industrial groups, it is fair to say that President Roosevelt and his advisers were relieved by the Court's decision of a policy they had come to find increasingly embarrassing. In view of the tenacity with which Mr. Roosevelt held to his major program, there can hardly be any doubt that had he wanted to pursue the major policy objective involved in the NRA codes, as he did, for example, with the labor provisions, he would not have been stopped by the Court's special theory of the Constitution. As to the seven other cases,[10] it is entirely correct to say, I think, that whatever some of the eminent justices might have thought during their fleeting moments of glory, they did not succeed in interposing a barrier to the achievement of the objectives of the legislation; and in a few years most of the constitutional interpretation on which the decisions rested had been unceremoniously swept under the rug.

The remainder of the thirty-eight cases where the Court has declared legislation unconstitutional within four years of enactment tend to fall into two rather distinct groups: those involving legislation that could reasonably be regarded as important *from the point of view of the lawmaking majority* and those involving minor legislation. Although the one category merges into the other, so that some legislation must be classified rather arbitrarily, probably there will be little disagreement with classifying the specific legislative provisions involved in eleven cases as essentially minor from the point of view of the lawmaking majority (however important they may have been as constitutional interpretations).[11] The specific legislative provisions involved in the remaining fifteen cases are by no means of uniform importance, but with one or two possible exceptions it seems reasonable to classify them as major policy issues from the point of view of the lawmaking majority.[12] We would expect that cases involving major legislative policy would be propelled to the Court much more rapidly than cases involving minor policy, and, as the table below shows, this is in fact what happens.

Thus a lawmaking majority with major policy objectives in mind usually has an opportunity to seek for ways of overcoming the Court's veto. It is an interesting and highly significant fact that Congress and the, president do generally succeed in overcoming a hostile Court on major policy issues.

---

8   Booth v. United States, 291 U.S. 339 (1934), involved a reduction in the pay of retired judges. Lynch v. United States, 292 U.S. 571 (1934), repealed laws granting to veterans rights to yearly renewable term insurance; there were only twenty-nine policies outstanding in 1932. Hopkins Federal Savings & Loan Ass'n v. Cleary, 296 U.S. 315 (1935), granted permission to state building and loan associations to convert to federal ones on a vote of fifty-one per cent or more of votes cast at a legal meeting. Ashton v. Cameron County Water Improvement District, 298 U.S. 513 (1936), permitting municipalities to petition federal courts for bankruptcy proceedings.

9   Schechter Poultry Corp. v. United States, 295 U.S. 495 (1935).

10 United States v. Butler, 297 U.S. 1 (1936); Perry v. United States, 294 U.S. 330 (1935); Panama Refining Co. v. Ryan, 293 U.S. 388 (1935); Railroad Retirement Board v. Alton R. Co., 295 U.S. 330 (1935); Louisville Joint Stock Land Bank v. Radford, 295 U.S. 555 (1935); Rickert Rice Mills v. Fontenot, 297 U.S. 110 (1936); Carter v. Carter Coal Co., 298 U.S. 238 (1936).

11 United States v. Dewitt, 9 Wall. (U.S.) 41 (1870); Gordon v. United States, 2 Wall. (U.S.) 561 (1865); Monongahela Navigation Co. v. United States, 148 U.S. 312 (1893); Wong Wing v. United States, 163 U.S. 228 (1896); Fairbank v. United States, 181 U.S. 283 (1901); Rassmussen v. United States, 197 U.S. 516 (1905); Muskrat v. United States, 219 U.S. 346 (1911); Choate v. Trapp, 224 U.S. 665 (1912); Evans v. Gore, 253 U.S. 245 (1920); Untermyer v. Anderson, 276 U.S. 440 (1928); United States v. Lovett, 328 U.S. 303 (1946). Note that although the specific legislative provisions held unconstitutional may have been minor, the basic legislation may have been of major policy importance.

12 Ex parte Garland, 4 Wall. (U.S.) 333 (1867); United States v. Klein, 13 Wall. (U.S.) 128 (1872); Pollock v. Farmers' Loan & Trust Co., 157 U.S. 429 (1895), rehearing granted 158 U.S. 601 (1895); Employers' Liability Cases, 207 U.S. 463 (1908); Keller v. United States, 213 U.S. 138 (1909); Hammer v. Dagenhart, 247 U.S. 251 (1918): Eisner v. Macomber, 252 U.S. 189 (1920); Knickerbocker Ice Co. v. Stewart, 253 U.S. 149 (1920); United States v. Cohen Grocery Co., 255 U.S. 81 (1921); Weeds, Inc. v. United States, 255 U.S. 109

Table 7.1.4 Number of Cases Involving Legislative Policy Other than Those Arising Under New Deal Legislation Holding Legislation Unconstitutional Within Four Years After Enactment.

Interval in Years		Major Policy	Minor Policy	Total
2 or Less	. . . .	11	2	13
3 to 4	. . . .	4	9	13
Total	. . . .	15	11	26

Table 7.1.5 Type of Congressional Action Following Supreme Court Decisions Holding Legislation Unconstitutional Within Four Years After Enactment (Other than New Deal Legislation).

Congressional Action		Major Policy	Minor Policy	Total
Reverses Court's Policy	. . . .	10[a]	2[d]	12
Changes Own Policy	. . . .	2[b]	0	2
None	. . . .	0	8[e]	8
Unclear	. . . .	3[c]	1[f]	4
Total	. . . .	15	11	26

Note: For the cases in each category, see footnote 13.

Thus the application of the majority criterion seems to show the following: First, if the Court did in fact uphold minorities against national majorities, as both its supporters and critics often seem to believe, it would be an extremely anomalous institution from a democratic point of view. Second, the elaborate "democratic" rationalizations of the Court's defenders and the hostility of its "democratic" critics are largely irrelevant, for lawmaking majorities generally have had their way. Third, although the Court seems never to have succeeded in holding out indefinitely, in a very small number of important cases it has delayed the application of policy up to as much as twenty-five years.

How can we appraise decisions of the third kind just mentioned? Earlier I referred to the criterion of Right or Justice as a norm sometimes invoked to describe the role of the Court. In accordance with this norm, it might be argued that the most important policy function of the Court is to protect rights that are in some sense basic or fundamental. Thus (the argument might run) in a country where basic rights are, on the whole, respected, one should not expect more than a small number of cases where the Court has had to plant itself firmly against a lawmaking majority. But majorities may, on rare occasions, become "tyrannical"; and when they do, the Court intervenes; and although the constitutional issue may, strictly speaking, be technically open, the Constitution assumes an underlying fundamental body of rights and liberties which the Court guarantees by its decisions.

Here again, however, even without examining the actual cases, it would appear, on political grounds, somewhat unrealistic to suppose that a Court whose members are recruited in the fashion of Supreme Court justices would long hold to norms of Right or Justice substantially at odds with the rest of the political elite. Moreover, in an earlier day it was perhaps easier to believe that certain rights are so natural and self-evident that their fundamental validity is as much a matter of definite knowledge, at least to all reasonable creatures, as the color of a ripe apple. To say that this view is unlikely to find many articulate defenders today is, of course, not to disprove it; it is rather to suggest that we do not need to elaborate the case against it in this essay.

So far, however, our evidence has been drawn from cases in which the Court has held legislation unconstitutional within four years after enactment. What of the other forty cases? Do we have evidence in these that the Court has protected fundamental or natural rights and liberties against the dead hand of some past tyranny by the lawmakers? The evidence is not impressive. In the entire history of the Court there is not one case arising under the First Amendment in which the Court has held federal legislation unconstitutional. If we turn from these fundamental liberties of religion, speech, press and assembly, we do find a handful of cases—something less than ten—arising under Amendments Four to Seven in which the Court has declared acts unconstitutional that might properly be regarded as involving rather basic liberties.[13] An inspection of these cases leaves the impression that, in all of them, the lawmakers and the Court were not very far apart; moreover, it is doubtful that the fundamental conditions of liberty in this country have been altered by more than a hair's breadth as a result of these decisions. However, let us give the Court its due; it is little enough.

Over against these decisions we must put the fifteen or so cases in which the Court used the protections of the Fifth, Thirteenth, Fourteenth and Fifteenth Amendments to preserve the rights and liberties of a relatively privileged group at the expense of the rights and liberties of a submerged group: chiefly slaveholders at the expense of slaves,[14] white people at the expense of colored people,[15] and property holders at the expense of wage earners and other groups.[16] These cases, unlike the relatively innocuous ones of the preceding set, all involved liberties of genuinely fundamental importance, where an opposite policy would have meant thoroughly basic shifts in the distribution of rights, liberties, and opportunities in the United States— where, moreover, the policies sustained by the Court's action have since been repudiated in every civilized nation of the Western world, including our own. Yet, if our earlier argument is correct, it is futile—precisely because the basic distribution of privilege *was* at issue—to suppose that the Court could have possibly acted much differently in these areas of policy from the way in which it did in fact act.

Thus the role of the Court as a policy-making institution is not simple; and it is an error to suppose that its functions can be either described or appraised by means of simple concepts drawn from democratic or moral theory. It is possible, nonetheless, to derive a few general conclusions about the Court's role as a policy-making institution.

National politics in the United States, as in other stable democracies, is dominated by relatively cohesive alliances that endure for long periods of time. One recalls the Jeffersonian alliance, the Jacksonian, the extraordinarily long-lived Republican dominance of the post-Civil War years, and the New Deal alliance shaped by Franklin Roosevelt. Each is marked by a break with past policies, a period of intense struggle, followed by consolidation, and finally decay and disintegration of the alliance.

---

13   The candidates for this category would appear to be Boyd v. United States, 116 U.S. 616 (1886); Rassmussen v. United States, 197 U.S. 516 (1905): Wong Wing v. United States, 163 U.S. 228 (1896); United States v. Moreland, 258 U.S. 433 (1922): Kirby v. United States, 174 U.S. 47 (1899); United States v. Cohen Grocery Co., 255 U.S. 81 (1921); Weeds, Inc. v. United States, 255 U.S. 109 (1921); Justices of the Supreme Court v. United States ex rel. Murray, 9 Wall. (U.S.) 274 (1870): United States ex rel. Toth v. Quarles, 350 U.S. 11 (1955).

14   Dred Scott v. Sandford, 19 How. (U.S.) 393 (1857).

15   United States v. Reese, 92 U.S. 214 (1876): United States v. Harris, 106 U.S. 629 (1883); United States v. Stanley (Civil Rights Cases), 109 U.S. 3 (1883); Baldwin v. Franks, 120 U.S. 678 (1887); James v. Bowman, 190 U.S. 127 (1903); Hodges v. United States, 203 U.S. 1 (1906); Butts v. Merchants & Miners Transportation Co., 230 U.S. 126 (1913).

16   Monongahela Navigation Co. v. United States, 148 U.S. 312 (1893); Adair v. United States, 208 U.S. 161 (1908); Adkins v. Children's Hospital, 261 U.S. 525 (1923): Nichols v. Coolidge, 274 U.S. 531 (1927); Untermyer v. Anderson, 276 U.S. 440 (1928); Heiner v. Donnan, 285 U.S. 312 (1932); Louisville Joint Stock Land Bank v. Radford, 295 U.S. 555 (1935).

Except for short-lived transitional periods when the old alliance is disintegrating and the new one is struggling to take control of political institutions, the Supreme Court is inevitably a part of the dominant national alliance. As an element in the political leadership of the dominant alliance, the Court of course supports the major policies of the alliance. By itself, the Court is almost powerless to affect the course of national policy. In the absence of substantial agreement within the alliance, an attempt by the Court to make national policy is likely to lead to disaster, as the *Dred Scott* decision and the early New Deal cases demonstrate. Conceivably, the cases of the last three decades involving the freedom of Negroes, culminating in the now famous decision on school integration, are exceptions to this generalization; I shall have more to say about them in a moment.

The Supreme Court is not, however, simply an *agent* of the alliance. It is an essential part of the political leadership and possesses some bases of power of its own, the most important of which is the unique legitimacy attributed to its interpretations of the Constitution. This legitimacy the Court jeopardizes if it flagrantly opposes the major policies of the dominant alliance; such a course of action, as we have seen, is one in which the Court will not normally be tempted to engage.

It follows that within the somewhat narrow limits set by the basic policy goals of the dominant alliance, the Court *can* make national policy. Its discretion, then, is not unlike that of a powerful committee chairman in Congress who cannot, generally speaking, nullify the basic policies substantially agreed on by the rest of the dominant leadership, but who can, within these limits, often determine important questions of timing, effectiveness, and subordinate policy. Thus the Court is least effective against a current lawmaking majority—and evidently least inclined to act. It is most effective when it sets the bounds of policy for officials, agencies, state governments or even regions, a task that has come to occupy a very large part of the Court's business.[17]

---

17 "Constitutional law and cases with constitutional undertones are of course still very important, with almost one-fourth of the cases in which written opinions were filed [in the two most recent terms] involving such questions. Review of administrative action ... constitutes the largest category of the Court's work, comprising one-third of the total cases decided on the merits. The remaining ... categories of litigation ... all involve largely public law questions." Frankfurter, op. cit. supra note 1, at 793.

Miranda v. Arizona

[...]

WARREN, C.J., OPINION OF THE COURT

MR. CHIEF JUSTICE WARREN delivered the opinion of the Court.

The cases before us raise questions which go to the roots of our concepts of American criminal jurisprudence: the restraints society must observe consistent with the Federal Constitution in prosecuting individuals for crime. More specifically, we deal with the admissibility of statements obtained from an individual who is subjected to custodial police interrogation and the necessity for procedures which assure that the individual is accorded his privilege under the Fifth Amendment to the Constitution not to be compelled to incriminate himself.

We dealt with certain phases of this problem recently in *Escobedo v. Illinois,* 378 U.S. 478 [...] (1964). There, as in the four cases before us, law enforcement officials took the defendant into custody and interrogated him in a police station for the purpose of obtaining a confession. The police did not effectively advise him of his right to remain silent or of his right to consult with his attorney. Rather, they confronted him with an alleged accomplice who accused him of having perpetrated a murder. When the defendant denied the accusation and said "I didn't shoot Manuel, you did it," they handcuffed him and took him to an interrogation room. There, while handcuffed and standing, he was questioned for four hours until he confessed. During this interrogation, the police denied his request to speak to his attorney, and they prevented his retained attorney, who had come to the police station, from consulting with him. At his trial, the State, over his objection, introduced the confession against him. We held that the statements thus made were constitutionally inadmissible.

This case has been the subject of judicial interpretation and spirited legal debate since it was decided two years ago. Both state and federal courts, in assessing its implications, have arrived at varying conclusions. A wealth of scholarly material has been written tracing its ramifications and underpinnings. Police and prosecutor have speculated on its range and desirability. We granted certiorari in these cases, 382 U.S. 924 [...], 925, 937, in order further to explore some facets of the problems thus exposed of applying the privilege against self-incrimination to in-custody interrogation, and to give concrete constitutional guidelines for law enforcement agencies and courts to follow.

We start here, as we did in *Escobedo,* with the premise that our holding is not an innovation in our jurisprudence, but is an application of principles long recognized and applied in other settings. We have undertaken a thorough reexamination of the *Escobedo* decision and the principles it announced, and we reaffirm it. That case was but an explication of basic rights that are enshrined in our Constitution—that "No person ... shall be compelled in any criminal case to be a witness against himself," and that "the accused shall ... have the Assistance of Counsel"—rights which were put in jeopardy in that case through official overbearing. These precious rights were fixed in our Constitution only after centuries of persecution and struggle. And, in the words of Chief Justice Marshall, they were secured "for ages to come, and ... designed to approach immortality as nearly as human institutions can approach it," *Cohens v. Virginia,* 6 Wheat. 264, 387 (1821).

[...]

The constitutional issue we decide in each of these cases is the admissibility of statements obtained from a defendant questioned while in custody or otherwise deprived of his freedom of action in any significant way. In each, the defendant was questioned by police officers, detectives, or a prosecuting attorney in a room in which he was cut off from the outside world. In none of these cases was the defendant given a full and effective warning of his rights at the outset of the interrogation process. In all the cases, the questioning elicited oral admissions, and in three of them, signed statements as well which were admitted at their trials. They all thus share salient features—incommunicado interrogation of individuals in a police-dominated atmosphere, resulting in self-incriminating statements without full warnings of constitutional rights.

An understanding of the nature and setting of this in-custody interrogation is essential to our decisions today. The difficulty in depicting what transpires at such interrogations stems from the fact that, in this country, they have largely taken place incommunicado. From extensive factual studies undertaken in the early 1930's, including the famous Wickersham Report to Congress by a Presidential Commission, it is clear that police violence and the "third degree" flourished at that time. In a series of cases decided by this Court long after these studies, the police resorted to physical brutality—beating, hanging, whipping—and to sustained and protracted questioning incommunicado in order to extort confessions. The Commission on Civil Rights in 1961 found much evidence to indicate that "some policemen still resort to physical force to obtain confessions," 1961 Common on Civil Rights Rep. Justice, pt. 5, 17. The use of physical brutality and violence is not, unfortunately, relegated to the past or to any part of the country. Only recently in Kings County, New York, the police brutally beat, kicked and placed lighted cigarette butts on the back of a potential witness under interrogation for the purpose of securing a statement incriminating a third party. *People v. Portelli,* 15 N.Y.2d 235, 205 N.E.2d 857, 257 N.Y.S.2d 931 (1965).

The examples given above are undoubtedly the exception now, but they are sufficiently widespread to be the object of concern. Unless a proper limitation upon custodial interrogation is achieved—such as these decisions will advance—there can be no assurance that practices of this nature will be eradicated in the foreseeable future. The conclusion of the Wickersham Commission Report, made over 30 years ago, is still pertinent:

To the contention that the third degree is necessary to get the facts, the reporters aptly reply in the language of the present Lord Chancellor of England (Lord Sankey):

It is not admissible to do a great right by doing a little wrong. ... It is not sufficient to do justice by obtaining a proper result by irregular or improper means.

Not only does the use of the third degree involve a flagrant violation of law by the officers of the law, but it involves also the dangers of false confessions, and it tends to make police and prosecutors less zealous in the search for objective evidence. As the New York prosecutor quoted in the report said, "It is a short-cut, and makes the police lazy and unenterprising." Or, as another official quoted remarked: "If you use your fists, you are not so likely to use your wits." We agree with the conclusion expressed in the report, that

The third degree brutalizes the police, hardens the prisoner against society, and lowers the esteem in which the administration of Justice is held by the public.

IV National Commission on Law Observance and Enforcement, Report on Lawlessness in Law Enforcement 5 (1931).

Again we stress that the modern practice of in-custody interrogation is psychologically, rather than physically, oriented. As we have stated before,

Since *Chambers v. Florida*, 309 U.S. 227 [...], this Court has recognized that coercion can be mental as well as physical, and that the blood of the accused is not the only hallmark of an unconstitutional inquisition.

Blackburn v. Alabama, 361 U.S. 199 [...], 206 (1960). Interrogation still takes place in privacy. Privacy results in secrecy, and this, in turn, results in a gap in our knowledge as to what, in fact, goes on in the interrogation rooms. A valuable source of information about present police practices, however, may be found in various police manuals and texts which document procedures employed with success in the past, and which recommend various other effective tactics.

These texts are used by law enforcement agencies themselves as guides.It should be noted that these texts professedly present the most enlightened and effective means presently used to obtain statements through custodial interrogation. By considering these texts and other data, it is possible to describe procedures observed and noted around the country.

The officers are told by the manuals that the principal psychological factor contributing to a successful interrogation is *privacy*—being alone with the person under interrogation.

The efficacy of this tactic has been explained as follows:

If at all practicable, the interrogation should take place in the investigator's office or at least in a room of his own choice. The subject should be deprived of every psychological advantage. In his own home, he may be confident, indignant, or recalcitrant. He is more keenly aware of his rights and more reluctant to tell of his indiscretions or criminal behavior within the walls of his home. Moreover his family and other friends are nearby, their presence lending moral support. In his own office, the investigator possesses all the advantages. The atmosphere suggests the invincibility of the forces of the law.

To highlight the isolation and unfamiliar surroundings, the manuals instruct the police to display an air of confidence in the suspect's guilt and, from outward appearance, to maintain only an interest in confirming certain details. The guilt of the subject is to be posited as a fact. The interrogator should direct his comments toward the reasons why the subject committed the act, rather than court failure by asking the subject whether he did it. Like other men, perhaps the subject has had a bad family life, had an unhappy childhood, had too much to drink, had an unrequited desire for women. The officers are instructed to minimize the moral seriousness of the offense, to cast blame on the victim or on society. These tactics are designed to put the subject in a psychological state where his story is but an elaboration of what the police purport to know already—that he is guilty. Explanations to the contrary are dismissed and discouraged.

The texts thus stress that the major qualities an interrogator should possess are patience and perseverance. One writer describes the efficacy of these characteristics in this manner:

In the preceding paragraphs, emphasis has been placed on kindness and stratagems. The investigator will, however, encounter many situations where the sheer weight of his personality will be the deciding factor. Where emotional appeals and tricks are employed to no avail, he must rely on an oppressive atmosphere of dogged persistence. He must interrogate steadily and without relent, leaving the subject no prospect of surcease. He must dominate his subject and overwhelm him with his inexorable will to obtain the truth. He should interrogate for a spell of several hours, pausing only for the subject's necessities in acknowledgment of the need to avoid a charge of duress that can be technically substantiated. In a serious case, the interrogation may continue for days, with the required intervals for food and sleep, but with no respite from the atmosphere of domination. It is possible in this way to induce the subject to talk without resorting to duress or coercion. The method should be used only when the guilt of the subject appears highly probable.

The manuals suggest that the suspect be offered legal excuses for his actions in order to obtain an initial admission of guilt. Where there is a suspected revenge killing, for example, the interrogator may say:

Joe, you probably didn't go out looking for this fellow with the purpose of shooting him. My guess is, however, that you expected something from him, and that's why you carried a gun—for your own protection. You knew him for what he was, no good. Then when you met him, he probably started using foul, abusive language and he gave some indication that he was about to pull a gun on you, and that's when you had to act to save your own life. That's about it, isn't it, Joe?

Having then obtained the admission of shooting, the interrogator is advised to refer to circumstantial evidence which negates the self-defense explanation. This should enable him to secure the entire story. One text notes that,

Even if he fails to do so, the inconsistency between the subject's original denial of the shooting and his present admission of at least doing the shooting will serve to deprive him of a self-defense "out" at the time of trial.

When the techniques described above prove unavailing, the texts recommend they be alternated with a show of some hostility. One ploy often used has been termed the "friendly-unfriendly," or the "Mutt and Jeff" act:

In this technique, two agents are employed. Mutt, the relentless investigator, who knows the subject is guilty and is not going to waste any time. He's sent a dozen men away for this crime, and he's going to send the subject away for the full term. Jeff, on the other hand, is obviously a kindhearted man. He has a family himself. He has a brother who was involved in a little scrape like this. He disapproves of Mutt and his tactics, and will arrange to get him off the case if the subject will cooperate. He can't hold Mutt off for very long. The subject would be wise to make a quick decision. The technique is applied by having both investigators present while Mutt acts out his role. Jeff may stand by quietly and demur at some of Mutt's tactics. When Jeff makes his plea for cooperation, Mutt is not present in the room.

The interrogators sometimes are instructed to induce a confession out of trickery. The technique here is quite effective in crimes which require identification or which run in series. In the identification situation, the interrogator may take a break in his questioning to place the subject among a group of men in a line-up.

The witness or complainant (previously coached, if necessary) studies the line-up and confidently points out the subject as the guilty party.

Then the questioning resumes "as though there were now no doubt about the guilt of the subject." A variation on this technique is called the "reverse line-up":

The accused is placed in a line-up, but this time he is identified by several fictitious witnesses or victims who associated him with different offenses. It is expected that the subject will become desperate and confess to the offense under investigation in order to escape from the false accusations.

The manuals also contain instructions for police on how to handle the individual who refuses to discuss the matter entirely, or who asks for an attorney or relatives. The examiner is to concede him the right to remain silent.

This usually has a very undermining effect. First of all, he is disappointed in his expectation of an unfavorable reaction on the part of the interrogator. Secondly, a concession of this right to remain silent impresses the subject with the apparent fairness of his interrogator.

After this psychological conditioning, however, the officer is told to point out the incriminating significance of the suspect's refusal to talk:

Joe, you have a right to remain silent. That's your privilege, and I'm the last person in the world who'll try to take it away from you. If that's the way you want to leave this, O. K. But let me ask you this. Suppose you were in my shoes, and I were in yours, and you called me in to ask me about this, and I told you, "I don't want to answer any of your questions." You'd think I had something to hide, and you'd probably be right in thinking that. That's exactly what I'll have to think about you, and so will everybody else. So let's sit here and talk this whole thing over.

Few will persist in their initial refusal to talk, it is said, if this monologue is employed correctly.

In the event that the subject wishes to speak to a relative or an attorney, the following advice is tendered:

[T]he interrogator should respond by suggesting that the subject first tell the truth to the interrogator himself, rather than get anyone else involved in the matter. If the request is for an attorney, the interrogator may suggest that the subject save himself or his family the expense of any such professional service, particularly if he is innocent of the offense under investigation. The interrogator may also add, "Joe, I'm only looking for the truth, and if you're telling the truth, that's it. You can handle this by yourself."

From these representative samples of interrogation techniques, the setting prescribed by the manuals and observed in practice becomes clear. In essence, it is this: to be alone with the subject is essential to prevent distraction and to deprive him of any outside support. The aura of confidence in his guilt undermines his will to resist. He merely confirms the preconceived story the police seek to have him describe. Patience and persistence, at times relentless questioning, are employed. To obtain a confession, the interrogator must "patiently maneuver himself or his quarry into a position from which the desired objective may be attained." When normal procedures fail to produce the needed result, the police may resort to deceptive stratagems such as giving false legal advice. It is important to keep the subject off balance, for example, by trading on his insecurity about himself or his surroundings. The police then persuade, trick, or cajole him out of exercising his constitutional rights.

Even without employing brutality, the "third degree" or the specific stratagems described above, the very fact of custodial interrogation exacts a heavy toll on individual liberty, and trades on the weakness of individuals. This fact may be illustrated simply by referring to three confession cases decided by this Court in the Term immediately preceding our *Escobedo* decision. In *Townsend v. Sain,* 372 U.S. 293 [...] (1963), the defendant was a 19-year-old heroin addict, described as a "near mental defective," *id.* at 307–310. The defendant in *Lynumn v. Illinois,* 372 U.S. 528 [...] (1963), was a woman who confessed to the arresting officer after being importuned to "cooperate" in order to prevent her children from being taken by relief authorities. This Court, as in those cases, reversed the conviction of a defendant in *Haynes v. Washington,* 373 U.S. 503 [...] (1963), whose persistent request during his interrogation was to phone his wife or attorney. In other settings, these individuals might have exercised their constitutional rights. In the incommunicado police-dominated atmosphere, they succumbed.

In the cases before us today, given this background, we concern ourselves primarily with this interrogation atmosphere and the evils it can bring. In No. 759, *Miranda v. Arizona,* the police arrested the defendant and took him to a special interrogation room, where they secured a confession. In No. 760, *Vignera v. New York,* the defendant made oral admissions to the police after interrogation in the afternoon, and then signed an inculpatory statement upon being questioned by an assistant district attorney later the same evening. In No. 761, *Westover v. United States,* the defendant was handed over to the Federal Bureau of Investigation by local authorities after they had detained and interrogated him for a lengthy period, both at night and the following morning. After some two hours of questioning, the federal officers had obtained signed statements from the defendant. Lastly, in No. 584, *California v. Stewart,* the local police held the defendant five days in the station and interrogated him on nine separate occasions before they secured his inculpatory statement.

In these cases, we might not find the defendants' statements to have been involuntary in traditional terms. Our concern for adequate safeguards to protect precious Fifth Amendment rights is, of course, not lessened in the slightest. In each of the cases, the defendant was thrust into an unfamiliar atmosphere and run through menacing police interrogation procedures. The potentiality for compulsion is forcefully apparent, for example, in *Miranda,* where the indigent Mexican defendant was a seriously disturbed individual with pronounced sexual fantasies, and in *Stewart,* in which the defendant was an indigent Los Angeles Negro who had dropped out of school in the sixth grade. To be sure, the records do not evince overt physical coercion or patent psychological ploys. The fact remains that in none of these cases did the officers undertake to afford appropriate safeguards at the outset of the interrogation to insure that the statements were truly the product of free choice.

It is obvious that such an interrogation environment is created for no purpose other than to subjugate the individual to the will of his examiner. This atmosphere carries its own badge of intimidation. To be sure, this is not physical intimidation, but it is equally destructive of human dignity. The current practice of incommunicado interrogation is at odds with one of our Nation's most cherished principles—that the individual may not be compelled to incriminate himself. Unless adequate protective devices are employed to dispel the compulsion inherent in custodial surroundings, no statement obtained from the defendant can truly be the product of his free choice.

We sometimes forget how long it has taken to establish the privilege against self-incrimination, the sources from which it came, and the fervor with which it was defended. Its roots go back into ancient times.

[...]

Thus, we may view the historical development of the privilege as one which groped for the proper scope of governmental power over the citizen. As a "noble principle often transcends its origins," the privilege has come rightfully to be recognized in part as an individual's substantive right, a "right to a private enclave where he may lead a private life. That right is the hallmark of our democracy." *United*

States v. Grunewald, 233 F.2d 556, 579, 581–582 (Frank, J., dissenting), *rav'd,* 353 U.S. 391 [...] (1957). We have recently noted that the privilege against self-incrimination—the essential mainstay of our adversary system—is founded on a complex of values, *Murphy v. Waterfront Common,* 378 U.S. 52 [...], 55–57, n. 5 (1964); *Tehan v. Shott,* 382 U.S. 406 [...], 414–415, n. 12 (1966). All these policies point to one overriding thought: the constitutional foundation underlying the privilege is the respect a government—state or federal—must accord to the dignity and integrity of its citizens. To maintain a "fair state-individual balance," to require the government "to shoulder the entire load," 8 Wigmore, Evidence 317 (McNaughton rev.1961), to respect the inviolability of the human personality, our accusatory system of criminal justice demands that the government seeking to punish an individual produce the evidence against him by its own independent labors, rather than by the cruel, simple expedient of compelling it from his own mouth. *Chambers v. Florida,* 309 U.S. 227 [...], 235–238 (1940). In sum, the privilege is fulfilled only when the person is guaranteed the right "to remain silent unless he chooses to speak in the unfettered exercise of his own will."*Malloy v. Hogan,* 378 U.S. 1 [...], 8 (1964).

The question in these cases is whether the privilege is fully applicable during a period of custodial interrogation. In this Court, the privilege has consistently been accorded a liberal construction. *Albertson v. SACB,* 382 U.S. 70 [...], 81 (1965); *Hoffman v. United States,* 341 U.S. 479 [...], 486 (1951); *Arndstein v. McCarthy,* 254 U.S. 71 ([...], 72–73 (1920); *Counselman v. Hitchcock,* 142 U.S. 547 [...], 562 (1892). We are satisfied that all the principles embodied in the privilege apply to informal compulsion exerted by law enforcement officers during in-custody questioning. An individual swept from familiar surroundings into police custody, surrounded by antagonistic forces, and subjected to the techniques of persuasion described above cannot be otherwise than under compulsion to speak. As a practical matter, the compulsion to speak in the isolated setting of the police station may well be greater than in courts or other official investigations, where there are often impartial observers to guard against intimidation or trickery.

[...] In addition to the expansive historical development of the privilege and the sound policies which have nurtured its evolution, judicial precedent thus clearly establishes its application to incommunicado interrogation. In fact, the Government concedes this point as well established in No. 761, *Westover v. United States,* stating:

We have no doubt ... that it is possible for a suspect's Fifth Amendment right to be violated during in-custody questioning by a law enforcement officer.

Today, then, there can be no doubt that the Fifth Amendment privilege is available outside of criminal court proceedings, and serves to protect persons in all settings in which their freedom of action is curtailed in any significant way from being compelled to incriminate themselves. We have concluded that, without proper safeguards, the process of in-custody interrogation of persons suspected or accused of crime contains inherently compelling pressures which work to undermine the individual's will to resist and to compel him to speak where he would not otherwise do so freely. In order to combat these pressures and to permit a full opportunity to exercise the privilege against self-incrimination, the accused must be adequately and effectively apprised of his rights, and the exercise of those rights must be fully honored.

It is impossible for us to foresee the potential alternatives for protecting the privilege which might be devised by Congress or the States in the exercise of their creative rulemaking capacities. Therefore, we cannot say that the Constitution necessarily requires adherence to any particular solution for the inherent compulsions of the interrogation process as it is presently conducted. Our decision in no way creates a constitutional straitjacket which will handicap sound efforts at reform, nor is it intended to have this effect. We encourage Congress and the States to continue their laudable search for increasingly effective ways of protecting the rights of the individual while promoting efficient enforcement of our criminal laws. However, unless we are shown other procedures which are at least as effective in apprising accused persons of their right of silence and in assuring a continuous opportunity to exercise it, the following safeguards must be observed.

At the outset, if a person in custody is to be subjected to interrogation, he must first be informed in clear and unequivocal terms that he has the right to remain silent. For those unaware of the privilege, the warning is needed simply to make them aware of it—the threshold requirement for an intelligent decision as to its exercise. More important, such a warning is an absolute prerequisite in overcoming the inherent pressures of the interrogation atmosphere. It is not just the subnormal or woefully ignorant who succumb to an interrogator's imprecations, whether implied or expressly stated, that the interrogation will continue until a confession is obtained or that silence in the face of accusation is itself damning, and will bode ill when presented to a jury. Further, the warning will show the individual that his interrogators are prepared to recognize his privilege should he choose to exercise it.

The Fifth Amendment privilege is so fundamental to our system of constitutional rule, and the expedient of giving an adequate warning as to the availability of the privilege so simple, we will not pause to inquire in individual cases whether the defendant was aware of his rights without a warning being given. Assessments of the knowledge the defendant possessed, based on information as to his age, education, intelligence, or prior contact with authorities, can never be more than speculation; a warning is a clear-cut fact. More important, whatever the background of the person interrogated, a warning at the time of the interrogation is indispensable to overcome its pressures and to insure that the individual knows he is free to exercise the privilege at that point in time.

The warning of the right to remain silent must be accompanied by the explanation that anything said can and will be used against the individual in court. This warning is needed in order to make him aware not only of the privilege, but also of the consequences of forgoing it. It is only through an awareness of these consequences that there can be any assurance of real understanding and intelligent exercise of the privilege. Moreover, this warning may serve to make the individual more acutely aware that he is faced with a phase of the adversary system—that he is not in the presence of persons acting solely in his interest.

The circumstances surrounding in-custody interrogation can operate very quickly to overbear the will of one merely made aware of his privilege by his interrogators. Therefore, the right to have counsel present at the interrogation is indispensable to the protection of the Fifth Amendment privilege under the system we delineate today. Our aim is to assure that the individual's right to choose between silence and speech remains unfettered throughout the interrogation process. A once-stated warning, delivered by those who will conduct the interrogation, cannot itself suffice to that end among those who most require knowledge of their rights. A mere warning given by the interrogators is not alone sufficient to accomplish that end. Prosecutors themselves claim that the admonishment of the right to remain silent, without more, "will benefit only the recidivist and the professional." Brief for the National District Attorneys Association as *amicus curiae,* p. 14. Even preliminary advice given to the accused by his own attorney can be swiftly overcome by the secret interrogation process. *Cf. Escobedo v. Illinois,* 378 U.S. 478 [...], 485, n. 5. Thus, the need for counsel to protect the Fifth Amendment privilege comprehends not merely a right to consult with counsel prior to questioning, but also to have counsel present during any questioning if the defendant so desires.

The presence of counsel at the interrogation may serve several significant subsidiary functions, as well. If the accused decides to talk to his interrogators, the assistance of counsel can mitigate the dangers of untrustworthiness. With a lawyer present, the likelihood that the police will practice coercion is reduced, and, if coercion is nevertheless exercised, the lawyer can testify to it in court. The presence of a lawyer can also help to guarantee that the accused gives a fully accurate statement to the police, and that the statement is rightly reported by the prosecution at trial. *See Crooker v. California*, 357 U.S. 433 [...], 443–448 (1958) (DOUGLAS, J., dissenting).

An individual need not make a pre-interrogation request for a lawyer. While such request affirmatively secures his right to have one, his failure to ask for a lawyer does not constitute a waiver. No effective waiver of the right to counsel during interrogation can be recognized unless specifically made after the warnings we here delineate have been given. The accused who does not know his rights and therefore does not make a request may be the person who most needs counsel. As the California Supreme Court has aptly put it:

Finally, we must recognize that the imposition of the requirement for the request would discriminate against the defendant who does not know his rights. The defendant who does not ask for counsel is the very defendant who most needs counsel. We cannot penalize a defendant who, not understanding his constitutional rights, does not make the formal request, and, by such failure, demonstrates his helplessness. To require the request would be to favor the defendant whose sophistication or status had fortuitously prompted him to make it.

People v. Dorado, 62 Cal.2d 338, 351, 398 P.2d 361, 369–370, 42 Cal.Rptr. 169, 177–178 (1965) (Tobriner, J.). In *Carnley v. Cochran*, 369 U.S. 506 [...], 513 (1962), we stated:

[I]t is settled that, where the assistance of counsel is a constitutional requisite, the right to be furnished counsel does not depend on a request.

This proposition applies with equal force in the context of providing counsel to protect an accused's Fifth Amendment privilege in the face of interrogation.[n39] Although the role of counsel at trial differs from the role during interrogation, the differences are not relevant to the question whether a request is a prerequisite.

Accordingly, we hold that an individual held for interrogation must be clearly informed that he has the right to consult with a lawyer and to have the lawyer with him during interrogation under the system for protecting the privilege we delineate today. As with the warnings of the right to remain silent and that anything stated can be used in evidence against him, this warning is an absolute prerequisite to interrogation. No amount of circumstantial evidence that the person may have been aware of this right will suffice to stand in its stead. Only through such a warning is there ascertainable assurance that the accused was aware of this right.

If an individual indicates that he wishes the assistance of counsel before any interrogation occurs, the authorities cannot rationally ignore or deny his request on the basis that the individual does not have or cannot afford a retained attorney. The financial ability of the individual has no relationship to the scope of the rights involved here. The privilege against self-incrimination secured by the Constitution applies to all individuals. The need for counsel in order to protect the privilege exists for the indigent as well as the affluent. In fact, were we to limit these constitutional rights to those who can retain an attorney, our decisions today would be of little significance. The cases before us, as well as the vast majority of confession cases with which we have dealt in the past, involve those unable to retain counsel.[n40] While authorities are not required to relieve the accused of his poverty, they have the obligation not to take advantage of indigence in the administration of justice. Denial of counsel to the indigent at the time of interrogation while allowing an attorney to those who can afford one would be no more supportable by reason or logic than the similar situation at trial and on appeal struck down in *Gideon v. Wainwright,* 372 U.S. 335 [...] (1963), and *Douglas v. California,* 372 U.S. 353 [...] (1963).

In order fully to apprise a person interrogated of the extent of his rights under this system, then, it is necessary to warn him not only that he has the right to consult with an attorney, but also that, if he is indigent, a lawyer will be appointed to represent him. Without this additional warning, the admonition of the right to consult with counsel would often be understood as meaning only that he can consult with a lawyer if he has one or has the funds to obtain one. The warning of a right to counsel would be hollow if not couched in terms that would convey to the indigent—the person most often subjected to interrogation—the knowledge that he too has a right to have counsel present.[n42] As with the warnings of the right to remain silent and of the general right to counsel, only by effective and express explanation to the indigent of this right can there be assurance that he was truly in a position to exercise it.[n43]

Once warnings have been given, the subsequent procedure is clear. If the individual indicates in any manner, at any time prior to or during questioning, that he wishes to remain silent, the interrogation must cease. At this point, he has shown that he intends to exercise his Fifth Amendment privilege; any statement taken after the person invokes his privilege cannot be other than the product of compulsion, subtle or otherwise. Without the right to cut off questioning, the setting of in-custody interrogation operates on the individual to overcome free choice in producing a statement after the privilege has been once invoked. If the individual states that he wants an attorney, the interrogation must cease until an attorney is present. At that time, the individual must have an opportunity to confer with the attorney and to have him present during any subsequent questioning. If the individual cannot obtain an attorney and he indicates that he wants one before speaking to police, they must respect his decision to remain silent.

This does not mean, as some have suggested, that each police station must have a "station house lawyer" present at all times to advise prisoners. It does mean, however, that, if police propose to interrogate a person, they must make known to him that he is entitled to a lawyer and that, if he cannot afford one, a lawyer will be provided for him prior to any interrogation. If authorities conclude that they will not provide counsel during a reasonable period of time in which investigation in the field is carried out, they may refrain from doing so without violating the person's Fifth Amendment privilege so long as they do not question him during that time.

If the interrogation continues without the presence of an attorney and a statement is taken, a heavy burden rests on the government to demonstrate that the defendant knowingly and intelligently waived his privilege against self-incrimination and his right to retained or appointed counsel. *Escobedo v. Illinois,* 378 U.S. 478 [...], 490, n. 14. This Court has always set high standards of proof for the waiver of constitutional rights, *Johnson v. Zerbst,* 304 U.S. 458 [...] (1938), and we reassert these standards as applied to in-custody interrogation. Since the State is responsible for establishing the isolated circumstances under which the interrogation takes place, and has the only means of making available corroborated evidence of warnings given during incommunicado interrogation, the burden is rightly on its shoulders.

An express statement that the individual is willing to make a statement and does not want an attorney, followed closely by a statement, could constitute a waiver. But a valid waiver will not be presumed simply from the silence of the accused after warnings are given, or simply from the fact that a confession was, in fact, eventually obtained. A statement we made in *Carnley v. Cochran,* 369 U.S. 506 [...], 516 (1962), is applicable here:

Presuming waiver from a silent record is impermissible. The record must show, or there must be an allegation and evidence which show, that an accused was offered counsel but intelligently and understandingly rejected the offer. Anything less is not waiver.

See also Glasser v. United States, 315 U.S. 60 [...] (1942). Moreover, where in-custody interrogation is involved, there is no room for the contention that the privilege is waived if the individual answers some questions or gives some information on his own prior to invoking his right to remain silent when interrogated.

Whatever the testimony of the authorities as to waiver of rights by an accused, the fact of lengthy interrogation or incommunicado incarceration before a statement is made is strong evidence that the accused did not validly waive his rights. In these circumstances, the fact that the individual eventually made a statement is consistent with the conclusion that the compelling influence of the interrogation finally forced him to do so. It is inconsistent with any notion of a voluntary relinquishment of the privilege. Moreover, any evidence that the accused was threatened, tricked, or cajoled into a waiver will, of course, show that the defendant did not voluntarily waive his privilege. The requirement of warnings and waiver of rights is a fundamental with respect to the Fifth Amendment privilege, and not simply a preliminary ritual to existing methods of interrogation.

[...]

The principles announced today deal with the protection which must be given to the privilege against self-incrimination when the individual is first subjected to police interrogation while in custody at the station or otherwise deprived of his freedom of action in any significant way. It is at this point that our adversary system of criminal proceedings commences, distinguishing itself at the outset from the inquisitorial system recognized in some countries. Under the system of warnings we delineate today, or under any other system which may be devised and found effective, the safeguards to be erected about the privilege must come into play at this point.

Our decision is not intended to hamper the traditional function of police officers in investigating crime. *See Escobedo v. Illinois*, 378 U.S. 478 [...], 492. When an individual is in custody on probable cause, the police may, of course, seek out evidence in the field to be used at trial against him. Such investigation may include inquiry of persons not under restraint. General on-the-scene questioning as to facts surrounding a crime or other general questioning of citizens in the factfinding process is not affected by our holding. It is an act of responsible citizenship for individuals to give whatever information they may have to aid in law enforcement. In such situations, the compelling atmosphere inherent in the process of in-custody interrogation is not necessarily present.

In dealing with statements obtained through interrogation, we do not purport to find all confessions inadmissible. Confessions remain a proper element in law enforcement. Any statement given freely and voluntarily without any compelling influences is, of course, admissible in evidence. The fundamental import of the privilege while an individual is in custody is not whether he is allowed to talk to the police without the benefit of warnings and counsel, but whether he can be interrogated. There is no requirement that police stop a person who enters a police station and states that he wishes to confess to a crime, or a person who calls the police to offer a confession or any other statement he desires to make. Volunteered statements of any kind are not barred by the Fifth Amendment, and their admissibility is not affected by our holding today.

To summarize, we hold that, when an individual is taken into custody or otherwise deprived of his freedom by the authorities in any significant way and is subjected to questioning, the privilege against self-incrimination is jeopardized. Procedural safeguards must be employed to protect the privilege, and unless other fully effective means are adopted to notify the person of his right of silence and to assure that the exercise of the right will be scrupulously honored, the following measures are required. He must be warned prior to any questioning that he has the right to remain silent, that anything he says can be used against him in a court of law, that he has the right to the presence of an attorney, and that, if he cannot afford an attorney one will be appointed for him prior to any questioning if he so desires. Opportunity to exercise these rights must be afforded to him throughout the interrogation. After such warnings have been given, and such opportunity afforded him, the individual may knowingly and intelligently waive these rights and agree to answer questions or make a statement. But unless and until such warnings and waiver are demonstrated by the prosecution at trial, no evidence obtained as a result of interrogation can be used against him.

The Effects of Miranda v. Arizona

Embedded in Our National Culture?

George C. Thomas III and Richard A. Leo

In 1966, the Supreme Court sought to revolutionize the judicial oversight of police interrogation. Prior to *Miranda v. Arizona*, 384 U.S. 436 (1966), the Court had typically examined the facts of individual cases to determine whether police pressure had rendered the confession "involuntary" and thus inadmissible as a violation of the Fourteenth Amendment Due Process Clause. A confession was deemed involuntary when the "will" of the suspect was "overborne" by police interrogators' use of coercion or compulsion. The classic example is the deputy sheriff in *Brown v. Mississippi*, 297 U.S. 278 (1936), who used physical torture (beatings with studded belts, hanging one suspect from a tree) to obtain confessions. But coercion analysis is more difficult when the pressure is simply the length and intensity of the interrogation. Does thirty-two hours of sustained interrogation, followed a few days later by another ten hours, coerce the defendant's confession as a matter of law? No, the Court held in *Lisenba v. California*, 314 U.S. 219 (1941). But three years later in *Ashcraft v. Tennessee*, 322 U.S. 143 (1944), the Court held that thirty-six continuous hours of interrogation did coerce the confession in that case. A thin distinction can be made between the facts of the two cases, but drawing such a fine line does not provide much guidance for lower courts faced with a steady stream of confession cases, each of which has facts at least a little different from all the others.[1]

Eschewing this case-by-case method, *Miranda* created a presumption of compulsion that can be dispelled only if the suspect receives a set of warnings, as set out above. *Miranda* was a bold stroke, one that sent shock waves throughout the United States. Police and prosecutors claimed that few would confess in the face of these warnings and that many crimes would go unsolved (Baker 1983, pp. 243–44). As a result, dangerous criminals

---

1 Indeed, a distinction between internal preferences and external acts that seek to shape preferences might always be elusive (Seidman 1990), suggesting that legal coercion may almost be impossible to discern in many individual cases.

would be freed to prey upon the innocent. Congress viewed the crime rate in 1966 as already too high, and the prospect of *Miranda* pushing it higher caused grave concern (Kamisar 2000, pp. 894–99). On the floor of the United States Senate, Senator John McClellan pointed to a graph of the crime rate and said, "Look at it and weep for your country" (Cong. Rec. 114:14,146 [1968]). Even normally staid Supreme Court Justices came close to outrage in their dissenting opinions in *Miranda*. For example, Justice Byron White wrote near the end of his dissent: "In some unknown number of cases the Court's rule will return a killer, a rapist or other criminal to the streets and to the environment which produced him, to repeat his crime whenever it pleases him. As a consequence, there will not be a gain, but a loss, in human dignity. ... There is, of course, a saving factor: the next victims are uncertain, unnamed and unrepresented in this case" (*Miranda*, pp. 542–43 [White, J., dissenting]).

[...]

Today's *Miranda* is subtly but importantly different from the *Miranda* that the Supreme Court decided in 1966. The rationale has evolved from encouraging suspects to resist police interrogation to informing suspects that they have a right to resist. The Warren Court saw *Miranda* as an active participant in the interrogation room, a regime that changes the psychology of the encounter between suspect and interrogator. Today's version is closer to a passive administrative requirement to be gotten out of the way so that the suspect can "tell his side of the story" to the police. This evolution resulted in part from the Court tilting more toward the law enforcement side of the balance in the 1970s and 1980s, relaxing the *Miranda* doctrine in some key ways. In addition, the police adjusted to *Miranda* and learned how to comply in a way that minimizes the chance that the suspect will resist interrogation. As *Miranda* became increasingly passive, a piece of furniture in the interrogation room, police became less hostile to its strictures. Though it is unclear why the *Dickerson* challenge arose when it did, the Court's ultimate judgment was unsurprising (Kamisar 2000; Thomas 2000): as it now exists, the *Miranda* rule does not seriously obstruct law enforcement interests. Indeed, in operation *Miranda* might further law enforcement interests more than it does the interests of suspects.

[...]

The Miranda Impact Studies

In the three decades prior to *Miranda*, there had been relatively little field research on police interrogation practices in America (see Leo [1996*b*] for a review). It was thus hardly surprising that the Warren Court in 1966 relied on police training manuals—rather than empirical studies—to describe the techniques and methods of police interrogation in America. Emphasizing the absence of firsthand knowledge of actual police interrogation practices at the time, the Warren Court in *Miranda* noted that "interrogation still takes place in privacy. Privacy results in secrecy and this in turn results in a gap in our knowledge as to what in fact goes on in the interrogation room" (*Miranda*, p. 448).

FIRST GENERATION STUDIES, 1966–73

In the years immediately following the *Miranda* decision, scholars published approximately a dozen empirical studies that sought to fill this gap (Younger 1966*a*, 1966*b*; Griffiths and Ayres 1967; Seeburger and Wettick 1967; Wald et al. 1967; Medalie, Zeitz, and Alexander 1968; Robinson

1968; Leiken 1970; Milner 1971; Schaefer 1971; Stephens, Flanders, and Cannon 1972; Witt 1973; Neubauer 1974). Undertaken in a variety of locations (e.g., Pittsburgh; New Haven, Conn.; Washington, D.C.; Los Angeles; Denver; Madison, Wisc.; and elsewhere), these studies sought to identify and analyze police implementation of, and compliance with, the new *Miranda* requirements; police attitudes toward *Miranda;* the effect of the *Miranda* warning and waiver regime on police and suspect behavior during interrogation; and the impact of *Miranda* on confession, clearance, and conviction rates.

These first-generation *Miranda* impact studies relied on a variety of methodologies (participant observation, surveys, interviews, analysis of case files), each with its own strengths, weaknesses, and limitations. One of the earliest and most widely cited studies was conducted by Yale law students, who observed 127 live interrogations inside the New Haven Police Department during the summer of 1966 (Wald et al. 1967) and then compared their observations to data they reviewed from approximately 200 cases from 1960 to 1965 in the New Haven Police Department. The researchers found that while the detectives failed to read all or part of the required warnings to custodial suspects in the immediate aftermath of *Miranda*, they eventually began to comply with the letter (but not the spirit) of the new *Miranda* requirements. The quality of the warnings varied inversely with the strength of the evidence (the stronger the evidence, the worse the warnings) and directly with the seriousness of the offense, suggesting that detectives delivered more adequate warnings when failure to do so might jeopardize the admissibility of a highly valued confession.

Most of the suspects appeared unable to grasp the significance of their *Miranda* rights, thus undermining *Miranda*'s effect on a suspect's decision to answer police questions. Only a few suspects refused to speak to police or requested counsel prior to questioning, and in only 5 percent of the cases did the *Miranda* requirements adversely affect the ability of police to obtain a confession that the researchers judged necessary for conviction. In addition, the researchers noted that *Miranda* appeared to have little impact on police behavior during interrogation, since detectives continued to employ many of the psychological tactics of persuasion and manipulation that the Warren Court had deplored in *Miranda*. Wald and colleagues (1967) concluded that the interrogation process had become "considerably less hostile" from 1960 to 1966 and that *Miranda* does not substantially impede successful law enforcement.

In addition to participant observation, several of the early *Miranda* researchers relied on broad surveys of existing police practices to assess the impact of *Miranda* on the apprehension and prosecution of criminal suspects. Less than a month after *Miranda* was decided, Evelle Younger (1966*a*, 1966*b*) administered a survey to the members of the Los Angeles County District Attorneys' Office. In the previous year (1965), the same office had compiled a similar survey to gauge the effect of *People v. Dorado*, 398 P.2d 361 (Cal. 1965), a California Supreme Court case that anticipated *Miranda* because it required California law enforcement officers to warn custodial suspects of their rights to counsel and to remain silent. Comparing the results of these two surveys, Younger concluded that police officers began complying with *Miranda* immediately after it became law; that the required warnings did not reduce the percentage of admissions and confessions made to officers in cases that reached the complaint stage; and that *Miranda* requirements did not decrease the percentage of felony complaints issued by prosecutors or their success in prosecuting cases at the preliminary stage. As Younger pointed out, the confession rate—in cases in which police requested that felony complaints be issued—rose approximately 10 percent (from 40 percent to 50 percent) after *Miranda*!

In addition to participant observation, field research, and surveys of police practices, some early researchers attempted to study *Miranda*'s impact on the processes and outcomes of custodial interrogation by interviewing custodial suspects, detectives, and lawyers. In one such study, Lawrence Leiken (1970) interviewed fifty suspects inside the Denver County jail in 1968. Leiken found that Denver police typically read the *Miranda* warnings to each suspect from a standard advisement form that the suspect was then asked to sign twice (to acknowledge that he understood his rights and to indicate the he wished to waive them). Nevertheless, Leiken argued that a large percentage of the suspects in his sample inadequately understood their rights because they could not recall the right to silence or counsel warnings and did not know that oral statements could be used against them in court or that their signatures on waiver forms had any legal effect in their cases. Paradoxically, however, those suspects who best understood their rights were most likely to speak to detectives. In addition, Leiken reported that the Denver police used the very psychological pressures deplored by the *Miranda* Court (including the use of promises and threats to obtain waivers and to elicit statements and confessions). Leiken concluded that the *Miranda* rights did not effectively achieve the Supreme Court's goal of dispelling the inherent pressures of interrogation because suspects could not make a meaningful, knowing waiver of their rights. Instead, police interrogators used the warnings to their advantage to create the appearance that a voluntary statement had been obtained.

The fourth method used in the first-generation of *Miranda* impact research was the analysis of case files and documents. In one study, for example, Witt (1973) analyzed 478 felony case files from 1964 to 1968 in an unidentified Southern California police department in a city with over 80,000 residents, which he dubbed "Seaside City." Witt found that although police officers believed they were receiving far fewer admissions and confessions as a result of the *Miranda* requirements, their confession rate declined only 2 percent, and the clearance rate only 3 percent, from the *pre-Miranda* period to the *post-Miranda* period. The conviction rate, however, declined almost 10 percent from the pre-*Miranda* to the *post-Miranda* period. Witt argued that *Miranda* had little impact on the effectiveness of police interrogations in the cases he studied, but that *Miranda* did have an impact on the collateral functions of interrogation: the police interrogated fewer suspects, implicated fewer accomplices, cleared fewer crimes, and recovered less stolen property through interrogation than prior to *Miranda*.

These four studies (Younger 1966*a*, 1966*b*; Wald et al. 1967; Leiken 1970; Witt 1973) exemplify the range, as well as the strengths and weaknesses, of the various methodologies employed in the first round of *Miranda* impact research. Wald et al.'s (1967) participant observation study broke new ground because these researchers directly witnessed and analyzed the interrogation process that, to that time, had been rarely observed. The downside of Wald et al.'s study, however, is that the researchers could never be certain whether their presence in the interrogation room altered the behavior of the detectives or the suspects, and, as with so many other *Miranda* impact studies, their focus on one jurisdiction limited the generalizability of their study. The *Miranda* impact studies that relied on interviews were able to ask probing questions to suspects, detectives, and other actors in the criminal justice system to better understand the perceptions, attitudes, and motivations of those who give and receive *Miranda* warnings. But these interview studies suffered from a different type of bias: the researcher never knew whether the subjects were distorting information—either intentionally or unintentionally—to portray themselves in a favorable light or to hide wrongdoing or perhaps simply due to ordinary errors of memory or recall. The problem of respondent bias inherent in the interviewing method is, of course, magnified by the adversarial context of American criminal justice. In the Leiken's study, for example, one may justifiably treat the statements of his incarcerated subjects with some skepticism (Thomas 1996*a*, pp. 828–29).

The two other methods of data gathering used in the first round of studies—surveys and documentary analysis—also provided researchers with useful information about *Miranda*'s impact on the process and outcomes of interrogation. The survey studies like Younger's allowed researchers to quantify and compare large numbers of case outcomes at different stages of the criminal process. The weakness of Younger's (and other survey studies of *Miranda*'s impact), of course, was that what they gained in coverage they sacrificed in depth: survey studies may provide useful information about trends and outcomes but do not tell us the "why's" that lay behind those trends and outcomes. The analysis of documents and case files to assess the processes and outcomes of police interrogation, as in the Witt (1973) study, proved to be among the most useful methods in parsing out *Miranda*'s impact, especially where pre- and post-*Miranda* data were available. As with Witt's study, the strengths and weaknesses of any documentary analysis depend primarily on the quality of the documents themselves—which tell a story that cannot be distorted (since the documents have been memorialized), but which may be incomplete or inaccurate. Regrettably, the problem with Witt's study of *Miranda*'s impact—as with several other first-generation studies—was that he failed to employ even the most elementary statistical techniques to evaluate whether any of the pre-*Miranda* versus post-*Miranda* differences that he observed were statistically significant.

The methodological problem of inferring the precise causal effects of a judicial decision on case outcomes goes beyond any particular data-gathering approach. Impact studies have been premised on a quasi-experimental model in which the impact of a single decision is evaluated as if all other factors could be held constant. But this assumption is rarely achieved since controlled experimentation is rarely, if ever, possible in the study of naturally occurring data. As a result, social scientists have traditionally relied on two positive strategies to measure judicial impact: before/after studies, and comparison-with-excluded-jurisdiction designs. While the latter method suffers from a lack of statistical comparability among jurisdictions (and in the case of *Miranda* there are no excluded jurisdictions—since all jurisdictions are required to follow the *Miranda* rules), the former suffers from the problem of intervening factors. Thus, our inability to hold constant extraneous and potentially confounding (independent) variables undermines our ability to draw precise causal inferences in the study of judicial impact. Though often imperfect, the best research designs in the study of *Miranda*'s impact have employed multiple approaches so that the strengths of one method may compensate for the weaknesses of another and the findings from one method may be triangulated against (and better understood by) the findings from another.

Several scholars have cataloged and analyzed the findings of the first-generation *Miranda* studies (Cassell 1996*b*; Leo 1996*a*; Schulhofer 1996*b*; Thomas 1996*a*). Although an in-depth discussion of these studies is beyond the scope of this essay, several general patterns are worth noting. First, in the initial aftermath of *Miranda* some police immediately began complying with *Miranda* (Younger 1966*b*), while others ignored the decision or failed to recite part or all of the required warnings to suspects in custody (Wald et al. 1967). After a brief adjustment period, virtually all police began to comply regularly with the letter, though not always the spirit, of the fourfold warning and waiver requirements (Wald et al. 1967; Leiken 1970). Despite their compliance, however, many detectives resented the new *Miranda* requirements (Wald et al. 1967; Stephens, Flanders, and Cannon 1972).

Second, despite the fourfold warnings, suspects frequently waived their *Miranda* rights and chose to speak to their interrogators. Some researchers attributed this largely unexpected finding to the manner in which detectives delivered the *Miranda* warnings, while others attributed it to the failure of suspects to understand the meaning or significance of their *Miranda* rights (Wald et al. 1967; Medalie, Zeitz, and Alexander 1968; Leiken 1970).

Third, once a waiver of rights had been obtained, the tactics and techniques of police interrogation did not appear to change as a result of *Miranda*. For example, Wald et al. (1967) observed in New

Haven that *Miranda* appeared to have little impact on police behavior during interrogation, since detectives continued to employ many of the psychological tactics of persuasion and manipulation that the Warren Court had deplored in *Miranda*. Stephens and colleagues (1972) reported that while most detectives in Knoxville, Tennessee, and Macon, Georgia, issued formalized warnings, *Miranda* did not change the nature and role of the interrogation process.

Fourth, suspects continued to provide detectives with confessions and incriminating statements. In some studies, however, researchers reported a lower rate of confession than prior to *Miranda*. For example, Seeburger and Wettick (1967) reported that in their study of Pittsburgh, the confession rate generally dropped from 54.4 percent prior to *Miranda* to 37.5 percent after *Miranda*, though the decline varied by the type of crime reported. Yet other researchers reported only a marginal decrease in the confession rate. For example, Witt (1973) reported that in "Seaside City" the confession rate dropped only 2 percent (from 69 percent before the *Miranda* decision to 67 percent after the *Miranda* decision). And one researcher even reported an increase in the confession rate of approximately 10 percent after *Miranda* (Younger 1966*b*).

Fifth, researchers reported that clearance and conviction rates had not been adversely affected by the new *Miranda* requirements. For example, even though Seeburger and Wettick (1967) found a 17 percent decline in the confession rate in Pittsburgh, they did not find a corresponding decline in the conviction rate. Other researchers reported significant, if temporary, declines in clearance rates, but conviction rates remained relatively constant (Milner 1971). To be sure, in some instances they too dropped, but not significantly. For example, in his study of "Seaside City," Witt (1973) reported a 3 percent decline in the clearance rate and a 9 percent decline in the conviction rate (from 92 percent to 83 percent) after *Miranda* became law. If there was a significant cost to *Miranda* according to first-generation impact researchers, it appeared to be that *Miranda* may have caused the interrogation rate to drop and may also have been responsible for lessening the effectiveness of the collateral functions of interrogation such as identifying accomplices, clearing crimes, and recovering stolen property (Witt 1973).

But the consensus that emerged from the first generation of *Miranda* impact studies was that the *Miranda* rules had only a marginal effect on the ability of the police to elicit confessions and on the ability of prosecutors to win convictions, despite the fact that some detectives continued to perceive a substantial *Miranda* impact (Witt 1973). The general view of these studies is not merely that *Miranda* failed to affect the ability of police to control crime, but also that, in practice, the requirement of standard *Miranda* warnings failed to achieve the Warren Court's goal of protecting the free choice of suspects to decide for themselves whether to answer police questions.

The generalizability and contemporary relevance of the first-generation *Miranda* impact studies are undermined by two key factors. First, these studies are largely outdated. The data in each of the first-generation *Miranda* impact studies was gathered during the first three years following the 1966 *Miranda* decision. More than three decades have now passed since that time. These studies likely captured only the initial effects of *Miranda* before police officers and detectives had fully adjusted to the new procedures (Schulhofer 1996*b*). Second, many of these studies are methodologically weak, perhaps because many were conducted by lawyers or law professors without any training in the research methods of social science (Leo 1996*a*).

SECOND-GENERATION STUDIES, 1996-PRESENT

The first generation of *Miranda* impact studies had run their course by 1973. For the next two decades, the social science and legal community, with few exceptions (Grisso 1980; Gruhl and Spohn 1981), appeared to lose interest in the empirical study of *Miranda*'s impact on criminal justice processes and outcomes. Gruhl and Spohn (1981) investigated the impact of *Miranda* (and post-*Miranda* rulings) on local prosecutors, while Grisso (1980) performed a couple of empirical studies of the legal and psychological capacities of juveniles and adults to waive their *Miranda* rights knowingly. Since the mid-1990s, however, there has been a second flurry of empirical *Miranda* impact studies. These studies might loosely be divided into two types: those that seek to assess the quantitative impact of *Miranda* on confession, clearance, and conviction rates; and those that qualitatively seek to assess *Miranda*'s real-world impact on police—whether they comply with or circumvent *Miranda*'s requirements, how they issue warnings and waivers, and how they approach interrogation after securing a waiver. Unlike their first-generation counterparts, however, the second-generation impact studies have generated considerable interpretive disagreement, debate, and commentary.

The best-known debate in the second-generation studies has been between Cassell and Schulhofer. Selectively reanalyzing first-generation impact studies, as well as unpublished surveys conducted by prosecutors' offices in several cities immediately prior to and after *Miranda*, Cassell speculated in 1996 that *Miranda* has caused a 16 percent reduction in the confession rate and that it is responsible for lost convictions in 3.8 percent of all serious criminal cases. Cassell arrived at these figures by reviewing the published and unpublished surveys, ignoring those that he claimed had major problems, and then averaging the change in confession rate in these studies before and after *Miranda*. Cassell did not always use the rate reported by the studies; he sometimes recalculated the rate, claiming that it was necessary to correct methodological errors or achieve comparability with other studies. Based on this selective reanalysis of some of these early published studies and unpublished surveys, Cassell posited that *Miranda* reduced confessions in approximately 16 percent of all cases. Cassell further posited that confessions are necessary for convictions in 24 percent of all cases. Multiplying the two figures (0.24×0.16), Cassell argued that *Miranda* is responsible for lost convictions in 3.8 percent of all serious criminal cases. Using the FBI's Uniform Crime Reports crime index for arrests (no figures are available for the number of individuals interrogated), Cassell concluded that approximately 28,000 violent crime and 79,000 property crime cases are lost each year as a result of *Miranda*, and that there are an equal number each year of more lenient plea bargains attributable to evidence weakened by *Miranda* (Cassell 1996*b*). Shortly after publishing these figures, Cassell substantially revised them and argued that each year more than one hundred thousand violent criminals (who would otherwise be convicted and incarcerated) go free as a direct result of the *Miranda* requirements (Cassell 1996*c*).

Reanalyzing the first-generation studies, Schulhofer speculated that *Miranda* may have initially caused a 4.1 percent drop in the confession rate in the immediate post-*Miranda* period. Arguing that confessions were necessary for conviction in 19 percent of all cases, Schulhofer multiplied these two figures together (0.041×0.19) to speculate that *Miranda* caused a 0.78 percent (seventy-eight hundredths of one percent) drop in the conviction rate, a decline, Schulhofer argued, that had probably been reversed as police learned how to comply with *Miranda* and still get confessions (Schulhofer 1996*b*). Schulhofer arrived at these figures by employing the same general approach as Cassell: Schulhofer reanalyzed the early *Miranda* impact studies, counting only those studies that he regarded as methodologically sound, and then averaging out their assessments of *Miranda*'s effect on the confession rate. Based on his analysis of these studies (as well as other adjustments such as large-city effects, trends in policing since *Miranda*, and a reanalysis of the "confessions-necessity-for-conviction figure"), Schulhofer concluded that "for all practical purposes, *Miranda*'s empirically detectable net damage to law enforcement is zero" (Schulhofer 1996*b*, p. 547).[2]

Despite Schulhofer's decisive refutation of Cassell's reanalysis of the first generation studies, Cassell continued to argue that *Miranda* has substantially depressed the confession rate and imposed significant costs on society by allowing tens of thousands of guilty suspects to escape conviction. In a study of prosecutor screening sessions involving a sample of 219 suspects, Cassell and Hayman (1996) found that 42.2 percent of the suspects who were questioned gave incriminating statements, a confession rate that they argued is far lower than pre-*Miranda* confession rates that they estimated to be in the range of 55–60 percent. Analyzing the same studies as Cassell, Thomas (1996*b*) found that the best estimate of the pre-*Miranda* confession rate was in the range of 45–53 percent. Arguing that Cassell and Hayman miscategorized some suspect responses that should have been counted as incriminating, Thomas speculated that the true confession rate in Cassell and Hayman's study was 54 percent, a rate similar both to Cassell and Hayman's estimate of the pre-*Miranda* confession rate as well as to the confession rate found in post-*Miranda* studies (Feeney, Dill, and Weir 1983; Leo 1996*b*).

In a subsequent law review article, Cassell and Fowles (1998) collected FBI national crime clearance rate data for violent and property crimes from 1960 (when such data first became available) to 1995. In addition, they estimated the national clearance rate data from 1950–59, thus producing a database of estimated and reported national crime clearance rates for violent and property crimes from 1950 to 1995. Cassell and Fowles visually identified a decline in national crime clearance rates in the mid-to-late 1960s and, through multiple-regression analysis, sought to test whether a variable they would call "*Miranda*" was responsible for the decline in clearance rates. Using an interrupted time series design, Cassell and Fowles developed a regression model that included thirteen other criminal justice and socioeconomic variables: number of crimes, number of law enforcement employees per capita, dollars spent on police protection per capita by state and local governments, changes to law enforcement manpower and expenditures, the interaction between these variables and the overall number of crimes (what they called "capacity of the system"), the number of persons in the crime-prone years or juveniles from ages fifteen to twenty-four, labor force participation, unemployment rate, disposable per capita real income, live births to unmarried mothers, percent of the resident population residing in urban areas, percentage of violent crimes committed in small cities, and a standard time trend variable. Cassell and Fowles then identified a dummy variable for the years 1966–68 that they called "*Miranda*," and, using an interrupted time series analysis, Cassell and Fowles found that this "*Miranda*" variable showed a statistically significant effect on estimated and collected aggregate crime clearance rates for violent and property crimes from 1950 to 1995. Disaggregating "violent" and "property" crimes and running separate regressions, Cassell and Fowles found that the only individual

---

2   Calling Cassell's analysis even further into question, Schulhofer pointed out that the studies on which Cassell relied suffer from significant methodological flaws and that we cannot so easily infer causation from correlation in any complex time-series analysis. Instead, Schulhofer suggested several competing alternative explanations for any decline in confession and conviction rates post-*Miranda* (long-term trends such as increasing professionalization of American police; trial courts' more rigorous reading of the Fourteenth Amendment to exclude involuntary confessions; competing causal events such as the trial rights applied to the states in *Mapp. v. Ohio*, Fourth Amendment, 367 U.S. 643 (1961), and Gideon v. Waintwright, Sixth Amendment, 372 U.S. 375 (1963); instability or random fluctuation in confession rates (i.e., regression to the mean); and shifting baselines against which to measure the effect of *Miranda*.

violent crime for which the *"Miranda"* variable showed a statistically significant effect was robbery,[3] and that the property crimes for which the *"Miranda"* variable showed a statistically significant effect were larceny, vehicle theft, and burglary.

Based on this interrupted time series, multiple-regression analysis, Cassell and Fowles argued that the *Miranda* requirements have, indeed, handcuffed law enforcement in the last thirty years. In particular, Cassell and Fowles stated that "our regression equations and accompanying causal analysis suggest that, without *Miranda*, the number of crimes cleared would be substantially higher—by as much as 6.6–29.7 percent for robbery, 6.2–28.9 percent for burglary, 0.4–11.9 percent for larceny, and 12.8–45.4 percent for vehicle theft. Moreover, applied to the vast numbers of cases passing through the criminal justice system, these percentages would produce large numbers of cleared crimes. As many as 36,000 robberies, 82,000 burglaries, 163,000 larcenies and 78,000 vehicle thefts remain uncleared each year as a result of *Miranda*" (1998, p. 1126).

Based on this analysis, Cassell and Fowles drew the more general conclusion that, "the clearance rate data collected in this study ... strongly suggest that *Miranda* has seriously harmed society by hampering the ability of the police to solve crimes ... *Miranda* may be the single most damaging blow inflicted on the nation's ability to fight crime in the last half century" (1998, p. 1132).

Yet as John Donahue (1998) has pointed out, there may be little relationship between *Miranda* and clearance rates since most crimes are cleared by arrest, and most interrogations occur after the arrest has been made. Moreover, Donahue cautioned that many other, unmeasured variables might be causing the effect that Cassell and Fowles attributed to *Miranda*.

> My sense is that there has been some drop in actual clearance rates owing to the dramatic changes in the nature of crime, drugs, and attitudes toward authority that emerged in the late 1960s, as well as to the changes in the criminal justice system ushered in by the Warren Court's many decisions in this area, not just *Miranda*. Moreover, measured clearance rates have probably dropped also as a result of the improved quality and reliability of crime and clearance rate data. We must query how much of the measured deviation from trend found in the regressions would remain once we subtracted out the effect of these factors. (Donahue 1998, pp. 1171–72)

Floyd Feeney has systematically and exhaustively analyzed the Cassell-Fowles hypothesis about *Miranda*'s impact on clearance rates (Feeney 2000). Feeney begins by pointing out two serious errors in the Cassell-Fowles hypothesis that, he argues, render it completely defective. First, and most fundamentally, Feeney demonstrates that there was no "sharp fall" for clearance rates in 1966 or 1966–68, contrary to the assertion of Cassell and Fowles. Feeney demonstrates that Cassell and Fowles did not rely on national-level clearance data, despite their claims but, instead, relied on city-level clearance data (and only a fraction of the available city-level clearance data). When one properly analyzes all of the available city-level clearance data, argues Feeney, the "sharp fall" in clearance rates in 1966–68 (the starting point of Cassell and Fowles's analysis) quickly disappears. As Feeney demonstrates, the Cassell-Fowles contention that there was a sharp fall "in every region of the country" during this period is simply false

---

3   In an earlier law review article analyzing national aggregate clearance data, Cassell has asserted that "about one out of every four violent crimes that was 'cleared' before *Miranda* was not 'cleared' after *Miranda*," arguing that *Miranda* was responsible for the trend of declining clearance rates (Cassell 1997).

(Feeney 2000, p. 40). Second, Feeney points out that even if the clearance rates had fallen from 1966–68, there would be no logial or empirical reason to attribute the fall to the *Miranda* decision. This is primarily because most primary clearances occur before any in-custody interrogation takes place (Feeney 2000, p. 41), and Cassell and Fowles fail to show how interrogation that takes place after a suspect has already been arrested (and thus the crime has already been cleared) leads to the initial identification and arrest itself. Clearances are driven by arrests, not the police interrogations that follow arrest. In addition, Feeney points out that other significant historical events—such as improved police management and police record keeping, a rising police workload, the 1965–68 race riots, and the heroin epidemic of the late 1960s—have been the major factors in the gradual decline in clearance rates in America, not court decisions. As a result of these logical and empirical errors in Cassell and Fowles's analysis, Feeney concludes that clearance rates are a "profoundly misleading and erroneous method" for measuring the effect of the *Miranda* decision on the ability of the police to combat crime, and that Cassell and Fowles "fail at every critical point of their argument" (Feeney 2000, p. 113).

Though he has garnered considerable attention from some of the nation's top law reviews, as well as the media, Cassell's quantitative claims have not been generally accepted in either the legal or the social science community. Instead, numerous scholars have disputed Cassell's findings or inferences and criticized his objectivity, methodology, and conclusions (Schulhofer 1996*a*, 1996*b*, 1997; Thomas 1996*b*, 1996*c;* Arenella 1997; Donahue 1998; Garcia 1998; Leo and Ofshe 1998; Weisselberg 1998; White 1998; Leo and White 1999). Schulhofer (1996*a*, 1996*b*, 1996*c*, 1997) has repeatedly criticized Cassell for selectively citing data, presenting sources and quotes out of context, and advancing indefensibly partisan analyses. Schulhofer (1996*a*, 1996*b*, 1997) has also disputed some of Cassell's factual assertions, provided alternative explanations for patterns in Cassell's data, and continued to argue that there is no empirical support for Cassell's claim that *Miranda* has measurably reduced confession rates. Other scholars have argued that Cassell oversimplifies complicated issues, presents speculation as fact, fails to discuss contrary evidence and interpretations, and, ultimately, fails to demonstrate that *Miranda* has caused a decline in confession, clearance, or conviction rates (Thomas 1996*b*, 1996*c;* Arenella 1997; Donahue 1998; Garcia 1998; Leo and Ofshe 1998; Weisselberg 1998; White 1998; Leo and White 1999).

Despite the disagreements between Cassell and his many critics, there appears to be relatively little dispute among second-generation researchers on several aspects of *Miranda*'s real-world effects. First, police appear to issue and document *Miranda* warnings in virtually all cases (Leo 1996*a*). Second, police appear to have successfully "adapted" to the *Miranda* requirements. In practice, this means that police have developed strategies that are intended to induce *Miranda* waivers (Simon 1991; Leo 1996*a*; Leo and White 1999). Third, police appear to elicit waivers from suspects in 78–96 percent of their interrogations (Leo 1998), though suspects with criminal records appear disproportionately likely to invoke their rights and terminate interrogation (Simon 1991; Cassell and Hayman 1996; Leo 1996*a*). Fourth, in some jurisdictions police are systematically trained to violate *Miranda* by questioning "outside *Miranda*"—that is, by continuing to question suspects who have invoked the right to counsel or the right to remain silent (Weisselberg 1998; Leo and White 1999). Finally, some researchers have argued that *Miranda* eradicated the last vestiges of third-degree interrogation present in the mid-1960s, increased the level of professionalism among interrogators, and raised public awareness of constitutional rights (Simon 1991; Leo 1996*a*).

The second generation of *Miranda* impact research has been far more spirited and engaging than the first round of studies. Yet despite the new energy that empirically oriented scholars have breathed into the *Miranda* debate and despite the renewed calls for more empirical research on *Miranda*'s real-world effects (Leo 1996*a*; Thomas 1996*a*; Meares and Harcourt 2001), the second generation of *Miranda* impact scholarship may be at a close. Now that the Supreme Court has resolved in *Dickerson* any question about *Miranda*'s constitutional status, it is highly unlikely that the Court will reconsider any constitutional challenges to *Miranda* for many years, if not decades, to come. As a result, there may be little incentive for either *Miranda*'s supporters or *Miranda*'s critics to continue the difficult task of gathering and interpreting data on *Miranda*'s measurable effects.

The *Dickerson* Court made its own empirical claim about *Miranda*'s impact when it stated that "*Miranda* has become embedded in routine police practice to the point where the warnings have become part of our national culture" (*Dickerson*, p. 2335). Yet it did so without considering any of the first- or second-generation research of *Miranda*'s real-world effects. This is particularly surprising in light of the fact that Paul Cassell litigated the challenge to *Miranda* before the Supreme Court in *Dickerson*. That the Court ignored even the *Miranda* impact research of one of the primary litigants might, understandably, dissuade scholars and advocates on both sides of the *Miranda* debate from pursuing another round of empirical research on *Miranda*'s real-world effects on the interrogation process, public attitudes, or confession and conviction rates. After all, *Miranda* appears to be here to stay for the foreseeable future, and the Court has made up its mind about its empirical effects.

[...]

REFERENCES

Ainsworth, Janet. 1993. "In a Different Register: The Pragmatics of Powerlessness in Police Interrogation." *Yale Law Journal* 103:259–322.

Akerström, Malin. 1991. *Betrayal and Betrayers: The Sociology of Treachery.* New Brunswick, N.J.: Transaction.

American Bar Association. 1988. *Criminal Justice in Crisis.* Washington, D.C.: American Bar Association.

Arenella, Peter. 1997. "*Miranda* Stories." *Harvard Journal of Law and Public Policy* 20:375–87.

Baker, Liva. 1983. Miranda: *Crime, Law and Politics.* New York: Atheneum.

Belsky, Martin. 1994. "Living with *Miranda*: A Reply to Professor Grano." *Drake Law Review* 43:127–47.

Burt, Robert A. 1969. "*Miranda* and Title II: A Morgananatic Marriage." *Supreme Court Review* 1969:81–134.

Caplan, Gerald M. 1985. "Questioning *Miranda*." *Vanderbilt Law Review* 38: 1417–76.

Cassell, Paul G. 1996*a*. "All Benefits, No Costs: The Grand Illusion of *Miranda*'s Defenders." *Northwestern University Law Review* 90:1084–124.

———. 1996*b*. "*Miranda*'s Social Costs: An Empirical Reassessment." *Northwestern University Law Review* 90:387–499.

———. 1996*c*. "True Confessions about *Miranda* Legacy." *Legal Times* (July 22, 1996), pp. 22–23.

———. 1997. "*Miranda*'s Negligible Effect on Law Enforcement: Some Skeptical Observations." *Harvard Journal of Law and Public Policy* 20:327–46.

———. 1999*a*. "Barbarians at the Gates? A Reply to the Critics of the Victims' Rights Amendment." *Utah Law Review* 1999:479–544.

———. 1999*b*. "The Statute That Time Forgot: 18 U.S.C. § 3501 and the Overruling of *Miranda*." *Iowa Law Review* 85:175–259.

———. 2000. Personal communication with George C. Thomas III, professor of law, University of Utah College of Law, August 31.

Cassell, Paul G., and Richard Fowles. 1998. "Handcuffing the Cops? A Thirty-Year Perspective on *Miranda*'s Harmful Effects on Law Enforcement." *Stanford Law Review* 50:1055–145.

Cassell, Paul G., and Brett S. Hayman. 1996. "Police Interrogation in the 1990s: An Empirical Study of the Effects *of Miranda* " *U.C.L.A. Law Review* 43:839–931.

Dallek, Robert. 1998. *Flawed Giant: Lyndon Johnson and His Times, 1961–1973.* New York: Oxford University Press.

Donahue, John. 1998. "Did *Miranda* Diminish Police Effectiveness?" *Stanford Law Review* 50:1147–80.

Feeney, Floyd. 2000. "Police Clearance: A Poor Way to Measure the Impact of *Miranda* on the Police." *Rutgers Law Journal* 32:1–114.

Feeney, Floyd, Forest Dill, and Adrianne Weir. 1983. *Arrests without Conviction: How Often They Occur and Why.* Washington, D.C.: U.S. Department of Justice, National Institute of Justice.

Garcia, Alfredo. 1998. "Is *Miranda* Dead, Was It Overruled, or Is It Irrelevant?" *St. Thomas Law Review* 10:461–505.

Graham, Fred P. 1970. *The Self-Inflicted Wound.* New York: Macmillan.

Grano, Joseph D. 1979*a*. "*Rhode Island v. Innis*: A Need to Reconsider the Constitutional Premises Underlying the Law of Confessions." *American Criminal Law Review* 17:1–51.

———. 1979*b*. "Voluntariness, Free Will, and the Law of Confessions." *Virginia Law Review* 65:859–945.

———. 1985. "Prophylactic Rules in Criminal Procedure: A Question of Article III Legitimacy." *Northwestern University Law Review* 80:100–164.

———. 1986. "Selling the Idea to Tell the Truth: The Professional Interrogator and Modern Confessions Law." *Michigan Law Review* 84:662–90.

———. 1988. "*Miranda*'s Constitutional Difficulties: A Reply to Professor Schulhofer." *University of Chicago Law Review* 55:174–89.

———. 1989. "The Changed and Changing World of Constitutional Criminal Procedure." *University of Michigan Journal of Law Reform* 22:395–424.

———. 1992. "Ascertaining the Truth." *Cornell Law Review* 77:1061–66.

———. 1993. *Confessions, Truth and the Law.* Ann Arbor: University of Michigan Press.

———. 1996. "Criminal Procedure: Moving from the Accused as Victim to the Accused as Responsible Party." *Harvard Journal of Law and Public Policy* 19:711–17.

Greenawalt, Kent. 1980. "Silence as a Moral and Constitutional Right." *William and Mary Law Review* 23:15–71.

Greenwood, Kate, and Jeffrey Brown. 1998. "Investigation and Police Practices: Custodial Interrogations." *Georgetown Law Journal* 86:1318–33.

Griffiths, John, and Richard Ayres. 1967. "Interrogation of Draft Protesters." *Yale Law Journal* 77:395–424.

Grisso, Thomas. 1980. "Juveniles' Capacities to Waive *Miranda* Rights: An Empirical Analysis." *California Law Review* 68:1134–66.

Gruhl, John, and Cassia Spohn. 1981. "The Supreme Court's Post-*Miranda* Rulings: Impact on Local Prosecutors." *Law and Policy Quarterly* 3:29–54.

Guy, Karen L., and Robert G. Huckabee. 1988. "Going Free on a Technicality: Another Look at the Effect of the *Miranda* Decision on the Criminal Justice Process." *Criminal Justice Research Bulletin* 4:1–3.

Herman, Lawrence. 1987. "The Supreme Court, the Attorney General, and the Good Old Days of Police Interrogation." *Ohio State Law Journal* 48: 733–55.

Hoffman, Jan. 1998. "Some Officers Are Skirting *Miranda* Restraints to Get Confessions." *New York Times* (March 29, 1998), p. Al.

Kamisar, Yale. 1965. "Equal Justice in the Gatehouses and Mansions of American Criminal Procedure." In *Criminal Justice in Our Time*, edited by A. E. Dick Howard. Published for the Magna Carta Commission of Virginia. Charlottesville: University Press of Virginia.

———. 1966. "A Dissent from the *Miranda* Dissents: Some Comments on the 'New' Fifth Amendment and the 'Old' Voluntariness Test." *Michigan Law Review* 65:59–104.

———. 1974. "Kauper's Judicial Examination of the Accused' Forty Years Later: Some Comments on a Remarkable Article." *Michigan Law Review* 73: 15–38.

———. 1977a. "*Brewer v. Williams*, *Massiah*, and *Miranda:* What Is 'Interrogation'? When Does It Matter?" *Georgetown University Law Journal* 67:1–101.

———. 1977b. "Fred E. Inbau: The Importance of Being Guilty." *Journal of Criminal Law and Criminology* 68:182–97.

———. 1990. "Remembering the 'Old World' of Criminal Procedure: A Reply to Professor Grano." *University of Michigan Journal of Law Reform* 23: 537–89.

———. 1996. "*Miranda* Does Not Look So Awesome Now." *Legal Times* (June 10, 1996):A22.

———. 1999. "Reflections: Retrospective on David Simon's *Homicide*" *Jurist* 2:1–6.

———. 2000. "Can (Did) Congress 'Overrule' *Miranda?*" *Cornell Law Review* 85:883–955.

Kant, Immanuel. 1998. *The Critique of Pure Reason.* Translated and edited by Paul Guyer and Allen W. Wood. New York: Cambridge University Press.

Leiken, L. S. 1970. "Police Interrogation in Colorado: The Implementation of *Miranda*." *Denver Law Journal* 47:1–53.

Leo, Richard A. 1994. "Police Interrogation and Social Control." *Social and Legal Studies* 3:93–120.

———. 1996a. "Inside the Interrogation Room." *Journal of Criminal Law and Criminology* 86:266–303.

———. 1996b. "The Impact of *Miranda* Revisited." *Journal of Criminal Law and Criminology* 86:621–92.

———. 1998. "*Miranda* and the Problem of False Confessions." In *The* Miranda *Debate: Law, Justice and Policing*, edited by Richard A. Leo and George C. Thomas III. Boston: Northeastern University Press.

Leo, Richard A., and Richard J. Ofshe. 1998. "Using the Innocent to Scapegoat *Miranda:* Another Reply to Paul Cassell." *Journal of Criminal Law and Criminology* 88:557–77.

Leo, Richard A., and George C. Thomas III, eds. 1998. *The* Miranda *Debate: Law, Justice, and Policing.* Boston: Northeastern University Press.

Leo, Richard A., and Welsh S. White. 1999. "Adapting to *Miranda:* Modern Interrogators' Strategies for Dealing with the Obstacles Posed by *Miranda*." *Minnesota Law Review* 84:397–472.

Malone, Patrick. 1986. "You Have the Right to Remain Silent: *Miranda* after Twenty Years." *American Scholar* 55:367–80.

Markman, Stephen J. 1987. "The Fifth Amendment and Custodial Questioning: A Response to 'Reconsidering *Miranda*.'" *University of Chicago Law Review* 54:938–49.

———. 1989. "Foreword: The 'Truth in Criminal Justice' Series." *University of Michigan Journal of Law Reform* 22:425–36.

Meares, Tracey, and Bernard Harcourt. 2001. "Transparent Adjudication and Social Science Research in Constitutional Criminal Procedure." *Journal of Criminal Law and Criminology* 90:733–98.

Medalie, Richard J., Leonard Zeitz, and Paul Alexander. 1968. "Custodial Police Interrogation in Our Nation's Capital: The Attempt to Implement *Miranda*" *Michigan Law Review* 66:1347–422.

Milner, Neal A. 1971. *The Court and Local Law Enforcement: The Impact of* Miranda. Beverly Hills, Calif.: Sage.

Monaghan, Henry P. 1975. "Foreword: Constitutional Common Law." *Harvard Law Review* 89:1–45.

Mosteller, Robert P. 1997. "Victim's Rights and the United States Constitution: An Effort to Recast the Battle in Criminal Litigation." *Georgia Law Journal* 85:1691–715.

Nardulli, Peter. 1983. "The Societal Cost of the Exclusionary Rule: An Empirical Assessment." *American Bar Foundation Research Journal* 3:585–609.

———. 1987. "The Societal Costs of the Exclusionary Rule Revisited." *University of Illinois Law Review* 2:223–39.

Neubauer, David W. 1974. *Criminal Justice in Middle America.* Morristown, N.J.: General Learning Press.

Nguyen, Alex. 2000. "The Assault on *Miranda.*" *American Prospect* (March 27–April 10, 2000), pp. 1–9.

Report to the Attorney General on the Law of Pretrial Interrogation. 1986. Truth in Criminal Justice, Report no. 1. Washington, D.C.: U.S. Department of Justice, Office of Legal Policy. Reprinted 1989 in *University of Michigan Journal of Law Reform* 22:437–572.

Robinson, Cyril D. 1968. "Police and Prosecutor Practices and Attitudes Relating to Interrogation as Revealed by Pre- and Post-*Miranda* Questionnaires: A Construct of Police Capacity to Comply." *Duke Law Journal* 3: 425–524.

Rosenfeld, Seth. 2000. "How an Improper Interrogation by Police Derailed a Murder Prosecution." *San Francisco Examiner* (June 18, 2000), p. A6.

Schaefer, Roger C. 1971. "Patrolman Perspectives on *Miranda.*" *Law and the Social Order. Arizona State Law Journal* 1971:81–101.

Schulhofer, Stephen J. 1987. "Reconsidering *Miranda*" *University of Chicago Law Review* 54:435–61.

———. 1996a. "*Miranda* and Clearance Rates." *Northwestern University Law Review* 91:278–94.

———. 1996b. "*Miranda*'s Practical Effect: Substantial Benefits and Vanishingly Small Social Costs." *Northwestern University Law Review* 90:500–563.

———. 1996c. "Pointing in the Wrong Direction." *Legal Times* (August 12, 1996), pp. 21, 24.

———. 1997. "Bashing *Miranda* is Unjustified—and Harmful." *Harvard Journal of Law and Public Policy* 20:347–73.

Seeburger, Richard H., and R. Stanton Wettick. 1967. "*Miranda* in Pittsburgh: A Statistical Study." *Pittsburgh Law Review* 29:1–26.

Seidman, Louis Michael. 1990. "Rubashov's Question: Self-Incrimination and the Problem of Coerced Preferences." *Yale Journal of Law and the Humanities* 2:149–80.

———. 1992. "*Brown* and *Miranda.*" *California Law Review* 80:673–753.

Simon, David. 1991. *Homicide: A Year on the Killing Streets.* Boston: Houghton Mifflin.

Skolnick, Jerome H., and Richard A. Leo. 1992. "The Ethics of Deceptive Interrogation." *Criminal Justice Ethics* 11:3–12.

Stephens, Otis, Robert Flanders, and J. Lewis Cannon. 1972. "Law Enforcement and the Supreme Court: Police Perceptions of the *Miranda* Requirements." *Tennessee Law Review* 39:407–31.

Stuntz, William. 2001. "*Miranda*'s Mistake." *Michigan Law Review* 99:975–99.

Thomas, George C., III. 1993. "A Philosophical Account of Coerced Self-Incrimination." *Yale Journal of Law and the Humanities* 5:79–111.

———. 1996a. "Is *Miranda* a Real World Failure? A Plea for More (and Better) Empirical Evidence." *U.C.L.A. Law Review* 43:821–37.

———. 1996b "Plain Talk about the *Miranda* Empirical Debate: A 'Steady-State' Theory of Confessions." *U.C.L.A. Law Review* 43:933–59.

———. 1996c. "Telling Half-Truths." *Legal Times* (August 12, 1996), pp. 20–24.

———. 2000. "The End of the Road for *Miranda v. Arizona?:* On the History and Future of Rules for Police Interrogation." *American Criminal Law Review* 37:1–39.

———. 2001. "Separated at Birth but Siblings Nonetheless: *Miranda* and the Due Process Cases." *Michigan Law Review* 99:1081–1120.

Toobin, Jeffrey. 1987. "*Viva Miranda.*" *New Republic* 196 (February 1987): 11–12.

Uviller, H. Richard. 1996. *Virtual Justice: The Flawed Prosecution of Crime in America.* New Haven, Conn.: Yale University Press.

Wald, Michael, R. Ayres, D. W. Hess, M. Schantz, and C. H. Whitebread. 1967. "Interrogations in New Haven: The Impact of *Miranda* Yale Law Journal* 76:1519–1648.

Walker, Samuel. 1993. *Taming the System: The Control of Discretion in Criminal Justice, 1950–1990.* New York: Oxford University Press.

Weisselberg, Charles. 1998. "Saving *Miranda.*" *Cornell Law Review* 84:109–92.

———. 2001. "In the Stationhouse after *Dickerson.*" *Michigan Law Review* 99: 1121–63.

White, Welsh. 1998. "What Is an Involuntary Confession Now?" *Rutgers Law Review* 50:2001–57.

———. 2001. "*Miranda*'s Failure to Restrain Pernicious Interrogation Practices." *Michigan Law Review* 99:1211–47.

Wigmore, John Henry. 1923. *A Treatise on the Anglo-American System of Evidence in Trials at Common Law.* 2d ed. Boston: Little Brown.

Witt, James W. 1973. "Non-coercive Interrogation and the Administration of Criminal Justice: The Impact of *Miranda* on Police Effectuality." *Journal of Criminal Law and Criminology* 64:320–32.

Younger, Evelle. 1966a. "*Miranda.*" *Fordham Law Review* 35:255–62.

———. 1966b "Results of a Survey Conducted in the District Attorney's Office of Los Angeles County regarding the Effect of the *Miranda* Decision upon the Prosecution of Felony Cases." *American Criminal Law Quarterly* 5: 32–39.

DISCUSSION QUESTIONS

1. Are the appellate courts policymakers?

2. What is the issue in assuming the Supreme Court as a political system versus an independent legal system?

3. How are the courts protectors of the minority?

4. Why are dominant policy views held by lawmakers usually held by the Court as well?

5. Discuss what safeguards could be implemented to prevent a suspect from incriminating himself.

6. What constitutes "free will" in an interrogation?

7. What was the goal of *Miranda,* and was it achieved?

8. Analyze the consequences of *Miranda*.

9. Explain the outcomes of the first generation *Miranda* studies. How are they similar to or different from the second-generation *Miranda* studies?

10. Some studies have shown an increase in confessions after the implementation of *Miranda*. What factors may have contributed to this?